Leaves of Faith:
The World of Jewish Living

VOLUME II

by
Rabbi Aharon Lichtenstein

KTAV PUBLISHING HOUSE, INC

Library of Congress Cataloging-in-Publication Data

Lichtenstein, Aharon
Leaves of faith: the world of Jewish living / by Aharon Lichtenstein.
v.cm.
Includes bibliographical references and index.
Vol 1. ISBN 0-88125-667-6
Vol 2. ISBN 0-88125-668-4
   1. Judaism—Study and teaching. 2. Jewish learning and scholarship.
   3. Rabbinical literature—History and criticism. 4. Jewish religious
   Education. I. Title.
BM 70.L49 2003
296.6'8—dc21
2002156791

Manufactured in the United States of America

Published by
KTAV Publishing House, Inc.
930 Newark Avenue
Jersey City, NJ 07306
Email: info@ktav.com
www.ktav.com
(201) 963-9524
Fax (201) 963-0102

Typesetting: Raphael Freeman, Jerusalem Typesetting

To Tovah:
With Appreciation and Admiration

Contents

Chapter 1

Religion and State:
The Case for Interaction

I.

Seen from a Jewish perspective, the question of religion and state is both very old and very new.[1] It goes back to the "generation of the wilderness," which constituted the first independent Jewish political community. This is so in a double sense. Textually and conceptually, the problem is rooted in sections of the Torah, Written or Oral, concerning the appointment of various governmental bodies; while historically, it finds its first concrete manifestation in the charismatic figure of Moses, at once king and prophet, judge and priest,[2] legislator and teacher. Yet in a very real sense, the problem is only decades old. Having lain dormant for centuries, upon the advent of the State of Israel it suddenly burst upon the scene with a vengeance, confronting us existentially with what had previously been purely theoretical issues – and largely quiescent issues at that.

A hiatus of fifteen or twenty centuries in the application of any halakhic area would pose severe difficulties, even if the practical situation in that area had remained relatively stable. How much greater the difficulty when the area has radically altered.

The nature of the change is twofold. First, the religious fabric of Jewry

---

This paper was originally published in *Judaism* 15:4 (Fall 1966) and reprinted in *Arguments and Doctrines,* ed. Arthur Cohen (Philadelphia: Jewish Publication Society, 1970).

has changed fundamentally. Our last previous political experience, whether in the Land of Israel or the Diaspora, occurred in the context of basic allegiance to Torah. Whatever his personal behavior, the Second Commonwealth or Babylonian Jew essentially subscribed to the idea of normative Judaism.[3] Needless to say, a substantial segment of contemporary Jewry, within or without the State of Israel, has rejected this concept in favor of some secular orientation. Second, the Western political climate has been thoroughly transformed. The ancient world assumed not only cooperation and liaison between the political and religious authorities but, at least to a limited extent, their actual identity. In the Greco-Roman world, who but a smattering of philosophers could even have imagined otherwise? The modern Western temperament, by contrast, considers separation the norm and at most tolerates some *pro forma* established church. Moreover, whereas the ancient world thought primarily in terms of the group, whether tribe, race, *polis*, or *civitas*, modern man instinctively thinks in terms of the individual. Regardless of what philosophers may hold, popular social thought is presently atomic rather than organic.

This change bears directly upon the current question of religion and the state. For, in the intervening centuries, the question has taken two distinct forms. In its medieval phase, it revolved around the relationship of church and state as two centers of power. The major issues concerned the demarcation of their respective provinces and the resolution of their recurrent conflicts. Since the seventeenth century, however, these themes, while still relevant, have gradually faded into the background. The emphasis has shifted to the consideration of personal liberty, its rights and its limits. In its modern formulation, therefore, the problem tends to pit both church and state against the individual citizen: public power versus private conscience. In this sense, it is reduced, not without some distortion, to one aspect of the broader question of authority versus the individual.

No doubt, any truly comprehensive exposition of the problem must come to grips with both its medieval and its modern aspects. Indeed, it must maintain a threefold perspective, viewing each issue with an eye to preserving the integrity of religion, of the state, and of the individual. Yet one can hardly overlook the fact that the question of religion and the state today is primarily one of the individual and his relation to authority. It is with this aspect, therefore, that the present analysis will be principally concerned.

II.

The quest for a sound Jewish position concerning the basic issues of religion and state can only be undertaken by reference to fundamental principles – principles not only social and political, but moral and religious. Given the secularist's premises, and hence his priorities, many of his contentions appear almost irrefutable. However, within a different axiological framework, from a religious and halakhic rather than a secular and nationalistic perspective, we may – nay, we must – read quite different conclusions.

What is this religious framework? Its basic components, each of which may in turn consist of a number of elements, are four:

1. Man was created by God as a spiritual being, a singular and unique person, endowed with freedom and vouchsafed a personal relation to God. Metaphysically, he is therefore a responsible moral and religious agent, capable of responding to an ethical norm or to a divine imperative.

2. The individual realizes himself and fulfills the purpose of his life only insofar as he adheres to God, whether this be understood in conative or contemplative terms, and freely gives himself to Him. Society attains its end to the extent that it becomes a vehicle for, and a manifestation of, personal and collective beatitude.

3. Although He is, in essence, wholly transcendent, God has chosen to reveal Himself to created beings and to relate to them through the very act of their creation, through the indirect expression of His will as manifested in nature and in history, through direct communication with man, and through an ongoing dialectical encounter with him.

4. Through the interaction of divine will and human aspiration, a single people, Israel, entered into a covenant with God and thus assumed

a unique position in history. As a result of both grace and merit, it became a holy nation, a community committed, individually and collectively, to God and His Torah, and thus invested with a special character and unique responsibilities.

These principles do not, in and of themselves, dictate a single political theory. Nor do they prescribe a specific solution to the problem of religion and state. They do, however, provide a basis and a frame of reference that serve, paradoxically, both to intensify the scope and difficulty of the problem and to point a direction for its resolution.

On the one hand, the opposition of personal liberty and social control assumes for the religious thinker a far more complex character than it may have for the secularist. Confronted by the dichotomy of the individual and the community, the secularist can opt for either. He can, with Mill and his followers, champion the absolute rights of the individual and relegate society and its rights to the role of a qualifying factor, a limit imposed upon one individual in the interest of collective preservation. Or he can, with totalitarian theorists, wholly subordinate the individual to the needs of the state, even sacrificing him, if need be, to satisfy the ravenous appetite of Leviathan. The religious thinker, on the other hand, and specifically the Jew committed to halakhic values and a Torah *Weltanschauung*, has no such latitude. He cannot abandon personal liberty or communal commitment; he cannot regard either the individual Jew or *Knesset Yisrael* as simply a limit of the other; neither can he be reduced to a merely negative factor preventing anarchy or automatism, restraining the excesses of either license or tyranny. To the Halakhah, both poles in the antinomy – the individual and the community, the moral freedom of the Jew and the historic destiny of Israel – are indispensable positive elements. At the practical level, their interests may no doubt clash, and some quasi-Hegelian synthesis or a transcendent *modus operandi* must be developed to harmonize them. As a value, however, each is self-validating, worthy of being preserved for its own sake. They exist in dialectical tension, and their reconciliation or integration must revolve around coordinate foci.

III.

The traditional importance of both elements is quite clear. The mishnah in Sanhedrin testifies of one:

> For this reason man was created alone...to proclaim the greatness of the Holy One, blessed be He. For when a man strikes many coins from one mold, they all resemble each other, but the King of the kings of kings, the Holy One, blessed be He, fashioned every man in the stamp of the first man, and yet not one of them resembles his fellow. Therefore, every individual is obligated to say: "The world was created for my sake."[4]

And innumerable texts, both Biblical and Rabbinic, concerning Israel's collective covenant and its spiritual nationality, speak eloquently of the other.

It should be emphasized, however, that Judaism does not regard the destiny and development of the individual and the community as merely independent desiderata. It sees them as inextricably intertwined, not only supplementary but complementary. A spiritually oriented society is not only necessary *per se* as a realization of divine purpose and collective destiny. It is an indispensable condition for the fulfillment of the individual Jew – not only in the obvious pragmatic sense that his total personality cannot properly mature in isolation, or that perhaps, as some would have it, the very notion of a wholly nonsocial human existence is inconceivable, but rather in the far dee*per se*nse that his identification with *Knesset Yisrael* is an integral aspect of the Jew's personal identity. His community is not only a context within which the Jew thrives and from which he derives sustenance; it is the vehicle through which his personal experience transcends the bounds of his own existence. It transmutes an isolated act into an aspect of a divinely ordered plan. It relates the Jew to history and to metahistory. The Rambam's strictures with respect to the *poresh mi-darkhei tzibbur,* "he who diverges from communal paths," speak for themselves:

> One who diverges from the communal paths, even though he has committed no transgressions but only separates himself from the congregation of Israel and does not do *mizvot* as one of them, does not participate in their trouble, and does not fast with them, but goes his own way like one of the Gentiles,

and as if he were not one of them [i.e., the Jews]: such a person has no portion in the world-to-come.[5]

This conception of the relation of the Jew to *Knesset Yisrael* is persistently reflected in the halakhic emphasis upon their practical interpretation. Both as a fact – "either fellowship or death"[6] – and as a value, the
social emphasis is writ large throughout the Halakhah. Not only political
or economic activity but even the Jew's spiritual existence is cast within a
social mold. There is little yearning for the nomadic or the monastic. We
encounter no idealization of the spiritual hermit, the *schöne Seele* that
cannot or will not come to grips with the world and resigns itself to becoming, in Byron's phrase, a "pilgrim of eternity." Indeed, the *talmid hakham*
is enjoined from living in a place that lacks basic social institutions.[7]
Moreover, innumerable *mizvot*, ranging from charity to the observance
of holy days, and including both those "between man and God" as well as
those "between man and his fellow," require a social framework for their
optimum fulfillment. Even prayer, "worship of the heart" though it be, has
a prominent public aspect. No doubt, in its essence religion is ultimately,
in Plotinus' phrase, "the flight of the alone to the Alone." Nevertheless, for
the Jew, the purpose and direction of his religious existence is defined by
his membership in *Knesset Yisrael*.

In one sense, then, the principles outlined above sharpen our problem,
for they compel us to consider the relation of religion and the state with
reference to not one ultimate goal but two. In another sense, however, they
attenuate it, or rather they indicate a direction for its resolution. In moving
from a homocentric to a theocentric context, they shift the focus from
rights to duties, from privileges to responsibilities, from endowments to
obligations. The question of religion and the state is thus largely shorn of
its quasi-juridical character. At the public level, the issue is no longer one
of defining the respective rights and provinces of civil and ecclesiastical
authority. It is rather a matter of discovering the social structure which,
at any given time, will best enable the community to attain its collective
spiritual ends. The accent is upon destiny rather than hegemony. On the
individual level, likewise, both the role and the character of personal

liberty are radically transformed. Personal liberty retains its immense significance – not, however, as an inalienable civil or natural right but as an essential factor, both an instrument and a condition, in the quest for beatitude. From a religious perspective, neither the concept nor the content of liberty resembles the secularist's *jus naturalis*. It is not a lack of restraint but a capacity for self-realization; not a freedom *from* but a freedom *to*.[8] For the Jew, liberty is the power to realize his spiritual potential as an individual, a being existing in special relation to God, and as a member of a community endowed with a unique historical destiny and charged with a singular commitment. Its ultimate point of reference lies beyond the order of rights or goods, on a plane where freedom and servitude are no longer polar opposites as man realizes himself in service to God. "They are My slaves, for I have taken them out of the land of Egypt;"[9] and yet "there is no free man but he who engages in Torah."[10]

To be sure, such a transcendent harmony is not ordinarily attained on the social and political level. However, even on this plane, the positive conception of a teleological freedom changes the problem of religion and the state from a theoretical and juridical issue of rights into a pragmatic issue of means. There is only one question to be asked: What, at any given time, is the social and political structure that will best preserve the spiritual integrity and identity of both the individual Jew and of *Knesset Yisrael,* and that will best promote the fulfillment of their historic destiny?

IV.

In addressing ourselves to the question of separation in its contemporary setting, we encounter formidable claims – I am speaking, of course, of religiously valid claims – on both sides. To begin with the arguments for separation, these are of two types: theological and practical. It may be contended, first, that there should be no link between religion and the state because they relate to wholly diverse areas of human experience, the sacred and the profane, and between the two there can be no real relationship. As a citizen, man lies within the order of nature; as a communicant, within the order of grace; and between the two there lies an unbridgeable chasm.

If one adopts this dichotomy, holding that nature and grace are not only distinct but disjunct, then, of course, there is little basis, if any, for the interaction of the political and the religious. The counsel of rendering unto God and Caesar their respective dues is very much in place. Indeed, it then matters little who Caesar may be. The radical separation of nature and grace is generally rooted in the conviction that the order of nature is a *massa perditionis,* inherently corrupt and lacking in ultimate spiritual relevance. So long, therefore, as there is no direct interference with the citizens' religious life – no ordinances, for instance, commanding the transgression of divine norms – does it really matter by whom and how this doomed carnal province is superintended? Thus, Calvin could demand absolute fealty and obedience to Francis I, holding that even martyrdom at the hands of the most tyrannous monarch was preferable to any resistance;[11] while English Puritans could argue for democracy on the ground that in the secular political sphere their own will could reign supreme.[12]

If we should reject this position, we are still confronted by a number of options. One is to assume the virtual identity of the sacred and the profane; or at least to assume it sufficiently so as to have both ruled by a single power. This is the basis of the institution of the king-priest prevalent in so many primitive societies.[13] A second is to assume that the sacred and the profane are neither identical nor disjunct but distinct on the one hand and integrated on the other. In Christianity, the political consequence of this position is the famous doctrine, dating from the patristic period and given modern formulation in Leo XIII's *Immortale Dei,*[14] of "two powers" that rule separate realms independently but, in theory at least, sustain and assist each other, so that their relations are governed by perfect concord.

From a Jewish point of view, none of these solutions is truly adequate. Judaism certainly has not espoused either the renunciation of the secular or its severance from the religious. On the contrary, the whole thrust of the Halakhah lies in its demand that all of life be redeemed and sanctified. Nor does Judaism identify the sacred and the profane. *Havdalah* ("Separation") is no less a *mizvah* than *Kiddush* ("Sanctification"). Indeed, according to the Rambam, they are both part of a single *mizvah.*[15] And, as regards our area specifically, we might recall the Ramban's strictures against the Hasmoneans' attempted union of royal and priestly authority.[16]

Nor yet can we be genuinely satisfied with the traditional Roman Catholic position. The Halakhah is not content with the integration of the secular and the religious into a single harmonious scheme. It demands their interpenetration. The sacred must not only relate to the profane but – even as the two remain distinct – impregnate it. Halakhah proclaims the central truth that while religion is, in one sense, an area of experience, in another sense it frames all of experience, inasmuch as it concerns man's relation to God, the ground and goal of life itself. It is not only a quantitative but also a qualitative aspect of existence, and as such it impinges upon every area. "All human activity," the Rambam insisted, "is subsumed under the fear of God, and every human act ultimately results in either a *mizvah* or a transgression."[17] Every act, therefore, does not merely lead *to,* but is itself, in the broader sense of the term, a part *of,* the religious life. Both the strength and the problematic of Halakhah derive precisely from its attempt to relate these two senses of religion and to grasp their often dialectical tension. Hence, the concept of the two realms, suggesting, as it does, the parceling out of spheres of influence to political and religious authority respectively, does not satisfy the radical demands of the Halakhah. The halakhic ideal would seem to call for a more organic relation.[18]

From a Jewish standpoint, therefore, the interaction of religion and state is theologically not only possible but desirable. But there remain formidable practical (I do not mean simply pragmatic) objections grounded upon the potential danger posed by such interaction. To the committed Jew, genuinely concerned with the maximal preservation of both religious values and moral freedom, the danger is twofold. It threatens Judaism, on the one hand, and the Jew, on the other. We are confronted first by the prospect of Erastianism, the facile system all too readily accepted by (to paraphrase C.D. Broad's description of Bacon) "sincere if unenthusiastic Jews of that sensible school which regards the Sanhedrin as a branch of the Civil Service, and the Chief Rabbi as the Israeli Minister for Divine Affairs." The Erastian danger is itself two-edged. There is, first, the external threat. The state may seek to impose its authority and values upon religion in order to advance its own secular, perhaps even antireligious ends. Medieval and modern European history is replete with instances of such

interference occurring in both Catholic and Protestant countries; and if
we go back somewhat in time, our own Second Commonwealth polity
offers a glaring example of the deleterious effects of political meddling in
religious life. Erastianism poses, secondly, an internal threat, the danger
that the spiritual quintessence of religion will be diluted, if not perverted,
by its official status. Quite apart from the threat of overt or covert state
interference, an establishment religion lives under a Damocles' sword of
worldliness, the perennial possibility that its public investiture will cor-
rode the fiber of its principles and purpose, that it will fall prey to spiritual
pride writ large.

As the marriage of religion to the state thus endangers organized religion, so it threatens the individual citizen spiritually. The loss of religious
liberty diminishes man's spiritual stature. It fractures the *zelem E-lohim,* the
"human face divine" within him. Man most fully realizes his potential when
he acts and exists as a subject and a person rather than as an object; and
to live as personality means to live freely, in consonance with conscience
and on the basis of moral choice. Consequently, the danger of tyranny is
not merely political or social. It is religious.

V.

The dangers posed by the interrelation of religion and state are no doubt
very real. A spiritual religion ignores them at its peril, and secularists are
quite right – indeed, perform a genuine service to religion – in calling
attention to them. From the perspective of Jewish history, they are only
half the story, however. Probing the problem in its entirety, I think we shall
find that the practical inferences secularism draws from these points are
both unwarranted and subversive.

The secularist prescription would avert some diseases but kill the
patient. It would preserve Jews, or rather some of their civil liberties, and
destroy Jewry; not only Judaism, but Jewry. For *Knesset Yisrael* is not just
a social and political entity. It is not merely what James Baldwin says he
found in Israel, a collection of individuals bound by the Hebrew language
and memories of the European Holocaust. *Knesset Yisrael* is, in its essence,
a spiritual community, or more specifically a religious community. It does

not simply consist of brothers bound by a common past – important as that may be – but of comrades committed to a common future. We are, by definition and constitution, a people of spiritual destiny and commitment. As Rav Saadia Gaon put it, "Our nation is a nation only by virtue of its *Torot*."[19]

Advocates of a secular State of Israel are therefore trying to put a square peg in a round hold. It is not only that the approach is wrong, that it will produce deplorable results. Secularization *ought* not take place, and it *cannot* take place – unless, that is, we are ready to dismantle the community of Israel as it has historically evolved and as it at present exists. For we must not underestimate the scope of the secularist's position. He does not simply argue for a secular state. He advocates a secular society – a society in which individuals could practice religion freely and religious institutions could exist, but that in character and structure would be essentially secular. If the issue were solely one of church and state, if it involved only the relations of organized government and organized religion, one could give the case for separation a sympathetic hearing. It might be argued that, from a tactical point of view, disestablishment is now in the interests of both religion and state. Indeed, some genuine advocates of Halakhah have at times inclined to this position, if not subscribed to it. The modern secularist plays for much higher stakes, however. Not only the organs of government but the fabric of Israeli society, ultimately the very fiber of the Jew himself, are to be gradually secularized. Of course, even in the political sphere the type of separation that would be motivated by religious considerations would perhaps be fundamentally different from what is envisioned by a secularist. But this is hardly the main point. The crux of the current Israeli *Kulturkampf* is clear and simple: Are we to adhere to our historic commitment and retain our identity as a spiritual community? Or are we to abjure our heritage and undergo, in Keble's famous phrase, "national apostasy"?

The danger that the total separation of religion and state will increasingly secularize society as a whole does not derive solely from secularists' demands. It is inherently rooted in the structure of modern society. So long as democratic theory and practice were dominated by the laissez-faire approach of classical liberalism, the effects of disestablishment were relatively minor. The church lost its privileged position, but the field was left fully open for its operation as a purely voluntary force. The French and American Revolutions ended government's patronage of religion, but they did not posit them as rivals. However, the century-old abandonment of laissez-faire has changed the situation drastically. The erosion of the private sector attendant upon the intrusion of the state into all walks of life has directly and materially affected church-state relations. The primary threat to religion posed by a secular state is no longer suppression but competition. The danger is not persecution but displacement. It is not the threat of being uprooted but that of becoming desiccated that is paramount.[20]

This is true in three ways: First, insofar as a sense of comfortable security, shallow as it may be, and the loss of private initiative and personal responsibility have deadened the individual's spiritual élan and religious verve. This torpor is by no means wholly due to the modern state. As Tocqueville and Mill emphasized, the sheer weight and breadth of a democratic society are likely to lead to conformist mediocrity, especially in an age of mass communications. Welfare-state paternalism has been of crucial importance, however. The Grand Inquisitor knew whereof he spoke. Not the bang but the whimper, not dissipation but ennui have become the spiritual dragons of the welfare age.

Second, the expansion of the state's activity has enabled it to make inroads upon the emotional attachment to religion. In one area after another – education, philanthropy, family counseling, and so on – government has preempted the former social role of religion. In so doing, it has not only reduced the church's hegemony; it has alienated the affections of its adherents. The modern state engages the emotions of its constituents in spheres undreamt of by Talleyrand and Palmerston. It is no mere accident that the notion of treason as a major crime, popularly regarded with an abhorrence reserved for few transgressions, is so relatively recent.[21]

Third, the omnivorous state competes with organized religion on a more pedestrian level – for money, for energy, above all, for time. The individual or nation with limited human and economic resources is confronted by government and religion with conflicting claims which are theoretically reconcilable but, practically speaking, mutually exclusive. To be sure, religion demands much more than material elements, and when it ossifies into demanding nothing else, a period of retrenchment and disengagement from the world is perhaps in order. As a viable institution, however, it does require material elements, too, in order to fulfill its distinctly spiritual function; and on this level it is in direct competition with the state. Needless to say, within a separatist structure in which the claims of government are binding and those of religion purely voluntary, the competition is rather unequal.

Such being the rivalry, conscious or unconscious, between government and religion, a purely "neutral" disestablished state is no more than a pipe-dream. In theory, there is a fine ring about it. The power of the state is to be exerted neither pro nor con religion, with reference to which a wholly voluntary approach is to prevail. In practice, however, things shape up somewhat differently. Religious education is voluntary, but only after a student has spent the lion's share of his time in state schools in which nary a prayerful syllable may be uttered. To be sure, there is an alternative. An American parent can forego the free education his tax dollars have bought for his children and spend thousands of dollars a year on tuition.[22] But just how voluntary is such a choice? Again, financial support for religious institutions is voluntary, but only with funds left over after the state has extracted its own sizable share!

Such a state is not neutral at all. A government that is deeply enmeshed in all spheres of life and yet operates in a purely secular manner is not just religiously inert. Beyond a certain point, omission is commission. To exercise significant control over society while remaining aloof from religion is, in effect, to oppose it. In a pluralistic democracy, this problem is aggravated by government's own tendency to become progressively more secular. Initially, assuming a generally religious society, even an avowedly disestablished state is likely to be involved in some aspects of religion. But in a religiously pluralistic society, a state committed to full separation will, at most, support only those aspects of religious life for which there is universal approval. In time, therefore, as any new form of dissent, however radical, crops up, the area of full consensus gradually contracts, and the state disengages itself more and more from religious involvement. With government directing so much of civic life, the public role of religion is gradually neutralized in one area after another, until it is whittled down to a private enclave within the overall social structure.

The American experience, especially in its recent phases, illustrates this pattern clearly,[23] and its possible Israeli counterpart can only be projected with trepidation. I am far from suggesting that the separation of religion and state in Israel would immediately produce so secular a society. Certainly religion is too potent a force at every level of Israeli life to disintegrate overnight. Yet before we set out on the path recommended to us by the advocates of separation, we would do well to scrutinize its direction and terminus. Moreover, separation would have greater repercussions in Israel than it has had in America. The specific practical demands of Christianity are, after all, relatively few, and thus the secular character of the state may not have so direct and extensive an impact upon the nature of society. Judaism, by contrast, imposes numerous practical demands in virtually all walks of life. Its distinctive quality is best characterized by its scope. Hence, the adverse religious effect of a purely secular government would be correspondingly more serious within a Jewish than within a Christian state. The withdrawal of the state from a number of crucial areas – which, practically speaking, is no withdrawal at all but a positive thrust in a secular direction – would directly undermine the Jewish character of Israeli society as a whole.

We should not be misled here by the apparent strength of the churches in America as reflected in recent social and political struggles. By and large, the churches have been able to exercise this power only where they have, in effect, whether consciously (as with Harvey Cox and his confrères) or unconsciously, worked on the terms of the secular gospel. One must entertain strong reservations as to whether they could muster widespread support over an issue that was purely religious and lacked secular sanction. It may not even be amiss to wonder whether, once their present social desiderata are attained, some church leaders will not find themselves somewhat adrift, groping – like many post-Depression liberals – for direction and purpose.

VI.

It is against this background that the problem of state religious coercion needs to be seen.[24] The problem has two aspects, for coercion may be opposed on two distinct grounds. The first is the general notion that the state has no business interfering in the personal affairs of private citizens. Every man's home is his castle, and so long as he tends his vineyard and does not disturb his neighbor, no one has the right to disturb him. This individualistic credo, which constituted the core of eighteenth- and nineteenth-century liberalism, once seemed almost irresistible. However, its contemporary force has been considerably blunted. The transition from laissez-faire to a welfare state has been attended by extensive governmental encroachment upon the so-called private sector. Even in the democracies, once inviolable property rights have been ignominiously trampled in the name of transcendent human rights; and once untouchable private enclaves have been subjected to extensive legislation and regulation. The century since *On Liberty* has eroded liberty in the interests of equality. Hence, if the argument against religious coercion rested solely on this general individualistic ground, it would have relatively little contemporary force. We could then indulge ourselves in the well-founded suspicion that modern latitudinarianism is more the result of religious indifference than of libertarian conviction.

There is, however, a second and more powerful argument against specifically religious coercion. Its contention is not so much that government *ought not* compel moral and religious action as that it *cannot*. Morality and religion depend upon inner conviction, and this lies beyond external control. Hence, as T.H. Green insisted,

> the question sometimes put, whether moral duties should be enforced by law, is really an unmeaning one; for they simply cannot be enforced. They are duties to act, it is true, and an act can be enforced: but they are duties to act from certain dispositions and with certain motives, and these cannot been forced. Nay, the enforcement of an outward act, the moral character of which depends on a certain motive and disposition, may often contribute to render that motive and disposition impossible.[25]

At best, the state can try to develop an environment within which morality can flourish.

On the whole, this argument is not directly relevant to the religious legislation now being attacked by Israeli secularists. The laws currently on the books have not sought solely or even primarily to impose a degree of religiosity upon all private citizens but rather to safeguard certain public areas. While the act of betrothal, *kiddushin,* constitutes a *mizvah,*[26] no one imagines that the purpose of the *Hok ha-Ishut* (Marriage Act) was to ensure that every eligible Jew would perform this one additional *mizvah.* Nor do the local Sabbath ordinances aim so much at compelling personal observance as at preserving the Sabbath's public character. Regardless of its lack of immediate relevance, however, no discussion of religion and state can ignore this problem, and at least a summary attempt to deal with it is, therefore, in order.

From a halakhic perspective, this argument should be considered on three levels: the ideal, the normative, and what, for lack of a better term, I shall call the tactical. Ideally, of course, religion should be spiritual in character. Religious acts should be motivated by the profoundest inner commitment, and religious existence should be permeated by the pervasive devotion of mind and will. "God desires the heart," said the rabbis.[27] Anyone with even a nodding acquaintance with Halakhah and endowed with any sensitivity to its values is fully aware of this; and hardly needs to be told that "religion should be a force by virtue of being a norm, not a norm by virtue of being a force." This is so self-evident, however, as to be almost tautological. The real question is entirely different. In the absence of the ideal motivation, does an act become morally and religiously worthless?

From a purist or from a Kantian perspective, this question should probably be answered in the affirmative. But the Halakhah thinks otherwise. While it has always emphasized the need to strive for an ideal motivation, it has never denigrated lower levels of commitment. It demands that the Jew engage in Torah and *mizvot lishmah,* out of a pure love of God. But it acknowledges the value of inferior motivation. "Let a man always engage in Torah and *mizvot,* though it be not for their own sake, for out of [doing them with] an ulterior motive he comes to [do them for] their own sakes."[28] On the one hand, it defines the *mizvah* of loving God as precluding not only serving Him for the sake of earthly rewards but even for theological hedonism: "Lest you say," explains the *Sifre*, "'I shall study Torah in order that I shall become wealthy, in order that I shall be called rabbi, or in order that I shall receive reward in the world-to-come,' therefore the text says, 'to love God, your Lord': all that you do, you should do solely out of love."[29] And yet, on the other hand, it can state that "Whoever says, 'Let this *selah* [coin] go to charity in order that I shall be a member of the world-to-come,' he is considered wholly virtuous."[30] However we resolve the apparent contradiction,[31] it should be clear that the Halakhah acknowledges both the ideal of selfless spirituality – "His *mizvot* he [i.e., the virtuous man] desires very much; but not the reward for His *mizvot*"[32] – and the inferior but nonetheless valid externally motivated virtue.

Hence, even actions that might otherwise not have been undertaken spontaneously, but are performed in response to promises or threats, may have some merit. Conceived simply as present actions, they may derive some value from their objective – one might almost say, their metaphysical – character. A *mizvah* performance, or contrarily a transgression, has intrinsic significance. This is a notion that the Greeks would have understood readily, but that the modern mind, since Descartes so subjectively and introspectively oriented, no doubt finds difficult to grasp. It seems more mystical than halakhic. And yet it ought not to be so inconceivable that objects, times, places, or actions, that have been singled out by divine command should be endowed, on a legal and not just on a mystical plane, with a certain character; and that acts which conform to certain external specifications could be described as objective religious acts even when their motivation is not impeccable. Moreover, such acts may have some value with reference to the future, as part of an educative process that can eventually lead the sluggish or recalcitrant Jew to a higher level of religious devotion. Under certain conditions, actual engagement in religious performances may turn initial reluctance into ultimate enthusiasm. It is altogether too easy to be a rigorous purist in this area. To contend, in Ernest Barker's words, "that true religion is a matter of the mind, to be sought and found in voluntary cooperation with others of like mind, and therefore to be sought and found in the area of Society,"[33] so that the state is, on the whole, effectively excluded, is to take far too simple a view of the complex interaction of the physical and spiritual aspects of human experience. In one sense, no doubt, opponents of civil rights legislation were right in arguing that morality cannot be legislated. Yet, quite apart from any objective attainments, we ought not underestimate the impact of external action and habit upon inner conviction. It is precisely because it avoids this pitfall that the Halakhah defines moral or religious acts in relatively liberal terms.

There is, however, a crucial proviso. The Halakhah, like Kant, does demand motivation, although not to the same total extent. In order to constitute a valid religious performance, a *mizvah* action must be accompanied by *kavvanah,* by an awareness on the part of the agent that he is acting in response to a divine imperative, and by a desire that the action constitute a proper fulfillment of his duty.[34] *Kavvanah* obviously involves moral and theological presuppositions of no little import; and the need for it reduces drastically the scope of any possible coercion. We are therefore inevitably led, first, to accept R. Meir Simhah's position that any religious coercion mentioned in the gemara is limited to situations in which it can be reasonably assumed that the application of external pressure will lead to an inner change of heart.[35] And second, we are led to ponder the conditions under which such a situation obtains. They do not admit of easy and precise definition, but at least their general outline may be indicated. The crucial principle, I believe, rests upon the distinction between two types of will – a specific and immediate will that resists a command or bridles at a restriction, and a more general and settled moral will that may acknowledge in principle the very authority which, on a different level, is then resented.[36] Broadly speaking, I know that I oughtn't double-park, and fundamentally I recognize the state's right to prevent me from so doing. But when I return from the dentist to find that my car has been towed away, I am genuinely, if temporarily, resentful. If we reject the notion that all sin or vice is simply error, and if we recognize the clear fact that we are regularly derelict in performing duties of whose essential value and normative character we are fundamentally convinced, then we shall grasp the essence of paradoxically convincing coercion. When agent and patient share a basic recognition of the law and of its authority to impose upon the individual, coercion, even in the moral and religious sphere, becomes possible. Where such recognition is lacking, it is wholly unworkable; and then, of course, as R. Meir Simhah emphasized, it becomes immoral. There is no middle ground here. Coercion either effects inner conviction, and then it may be justified, or else it is not simply neutral but halakhically forbidden.

On the ideal level, then, the Halakhah strives for maximal spirituality. On another level, it asserts that in principle external pressure may sometimes be morally justified. What are we to assume, however, on a third level – the tactical? Even if the power and the authority to impose Halakhah still existed or once existed, would it be wise and moral to exercise them now?

The answer must be sought in the light of the principles outlined above and with an eye to contemporary conditions.[37] Quite obviously, with respect to many, if not most, halakhic demands, fundamental acceptance by non-observant Israelis simply does not exist. This is not solely due to the fact that non-observant Jews are now so much more numerous than they were before the Enlightenment, although that is a factor. It is due, in large measure, to the fact that the recalcitrant Jew is now differently motivated. Whereas dereliction in fulfilling religious duties would previously have been probably due to frailty and backsliding, i.e., a volitional failing, it is now generally the result of unbelief, an intellectual failing. The type of resistance encountered is entirely different, therefore, and is not amenable to formerly effective modes of response. Moreover, in the generally libertarian climate of modern Western society, attempts at coercion are usually not only ineffectual but destructive. Inasmuch as they generate resentment, they do not simply fall short but backfire. In the present context, therefore, coercion, as a technique of stimulating positive religious observance, cannot generally succeed.

VII.

Lest I be misunderstood, let me emphasize that I am not suggesting that all religious legislation is now *ipso facto* out of court. Some laws may aid in preserving our public national character even if they do not materially promote individual observance. And for others there may be general basic acceptance. I simply point out that by and large, coercion is no longer a feasible and justifiable *modus operandi*; and that now more than ever, our main thrust must be educational. This does not mean that we should introduce total separation of religion and state, a step that could entail the gravest consequences. The modern state has many other means at its disposal besides coercion. The schools are no less a part of its apparatus than the courts. I think it would be a great mistake to totally sever the state from religion. From both a moral and a pragmatic point of view, however, we need to be most careful about the stress and scope of its involvement.

It should be clear that such reservations about the present value of much specific legislation are radically different from the total opposition in principle espoused by secularists. Before a Jewish state institutes religious ordinances, it must evaluate empirically the overall impact of a given law upon the quality of national and individual religious life. It must ascertain whether the game is worth the candle. The possibility that the resistance engendered will outweigh any gain in observance or commitment; that individual personality will be impaired by the impingement upon civil liberties; that the spirituality and the independence of organized religion will be diluted by its increased affiliation with the state – all must be carefully considered, spiritual gain in one sector being balanced against possible loss in another. However, the right of legislation *per se* does exist. We cannot ignore valid objections to religious legislation; but if we are to maintain a viable Jewish society, neither can we assume that they must always be decisive.

The realities of life will not let us eat our cake and have it too. We cannot be both wholly free and truly committed. No society can be fully open unless it is genuinely open-ended. Most modern Western readers are no doubt revolted by the middle books of Plato's *Republic*. Even while sharing in this revulsion, however, we need to realize what drove the greatest of classical thinkers to such extremes. It was, of course, commitment: commitment to the true, the beautiful, and the good, to the idea of virtue, the ideal of a *polis* saturated with *arete*. We must realize further that, unless it wishes to rely upon Pollyannish hopes, any society committed to any ideal will have to take some step down this Platonic road. It will have to encourage, perhaps even compel, action it deems necessary to preserve that ideal and maintain its character; and to this end it will almost inevitably involve its political arm, the state. If we agree with Aristotle that the state does not exist solely for the sake of life but for the sake of the good life – taking "good" to be in some sense ideal rather than utilitarian – then we must recognize that at some point the state will have to act in order to promote that life. In so doing, it will employ its two principal weapons: the carrot and the stick. The only question is how much use will be made of one or the other. To us the question is crucial, but from the point of view of those who would divorce a state's political activity from its ultimate commitment, it is thoroughly irrelevant. The principle of separation is breached by blandishment or education no less than by threat.

Hence, the only truly neutral state is one governed by a relativist ethic. If no absolute values are assumed, then a fully open society is quite feasible. However, if a society wishes to lead its members, and therefore itself, in a certain direction, it must be prepared at some point to act to this end politically. No doubt, the main thrust should always be educational, the basic language always spiritual, the primary appeal always to minds and hearts rather than to bodies or pockets. Nevertheless, we cannot *a priori* eschew a political approach entirely. Let us make no mistake: ultimately, we are not only confronted with the problem of religion and state but with the broader question of morality and state. Philosophically, the same arguments that militate against the state's involvement in the one apply likewise to the other.

These remarks have a particular relevance for a Jewish society – by definition, to use Rav Soloveitchik's phrase, "the community of the committed." Ours is, moreover, a specific commitment, rooted in our history and revolving around an apocalyptic experience. We are not just committed to some abstract Platonic idea but to the God of Abraham, Isaac, and Jacob. Indeed, our moral claim to the possession of the Land or the State of Israel rests solely on the historic destiny growing out of that historical commitment. The commitment and the experience must be created anew in every generation: "Let them [the words and commands of the Torah] be treasured by you as if you had received them this very day from Sinai; and let them be as regularly upon your tongue as if you had heard them this very day."[38] But at the same time they must be transmitted and inculcated, and to this end we cannot *a priori* reject governmental assistance entirely. Even if we should be sufficiently optimistic to imagine that such assistance would never be extended in the interests of natural religion or morality (and one need hardly be a Hobbesian to reject such a judgment), we cannot assume the same with reference to Judaism. Without external guidance and with no knowledge of tradition whatsoever, a spiritually minded person may perhaps become a devotee of Bahai; but a Jew – hardly. He must somehow learn that God has spoken to Israel and receive the content of the divine message; and to this end he needs some guidance. To establish a purely secular State of Israel at present would mean to preclude such guidance from the vast areas of life influenced, if not controlled, by government. This could not be countenanced by the *Knesset Yisrael* out of whose past we have evolved and in whose future we have devout faith. It was not for this that our forefathers lived and died, and it is not through this that our children can hope to survive. Ours is a unique destiny: to serve as a vehicle of God's purpose in history, and this entails not just glory but responsibility.

VIII.

Midway through his essay, "Secularism and Religion in Israel," Professor Nathan Rotenstreich quietly executes a remarkable *volte-face*.[39] Whereas he had previously appeared to champion not only a secular state but the secularist gospel *in toto*, he now proceeds to advise religionists how they ought best to promote their cause. We are no longer told that a state should be secular *per se* but that it must be secular because this is in the best interest of religion; and we are told further how religion – or more specifically, Halakhah – must reform or transform itself if it is to survive in the modern world. This section, therefore, goes far beyond political problems, and its challenge to traditional Judaism is very different from what we have hitherto encountered. Precisely for this reason, however, the issues it raises, serious and fundamental as they are, require much fuller treatment, both more intensive and more extensive, than can be presented if the present essay is to remain within reasonable bounds. Nevertheless, the issues cannot and should not be ignored entirely; and I shall attempt, if only in brief summary, to come to grips with the heart of the argument.

Professor Rotenstreich's critique of Halakhic Judaism opens with the observation, borrowed from Solomon Schiller, that "the development of Orthodox Judaism is governed by the law of inertia." If I remember my physics correctly, the classical law of inertia simply reads: "Every body continues in its state of rest or uniform motion in a straight line except insofar as it is compelled by external forces to change that state." Secularists, observing Halakhic Judaism from without, apparently assume it to be in a state of continuous rest; hence the intended criticism. Traditional Jews, however, who have known and lived Halakhah from within, and who experience it as a vibrant and dynamic force, see it as being constantly in motion – or perhaps (shades of Zeno!) as being, paradoxically, both at rest and in motion. They might therefore find Schiller's remark not quite so damning. Indeed, if we can disregard the mechanical overtones of the metaphor, it is downright flattering.

These remarks are not made in jest. They cut to the root of professor Rotenstreich's argument, for he fails to appreciate properly what to the traditional Jew is the most pulsating reality of all, Divine Revelation. What the halakhist finds succulent and vital is for him arid and sterile; and the failure to grasp both the vibrancy and the significance of revelation lies at the heart of his critique. Professor Rotenstreich advances two contentions, one historical and the other normative. He claims that Jewish thought has always been isolationist in character, and that this is due primarily to the intrinsic nature of Halakhah, and secondarily, in recent times, to the dominance of Eastern European (i.e., Halakhah-saturated) Jewry. He also argues that Judaism should abandon the traditional, limited, objective framework of Halakhah in favor of a more general approach.

Underlying both statements is the failure to regard seriously either Halakhah or the revelation upon which it is grounded. As a matter of bare fact, it is no doubt true that "throughout its history, the primary concern of Jewish thought has been self-interpretation, interpretation of the heritage of Judaism, interpretation of the relation between Judaism and other religious or philosophical world-outlooks and traditions." But why? Partly, no doubt, because of the inherently separatist nature of the Jew: "the whole world is on one side and he [i.e., Abraham] is on the other;"[40] and partly because of the lengthy sojourn in a Diaspora whose alien environment drew Jewry inward upon itself and assigned top priority to the sheer preservation of distinctive identity and values. Primarily, however, this concern derived from the utter and genuine earnestness with which both the idea and the content of revelation were taken. Can those who are convinced that the heritage of Judaism is grounded in the Divine Word make anything but that their primary concern? Such concentration does not constitute a flight from reality. On the contrary, it is rooted in the quest for a higher reality to which the Jew can relate both himself and his world. It is, however, admittedly confining. In the very process of revelation, God limited Israel, closing some options even as He opened others; and to the extent that he seeks to respond to that revelation and to interpret it, the Jew *does* limit himself somewhat. To be sure, the degree of confinement has varied. Medieval Ashkenazic Jewry was more intense and narrow than its Sephardic counterpart. In some measure, however, confinement has persisted throughout.

Nevertheless, it would be wrong to assume that traditional Jewry cannot or should not come to grips with contemporary problems. Its primary concern with the heritage of Judaism has not constituted a deliberate aversion from the world but rather a yearning for the Word and for the Divine Presence revealed through it. The possibility, indeed the obligation, of dealing with general contemporary issues within a halakhic framework is very much alive, however. Inasmuch as we are enjoined not only to understand Halakhah but to experience it, and not only to experience but to apply it, we shall – even as the interpretation of our heritage remains our primary concern – strive to understand the modern world, to grapple with its problems, and to cope with its inexorably increasing impingement upon Jewry and its values. And we shall not assume, *a priori,* that these tasks cannot be performed.

Professor Rotenstreich's second contention, that Judaism and Halakhah should be less objective in character, likewise ignores the full implications of our commitment to revelation. He laments the rigidity of Halakhah and contends that "only a view which transcends the Halakhah can constitute a foundation for suggested innovation;" and he goes on to complain that even critics of the "current interpretation of the Halakhah in Israel generally base their criticism upon the Halakhah itself rather than upon a more comprehensive view which transcends it. If, accordingly, the Halakhah is a realm in which Jewish thought is confined, how can the Halakhah itself make available to its dwellers the means of breaking through its walls?" Well, why not go a step further? Since Judaism is a realm within which Jewish thought is confined, how can Judaism itself make available to its dwellers the means of breaking through those walls? And ought we not, therefore, opt for a universal religion?

This is not merely an exercise in one-upmanship but an attempt to point out the obvious. If we take seriously the idea of revelation – and of Halakhah as its explication – we cannot look for ways of transcending it. We *can* properly speak of values that are both the basis and the *telos* of Halakhah and that transcend specific normative sections; and we can validly attempt, on the practical plane and in accordance with halakhic processes, to harmonize the values and the norms, the spirit and the letter, of Halakhah when changed conditions tend to rend them asunder. But this is hardly the same as transcending the Halakhah in its entirety.

This is not to deny the possibility of a certain type of development or change within Halakhah. Change does take place, and anyone who doubts this should try to decide halakhic questions by referring solely to the Gemara. However, the change grows out of creative insight, disciplined interpretation, occasional legislation, and perceptive application to contemporary conditions – all operating in accordance with valid halakhic procedure. It cannot result from random tampering. We can hardly tinker with a system grounded in Divine Revelation.

To be sure, Halakhah does contain a human element, and the rabbis not only acknowledged it but, in a sense, glorified it.[41] But this element cannot take the form of casuistic engineering or self-willed revision. Rather, it consists of an honest attempt to explicate and apply the Divine

Word and the legal corpus grounded upon it in accordance with one's best human lights; and at the same time, within certain limits and in the spirit of Halakhah, of the promulgation of new laws by recognized authorities endowed with sound scholarship and developed halakhic intuition. It may be argued that in certain areas the authority for change properly available within the Halakhah has been insufficiently exercised. But this is hardly the same as to criticize its essentially objective character. To make subjectivism its conscious operative principle is not so much to transcend Halakhah as to abandon it.[42]

The very nature of the human element in Halakhah demands that definitive interpretation be left to acknowledged authorities, *talmidei hakhamim* whose informed scholarly judgement and profound commitment to tradition qualify them for competent decision. Since this element is not a matter of sheer fiat but of insight and interpretation, it must meet a certain standard of knowledge and responsibility vis-à-vis the tradition. While the obligation to study Torah and to attempt to interpret it is universal, the right to make definitive decisions is not. Luther's principle of private judgment, short-lived even in the more limited domain of scriptural explication, hardly applies to more complex halakhic interpretation. In the final analysis, undemocratic as it may sound, halakhic decision does indeed rest with halakhists. With whom else?

IX.

At this point, we are confronted by the specter of ecclesiasticism, with all its attendant overtones of overcentralization and worldliness. Professor Rotenstreich is perfectly right to call attention to these dangers, although I think he errs in asserting that the Israeli rabbinate's current status has no Jewish precedent. The ancient Sanhedrin is one, the structure of Babylonian Jewish society is a second, and the more recent *Va'ad Arba Ha-Arazot* is a third. Whether or not there are precedents, however, the dangers inherent in ecclesiasticism are ever present and very real, and proponents of spiritual religion must be constantly ready to detect and denounce any onset of ossification or creeping worldliness. It does not therefore follow, however, that the abrogation of rabbinic authority is the proper alternative. At most, we have here an argument, not necessarily decisive, against *centralized* halakhic authority, the transposition to another milieu, as it were, of the struggle between the Congregationalists and the Presbyterians. This position can be argued, but let us recognize the argument for what it is worth. It hardly militates for taking halakhic authority out of the hands of those who, by knowledge and commitment, are best qualified to exercise it.

The failure to appreciate the significance of revelation also underlies Professor Rotenstreich's comments concerning the Orthodox attitude toward the secular segment of the community. Rotenstreich lays great stress on the secularist's voluntary renunciation and demands that it be acknowledged. In one sense, I agree with him wholeheartedly. As a Jew committed to the halakhic tradition, I naturally make it the basis of my action; and its truth, values, and interest serve as a point of departure for my thinking. However, I know full well that many Jews – very often through no fault of their own – lack this commitment, and that any concession they make to its normative demands is, more likely than not, purely voluntary. To the extent that such renunciation is ethically motivated, say, by a desire for national unity or out of deference to one's fellow, I not only acknowledge this voluntary element but salute it. However, if Professor Rotenstreich means not only that the secularist's renunciation, given his rejection of tradition, is to be lauded, but that we should recognize his right to reject the tradition in the first place, then an Orthodox Jew cannot but demur. We must no doubt be charitable in evaluating the subjective reasons for such rejection, but we can hardly assume, given our acceptance of revelation, that a Jew has the right to renounce it. We recognize, of course, that secularism is one approach, and that secularists are not all profligate libertines. But is it a Jewish approach? Something more was demanded and committed at Sinai. I am perfectly willing, again, to consider Professor Rotenstreich's statement that it is tactically and psychologically wiser, and hence morally and religiously purer, to ask the secularist to renounce voluntarily rather than to attempt to impose upon him. However, I cannot do so without holding that he ought to be bound by Halakhah even while I know he is not. The basic principle that normative Judaism, as a divinely ordained order, is binding upon *Knesset Yisrael* is not my personal possession to renounce.

A similar flaw pervades Rotenstreich's comments concerning the halakhic attitude toward "the problem of non-Orthodox piety." Orthodox Jews recognize that heterodox piety does exist, just as they realize that secularists may lead genuinely ethical lives (albeit only because they are unwittingly inconsistent with their own principles). I hope that Professor Rotenstreich does not seriously believe that the attitude he ascribes to Orthodox Jews – "better an atheist than a non-Orthodox Jew" – is a genuinely halakhic position.[43] Particularly in an age when belief is so largely conditioned by environmental influences and prevalent intellectual currents, it would be both unwise and immoral to deny the genuine reality of heterodox religious experience. It does not therefore follow, however, that the distinction between Orthodox and non-Orthodox Judaism can be safely ignored. Viewed as a subjective phenomenon, heterodox piety may constitute invaluable religious experience, and this consideration is crucial for any intelligent assessment of the individual involved. However, as interpretations of revelation and the tradition that explicates it, heterodox versions are quite invalid. If we take seriously the idea of an objective revealed divine will, then no matter how charitably or tolerantly we may wish to regard our fellow Jews, we cannot treat all readings of it equally. Beyond a certain point, sincerity and goodwill are not enough. We have a responsibility not only to preserve our own moral integrity but also to see that the revealed will of God prevails. That the existence of an objective element in Halakhah may occasionally produce apparent anomalies is unquestionable (whether or not the case of Brother Daniel is one).[44] This is inherent in the nature of law. But Professor Rotenstreich's alternative to the halakhic dialectic between subjective and objective poles poses far graver problems than it resolves. He would, as Sterling said of Carlyle, take us into the desert and leave us there. In any event, however, if we scratch Rotenstreich's essay enough, I think we encounter not only opposition to Halakhah but universalistic repugnance to the notion of Special Revelation.

Yet Special Revelation, paradoxical a doctrine though it may seem, is the core of Judaism. It assisted at our birth, it defined our essence, and it molds our destiny. To constitute, in some particular sense, a "dwelling" for the suffusive Presence of the *Shekhinah*, to testify to a singular divine message, received, on the one hand, and to be borne, on the other: this is the essence of Jewish history. Covenants ago, in a land by rivers bounded, two roads diverged in a wood. We took the one as yet untraveled – and that has made all the difference.

Notes

1. Throughout this essay I assume that the concept of a state in the modern sense of the term, distinct from either a city or a kingdom, is halakhically valid. I have no doubt that this is so, but I should point out that its precise halakhic character and status require careful formulation. This is not my present purpose, however.
2. See Zevahim 101b and Shevuot 15a.
3. Historians have disagreed on the degree of actual observance in these periods. But apart from the fact that I am inclined to assume that it was reasonably widespread, the general profession or assumption of commitment is in itself crucial.
4. Sanhedrin 37a. See also ibid. 38a, and *Tosefta*, Berakhot 6:2.
5. Mishneh Torah, Hilkhot Teshuvah 3:11.
6. Ta'anit 25a.
7. See Sanhedrin 17b.
8. While this view of freedom is deeply Jewish, it is by no means exclusively so; and while, in a certain sense, it implies a more restricted freedom than the eighteenth-century Enlightenment envisioned, it has been espoused by some liberal as well as conservative thinkers. A prime example would be T.H. Green, for whom the concept of what he called "positive freedom" was central. See Guido de Ruggiero, *The History of European Liberalism,* trans. R.G. Collingwood (Oxford, 1927), especially pp. 347–357.
9. Vayikra 25:42.
10. Avot 6:2. Cf. Eruvin 54a, where the same idea is developed with reference to the collective, national scope. The conflict between organic and democratic theory, so irreconcilable in secular terms (see T.D. Weldon, *State and Morals* [London, 1946], pp. 26–61), assumes an entirely different character in a religious framework.
11. See the selections from his writings published under the title *On God and Political Duty,* ed. John T. McNeill (New York: Liberal Arts Press, 1950). It should be pointed out, however, that Calvin's acceptance of even the most tyrannous civil authority and his insistence that martyrdom was preferable to resistance was due, in large measure, to his acknowledgment of the former's existence as providentially ordained. The bifurcation of nature and grace was not the only factor.
12. This position was not adopted by all Puritans. One should beware of oversimplifying generalizations. See A.S.P. Woodhouse's introduction to *Puritanism and Liberty,* 2nd ed. (London, 1950), especially pp. 35–60.

13. See Christopher Dawson, *Religion and Culture* (London, 1949), chap. 6.
14. See *The Church Speaks to the Modern World: The Social Teachings of Leo XIII*, ed. E. Gilson (Garden City, NY: Image Books, 1954), pp. 167–168.
15. See Mishneh Torah, Hilkhot Shabbat 29:1.
16. See his comment on Bereshit 49:10.
17. *Teshuvot Ha-Rambam*, ed. J. Blau (Jerusalem, 1960), p. 715.
18. The scope of the Halakhah could conceivably assign a far-reaching social role to a religious court (*bet din*). However, the definition of the proper role of a *bet din* and of its practical relations to civil government requires fuller and more precise halakhic formulation than can here be undertaken. I might just refer to the radically different definitions of the *mizvah* of appointing a *bet din* formulated by the Rambam in *Sefer Ha-Mizvot, mizvot assei*, 176, and by the Ramban in his commentary on Devarim 16:18, and to the eleventh of Rabbenu Nissim's twelve *derushim* in *Derashot Ha-Ran*, which deals specifically with the delineation of civil and religious authority.
19. *Ha-Emunot ve-ha-De'ot* III:7.
20. See Christopher Dawson, *Religion and the Modern State* (New York, 1936), chap. 3.
21. See Margaret Boveri, *Treason in the Twentieth Century*, trans. Jonathan Steinberg (London, 1961), pp. 13–18, 33–44.
22. The situation is somewhat different in Israel, where, as in early Victorian England, the government supports a number of educational channels. But this pluralism is precisely part of what advocates of separation are attacking.
23. For a lucid and compact account of the legal history of this area prior to the ban on prayer in public schools, see Harry W. Jones, "Church-State Relations: Our Constitutional Heritage," in *Religion and Contemporary Society*, ed. Harold Stahmer (New York, 1963), pp. 156–214.
24. It should be emphasized that the question of coercion is not the same as the problem of separation. A state can be involved in religion in a noncoercive manner (even though there is ultimately an indirect coercive element, since taxes are used to finance all state endeavors), and coercion can be exercised by a voluntary society, such as a union, or, in an indirect manner, by society at large. This fact is added reason for proceeding carefully in defining the concepts of consent and coercion.
25. *Lectures on the Principles of Political Obligation* (London, 1895), p. 34 (sec. 10).
26. See Kiddushin 41a, where it is stated that one should betroth in person rather than through an agent because the *mizvah* is greater.
27. Sanhedrin 106b.
28. Pesahim 50b. As the Netziv pointed out, this should be understood to mean that the involvement has present intrinsic merit, even if *lishmah* is never attained, and not just as an advisable ploy because it can lead to greater heights; see *Meshiv Davar*, I, 44.
29. *Parshat Ekev* 41, commenting on Devarim 11:13; cf. Nedarim 62a.
30. Pesahim 8a.
31. Various solutions have been propounded for reconciling the citation from Pesahim with

other texts which clearly demand that the individual purge himself of ulterior motivation; see the commentaries ad loc., and in parallel texts. I might only mention that R. Hananel (Rosh Hashanah 4a) reads *tzedakah gemura* rather than *tzadik gamur,* suggesting that the act is valid or meritorious even if the agent is spiritually deficient.

32. Avodah Zarah 19a.

33. *Principles of Social and Political Theory* (Oxford, 1951), p. 46.

34. These remarks assume the view of the tannaim and amoraim who held that *mizvot* are invalid if performed without *kavvanah;* see especially Pesahim 114b–115a and Rosh Hashanah 28a–29a. This view was accepted in the *Shulhan Arukh,* Orah Hayyim 60:4, but not all of the Rishonim accepted it. My basic position here would not be severely affected in any event, since many Rishonim stressed that everyone would agree that acts done with rebellious or resistant intention could certainly not be considered fulfillment of a *mizvah.* The whole problem of objective and subjective elements in Judaism, the role of inwardness, and especially the crucial relation of law and morality require much fuller treatment. It should be added that these remarks deal with coercion as a stimulus to positive religious behavior. Punishments for transgressions and their use as a deterrent would pose a somewhat different problem. The argument with reference to them would therefore follow a different, albeit in some respects parallel, course. The conclusion on the tactical level would be pretty much the same, however.

35. *Or Same'ah,* Hilkhot Gerushin 2:20.

36. The distinction is by no means my own discovery, for it has classical origins and was prominent in Burke. See Charles Parkin, *The Moral Basis of Burke's Political Thought* (Cambridge, 1956). It was especially developed and applied in Bernard Bosanquet, *The Philosophical Theory of the State,* 3rd ed. (London, 1920), chaps. 3, 5–6.

37. I have omitted any discussion of the most obvious tactical argument for pluralism; namely, that if generally pursued, the insistence on spreading one's truth leads to conflict and instability, resulting finally in the situation commended by Dr. Johnson to Boswell: "Every man has the right to speak his mind, and every other man has the right to knock him down for it." On the assumption that one has the truth, however, this is primarily a pragmatic rather than a moral argument; and the possibility that a system may be false (one of Mill's arguments) cannot itself be part of the meaning of that system. Of course, from the perspective of Kant's categorical imperative, this *is* a moral argument, and a most persuasive one, but only within a philosophic framework that rejects the concept of particular revelation. To say that the argument is pragmatic rather than moral is not to dismiss it, and the various factors in any given situation (e.g., what the effect of religious legislation in Israel would be upon Jews potentially subject to equivalent legislation in non-Jewish countries) need to be weighed. Such calculation occurs on a different level, however, and lies outside the purview of this paper.

38. *Sifre,* Parshat Re'eh 58, commenting on Devarim 11:32.

39. *Judaism* 15, no. 3 (Summer 1966).

40. Bereishit Rabbah 13:42.

41. See Makkot 22b and *Hiddushei Ha-Ritva,* Eruvin 13b.

42. Within certain limits, there is some leeway for deciding objectively and legally questionable matters on the basis of one's subjective ethical inclinations. But while this point is important, it constitutes a nuance within an objective framework rather than a general denial of that framework.

43. In one sense, of course, one might think that atheism *is* better than heterodoxy inasmuch as it poses a clear alternative to Orthodoxy rather than an adulteration or dilution of it, so that it does not threaten it in quite the same way. It is precisely for this reason that personal and institutional relations between Orthodox and non-Orthodox Jews are often more strained than the relations of either with atheists. In this sense, however, the term "better" has political (I use the term in a good sense) rather than moral and theological overtones.

    As to whether anyone ought rather be an atheist than a non-Orthodox Jew, it is inconceivable that any advocate of Halakhah would assume the position ascribed to him by Rotenstreich. One should not be misled by R. Tarfon's statement that, "If someone were pursuing me, I would rather escape into houses of *avodah zarah* [idolatry] than into houses of *minim* [heretics]. For worshippers of *avodah zarah* reject Him without knowing Him, but the *minim* know Him and yet reject Him" (Yerushalmi, Shabbat 16:2). As the text specifies, the distinction is not between two degrees of remoteness from God but two types of motivation, one conscious rebellion and the other unwitting rejection. Wherever, because of different circumstances than R. Tarfon's, the distinction in motivation does not exist, the statement would not apply.

44. See my discussion of the Brother Daniel case in chapter 3 of this volume.

.

Chapter 2

Does Judaism Recognize an Ethic Independent of Halakhah?

Does Jewish tradition recognize an ethic independent of Halakhah? My subject is a simple factual question presumably calling for a yes-or-no answer. But what kind of Jew responds to salient questions with unequivocal monosyllables? Certainly, not the traditional kind. Moreover, as formulated, this particular query is a studded minefield, every key term an ill-defined booby trap. Who or what represents the tradition? Is the recognition *de facto* or *de jure*? How radical is the independence? Above all, what are the referents of "ethic" and "Halakhah"? A qualified reply is obviously required.

Before presenting it in detail, however, I must confess that, on one level, an unequivocal response could be easily mounted. If the issue is reduced to natural morality in general, it need hardly be in doubt. "Rabbi Yohanan stated," says the gemara in Eruvin, "If the Torah had not been given, we would have learned modesty from the cat, [aversion to] robbery from the ant, chastity from the dove, and [conjugal] manners from the cock."[1] The passage implies, first, that a cluster of logically ante-halakhic virtues exists; second, that these virtues can be inferred from natural phenomena; and, probably, third – with Plato and against the Sophists – that they relate to *physis* rather than *nomos,* being not only observable through

---

Reprinted from *Modern Jewish Ethics,* ed. Marvin Fox (Columbus, 1975).

nature but inherent within it. Nor does the passage stand alone. The wide-ranging concept of *derekh eretz* – roughly the equivalent of what Coventry Patmore called "the traditions of civility" – points in the same direction.[2] Its importance again, not as descriptively synonymous with conventional conduct but as prescriptive *lex naturalis* should not be underestimated. The Mishnah cites Rabbi Eliezer b. Azariah's view that "without Torah, there is no *derekh eretz,* and without *derekh eretz,* there is no Torah;"[3] and the Midrash goes beyond this dialectical reciprocity, stating that "*derekh eretz* preceded Torah."[4] In context, the primary reference is to chronological priority. Nevertheless, one senses that the common tendency, especially prevalent among the mussar masters, to include logical, if not axiological, precedence as well, is a response to clearly present undertones; and, in this sense, the two texts are closely related. As the Maharal put it, "From this [i.e., the Mishnah], we learn that *derekh eretz* is the basis of Torah, which is," as explained by the Midrash, "the way of the tree of life."[5] Their link reinforces our awareness of the rabbis' recognition of natural morality.

There is, however, little need to adduce proof texts. Even if one assumes that the rabbis' awareness of natural law as an explicit philosophical and historical doctrine was limited, a point that Baer and Lieberman have debated,[6] this would be, for our purposes, quite irrelevant. Indeed, even if one accepts the thesis, recently advanced by Marvin Fox,[7] that the concept of natural law, in its classical and Thomistic sense, is actually inconsistent with the thought of the rabbis and the Rishonim, our problem is very little affected. The fact remains that the existence of natural morality is clearly assumed in much that is quite central to our tradition. All discussion of theodicy is predicated upon it. As Benjamin Whichcote,[8] the seventeenth-century Cambridge Platonist, pointed out, one cannot ask, "Shall, then, the judge of the whole earth not do justice?"[9] unless one assumes the existence of an unlegislated justice to which, as it were, God Himself is bound; and which, one might add, man can at least apprehend sufficiently to ask the question. Or again, any attempt at rationalizing Halakhah, an endeavor already found in Hazal, although much more fully elaborated by the Rishonim, presupposes an axiological frame of reference, independent of Halakhah, in the light of which it can be interpreted. It makes no sense to say, with Abbaye, that "the whole of the Torah... is for the purpose of promoting peace,"[10] unless the ethical value of peace can be taken for granted. The same holds true with respect to suggesting reasons for specific *mizvot*. The intensity of Maimonides' efforts on this front is consistent with the position – advanced by Rav Saadia Gaon[11] and, in broad outline, adopted by Rabbenu Bahya[12] and probably by Maimonides[13] – that, given sufficient time, ability, and interest, the bulk of revealed Torah could have been naturally and logically discovered.

Any supposed traditional rejection of *lex naturalis* cannot mean, therefore, that apart from Halakhah or, to put it in broader perspective, in the absence of divine commandment, man and the world are amoral. Nor does it entail a total relativism or the view (evidently ascribed to Maimonides by Professor Fox)[14] that social convention or utility is the sole criterion for action. At most, the rabbis rejected natural law, not natural morality. They may conceivably have felt that one could not ground specific binding and universal rules in nature, but they hardly regarded uncommanded man as ethically neutral. They could have accepted, on the natural plane, the position summarized by Whitehead:

> There is no one behaviour-system belonging to the essential character of the universe, as the universal moral ideal. What is universal is the spirit which should permeate any behaviour-system in the circumstances of its adoption.... Whether we destroy, or whether we preserve, our action is moral if we have thereby safeguarded the importance of experience so far as it depends on that concrete instance in the world's history.[15]

But they would surely have gone no further. One might contend, maximally, that natural morality is contextual rather than formal. It does, however, exist.

Inasmuch as the traditional acceptance of some form of natural morality seems to me beyond doubt, I could, were I literally minded, simply answer our original question in the affirmative and close up shop. I presume, however, that its framers had something more in mind. If I read their concern rightly, the issue is not whether the tradition accords a non-halakhic ethic some theoretical standing by acknowledging its universal validity and provenance. Rather, in light of Hazal's statement that "Torah has been given and Halakhah innovated,"[16] it is whether that standing is of any practical significance to us; whether, for the contemporary Jew, an ethic independent of Halakhah can be at all legitimate and relevant on an operative level.

On this plane, the issue resolves itself, in turn, into the problem, both historical and analytic, of the relation between the pre- and post-Sinai orders, somewhat akin to the question of the relation between nature and grace that has exercised so much Christian theology. On this score, traditional thought has focused upon two complementary points. The first is that natural morality establishes a standard below which the demands of revelation cannot possibly fall. Thus, in proving that the killing of a Gentile constitutes proscribed murder (although the Torah at one point speaks of a man killing "his fellow," i.e., a Jew; Shemot 21:14), the Mekhilta explains: "Issi b. Akiba states: Prior to the giving of the Torah, we were enjoined with respect to bloodshed. After the giving of the Torah, instead of [our obligation's] becoming more rigorous [is it conceivable] that it became less so?"[17] Moreover, this limit does not just reflect a general attitude but constitutes a definitive legal principle to be applied to specific situations. "Is there anything, then," the gemara asks, "that is permitted to the Jew but prohibited to the Gentile?"[18] And it uses the implicit rhetorical denial to clinch a fine point in the course of an intricate discussion.

The second point is most familiarly associated with a statement – frequently quoted, and never, to the best of my knowledge, seriously challenged – made by Maimonides in his Commentary on the Mishnah. Taking his cue from a mishnah in Hullin concerning the prohibition against eating the sciatic nerve (*gid ha-nasheh*), he goes on to postulate a general principle:

> And pay attention to the great principle conveyed by this mishnah when it states that it [i.e., the sciatic nerve] was "proscribed from Sinai." What you must know is that [as regards] anything from which we abstain or which we do today, we do it solely because of God's commandment conveyed through Moses, [and] not because God commanded thus to prophets who preceded him. For instance we do not circumcise because Abraham circumcised himself and the members of his household, but because God commanded

us, through Moses, to become circumcised as did Abraham.... Take note of
their [i.e., the rabbis'] comment, "Six hundred and thirteen *mizvot* were stated
to Moses at Sinai, and all of them are among those *mizvot*."[19]

On this view, although the substance of natural morality may have
been incorporated as a floor for a halakhic ethic, it has nevertheless, as a
sanction, been effectively superseded.

On another level, however, we are confronted by an issue of far wider
scope. The question is not what vestiges of natural morality continue to
bind the Jew or to what extent receiving the Torah abrogated any antecedent ethic. It is, rather, whether the demands or guidelines of Halakhah,
quite apart from the ground common to natural and halakhic morality,
are both so definitive and so comprehensive as to preclude the necessity for – and therefore, in a sense, the legitimacy of – any other ethic.
In translating my assigned topic into these terms (so strikingly familiar
to readers of Hooker's *Ecclesiastical Polity*),[20] I am taking two things for
granted. I assume, first, that Halakhah constitutes or at least contains an
ethical system. This point has sometimes been challenged – most notably,
in our day, by Professor Yeshayahu Leibowitz; but I do not think that the
challenge, albeit grounded in healthy radical monotheism, can be regarded
seriously. The extent to which Halakhah as a whole is pervaded by an ethical moment or the degree to which a specific *mizvah* is rooted, if at all, in
moral considerations is no doubt debatable. If evidence were necessary,
we need only remember the conflicting interpretations of the Mishnah
concerning "he who says, May your mercies encompass the bird's nest"[21]
and the attendant controversy over the rationalization of *mizvot* en bloc.[22]
As for the outright rejection of the ethical moment, however, I cannot find
such quasi-fideistic voluntarism consonant with the main thrust of the
tradition. One might cite numerous primary texts by way of rebuttal, but
a single verse in Jeremiah should suffice: "But let him that glorieth, glory
in this, that he understandeth and knoweth Me, for I am the Lord who
exercise mercy, justice, and righteousness, in the earth; for these I desire,
saith the Lord."[23] The ethical element is presented as the reason for seeking knowledge of God, or, at the very least, if we translate *ki ani* as "that

I am" rather than "for I am,"[24] as its content. In either case, the religious
and the ethical are here inextricably interwoven; and what holds true
of religious knowledge holds equally true of religious, that is, halakhic,
action. This fusion is central to the whole rabbinic tradition. From its perspective, the divorce of Halakhah from morality not only eviscerates but
falsifies it.

Second, I assume that, at most, we can only speak of a complement to
Halakhah, not of an alternative. Any ethic so independent of Halakhah as
to obviate or override it clearly lies beyond our pale. There are, of course,
situations in which ethical factors like the preservation of life, the enhancement of human dignity, the quest for communal or domestic peace, and
the mitigation of anxiety or pain sanction the breaching, by preemptive
priority or outright violation, of specific norms. However, these factors
are themselves halakhic considerations, in the most technical sense of the
term, and their deployment entails no rejection of the system. Admittedly,
advocates of such rejection are no strangers to Jewish history; but they are
hardly our present concern. However elastic the term "tradition" may be to
some, it does have its limits, and antinomianism, which for our purposes
includes the rejection of Torah law, lies beyond them. As a prescriptive
category, the currently popular notion of *averah lishmah* (idealistic transgression) has no halakhic standing whatsoever.[25]

Essentially, then, the question is whether Halakhah is self-sufficient.
Its comprehensiveness and self-sufficiency are notions many of us cher-
ish in our more pietistic or publicistic moments. For certain purposes, it
would be comfortable if we could accept Professor Kahana's statement
"that in Jewish civil law there is no separation of law and morals and that
there is no distinction between what the law *is* and what the law *ought*
to be."[26] If, however, we equate Halakhah with the *din*, if we mean that
everything can be looked up, every moral dilemma resolved by reference
to code or canon, the notion is both palpably naive and patently false.
The Hazon Ish, for one, and both his saintliness and his rigorous halakhic
commitment are legend, had no such illusions. "Moral duties," he once
wrote, "sometimes constitute one corpus with halakhic rulings, and it is
Halakhah that defines the proscribed and permitted of ethical thought."[27]

Sometimes but not, evidently, always. There are moments when one must seek independent counsels. Recognition of this element rests upon both textual and practical evidence. In this setting, I presume, little need be said with reference to the latter. Which of us has not, at times, been made painfully aware of the ethical paucity of his legal resources? Who has not found that the fulfillment of explicit halakhic duty could fall well short of exhausting clearly felt moral responsibility? The point to be emphasized, however – although this too, may be obvious – is that the deficiency is not merely the result of silence or ambiguity on the part of the sources. That may, of course, be a factor, requiring, as it does, recourse to inference and analogy to deal with the multitude of situations that, almost *a priori,* are not covered by basic texts. The critical point, however, is that even the full discharge of one's whole formal duty as defined by the *din* often appears palpably insufficient.[28]

Lest this judgment appear excessively severe, let me hasten to add that it is precisely this point that is stressed by the second source of evidence: the textual. Consider the gemara in Bava Metzia:

> Rav Yohanan said, "Jerusalem was destroyed because they [i.e., its inhabitants] judged [in accordance with] Torah law within it." Well, should they have followed the law of the Magians instead?! Say, rather, because they based their judgments solely upon Torah law and did not act *lifnim mi-shurat ha-din* [i.e., beyond the line of the law].[29]

Nahmanides was even more outspoken. In a celebrated passage, he explains that the general command "Ye shall be holy" was issued because, the scope of the Torah's injunctions regarding personal conduct notwithstanding, a lustful Sybarite could observe them to the letter and yet remain "a scoundrel with Torah license." The same holds true, he continues, with respect to social ethics. Hence, in that area, too, the Torah formulates a broad injunction:

> And this is the Torah's mode: to detail and [then] to generalize in a similar vein. For after the admonition about the details of civil law and all interpersonal dealings… it says generally, "And thou shalt do the right and the good," as it includes under this positive command justice and accommodation and all *lifnim mi-shurat ha-din* in order to oblige one's fellow.[30]

This position is further elaborated in Nahmanides' explication of the phrase "the right and the good." He suggests, initially, that it may refer to the collective body of specific *mizvot*, but then presents an alternative:[31]

> And our rabbis have a fine interpretation of this. They said: "This refers to compromise and *lifnim mi-shurat ha-din.*"[32] The intent of this statement is that, initially,[33] He had said that you should observe the laws and statutes which He had commanded you. Now He says that, with respect to what He has not commanded, you should likewise take heed to do the good and the right in His eyes, for He loves the good and the right. And this is a great matter. For it is impossible to mention in the Torah all of a person's actions toward his neighbors and acquaintances, all of his commercial activities, and all social and political institutions. So after He had mentioned many of them, such as "thou shalt not go about as a tale-bearer," "thou shalt not take vengeance or bear a grudge," "thou shalt not stand idly by the blood of thy fellow," "thou shalt not curse the deaf," "thou shalt rise up before age,"[34] and the like, He resumes to say generally that one should do the good and the right in all matters, to the point that there are included in this compromise, *lifnim mi-shurat ha-din,* and [matters] similar to that which they [i.e., the rabbis] mentioned concerning the law of the abutter,[35] even that which they said, "whose youth had been unblemished,"[36] or "he converses with people gently,"[37] so that he is regarded as perfect and right in all matters.[38]

These passages contain strong and explicit language, and they answer our question plainly enough. Or do they? Just how independent of Halakhah is the ethic that ennobles us above the "scoundrel with Torah license"? If we regard *din* and Halakhah as coextensive, very independent. If, however, we recognize that Halakhah is multiplanar and many-dimensional; that, properly conceived, it includes much more than is explicitly required or permitted by specific rules, we shall realize that the ethical moment we are seeking is itself an aspect of Halakhah. The demand or, if you will, the impetus for transcending the *din* is itself part of the halakhic corpus. This point emerges quite clearly from the primary rabbinic source for the concept of *lifnim mi-shurat ha-din.*

> "'And thou shalt show them the way': this is the study of Torah; 'and the action they should take': good conduct." These are the words of Rabbi Yehoshua. Rabbi Eleazar of Modi'im says: "'And thou shalt show them': teach them their life's course; 'the way': this alludes to visiting the sick; 'they shall walk':

to burying the dead; 'therein': to exercising kindness; 'and the action': to *din* proper; 'which they shall do': to *lifnim mi-shurat ha-din.*"[39]

Whether we accept Rabbi Yehoshua's generalization or Rabbi Eleazar's more specific catalogue, the conjunction of either "good conduct" or *lifnim mi-shurat ha-din* with thoroughly mandatory elements clearly indicates that it is no mere option.

The obligatory character of *lifnim mi-shurat ha-din* stands revealed in the verses Nahmanides saw as related to it: "And thou shalt do the right and the good" and "Ye shall be holy." Neither was expressed in the indicative or the optative. With respect to the degree of obligation, however, the Rishonim admittedly held different views. Perhaps the most rigorous was advanced by one of the Tosafists, Rabbi Isaac of Corbeille. In his *Sefer Mizvot Katan,* one of the many medieval compendia summarizing and enumerating the *mizvot,* he lists "to act *lifnim mi-shurat ha-din,* as it is written, 'which they shall do' "[40] as one of the 613 commandments; and he goes on to cite the gemara in Bava Mezia 30b as a proof-text. Nahmanides did not go quite this far, as he does not classify *lifnim mi-shurat ha-din* as an independent *mizvah,* as binding as shofar or tefillin. However, he does clearly posit it as a normative duty, incumbent upon – and expected of – every Jew as part of his basic obligation. Failure to implement "the right and the good" would obviously not be regarded as mere insensitivity to the music of the spiritual spheres. It is villainy: with the Torah's license, but villainy nonetheless.

Maimonides, however, does apparently treat *lifnim mi-shurat ha-din* in a more rarefied context. After presenting his account of the golden mean in the opening chapter of Hilkhot De'ot, he concludes: "And the early pietists would incline their traits from the median path toward either extreme. One trait they would incline toward the farther extreme, another toward the nearer; and this is *lifnim mi-shurat ha-din.*"[41] On this view, supralegal conduct appears as the hallmark of a small coterie of hasidim. Postulated as an aristocratic rather than as a popular ideal, *lifnim mi-shurat ha-din* thus represents a lofty plane whose attainment is a mark of eminence but whose neglect cannot be faulted as reprehensible.

This is drastically different from Nahmanides and may be construed as indicating, contrary to my earlier statement, that according to Maimonides, *lifnim mi-shurat ha-din* is purely optional; that it constitutes a kind of supererogatory extra-credit morality rather than an obligation, strictly speaking. Even if the argument is accepted, it would not render *lifnim mi-shurat ha-din* wholly voluntary. It would merely shift it, to use Lon Fuller's distinction, from the "morality of duty" to the "morality of aspiration."[42] But a Jew is also commanded to aspire. More important, however, this point has little impact upon our present broader purposes. The semantics and substance of the term *lifnim mi-shurat ha-din* aside, Maimonides most certainly does not regard character development, ethical sensitivity, or supralegal behavior as nonhalakhic elements, much less as optional. He simply subsumes them under a different halakhic rubric, the demand for *imitatio dei*. "And we are commanded," he writes, "to walk in these median paths, and they are the right and the good paths, as it is written, 'And ye shall walk in His ways.'"[43] The command refers to the golden mean rather than to *lifnim mi-shurat ha-din*,[44] but we are confronted by the same normative demand for "the right and the good."

The difference in terminology and source is significant, and, were my present subject *lifnim mi-shurat ha-din per se*, I would discuss it in detail. For our purposes, however, Maimonides' and Nahmanides' views point in the same general direction: Halakhah itself mandates that we go beyond its legal corpus. Were I to follow Fuller's example and chart a spectrum running from duty to aspiration,[45] I think that, on Maimonides' view, so-called nonhalakhic ethics would be a couple of notches higher than for Nahmanides. Even after we have taken due account of the imperative of pursuing "His ways," we are still imbued with a sense of striving for an ideal rather than of satisfying basic demands. Nevertheless, the fundamental similarity remains. The ethic of *imitatio* is not just a lofty ideal but a pressing obligation. The passage previously cited from Maimonides explicitly speaks of our being "commanded" (*u-mezuvim anu*) to pursue the golden mean; and subsequent statements are in a similar vein. Thus, he asserts that Scripture ascribes certain attributes to God "in order to inform [us] that they are good and right ways and [that] a person is obligated [*hayav*] to guide himself by them and to resemble Him to the best of his ability." Or again, he speaks of the attributes as constituting collectively "the median path that we are obligated [*hayavim*] to pursue."[46] Furthermore, it is noteworthy that in describing this ethic, Maimonides uses the very adjectives fastened upon by Nahmanides: "right and good." It can be safely assumed that both, in principle, recognize the imperative character of supralegal conduct.[47]

This exposition is admittedly partial. It rests upon two assumptions: first, that Maimonides recognizes an elitist ethic of the hasid, which, though grounded in *din*, nevertheless transcends it; second, that even the universal median ethic demands much that has not been specifically legislated, and, according to Nahmanides' definition, would be subsumed under *lifnim mi-shurat ha-din*. I think both points emerge unequivocally from the account in Mishneh Torah; but in the earlier *Shemonah Perakim* we get a distinctly different impression.[48] In this work, action *lifnim mi-shurat ha-din* is not described as inherently superior to the golden mean but as a propaedeutic technique for attaining it. As in Aristotle's familiar example of straightening the bent stick,[49] one excess is simply used to correct another, this corresponding to standard medical practice. Second, Maimonides suggests that adherence to *din* proper produces the ideal balance, so that deviation in any direction, except when dictated by the need to "cure" the opposite deficiency, becomes not only superfluous but undesirable.

The brunt of this argument is directed against asceticism, and the excesses decried by Maimonides all concern material self-denial.[50] However, the list of examples adduced to prove the sufficiency of Torah law includes *mizvot* that relate to a whole range of virtues and vices: munificence, anger, arrogance, timidity. The net impact of the passage, therefore, is clearly to diminish somewhat the role of an independent ethic. Nevertheless, I am inclined to regard the later and fuller exposition in Hilkhot De'ot as the more definitive. The difference between Maimonides and Nahmanides, though significant, does not strike me as radical.

The variety of conceptions of a supralegal ethic held by the Rishonim may be judged from another perspective, in light of a very practical question: Is *lifnim mi-shurat ha-din* actionable?[51] The gemara records at least one instance in which it was enforced. It tells the story of some porters who had been working for Rabbah the son of Rav Huna and who had broken a barrel of wine while handling it. Inasmuch as they had evidently been somewhat negligent, the strict letter of the law would have held them liable for the damage; and since they had been remiss in performing their assigned task, it would have allowed them no pay. By way of guaranteeing restitution, Rabbah held onto their clothes, which had apparently been left in his possession, as surety;

> whereupon they came and told Rav, [who in turn] told [Rabbah], "Return their clothes to them." "Is this the *din*?" [Rabbah] asked. "Yes," [Rav] answered, "'that thou mayest walk in the way of good men.'" [Rabbah] then returned their clothes, whereupon they said to him, "We are poor, we have labored all day, and [now] we are hungry and left with nothing!" [So Rav] said to [Rabbah], "Go and pay their wages!" "Is this the *din*?" [Rabbah] asked. "Yes," [Rav] answered, "'And keep the path of the righteous.'"[52]

Moreover, in the Palestinian Talmud,[53] a similar story is told, not about an amora, from whom a higher ethical standard could presumably be exacted, but about an ordinary potter. However, the pathetic circumstances as well as the omission of the term *lifnim mi-shurat ha-din*[54] suggest this may have been an isolated instance. In any event, the Rishonim divided on the issue. The Rosh held that "we do not compel action *lifnim mi-shurat ha-din*";[55] and inferring *de silentio*, I think it safe to assume that this was the prevalent view of the Spanish school. However, a number of Tosafists, notably Ravya and Ravan,[56] held that such action could indeed by compelled. Of course, such a position could not conceivably be held with reference to all supralegal behavior. *Din* has many ethical levels; and so, of necessity, must *lifnim mi-shurat ha-din*. Surpassing laws grounded in, say, the concept that "the Torah has but spoken vis-à-vis the evil inclination"[57] is hardly comparable to transcending those with a powerful moral thrust. Nevertheless, the fact that some Rishonim held *lifnim mi-shurat ha-din* to be, in principle, actionable, indicates the extent to which it is part of the fabric of Halakhah.

The possibility of compulsion arises in yet another, and possibly surprising, context. Hazal state that *kofin al midat Sodom*, "we coerce over a trait of Sodom."[58] As defined by most Rishonim, this refers to an inordinate privatism that leaves one preoccupied with personal concerns to the neglect of the concerns of others; a degree of selfishness so intense that it denies the other at no gain to oneself. There need be no actual spite. Simple indifference may suffice. Nor is *midat Sodom,* despite the severity of the term, confined to what popular morality might regard as nastiness or mindless apathy. One view in the Mishnah – the definitive view according to most Rishonim – subsumed under it the attitude that "mine is mine and yours is yours."[59] Thus, it broadly denotes obsession with one's private preserve and the consequent erection of excessive legal and psychological barriers between person and person.

This posture the rabbis both condemned and rendered actionable. To the best of my knowledge, however, Hazal nowhere explicitly formulated the basis of this Halakhah. I would therefore conjecture that it is most likely subsumed under *lifnim mi-shurat ha-din*; and if this be so, we have here a striking instance of its scope and force. Admittedly, most of us do not instinctively associate the two concepts. However, this is simply another manifestation of our failure to grasp the full range of supralegal obligation. So long as *lifnim mi-shurat ha-din* is regarded as the sphere of supererogatory extra-credit morality, it can hardly include rejection of actions so reprehensible as to earn the opprobrium of *midat Sodom.* However, once we appreciate its true scope, from rigorous obligation to supreme idealism, we should have little difficulty with the association.

The Maharal, at any rate, had none – precisely because he emphasized the centrality and force of *lifnim mi-shurat ha-din.* This emphasis was clearly expressed in the course of his discussion of *gemilut hasadim* (loosely translatable as "benevolent action"). "The antithesis of this trait," he writes, "is [a person] who does not want to do any good toward another, standing upon the *din* and refusing to act *lifnim mi-shurat ha-din.*" This virtual equation of *hesed* and *lifnim mi-shurat ha-din* then becomes the basis for an explanation of the gemara's comment regarding the destruction of Jerusalem. This was not, the Maharal explains, retributive punishment. It was a natural consequence, for a wholly legalistic community simply cannot exist. Supralegal conduct is the cement of human society. Its absence results in disintegration: "Standing upon *din* entails ruin." Likewise, excessive commitment to law invites disaster on a broader scale, for, by correspondence, it both recognizes and enthrones natural law as cosmic sovereign, thus rejecting the providential grace of miracles that deviate from it. Finally, rejection of *lifnim mi-shurat ha-din* is defined as the hallmark of Sodom, whose evil, although it issued in corruption, nevertheless was grounded in total fealty to legal nicety: "For this was their nature, to concede nothing, as the rabbis said, 'Mine is mine and yours is yours: this is the trait of Sodom.' And they have everywhere said, *kofin al midat Sodom.*"[60] The identification of *lifnim mi-shurat ha-din* as the source of such coercion is here fairly explicit; and the conjunction of its denial with the biblical apotheosis of malice reflects the importance that the Maharal attached to supralegal conduct.

This exposition is open to two obvious objections. First, if *lifnim mi-shurat ha-din* is indeed obligatory as an integral aspect of Halakhah, in what sense is it supralegal? More specifically, on the Ravya's view, what distinguishes its compulsory elements from *din* proper? Second, isn't this exposition mere sham? Having conceded, in effect, the inadequacy of the halakhic ethic, it implicitly recognizes the need for a complement, only to attempt to neutralize this admission by claiming the complement has actually been a part of Halakhah all along, so that the fiction of halakhic comprehensiveness can be saved after all. The upshot of this legerdemain does not differ in substance from the view that the tradition recognizes an ethic independent of Halakhah, so why not state it openly?

These are sound objections; but they do not undermine the position I have developed. They only stimulate a more precise definition. As regards the first question, a comment made, interestingly, by the Ravya points toward the solution. The Ravya is explaining why Rav Nahman did not compel the finder of a lost object whose owner despaired of its recovery to return it. Rav Nahman holds that the finder is legally free to retain the object, but the gemara notes that the object is returnable *lifnim mi-shurat ha-din.*[61] The Ravya suggests that in this instance, "perhaps the finder was poor, whereas the object's owner was well-to-do."[62]

Within the framework of *din,* this would be a startling distinction.

Powerful as is the obligation of the affluent to help the relatively disadvantaged, it is a general responsibility to a group and enforceable only through a third party, the community and its *bet din*. Although many *poskim* regard charity as a legal and collectible debt rather than a mere act of grace,[63] an individual pauper certainly has no right, except with respect to one type of charity, *ma'aser ani* (tithe for the poor),[64] to seize his more affluent neighbor's property.

That such a point could be made with reference to *lifnim mi-shurat ha-din* suggests its crucial distinction from *din*. It is less rigorous not only in the sense of being less exacting with respect to the degree and force of obligation – and there are times, as has been noted, when it can be equally demanding – but in the sense of being more flexible, its duty more readily definable in light of the exigencies of particular circumstances. This has nothing to do with the force of obligation. Once it has been determined, in a given case, that realization of "the right and the good" mandates a particular course, its pursuit may conceivably be as imperative as the performance of a *din*. However, the initial determination of what moral duty requires proceeds along different lines in the respective spheres. *Din* consists of a body of statutes, ultimately rooted in fundamental values, that, at the moment of decision, confront the individual as a set of rules. It is highly differentiated, numerous variables making the relevant rule very much a function of the situation. Yet, the basic mode is that of formulating and defining directives to be followed in a *class* of cases; it is precisely the quality of generality that constitutes a rule and applies them to situations marked by the proper cluster of features. Judgments are essentially grounded in deductive, primarily syllogistic reasoning. Metaphors that speak of laws as controlling or governing a case are therefore perfectly accurate.

Lifnim mi-shurat ha-din, by contrast, is the sphere of contextual morality. Its basis for decision is, paradoxically, both more general and more specific. The formalist is guided by a principle or a rule governing a category of cases defined by n number of characteristics. The more sensitive and sophisticated the system, the more individuated the categories. Whatever the degree of specificity, however, the *modus operandi* is the same:

action grows out of the application of class rules to a particular case judged to be an instance of that class or of the interaction of several classes, there being, of course, principles to govern seemingly hybrid cases as well. The contextualist, by contrast, will have nothing to do with middle-distance guidelines. He is directed, in theory, at least, only by the most universal and the most local of factors – by a minimal number, perhaps as few as one or two, of ultimate values, on the one hand, and by the unique contours of the situation at hand, on the other. Guided by his polestar(s), the contextualist employs his moral sense (to use an outdated but still useful eighteenth-century term) to evaluate and intuit the best way of eliciting maximal good from the existential predicament confronting him. A nominalist in ethics, he does not merely contend that every case is phenomenologically different. That would be a virtual truism. He argues that the differences are generally so crucial that no meaningful directives can be formulated. Only direct ad hoc judgment, usually – although this is, logically, a wholly separate question – his own, can serve as an operative basis for decision. Between ultimate value and immediate issue, there can be no other midwife.

It goes without saying that Judaism rejects contextualism as a self-sufficient ethic. Nevertheless, we should recognize that it has embraced it as the *modus operandi* of large tracts of human experience. These lie in the realm of *lifnim mi-shurat ha-din.* In this area, the halakhic norm is itself situational. It speaks in broad terms: "And thou shalt do the right and the good"; "And thou shalt walk in His ways." The metaphors employed to describe it, "the ways of the good" and "the paths of the righteous," denote purpose and direction rather than definitively prescribed acts. And, finally, the distinction from *din* is subtly recognized in the third source we have noted: "'And the action': this [refers to] the line of *din;* 'that they shall take': this [refers to] *lifnim mi-shurat ha-din*" – the reified static noun being used in relation to one and the open-ended verb in relation to the other. In observing *din,* the Jew rivets his immediate attention upon the specific command addressed to him. His primary response is to the source of his prescribed act. With respect to *lifnim mi-shurat ha-din,* he is, "looking before and after," concerned with results as much as with origins. His focus is axiological and teleological.

Quite apart from the severity of obligation, therefore, there is a fundamental difference between *din* and *lifnim mi-shurat ha-din*. One, at a more minimal level, imposes fixed objective standards. The demands of the other evolve from a specific situation; and, depending upon the circumstances, may vary with the agent.

This point was clearly recognized by a late Rishon, the author of a fourteenth-century commentary on the Mishneh Torah. In explaining why Maimonides both expanded and differentiated the concept of *dina de-bar mezra*, making it legally enforceable in some cases but only obligatory *ante facto* in others,[65] the *Maggid Mishneh* both echoes Nahmanides and goes beyond him.

> The point *of dina de-bar mezra* is that our perfect Torah has laid down [general] principles concerning the development of man's character and his conduct in the world; as, in stating "Ye shall be holy,"[66] meaning, as they [i.e., the rabbis] said, "Sanctify yourself with respect to that which is permitted you,"[67] that one should not be swept away by the pursuit of lust. Likewise, it said, "And thou shalt do the right and the good," meaning that one's interpersonal conduct should be good and just. With regard to all this, it would not have been proper to give detailed instructions. For the Torah's commands apply at all times, in every period, and under all circumstances, whereas man's characteristics and behavior vary, depending upon the time and the individual. The rabbis [therefore] set down some relevant details subsumed under these principles, some of which they made [the equivalent of] absolute din and others [only] *ante facto* and by way of *hasidut,*[68] all [however] ordained by them. And it is with reference to this that they said, "The words of consorts [i.e., the rabbis] are more beloved than the wine of Torah, as stated, 'For thy love is better than wine.'"[69]

The *Maggid Mishneh* is certainly not espousing an exclusively relativistic or situational ethic. No conscientious halakhist could even countenance the possibility. He is, rather, defining the character of *dina de-bar mezra*, and, more generally, of "the right and the good"; and beyond this, noting that, from a certain perspective, the greater flexibility and latitude that characterize this class of rabbinic legislation give it an edge, as it were, over the Torah's absolutely rigorous law. The concluding statement is of considerable interest in its own right. Comparisons aside, however, the passage clearly reveals the respective characters of *din* and *lifnim mi-shurat ha-din*.

The second objection – that I am either playing games or stalking a Trojan horse, and possibly both – can likewise be parried. Whether supralegal behavior is regarded as an aspect of, and in relation to, Halakhah does matter considerably. The difference, moreover, concerns not so much the prestige of Halakhah as the substance of the supralegal behavior. And this in three respects. First, integration within Halakhah helps define the specifics of supralegal conduct. One of its principal modes entails the extension of individual *dinim* by (1) refusal to avail oneself of personal exemptions; (2) disregard of technicalities when they exclude from a law situations that, morally and substantively, are clearly governed by it; and (3) enlarging the scope of a law by applying it to circumstances beyond its legal pale but nevertheless sufficiently similar to share a specific *telos*. All three, however, constitute, in effect, the penumbra of *mizvot*. To this end, relation to a fundamental law, which posits frontiers and points a direction, is obviously essential.

Not all supralegal conduct has this character, however. It may, alternatively, either fill in a moral lacuna at a lower level – *kofin al midat Sodom* is an excellent example; or, on a higher plane, aspire to attainments discontinuous with any specific practical norm. Even at these nether and upper reaches, however, relation to the overall halakhic system is important both for the definition of general goals and by way of molding orientation, context, and motivation. Even while closing an interstice or reaching for the stars, one does not move in a vacuum. The legal corpus here, to adapt Ben Jonson's remark about the ancients, is more guide than commander; but it is vital nonetheless.

Finally, the halakhic connection is relevant at a third level, when we are concerned with an ethic neither as decisor of specific actions nor as determinant of a field of values but as the polestar of life in its totality. Halakhic commitment orients a Jew's whole being around his relation to God. It is not content with the realization of a number of specific goals but demands personal dedication – and not only dedication, but consecration. To the achievement of this end, supralegal conduct is indispensable.

Integration of the whole self within a halakhic framework becomes sub-stantive rather than semantic insofar as it is reflected in the full range of personal activity. Reciprocally, however, that conduct is itself stimulated by fundamental halakhic commitment.

Let me emphasize that in speaking of the investiture of an indepen-dent ethic with a halakhic mantle, I hold no brief for terminology *per se*. I would readily concede that we can, if we wish, confine the term "halakhah" to *din* and find some other term to cover what lies beyond. A limitation of this kind would probably be consonant with the use of the term by Hazal. In classical usage, "halakhah," properly lower-case and commonly used without the definite article, generally denotes a specific rule (hence, the frequent appearance of the plural, *halakhot*) or, in broader terms, the body of knowledge comprising Torah law. It does not convey the common contemporary sense in which it is roughly the equivalent of halakhic Juda-ism – the *unum necessarium* of the Jew committed to tradition, in which, as a commanding presence, magisterial to the point of personification, it is regarded as prescribing a way of life; in which, as with the term "Torah" in Hazal, Halakhah and its Giver frequently become interchangeable. Hence, we ought not to be surprised if we find that Hazal did differentiate between *halakhot* and other normative elements. Thus, in commenting upon the verse "If thou wilt diligently hearken to the voice of the Lord thy God, and wilt do that which is right in His eyes, and wilt give ear to His command-ments, and keep all his statutes,"[70] the Mekhilta notes:

> "And wilt do that which is right in His eyes": these are wonderful aggadot which hold every one's ear; "and wilt give ear to His commandments": these are orders; "and keep all His statutes": these are *halakhot*.... These are the words of Rabbi Yehoshua. Rabbi Eleazar of Modi'im says... "And wilt do that which is right in His eyes": this is commercial dealings. [The verse thus] teaches [us] that whoever deals honestly and enjoys good relations with people is regarded as having realized the whole Torah. "And wilt give ear to His commandments": these are *halakhot*; "and keep all His statutes": these are [prohibitions concerning] forbidden sexual relations.[71]

This exposition I understand readily and, semantics apart, find fully consistent with the view I have outlined above. At most, it requires that we adjust our customary terminology somewhat and assent to the thesis that traditional halakhic Judaism demands of the Jew both adherence to Halakhah and commitment to an ethical moment that, though different from Halakhah, is nevertheless of a piece with it and in its own way fully imperative.[72] What I reject emphatically is the position that defines the function and scope of Halakhah in terms of the latitude implicit in current usage, yet identifies its content with the more restricted sense of the term. The resulting equation of duty and *din* and the designation of supralegal conduct as purely optional or pietistic is a disservice to Halakhah and ethics alike.

In dealing with this subject, I have, in effect, addressed myself both to those who, misconstruing the breadth of its horizons, find the halakhic ethic inadequate, and to those who smugly regard its narrower confines as sufficient. In doing so, I hope I have presented my thinking clearly. But for those who prefer definitive answers, let me conclude by saying: Does the tradition recognize an ethic independent of Halakhah? You defines your terms and you takes your choice.

Notes

1. Eruvin 100b. Soncino translates "we could have learnt," but I think "would have" is more accurate. Rabbenu Hananel, it might be noted, has *lamadnu.*

2. In the passage cited from the gemara in Eruvin, the term has a rather narrow meaning, referring, in context, to proper conjugal gallantry. Elsewhere, however, it clearly denotes far more, sometimes civility or culture generally. The *Mahzor Vitry,* commenting on Avot 3:17 (ed. Horowitz, p. 517), renders it as *nourriture,* and the Maharal of Prague spells out its latitude quite clearly: "The things that are *derekh eretz* are all ethical matters included in Avot, those mentioned in the Talmud, and all other ethical matters. It is conduct that is right and fitting toward [possibly, 'in the eyes of'] people; and failure to pursue some of its elements is sinful and a great transgression" (*Netivot Olam,* Netiv Derekh Eretz, chap. 1). See also N.S. Greenspan, *Mishpat Am Ha-Aretz* (Jerusalem, 1946), pp. 1–5; the references cited in Boaz Cohen, *Law and Tradition in Judaism* (New York, 1959), p. 183n.; and *Encyclopedia Talmudit,* vol. 7, pp. 672–706. One might add that the flexible range of *derekh eretz* parallels that of "curteisie" and "manners," respectively, in their Middle English and Elizabethan senses.

3. Avot 3:17. Cf. ibid. 2:2, and Tosafot Yeshanim, Yoma 85b, s.v. *teshuvah.*

4. Vayikra Rabbah 9:3 (Tzav); cf. Tanna Debei Eliyahu Rabbah, chap. 1.

5. *Netivot Olam,* Netiv Derekh Eretz, chap. 1.
6. See Saul Lieberman, "How Much Greek in Jewish Palestine?" in *Biblical and Other Studies,* ed. A. Altmann (Cambridge, Mass., 1963), pp. 128–29.
7. M. Fox, "Maimonides and Aquinas on Natural Law," *Dine' Israel 3* (1972): 5–27. Cf. Ralph Lerner, "Natural Law in Albo's *Book of Roots,*" in *Ancients and Moderns,* ed. Joseph Cropsey (New York, 1964), pp. 132–44.
8. The statement appears in one of his *Discourses,* but the exact reference eludes me at present.
9. Bereshit 18:25.
10. Gittin 59b. This passage was cited by Maimonides in the concluding lines of *Sefer Zemanim*: "Great is peace, for the whole Torah was given in order to promote peace in the world, as it was stated: 'Her ways are the ways of pleasantness, and all her paths are peace'" (Mishneh Torah, Hanukkah 4:14). There may be a shift in focus, however, as Maimonides dwells upon the reason the Torah was given, while the gemara may conceivably refer to its content and the *telos* to which its inner logic leads. In either case, Torah is regarded as serving the interests of peace and, therefore, presumably, as axiologically ancillary to it. In the *Guide* (III:27; and cf. III:52), this nexus is reversed. Peace and social stability are subsumed under the welfare of the body that is merely a condition for attaining man's ultimate perfection via the soul's intellectual apprehension. There is no contradiction, however, as the passage in the Mishneh Torah probably refers to the specific corpus of revealed Torah and the regimen prescribed by it rather than, as in other contexts, to the full range of spiritual perception.
11. See *Ha-Emunot Veha-Deʾot,* Introduction, sec. vi; and cf. III:iii.
12. See *Hovot Ha-Levavot* III:i–iii.
13. This point is not explicitly developed in Maimonides' discussions of prophecy, which focus upon its nature rather than upon the need for it. However, it is implicit in the substance and tone of numerous passages concerning the Torah's revelation and dovetails with Maimonides' faith in the spiritual capacity of singular individuals, on the one hand, and his conviction about the average person's indolence, on the other.
14. See Fox, "Maimonides and Aquinas on Natural Law," pp. 15–17.
15. Alfred North Whitehead, *Modes of Thought* (New York, 1938), p. 20.
16. Shabbat 135b.
17. *Mishpatim,* Massekhta di-Nezikin IV (ed. Horowitz-Rabin), p. 263.
18. Hullin 33a; cf. Sanhedrin 59a.
19. *Perush Ha-Mishnahyot,* Hullin 7:6. The talmudic citation is from Makkot 23b.
20. See, especially, Book 2.
21. Berakhot 5:3 and Megillah 4:9.
22. See Maimonides, *Guide* III:26, III:31, and III:48; Nahmanides' comment on Devarim 22:7; and Maharal, *Tiferet Israel,* chaps. 5–7. See also Yizhak Heinemann, *Taʾamei Ha-Mizvot Besafrut Yisrael* (Jerusalem, 1954), vol. 1, pp. 46–128.
23. Yirmiyahu 9:23.
24. The Jewish Publication Society translation, following the Authorized Version (i.e., the King James

Version), has "that I am," an interpretation implicitly supported by *Ikkarim* 3:5. However, Radak is closer to "for I am," which I am more inclined to accept. The Septuagint's *hoti* is inconclusive, but the Vulgate's *quia* parallels "for." For a discussion of the verse, see Maimonides, *Guide* III:54.

25. The term *averah lishmah* appears in the gemara that cites Rabbi Nahman b. Yizhak's statement that "an *averah lishmah* is greater than a *mizvah* performed with an ulterior motive" (Nazir 23b and Horayot 10b). However, this apparent priority of *telos* and motivation over formal law has no prescriptive or prospective implications. At most, it means that we can sometimes see, after the fact, that a nominal violation was superior to a licit or even required act; but it gives no license for making the jump. Moreover, in the case at hand, Yael's sexual relations with Sisera, there most likely was no formal violation. Most Rishonim assume that a woman, inasmuch as she can be regarded as passive during coitus, is not obligated to undergo martyrdom rather than engage in incest or adultery (see Sanhedrin 74b). This is true even when she is threatened but not assaulted, as it is the element of willful involvement that defines her sexual participation as a human action. Hence, when motivated by the need to save her people, Yael's relations with Sisera, even though she may have initially seduced him, may very well be regarded as passive and therefore no formal violation whatsoever; see Tosafot, Yevamot 103a, s.v. *veha* and Yoma 82b, s.v. *ma*. The term *averah* refers, then, to an act that is proscribed under ordinary circumstances, but that here, its usual sinful character notwithstanding, becomes superior to a *mizvah*. Likewise, Raba's remark that the verse "In all thy ways know Him and He will direct thy paths" (Mishlei 3:6) is to be understood "even with regard to a matter of *averah*" (Berakhot 63a), may refer to acts that are ordinarily forbidden but in certain cases have formal dispensation. See, however, Maimonides, *Shemonah Perakim,* chap. 5. [See, my Hebrew article, "*Averah Lishmah,*" in *Ha-Aher: Bein Adam le-Azmo u-le-Zulato: Asufat Ma'amarim le-Zekher Dudi Deutch z"l,* ed. Hayim Deutch and Menahem Ben-Sasson (Tel Aviv, 2001).]

26. K. Kahana, *The Case for Jewish Civil Law in the Jewish State* (London, 1960), p. 28n (his emphasis).

27. *Hazon Ish: Emunah U-Vitahon* (Jerusalem, 1954), p. 21. The point is illustrated by a discussion of economic competition, aspects of which are very differently evaluated, depending upon their being regarded as aggressive or defensive; and this, in turn, is a function of legal right. Of course, in such a case, the moral duties include many outright *dinim*. However, the implication of the sentence stands and is clearly accepted in the following chapter, pp. 44–46. Cf., however, p. 49.

28. Many of the leaders of the mussar movement, who criticized what they regarded as the ethical shortcomings of their contemporary Torah community, ascribed many of these failings to the fact that the relevant *halakhot* had been insufficiently developed. They urged the fuller analysis and exposition of these categories as a remedy; see J.D. Epstein, *Mizvot Ha-Bayit* (New York, 1966), pp. 34–57. I am inclined to think that while such neglect could have been a factor in causing the alleged failings, its importance, and the potential for resolution via fuller halakhic exposition, has been exaggerated by the mussar movement.

29. Bava Mezia 30b.

30. Vayikra 19:2.
31. In his edition of Nahmanides' commentary, *Perush Ha-Ramban al Ha-Torah* (Jerusalem, 1960), II, 376n., C.B. Chavel notes that no extant source of this comment is known.
32. Rashi, Devarim 6:18, comments, "This is compromise *lifnim mi-shurat ha-din.*" This reading he is presumably quoting from the same source as Nahmanides narrows the scope of the remark considerably.
33. In the preceding verse, 6:17.
34. The verses cited are from Vayikra 19:16, 18, 16, 14, and 32, respectively.
35. A rabbinic ordinance that requires a seller to give first option to any prospective customer who already owns property adjacent to that to be sold; see Bava Mezia 108.
36. Ta'anit 16a.
37. Yoma 86a.
38. Devarim 6:18.
39. Mekhilta, Yithro, Massekhta de-Amalek, II (ed. Horowitz-Rabin), p. 198. The phrase I have rendered as "their life's course" is *bet ha-yehem*. Rashi interprets it variously as "the study of Torah" (Bava Kama 100a, s.v. b*et*) and as "a trade from which to derive a livelihood" (Bava Mezia 30b. s.v. *zeh*).
40. Semak, 49.
41. Mishneh Torah, De'ot 1:5.
42. See his *The Morality of Law* (New Haven, 1964), pp. 5–9; cf. A.D. Lindsay, *The Two Moralities* (London, 1940), passim.
43. De'ot, 1:5.
44. Thus, Maimonides distinguishes here between "the right and the good" and *lifnim mi-shurat ha-din*. Elsewhere, however, he seems to identify them. See Rabbi M. Krakowski's commentary, *Avodat Ha-Melekh* (Vilna, 1931), ad loc., and S. Rawidowicz, *Iyyunim Be-Mahashevet Yisrael* (Jerusalem, 1969), vol. 1, pp. 430–31.
45. See Fuller, *Morality of Law,* pp. 9–13.
46. De'ot 1:6 and 1:7, respectively.
47. See, however, *Avodat Ha-Melekh,* De'ot 1:5, which expresses some uncertainty on this point.
48. See chap. 4; cf. *Perush Ha-Mishnahyot,* Avot 4:4.
49. See Nicomachean Ethics, 1 109b.
50. Most involve actual physical deprivation, so that the passage largely anticipates Mishneh Torah, De'ot 3:1. However, it also criticizes excessive munificence; cf. Mishneh Torah, Arakhin 8:13.
51. There is, of course, no question about practices like *dina de-bar mezia* (i.e., "the law of the abutter") that were instituted by Hazal on the basis of the principle of "the right and the good"; see Bava Mezia 108. The question concerns situations that have not been singled out for rabbinic prescription.
52. Bava Mezia 83a. The citations are from Mishlei 2:20.
53. Yerushalmi, Bava Mezia 6:6.
54. However, Rashi, ad loc., does use the term.

55. *Pesakim*, Bava Mezia 2:7.
56. This view was advanced by the author of the *Mordecai, Bava Mezia*, sec. 327, who cites his predecessors, the Ravan and the Ravya, as support, but it is usually associated with the latter and cited in his name by *Hagahot Maimuniyot*, Hilkhot Gezelah 11:3. The Ravya's original text is, as yet, unpublished, however. The reference to the Ravan is presumably to *Sefer Ravan* (ed. Ehrenreich), 11:198, but that passage, while it unequivocally states that the finder, in the case in question, is fully obligated to return the lost object, says nothing of juridic coercion. Perhaps the *Mordecai* drew upon another, more explicit source. See also Z.Y. Meltzer, "Lifnim Mishurath Hadin," in *Mizkeret: In Memory of Rabbi I.H. Herzog* (Jerusalem, 1962), pp. 310–15.
57. Kiddushin 21b.
58. Ketubbot 103a. For an analysis of this Halakhah, see my "Le-Verur Kofin al Midat Sodom," in *Hagut Ivrit Be-'Amerika*, ed. M. Zohori et al. (Tel Aviv, 1972), vol. 1, pp. 362–82.
59. Avot 5:10.
60. *Netivot Olam*, "Netiv Gemilut Hasadim," chap. 5.
61. See Bava Mezia 24b.
62. Quoted in *Mordecai, Bava Mezia*, sec. 327.
63. See *Kezot Ha-Hoshen* 290:3.
64. See Tosafot, Yevamot 100a, s.v. *ma'aser*, and Maimonides, Matnot Aniyim 1:8.
65. The Halakhah in question concerns criteria for assignment of priorities among various prospective purchasers, none of whom is an abutter. In such cases, Maimonides states that while "this, too, is included within the good and the right," the priority is not enforceable, "for the rabbis only commanded regarding this by way of *hasidut*, and it is a virtuous soul that acts thus" (Shekhenim 14:5).
66. Vayikra 19:2.
67. Yevamot 20a.
68. I know of no satisfactory English equivalent for this term. It suggests a blend of spiritual elevation and refinement with scrupulousness and pietism. Perhaps "saintliness" comes closest, though more in the Jamesian than in the popular sense of total selflessness or other-worldiness; but that, also, has too ethereal a ring.
69. Shekhenim 14:5. The concluding talmudic quotation is from Avodah Zarah 34a, the verse from Kohelet 1:3.
70. Shemot 15:26.
71. Beshalah, Massekhta de-Vayissa 1 (ed. Horowitz-Rabin), pp. 157–58; see also the notes there.
72. This is pointed up by the fact that Nahmanides (Shemot 15:26) quotes Rabbi Eleazar's statement and yet, in the same passage, refers the reader to his subsequent discussions of "the right and the good."

Chapter 3

Brother Daniel and the Jewish Fraternity

I.

"Who is a Jew?" Twice in recent years, this troublesome question has been a matter of public Jewish concern. Hardly had the reverberations from its initial appearance four years ago died down, when it made a dramatic recurrence several months back with the case of Brother Daniel. On the earlier occasion, the issue was the status of born Gentiles who wanted the State of Israel to recognize them as Jews without their converting; the later debate revolved around a born Jew who apostatized to Christianity but demanded that the State of Israel continue to recognize him as a Jew. For reasons probably more emotional than philosophic, the second controversy was aired in a markedly different climate. Four years ago, discussion of the explosive issue was marked by bitterness and dissension that rocked secular and religious Jewry throughout the world. With regard to the Israeli court's rejection of Brother Daniel's petition, however, the consensus of opinion, both within and without the State of Israel, was striking in its near-unanimity. The fundamental problem remains the same, however; the common vortex is a continuing attempt, of which these instances are only two aspects, to define the Jew in terms of race, nation, and religion.

The recurrence of the problem is hardly surprising. While it had always had a general relevance – increased somewhat by the growing

Reprinted from *Judaism: A Quarterly Journal of Jewish Life and Thought* 12, no. 3 (Summer 1963):260–280.

secularization of European Jewry in the wake of the Haskalah – the emergence of the State of Israel as an independent sociopolitical entity defined by fixed geographical bounds has lent its treatment a rather different and generally sharper character. The problem has acquired, first, immediacy. What before was often a theoretical academic question has become a pragmatic political, and especially legal, issue. Furthermore, it has become a pragmatic issue on a national scale. Whereas whatever practical application the question "Who is a Jew?" had earlier was generally local – whether or not to admit such-and-such a person into the Kehillah – it now became the subject of national policy decisions. Second, the problem has acquired a centrality which derives, in part, from the issue's full scope. The very fact that decisions defining a Jew have become national in character has inevitably embroiled them in intramural conflict. As long as divergent elements of the Jewish people were not necessarily bound within a common polity, they could each – theoretically, at least, and, sometimes, practically as well – decide the matter for themselves. In the context of a state, however, a single decision affecting all applicants would obviously have to be rendered; hence, the increased interest in its formulation.[1]

In part, the increased prominence of "Who is a Jew?" is perhaps the result of another factor. Paradoxical as it may seem, this is probably attributable to the social and political emancipation deriving from the development of a homeland and the establishment of a state. As long as the Jew was in the Galut, continually bludgeoned and harassed, he generally had neither the leisure nor the inclination to define himself. Within the confines or the shadow of the ghetto and the concentration camp, simply being a Jew was difficult enough. In the face of the Crusader, the Cossack, and the Nazi, it was all the Jew could do merely to maintain his identity. As for the rest, there existed a complex of elements that somehow defined and constituted Jewishness; one felt them, accepted them, strove against terrible odds to implement them – and did not speculate excessively. With the advent of the state, however, the situation has changed somewhat. With Innocent III, Chmielnicki, and Hitler no longer on one's back, it suddenly became easier to forget both that one was Jewish and what Jewishness meant. On the one hand, the maintenance of Jewish consciousness became a problem. And on the other, the task of determining "Who is a Jew?" became a much more pressing need.[2]

Finally, the existence of the state has radically changed the character of the problem. Its establishment opened up the possibility that political and geographic elements might supplement or supplant ethnic and religious factors in determining membership in the community of Israel. The possibility is two-edged. On the one hand, it might be contended that Jews living in Israel were somehow "more Jewish" than their co-religionists elsewhere – a contention which is not merely the source of political in-fighting between Ben-Gurion and the Zionist Organization, but has important philosophical implications. On the other hand, arguing for inclusion rather than exclusion, one might hold that non-Jewish residents of the state are also, in a sense, within the community of Israel. This disturbing tendency – not necessarily pursued ruthlessly to either logical conclusion – to distinguish between Israelis and Jews has been noted by a number of observers. Its existence, potential and actual, is another factor rendering more urgent and more difficult the quest for a definition of the Jew.

In assessing the Brother Daniel case, it is important to keep this broader background in mind. For the case can and should be seen from two perspectives. It constitutes, first, a self-contained *she'elah*, a technical halakhic problem to be judged in the light of specific halakhic principles governing the relation of a *meshumad* to *Knesset Yisrael*.[3] At the same time, however, it is part of a broader philosophic attempt – timeless and yet accentuated in our own day – to define the matrix and the essence of Jewishness. The two approaches do not conflict; indeed, the second can only be based upon the first. They are, however, different, and we should keep both in mind. In discussing the issues raised by the case, I should like therefore, first, to determine the bare halakhic facts; and second, to analyze the broader implications and premises of the relevant *halakhot*.[4] I do not presume to pass judgment on the specific case: one could hardly do this without a full mastery of all the evidence. It is to be hoped, however, that the basic principles involved will be clarified somewhat.

II.

The moment we ask whether, halakhically, a *meshumad* is considered a Jew, we realize that the question – and the larger one of "Who is a Jew?" – admits of no simple answer.[5] A *meshumad* – of what type? A Jew – for what purpose? On the one hand, the Halakhah distinguishes between different types of apostates, the distinction depending on either the mode or the motivation of the apostasy; on the other hand, it varies the *meshumad*'s treatment. The problem of the *meshumad*'s status is equally relevant to all areas with respect to matters whose Jew and non-Jew have been differentiated. However, its determination is not the same in regard to all issues. Furthermore, these two distinctions often intertwine, so that one type of apostate may be considered a Jew with regard to one area of life or Halakhah but not with respect to another, while for a second type the situation may be reversed. Some classification is therefore in order.

Basically, the Halakhah operates with five categories of apostates. The first, and least culpable, is a *meshumad okhel nevelot le-te'avon,* an individual who, in order to satisfy some appetite, habitually transgresses one of the Torah's injunctions. A second type, *meshumad okhel nevelot le-hakh'is,* is identical with the first except that, in this far graver case, the motivation is not the gratification of desire but sheer rebellious spite. The next two types are distinguished from these not by the subjective motive but by the gravity of the objective sin. One is the *mehallel shabbatot be-farhesia,* an individual who brazenly, publicly, and willfully desecrates the Sabbath.[6] The other is the *meshumad la-avodah zarah,* the polytheistic believer and worshipper. Finally, there is the *meshumad le-khol ha-Torah kulah,* or "apostate with regard to the whole Torah," one who simply abandons everything and rejects Judaism entirely; or, as the Rambam would have it: "One of those who turn to Gentile ways when they are pressed and who adheres to them [i.e., the Gentiles] and says, 'What profits it me to adhere to Jews who are lowly and oppressed; it is better for me to adhere to these whose might is superior.'"[7]

A converted monk comes very close to personifying all five types,[8] and a full assessment of his status demands at least some basic knowledge of the halakhic categories of apostasy and their respective consequences.

For our specific purpose, however, it is only the last two classes that are relevant. With respect to the first three groups, the possibility of exclusion from *Knesset Yisrael* does not even arise. It does arise, however, with respect to a convert to another religion.[9] An examination of the apostate's status with respect to various areas of Halakhah may indicate whether and to what extent this possibility is realized.

In its most limited form, the question of an apostate's status relates to specific *mizvot* – or, more precisely, to his qualification to perform certain functions. Halakhically, a *meshumad* is barred from fulfilling certain tasks. Thus, an animal slaughtered by him, even in accordance with the specifications of *shehitah,* is considered non-kosher; and a *Sefer Torah* or a mezuzah – perhaps even a bill of divorcement – written by him, has no significance whatsoever.[10] He cannot and may not offer a sacrifice, either as a priest or a layman; he may not partake of the paschal sacrifice;[11] nor, according to some, can he serve as a *mohel.*[12] Inasmuch as he has turned his back upon these *mizvot,* or upon *mizvot* generally, the *meshumad* is barred from serving as an agent with respect to them.

Halakhah's rejection of the apostate in these areas does not necessarily imply, however, that, either here or elsewhere, he is considered a Gentile. It simply means that, not being a fully committed Jew, he is not considered qualified to fill various offices or perform certain functions. Indeed, some of the disqualifications apply even to transgressors who are very definitely recognized as full-fledged Jews. Thus, even a *meshumad okhel nevelot le-hakh'is,* who *is* unquestionably considered a Jew,[13] is not permitted to write a *Sefer Torah;* and a *mehallel shabbatot be-farhesia* cannot perform a valid *shehitah.*[14] Conversely, an apostate may be disqualified not because he is classified as a non-Jew but because, even in a Jew, apostasy is, in itself, a basis for exclusion. Thus, the *meshumad* may be disqualified beyond the Gentile. Sacrifices, for instance, may be brought either by an ordinary Jew or by any Gentile, even an idolater, but not by the renegade and unrepentant apostate.[15] Moreover, even if we should assume that the *meshumad's* exclusion from the aforementioned functions is identical with the non-Jew's, it does not follow that he has actually become a Gentile. It could simply mean that in these areas we treat him as if he were. We have yet to consider, therefore, the broader question of the status of the *meshumad* with reference to a plethora of *halakhot* that may not involve any personal qualification. What, considered almost as an object, *is* the apostate: Jew or non-Jew? Or at least, how is he to be treated in all areas? Can he, like a Jew, become defiled, or is the law inapplicable to him? Is his produce, like the Jew's, subject to tithes? Do all the *halakhot* concerning the guardianship of property apply to him? Can his marriage to a Jewess have validity? What, in short, is his universal halakhic status?

With respect to at least one area, the answer is clear. Wherever the Torah has formulated a Halakhah with reference to *ahikha*, "thy brother," the apostate is excluded. Inasmuch as the term clearly does not signify con-sanguinity, it refers to spiritual kinship, *ahikha be-mizvot,* and the apostate hardly falls into this category. Most Rishonim, for example, held – with Rabbenu Tam and against Rashi – that one may charge interest on a loan to a *meshumad.*[16] Here again, however, one might conceivably argue that the exclusion of the *meshumad* does not derive from his being outside the pale of Jewry generally. Rather, he is only excluded from the more limited community of *ahim be-mizvot,* those who share a spiritual commitment that he has renounced. That such is the case is evidenced by the fact that the exclusion applies in some instances to a *meshumad le-hakh'is* as well as to a convert to another faith,[17] and also by the fact that with respect to some of these *halakhot,* the non-idolatrous Gentile is included but the *meshumad* is not.[18] It is entirely possible, therefore, that the apostate may essentially be a Jew; that, for instance, although excluded from the cat-egory of *ah,* "brother," he may be included in the broader category of *re'a,* "fellow." To come to grips, finally, with this fundamental question, we must venture into another area, one in which intrinsic personal status is most crucial – *ishut,* marital status. Halakhically, intermarriage between Jew and Gentile is not only forbidden but invalid. What of marriage between Jew and *meshumad?*

The gemara's evidence would appear to be rather clear-cut. Comment-ing on the statement "as soon as he [i.e., a proselyte] rises from immersion he is a full-fledged Jew," it asks: "why was it necessary to state this?" The answer given is that the statement was intended to emphasize that the conversion was irreversible; like a native Jew, the convert could not leave the fold. By way of underscoring the point, the gemara refers us to what is apparently the acid test: "If he should reverse himself and then marry a Jewess, we consider him an apostate [rather than a Gentile], and the marriage is valid."[19] On the basis of this text, paralleled by a similar passage elsewhere,[20] the Rambam and the great majority of Rishonim asserted that *all* marriages of apostates to Jews were legally binding.[21] Indeed, R. Joseph Karo was almost violently emphatic in insisting that the contrary view could not even be entertained.[22] As a matter of fact, it was entertained, but only by a small minority,[23] and only by drastically reinterpreting the previously cited text.[24] The prevailing view is clear: the *meshumad's* marital status is that of a Jew.

We have apparently reached the conclusion, then, that, although he may be disqualified from performing certain functions, and although he is subject to certain strictures and liabilities, the apostate remains, essentially, a Jew. The conclusion would appear to be reinforced by another text, used by some to support the validity of an apostate's marriage, and which, more than any other single source, has given rise to the popular impression that once a Jew, always a Jew. "Even though [the people] have sinned, they are still [called] Israel."[25] Such a conclusion cannot yet be accepted as final, however, and we may still find ourselves countenancing the view that under certain conditions, a Jew's status may be rescinded after all.

For there is another text, also dealing with an apostate's marital status. Elsewhere, the gemara cites an opinion that if a presumed Gentile married a Jewess, she could not remarry without a divorce because, where the chances are considered halakhically even, we must consider the possibility that he is a member of the lost ten tribes. The opinion is subsequently rejected, however, and the primary reason given is that, even if he were a member of one of the lost tribes, it would make no difference. "They[26] immediately declared them to be complete heathens, for it is written, 'They have betrayed God, for they have begotten alien children.'"[27] Identical language is employed elsewhere with reference to the Kuthim (Samaritans). We are told that even if we should assume that their initial conversion was valid (there are differences of opinion regarding this),[28] their present status is that of full-fledged Gentiles.[29] Presumably, then, a Samaritan-Jewish marriage would also be invalid.[30] Thus we are confronted with an apparent contradiction. On the one hand, the marriage of a proselyte who defects is valid because he remains a Jew. On the other hand, members of the lost tribes and Samaritans cannot marry Jews because they are considered Gentiles.

The contradiction is only apparent, however. The solution to the dilemma lies in the clear realization that we are dealing with two types of apostates. The term employed in Scriptures to refer to an apostate is *ben nekhar*, an alien, and the essence of apostasy is indeed estrangement and dissociation. This alienation may take two forms, however. There is, first, an apostasy of action, a *ben nekhar* described by the phrase *she-nitnakru maʾasav le-aviv she-ba-shammayim*, "one whose actions have become alien to his Father in Heaven."[31] The apostasy we have heretofore treated, whether it be manifested through public Sabbath desecration, idolatry, or spiteful transgression of any injunction, generally falls into this category. As far as such an apostate, "a Jew who has sinned," is concerned, he remains a Jew. There is, however, a second *ben nekhar*. There is an apostasy not of action but of person, an estrangement manifested not merely by the commission of various sins but by the complete severance of personal bonds with Jewry; by total alienation from the Jewish people and its history as a spiritual and physical community; and finally, by thorough assimilation into the mainstream of Gentile society. Such persons are not simply disqualified because of some apostate act. Nor are they merely treated as if they were foreign. They are people who have "betrayed God, for they have begotten strange children."

There is, then, a point beyond which the apostate cannot go and yet remain a Jew. The account can be overdrawn, and the rubber band can burst. This principle was underscored and elucidated by Rav Hayyim Soloveitchik, one of the greatest rabbis of recent generations, in connection with a specific incident. An eminent apostate was being honored on having reached a milestone, and some leaders of the Russo-Polish Jewish community, whom he had helped on occasion, were anxious to send greetings. Rav Hayyim, an inflexible ramrod on matters of principle, refused to participate. Intimates recalled that not long before this he had personally gone to great lengths to help a young Bundist who was known to be an avowed opponent of religion, and they questioned him about the apparent inconsistency. Rav Hayyim's reply was immediate and to the point: "That one was a sinner, this one is a *meshumad*; his children won't even know they are Jewish." He then referred them to the previously cited gemara and proceeded to spell out its implications.[32]

The halakhic principle that an apostate *can* become a Gentile, and that Jewishness is not an absolutely irrevocable status, should thus be clear. Having come this far, however, I should like to make a qualifying distinction. Let us ask ourselves a simple question: Are these estranged figures truly full-fledged Gentiles with no vestige of Jewishness whatsoever? Or, to be more specific: Theoretically, ought they to be acting as Jews, or are they, like true Gentiles, wholly relieved from any responsibility for a Torah discipline, so that they are absolved – not because of duress and incapacity but as non-Jews – from any guilt for their failure to maintain it? Or again, suppose that one of these lost souls, or one of their descendants, should subsequently want to "convert" to Judaism. Even if he, and everyone else, were totally ignorant of his Jewish origins, would he – again, theoretically – remain a full-fledged Gentile until he had undergone the regular process of conversion? Instinctively, I think, we feel that these aliens are *not* simply like Russian Cossacks or Mexican mestizos. We feel that halakhic obligations *are* relevant to them, and that, should they return to the fold, they would represent reformed prodigal children rather than fresh converts.[33] What of their total alienation and their loss of personal status, however? Why do we completely disregard a marriage to a Jew(ess)?

The solution may be best introduced via an analogy. As is generally known, Eretz Yisrael – the land proper – is halakhically sacred. Technically, its sanctity derives from the consecration implicit in its settlement by Jews at the time of their entry into it in the days of Joshua and then of Ezra. Now, in the opinion of virtually all authorities, "the first hallowing" (i.e., Joshua's) was only in effect as long as Jews continued to live in Eretz Yisrael, and it was therefore terminated by the First Exile. The question then arises: What was the status of the Land during the Babylonian Exile?

Was it simply identical with Iceland's or Manchuria's? Or, to put the same
question differently: What of areas settled by Joshua and during the First
Commonwealth but not during the Second? Are they now simply part of
hutz la-aretz, their past dead and forgotten? We recoil from these possibilities instinctively, and our instincts are right. The continuity of our
presence in Eretz Yisrael, devolving from the covenant with Abraham[34]
("unto thee, and to thy seed after thee ... for an everlasting possession"),[35]
is clearly maintained in the Scriptures; Ezra did not merely start afresh in
some virgin territory. Furthermore, the Rambam states that with regard to
certain *halakhot* – the requirement that classical ordination take place in
Eretz Yisrael, for instance – any area settled by Joshua or during the First
Commonwealth (any area, that is, that was ever part of Eretz Yisrael) is
included, even though it is no longer hallowed.[36] In order to understand
this, then, we must, as I have often heard from Rav Soloveitchik, introduce a
basic distinction. We must distinguish between territory endowed with the
full status and sacredness of Eretz Yisrael and territory that descriptively
bears its name even though it lacks its sanctity. With respect to "*mizvot*
that are dependent on the land" – the tithing of produce, for instance – the
land must be sacred, and for this, full present sanctity (resulting, of course,
from past sanctification) must still be in effect. However, with regard to
some other *halakhot* – such as the site of ordination or the locus of discovery of a corpse which mandates the ritual of *eglah arufah* (the beheaded
sacrificial calf) – we need only know whether the area in question is part
of the country of Eretz Yisrael, and for this the fact of previous sanctity,
perhaps even the bare fact that this territory is part of the area covenanted
to Abraham, is sufficient. To put it succinctly, we must distinguish between
shem Eretz Yisrael and *kedushat Eretz Yisrael.*[37]

I think a similar distinction should be established with reference to
an apostate. If we ask, in purely descriptive terms, whether anyone born
of Jewish parents is a Jew, the answer must be yes. As an epithet, the term
"Jew" remains applicable to any individual who was ever endowed with
Jewish status – even to a *meshumad.* Hence, he is obligated to pursue a
Torah life, and should he decide to return, he would perhaps require no
new conversion.[38] However, if we ask whether a *meshumad* has anything of

a Jewish personality and character, and whether, therefore, he continues to be endowed with the personal status of a Jew, the answer is a ringing no. He remains a Jew without Jewishness. What he retains is simply the descriptive epithet: *shem Yisrael*. Of *kedushat Yisrael*, however – of the sacredness of the Jewish personality, that which essentially constitutes being a Jew – he is bereft. And let us remember that *kedushat Yisrael* is not simply a psychological condition or even a legal status. It is also a metaphysical state. Of this, the *meshumad* is divested completely. As he has renounced Jewry, so Jewishness is divorced from him.

The principle established by the gemara in Yevamot is thus clear. Wherever there is complete personal alienation resulting in total lack of identification with Jewry, *kedushat Yisrael* expires. There is room for argument, however, over how far the principle can be pushed, depending on what we understand by lack of identification. It might be argued that it only applies to a mass secession whereby not only an individual but his whole social context becomes uprooted. Or one might contend that only the children, born in complete ignorance of their origins, are affected, whereas the apostate himself, paradoxically, might remain a Jew.[39] And even if we assume that the Halakhah applies to the *meshumad*,[40] even though he is aware of his Jewish descent, we might disagree on the criterion to be employed. What is primarily important, however, is that the principle be recognized.

In assessing whether to apply the principle to the specific case of Brother Daniel, there is, finally, one important factor to be considered. The idolatrous *meshumad* of which the gemara speaks would ordinarily have been a devotee of one of the numerous pagan deities whose worship flourished in the Near East during the early centuries of the Christian era. As such, he might have participated in certain rites, become attached to some cult, perhaps even initiated into some mysteries. However, he would not have considered this attachment exclusive, nor would he have been expected to. The various cults were, on the whole, treated pretty much as local affairs which could enjoy peaceful coexistence without being mutually exclusive. Hence, participation in Mithraic or Olympian worship, while unquestionably a mortal sin, did not necessarily call for a complete personal break with the Jewish people. With Christianity, however, the case is radically different. From the outset, it has been, like its parent, sharply exclusive. Membership in the Christian communion was presented as calling for a radical break with one's past (Paul's "dying to the old man") and with all other religious bodies. Indeed, the late A.D. Nock saw the very intensity of this call to exclusive devotion as the major cause of Christianity's triumph over its rivals for the spiritual hegemony of the Roman Empire.[41] It demanded transformation where they only required adaptations. Christians therefore constituted a distinct social group in a sense in which other religious societies did not. "They were not," as Christopher Dawson put it, "like the other religious bodies of the time, a group of individuals united by common beliefs and a common worship, they were a true people. All the wealth of historical associations and social emotion which were contained in the Old Testament had been separated from its national and racial limitations and transferred to the new international spiritual community."[42] For the Jewish convert to Christianity, therefore, the personal alienation from *Knesset Yisrael* is incomparably greater than it would have been for the idolaters of whom the gemara spoke. Consequently, the possibility that such a convert would lose his *kedushat Yisrael* is correspondingly greater. A Jewish Christian, the church contends, is a contradiction in terms. We would do well to consider the point seriously.

Of course, we should not make the mistake of equating all apostates. There are converts, and there are converts. The Russian student who adopted Christianity in order to gain admission to a university but who remained, as far as he could, socially and emotionally, a Jew is one thing; the social climber who kicks over the traces to enter Christian society with a vengeance is something else entirely. And a monk, fully absorbed in the mainstream of a monastic order, represents a still further departure. Between a Heine and a Disraeli there lies an immense gap; and between Disraeli and Pablo Christiani still another gap. Everything considered, just where Brother Daniel stands must be judged on the evidence. The important thing is to recognize the fatal fallacy of the notion that *ad aeternitatem*, the crown of Jewry can never fall off, no matter how ill it is worn.

III.

So much for the pure Halakhah. What, in more general terms, are its implications and premises? The crux of our problem derives from a single phenomenon: the dual nature of *Knesset Yisrael*, the Jewish people. Jewry is, so to speak, both spiritual and material. It is a community as well as a communion, not only an *eccelesia* but a *polis*. As a religious body, it includes believers sharing a common faith and a joint commitment. As a social unit, it consists of individuals bound by national and/or ethnic ties and sharing a common history. What is more, these two aspects are closely interwoven. For the individual, the material element defines the spiritual. Halakhically, the purely biological factor of birth from a Jewish mother determines one's Jewishness.[43] Its presence inexorably confers all the attendant privileges and responsibilities; its absence renders their attainment extremely difficult. A proper understanding of the twofold nature of Jewry is therefore essential to an appraisal of the position of the apostate, as well as to an answer to the larger question: "Who is a Jew?"

We are immediately confronted by two related but independent problems. One, of a more general nature, simply concerns the concept of a formal and exclusive religious community. The second, whose implications bear more immediately upon the Brother Daniel case, calls for a fine appreciation of the interrelationship of the spiritual and material components of Jewry. Through the telescoping of both questions, finally, we might be able to see our more specific issue in sharper focus.

As critics, classical and modern, have often charged, Judaism is strongly exclusive. It thinks in terms of a limited group.[44] As Haman, Paul, and a host of successors realized, this sense is largely engendered by the strict halakhic regimen in which it is implicit. Most obviously, of course, this spirit finds manifest expression in the concept of chosenness, the idea of a charismatic community endowed with a specific character and special responsibilities. The concept of separation requires some elucidation, however. Ideally speaking, after all, the advocates of universalism are right. Religion is, in its essence, catholic; it knows bounds of neither time nor place. Its obligations are universal, deriving from the bare fact of humanity. Moreover, as the traditional argument from *consensus gentium* insisted, and as modern anthropologists have increasingly come to recognize, its power is universal, too. It neither can nor should be confined to any race or nation. Its appeal is to mankind.

Most strikingly, the idea of universality lies at the heart of the religious conception of the historical terminus. To the millennial vision, unity is indispensable. It looks to the unity of mankind in the worship of one God, under conditions in which, *salve reverentia,* God Himself – not, of course, His essence or existence (their initial fragmentation is inconceivable) but His immanent presence – is to be, as it were, reintegrated. With the universal recognition of the one God, the revelation of nature, Scripture, and history, distorted by evil and error, is to be rendered whole. The broken image is to be repaired, the fractured picture to be restored. The divine "Name," the symbol through which mundane man grasps and experiences a transcendent God become his interlocutor, will once again be one: "And the Lord shall be King over all the earth; in that day shall the Lord be One and His name One."[45] The vision of universality, moreover, is thoroughly Jewish. It is a central theme of *Aleinu,* the hymn with which prayer services are always concluded, and of our Rosh Hashanah prayers, especially the *Malkhuyot,* from which *Aleinu* is, in fact, excerpted.

> May all the inhabitants of the world realize and know that to Thee every knee must bend, every tongue must vow allegiance. May they bend the knee and prostrate themselves before Thee, Lord our God, and give honor to Thy glorious name; may they all accept the yoke of Thy kingdom, and do Thou reign over them speedily forever and ever.... Let Thy works revere Thee, let all Thy creatures worship Thee; may they all blend into one brotherhood to do Thy will with a perfect heart.... Reign over the whole universe in Thy glory; be exalted over all the earth in Thy grandeur; shine forth in Thy splendid majesty over all the inhabitants of Thy world.[46]

From the ideal perspective, certainly, catholicity is the keynote of a religious *Weltanschauung.* Only from the ideal perspective, however. When confronted on the plane of pragmatic reality, the lofty vision of universality that inspires abstract thought gives way to something else entirely. At this level, change and struggle are more evident than contemplated abstract or theoretical perfection, the strident tones of strife and conflict more audible than a universal paean. We recognize that, whatever its ideal resolution, the historical drama requires real protagonists, requires, therefore, differentiated characters. The vision of universality remains, but we realize that unity is not to be confused with uniformity, and that the attainment of the universal ideal depends upon particular providential vehicles. *Malkhuyot* leads to *Shofarot*, philosophic homogeneity to historical multiplicity. Hence the possibility of *Knesset Yisrael* as a special religious community.[47]

But of course *Knesset Yisrael* is not merely a philosophic possibility. It is a historical reality; and here we come to our second problem – understanding the relationship of the spiritual and material components of Jewry. Dualists are scandalized to think that there should be any relationship at all. Relationship there must be, however, and the Halakhah characteristically insists that it must be significant. Judaism has therefore adhered to a relatively vigorous separatism. Particular religious communities, let us remember, may be variously conceived. One may reject the extreme universalist position – the notion that no visible *eccelesia* exists, and that believers are only bound by a common, individually developed, natural faith[48] – and still conceive of a worldwide religion. This has been the traditional Roman Catholic attitude. Catholicism has pursued a particular path within a specific corporate structure and yet has sought to encompass all mankind; indeed, until recently, it even insisted that no salvation was possible outside the church. Or one may adopt the widespread Anglican position that religion is universal but the church national.[49] On this view, a single faith is proclaimed for all mankind, but believers are organized in national communities.

Judaism has gone much further, however;[50] it conceives of Jewry as a distinct socio-racial unit divinely endowed with a unique religion, and charged with a special historical function. The religion is confined to the group, and the group to the religion. For members, determined by the strongest of natural ties but by a natural tie still, the religious obligations are binding. Upon outsiders, who are hardly encouraged to join, they have no claim whatsoever. Finally, the historical course of Judaism is seen as dependent upon the fortunes of Jewry. They share, at least within history, a common destiny.

The physical basis of *Knesset Yisrael* is only one side of the coin, however. It needs to be completed, if not indeed explained, by the obverse: its spiritual character. If we are confronted, on the one hand, by a national religion, we have, on the other hand, a distinctively religious nation. With reference to *Knesset Yisrael,* however, "religious" is not merely an attribute. It is the essential, the definitive, characteristic. It is that and that alone which constitutes us as a nation. To use a phrase once employed by Rav Soloveitchik, we are a "community of the committed," and our commitment is not only the source of our chosenness; it is the cause of our being a people at all.

Our spiritual character is reflected in our history, out of which, indeed, it grows. The crucial period in that history was the formative one, the period of national gestation beginning with Abraham and culminating at Sinai. It was this which determined all the rest, which fixed once and for all the character of Jewish existence. The lonely quest of a God-ridden soul initiated a development that led, from covenant to covenant, to the tablets and beyond. At the Giving of the Torah, that moment in and out of time at which human virtue and divine grace conjoined in our election, our chosen course was sealed by a divine fiat. Halakhically, the assembly at Sinai was an act of personal and national conversion;[51] and it was irrevocable. Henceforth, to be a Jew was to mean to pursue an ideal, to follow a regimen, to be committed to a divine order and a divine purpose. We had been chosen because we aspired, and now we would have to aspire because we had chosen – and had been chosen.

In a sense, such a spiritual nature is perhaps characteristic of any nation. "What is a nation?" asked Renan.

> A nation is a soul, a spiritual principle. Two things, which actually are but one, constitute this soul, this spiritual principle. The one is in the past, the other in the present. The one is the common possession of a rich legacy of remains; the other is the present consent, the desire of cohabitation, the will to continue to make one's heritage as valuable as what has been received.[52]

Or, as Ernest Barker put it more recently:

> Neither a physical fact of common blood, nor a political structure of common law and order, a nation is essentially a spiritual society. It is what it is in

virtue of a common mental substance resident in the minds of all its members – common memories of the past, common ideas in the present, common
hopes for the future, and, above all, a common and general will issuing from
the common substance of memories, ideas, and hopes.[53]

Nevertheless, the definition of the nation as a spiritual community has
a special relevance for *Knesset Yisrael*. Our spiritual character is not simply
an accretion that we have acquired in the course of our material existence.
It is not as if we were first incorporated in some other way and then went
on to develop a national soul. *Kedushat Yisrael* is not a shoot that twined
itself around a sociopolitical trunk. It is the very essence of our constitution, our article of confederation, so to speak. Chronologically and logically,
Knesset Yisrael is, *ab initio,* a spiritual community. It was this character,
in turn, which gave birth to its material development, along either racial
or geographical lines. In a sense, it is no doubt universally true, as Acton
said, that "there is a moral and political country, in the language of Burke,
distinct from the geographical, which may be possibly in collision with
it."[54] The base is generally geographical, however, and if the collision should
last too long, the nation will dissolve. With us, however, the causal nexus
is reversed. From Abraham down, neither contiguity nor consanguinity
has made us a people, although the latter provides the formal criterion
for membership. What has made us such is an ideal: *mamlekhet kohanim
ve-goy kadosh,* "a priestly kingdom and a holy people." Abraham started
us on a spiritual odyssey, and, to this day, we have continued it.

The relevance of our spiritual character for the individual modern
Jew derives first from his relation to history, and second from Judaism's
almost overpowering sense of organic community. The Jew is not born
into a vacuum. Nor does he merely enter a contemporary sociological
complex. He is born to a history, and consciousness of it is ingrained into
his very fiber. "Not in utter nakedness" – but with a historical heritage
and a historic destiny. The modern Jew's bond with his past is not merely
psychological or sociological, however. He is related to it as a member of
the organic community of *Knesset Yisrael*. Halakhah has, of course, always
thought of Jewry as an organic rather than an atomic society. We are not
merely the sum total of individual fishes contemporaneously confined

in the same aquarium. We are members of a timeless and universal body which constitutes an organic whole. To be sure, Halakhah does not deny the limitations of time and place entirely. For certain purposes, the Jewish people is defined as the body of Jews living in Eretz Yisrael at any given time.[55] However, this definition only pertains to the pragmatic level of joint action. At the much deeper level of joint existence, the conception of *Knesset Yisrael* as a timeless and universal community is paramount.

It is this membership in an organic spiritual community – determined, to be sure, by a physical bond – which binds the Jew to our historical destiny and to his personal responsibility. The covenant at Sinai was not accepted solely by those who were physically present. It was accepted by *Knesset Yisrael* as an organic entity: "with him that standeth here with us this day before the Lord our God, and also with him that is not here with us this day."[56] We need not resort to this, as some have, in order to "justify" the obligation of posterity to honor commitments made by its forefathers at Sinai. No justification is required. It is rather difficult to grasp in what sense volition in the ordinary sense applies to obedience to God. Is one free – morally, that is, not practically – to reject a divine fiat? Regardless of its application, however, the concept of the collective nature of the Jewish experience is significant in itself. In its essence, religious experience is intensely personal, but this does not preclude the relevance of its communal roots or the importance of its collective context.

The relation of personal obligation to membership in an organic community is underscored by a striking fact. The religious experience of the patriarchs, Abraham, Isaac, and Jacob, lacked a communal context.[57] Being purely individual in character, it was therefore a matter of choice, and the possibility of defection, as in the cases of Ishmael and Esau, was open. With the migration to Egypt, however, Jewry as a community came into existence, and this possibility was henceforth eliminated. Within an organic *Knesset Yisrael*, spiritual obligation became inexorable.

The interrelationship of the spiritual and the material as constituent elements of Jewry is thus thrown into bolder relief. *Knesset Yisrael* is a material corpus. The formal criterion for membership is ordinarily biological, and it is Jewish parentage that confers the halakhic status of

Jewry. This is only the formal side, however; an important side, no doubt, and one to which Halakhah, as a legal system concerned with form (Halakhah is far more than this, but surely it is this too), must pay attention. The substantive essence of *Knesset Yisrael,* though, is spiritual. Membership in the nation confers a religious status, but only because the nation itself is, in its definitive essence, a spiritual community. Conversely, participation in the religion is limited to members of the nation. For form and substance, matter and spirit, cannot – much as our Platonic inclinations may desire it – be wholly divorced. That is the metaphysical condition of human life, and it is the condition of our national existence. They can be separated logically, and the distinction is of paramount importance. In practice, however, they are intertwined, as they exert a mutual influence upon each other. Collectively, therefore, we are both religion and nation. The begetting of alien children – i.e., uprooting oneself from Jewry so completely that one's children don't even know they are Jewish – is itself an apostasy which causes the loss of Jewish status. In this case, the gemara's principle would apply to the father. However, the gemara may only be inferring from the use of the epithet "alien" that the children in this situation really are alien and not Jews. If so, it is possible to assume that the father remains a Jew.

The dual nature of *Knesset Yisrael* pertains to its collective character. It leaves us, however, with one obvious problem. How are we to deal with an individual in whom one element is present and the other wholly lacking? There are two possibilities: the native Jew who renounces his heritage and the born Gentile who wants to embrace Judaism; or, to put it simply, the apostate and the proselyte. Superficially, we might assume that the acknowledgment of one or the other as a Jew would destroy the dual conception of Jewishness that I have heretofore suggested. A more careful scrutiny, especially of some relevant *halakhot,* quickly dispels this impression, however. Indeed, the conception is reinforced.

> If at the present time a man desires to become a proselyte, he is to be addressed as follows: "What reason have you for desiring to become a proselyte; do you not know that Israel at the present time are persecuted and oppressed, despised, harassed, and overcome by afflictions?" If he replies, "I

know and yet am unworthy," he is accepted forthwith, and is given instruction in some of the minor and some of the major commandments.[58]

Thus the gemara. The instruction in religious law – and, the Rambam adds, philosophical principles – seems apt enough; but why, we wonder, the account of Jewry's present fortunes – and as the significant opening thrust, at that? Partly, no doubt, to test the prospect's mettle. Judaism has always been wary of easy conversion; it would agree with Shaw that, under all too many conditions, "the conversion of a savage to Christianity is the conversion of Christianity to savagery."[59] But only partly. There are deeper implications here, and I think they are clear. The *ger* cannot embrace Judaism as a religion without simultaneously becoming a member of the Jewish people. He cannot, that is, accept the spiritual aspect of Jewry without the material. And we must go a step further. Rabbi Yehudah laid down the view – later generally accepted – that a proselyte's prayers may refer to the patriarchs as "our fathers" even though he is not their descendant. The reason given is that the Torah describes Abraham as *av hamon goyim*, "the father of a multitude of nations," and the epithet justifies including proselytes (not, of course, all Gentiles) as his "children."[60] To put it in more general terms, the proselyte embraces not only Jewry's present fortunes but its history as well. Even though born outside *Knesset Yisrael,* he becomes, through strenuous spiritual and psychological effort, a member of its organic community; hence, the gemara's comment that all future proselytes were implicit participants at Sinai.[61] He does so, however, precisely because, through conversion, he identifies with both a concrete reality and an abstract ideal, not only with a future but with a past, with a historical consciousness as well as with a historic destiny.

The Rambam put the matter most vigorously, in a letter to a proselyte in which he cited and explained Rabbi Yehudah's opinion:

> Therefore, until the end of time, whoever converts and whoever hallows the name of God as it is written in the Torah is a student of our father, Abraham, and they are all members of his household, and it is he who restored them to the right path. Just as he restored his contemporaries through his speech and instruction, so he restored all future converts through the guidance which

he gave his children and household successors; so that our father, Abraham, is a father to all his righteous descendants who pursue his ways, and a father to all his disciples and to all proselytes who will ever convert.... Since you have entered God's fold and become a member of it, there is no distinction between us and you, and all the miracles that occurred, it is as if they happened to us and to you.... There is no distinction whatsoever between us and you. Certainly you should say [in blessings] "Who chose us," "Who gave to us," "Who endowed us," and "Who elected us." For God has indeed chosen you and elected you from among the Gentiles and given you the Torah, for the Torah is for us and converts alike.[62]

In coming, finally, to deal with the converse situation, that of the apostate, we find the same basic principles at work. We find them operative, moreover, at every level of apostasy and its consequences. First, where an apostate, whether only a *meshumad le-hakh'is* or a *mehallel le-shabbatot be-farhesia,* is disqualified for a given function, he is not rejected simply qua sinner. "If Thou, God, shouldst mark iniquity, O Lord, who could stand?" He is rejected because, as a result of his sin, he has, as regards that area, withdrawn from the spiritual community of *Knesset Yisrael.* He is not, for instance, a *bar keshirah* or a *bar zevihah.* Or he is barred from presenting a votive offering because he is not, for this purpose, one of the *Benei Yisrael,* "children of Israel," designated by the Torah: "*Benei Yisrael –* just as [we include] *Benei Yisrael* who receive the covenant, so we include proselytes who receive the covenant, to the exclusion of apostates who do not receive the covenant."[63] Second, where the *meshumad* is rejected as *ahikha,* "thy brother," it is because he is not *ahikha be-mizvot,* a brother of the spirit. There may be consanguinity, but there is hardly confraternity.

As regards the complete loss of personal Jewish status, finally, nothing short of total personal alienation will bring it off. Sinfulness, no matter how intense, degradation, no matter how extreme, will not accomplish it. If the apostate is to be expelled, he must first reject not only Judaism as a religion, but *Knesset Yisrael –* Jewry as a people. And he must reject not only its future but its past. As the proselyte enters *Knesset Yisrael* by embracing not only its destiny but its history, so the *meshumad* departs when and because he is alienated from both, when, by whatever criteria we employ, the lack of identification is complete. Even then, his physical roots in the community are sufficient to make him liable for all obligations and to keep the door open for his return. However, total loss of spiritual contact through alienation from our people and its history means that, for the present, he must be considered a non-Jew. As long as there is an identification with *Knesset Yisrael,* and not merely with a political state, the gravest of sinners remains a Jew. As a member of a spiritual community (even though he may not acknowledge and appreciate its true nature), he retains its quintessential character, at once a spiritual quality and a legal status – *kedushat Yisrael,* the personal sanctity of the Jew. With the loss of identification, however, there is a loss of identity. Personal status as a Jew – be it for marriage or for any other purpose – is lost. The distinctive mark of Jewry, what being a Jew essentially means, is effaced. *Kedushat Yisrael* is destroyed.

Halakhic discourse and philosophic analysis thus arrive at the same conclusion because they departed from the same terminal. *Kedushat Yisrael* may be a native endowment, but it is not an irrevocable patrimony. It is received, but it must also be taken; and it can be thrown away. It courses through the veins, but it must be lodged in the heart. For above all, *kedushat Yisrael* carries with it a spiritual challenge. As chosenness is, collectively, as much a responsibility as a privilege, so *kedushat Yisrael* calls upon the individual Jew to live up to his status. It is a position to be attained as much as a gift to be enjoyed. Hence, if it is to be retained at all, there must be a minimum of spiritual identification. The ideal is, of course, beyond fulfillment. The heights to which *kedushat Yisrael* calls the Jew are immeasurable; the mountain of the Lord is infinitely high. But if there is no ceiling, there is a floor – and beneath it the abyss. Willy-nilly, the Jew has been called. It is for him to frame the nature and direction of the response. Jewish consciousness is the first stage of the Jew's transmutation of inexorable fate into glorious destiny.

Notes

1. In many Eastern European communities, the Kehillah was an organized polity in a sense, and would have been faced with the same problem. However, the Kehillah did not cover all areas

of life as comprehensively as a state; its decisions were not as final (potentially at least, as happened in some parts of Germany, it could break up into several factional groups); and in any event, it dealt with the issue on a much smaller scale.

2. The relative security of Jews in the United States has had the same effect upon some American-Jewish intellectuals. I do not mean to suggest that the problem was previously ignored completely. It was not, and some nineteenth-century *maskilim*, for instance, were very much concerned with it. Relatively speaking, however, it was less prominent than at present.

3. In published halakhic texts, the term employed for an apostate is generally *mumar* rather than *meshumad*. This was due to censorship, however, and all uncensored texts regularly have *meshumad*. I have used the latter term partly because of its genuineness, and partly because, in popular parlance, it has much more powerful connotations.

4. From the polemical point of view, to approach the problem from the perspective of Halakhah is largely to beg the question. For much of the controversy surrounding the case has turned precisely on this point: how much weight shall be assigned to the authority of Halakhah? The polemical point of view is not necessarily the best, however; and in any event, for anyone committed to traditional Judaism, any other approach is unthinkable.

5. A full discussion of the halakhic position of the apostate would require an analysis of his status not only as a *meshumad* but as a *min* and an *apikoros*. However, while the latter two conditions carry certain liabilities and disqualifications, they do not raise the possibility of total exclusion from Jewry. I have therefore omitted mention of them and have concentrated on discussing the apostate's status as a *meshumad*, which does raise that possibility.

6. Desecration of the Sabbath is accorded special status because it implies a denial of Creation and Providence, and perhaps, therefore, of the existence of God (Rashi to Hullin 5a, and cf. Rambam, Hilkhot Shabbat 30:15). It has been argued that where these implications are lacking, as is now often the case, the law does not apply.

7. Hilkhot Teshuvah 3:9.

8. He could conceivably avoid the third group if he had converted for lucrative or appetitive reasons. If he had become a Unitarian rather than a Catholic, he would also have avoided the fourth group. Even those authorities who held, against the Rambam, that trinitarianism is not considered *avodah zarah*, spoke only with reference to Gentiles, for whom, they felt, the injunction against polytheism had been less vigorously formulated. With reference to Jews, however, the Athanasian Creed certainly is considered *avodah zarah*; see Sanhedrin 63a. Even a convert to Unitarianism – or to Islam, for that matter – would come under the fifth category, however.

9. Unless otherwise qualified, the term *meshumad* hereinafter simply designates a convert to another religion.

10. Hullin 5a, Gittin 45b, and Rambam, Hilkhot Gerushin 3:15, respectively.

11. Zevahim 22b, Hullin 5a, and Mekhilta 15 (on Shemot 12:43), respectively.

12. *Or Zaru'a*, Milah 97; Tosafot Rabbenu Elhanan, Avodah Zarah 27a. See also Yoreh De'ah 264:1, and commentaries.

13. See Sanhedrin 27a.

14. *Bet Yosef,* Orah Hayyim 39, and Hullin 5a, respectively.

15. See Hullin 5a for the source of the invalidation of an idolatrous Jew's sacrifice. No mention is made there of an idolatrous Gentile's sacrifice, but the Rambam, Ma'asseh Ha-Korbanot 3:2 explicitly states that it may be offered. Cf, however, Rambam, Melahkim 10:10.

   Similarly, Rabbenu Elhanan (Avodah Zarah 27a) holds that even if we assume that a Gentile can perform a valid circumcision, an apostate cannot.

16. Tosafot, Avodah Zarah 26b; Rosh and *Shiltei Ha-Gibborim,* ibid.; *Mordekhai* 814; and especially Ramban, Bava Metzia 71a. See also Yoreh De'ah 159:3, and commentaries.

17. See Gittin 47a.

18. See Pesahim 21b.

19. Yevamot 47b.

20. Bekorot 30b.

21. Rambam, Hilkhot Issurei Bi'ah 13:17 and Hilkhot Ishut 4:15; *Behag,* Kiddushin (p. 84 in Traub's edition); *Ittur,* Kiddushin 2; *Or Zaru'a* 604; and others.

22. *Bet Yosef,* Even Ha-Ezer 157.

23. An "early responsum" cited by the *Ittur,* Kiddushin 2; R. Samson, quoted in *Haggahot Mordekhai,* Yevamot 107, mentioned as one opinion in *Tur,* Even Ha-Ezer 44. A much larger number of authorities held that the bond of *yibbum* did not apply to the apostate, i.e., if a man dies childless and the surviving brother is an apostate, the wife does not require *halitzah.* However, this may be accounted for by reasons which are, for our purposes, irrelevant; e.g., we can assume (on the basis of Bava Kamma 110b) that the marriage was invalid because the woman would never have consented to it if she had foreseen this development (R. Meir of Rothenburg, quoted in *Teshuvot Maimuniyyot,* Ishut 29); or that an apostate is excluded because the Halakhah applies to brothers (*Or Zaru'a* 605; *Be'urei Ha-Gra,* Even Ha-Ezer 157. But see *Terumat Ha-Deshen* 123, who argues very effectively that the brotherhood mentioned here only means literal consanguinity).

24. See *Haggahot Mordekhai,* Yevamot 107. But cf. *Ittur,* Kiddushin 2.

25. See Sanhedrin 44a.

26. It is unclear whether this refers to the present disputants or to some earlier group.

27. Yevamot 17a. The biblical verse is from Hoshea 5:7.

28. Kiddushin 75b.

29. Hullin 6a. Some authorities hold that this change was only made *mi-de-rabbanan* and *le-humra,* i.e., where its application has the effect of superimposing a fresh injunction by rabbinic authority, but with no violation of Torah law. On this view, wherever the change in status would operate *le-kula,* i.e., relieve us of a Torah injunction, we do not apply it and we continue to regard the Samaritans as Jews. However, the Rambam (*Perush Ha-Mishnayot,* Niddah 7:4) explicitly applies the principle in the latter case as well. See also *Shakh* and *Havvot Da'at,* Yoreh De'ah 159.

30. Some of the Geonim held differently – see *Tur,* Even Ha-Ezer 44, and *Behag,* Kiddushin (p. 84) – but there is no doubt that this would be the case according to the Rambam.

31. Zevahim 22b.
32. The story comes to me on the authority of Rav Hayyim's grandson and my rebbe, Rav Joseph B. Soloveitchik.

    In all candor, I should point out, first, that the *Behag* drastically reinterpreted the gemara in such a way that it would have no bearing on our problem, and second, that the *Bah* (Even Ha-Ezer 44) holds that the declaration mentioned in the gemara is not a mere judgment but a promulgation made in that specific case and inapplicable to apostates generally. See also *Keren Orah*, Yevamot 17b.

33. According to the Geonim, who required reconversion even for apostates who did not become completely cut off from Jewry, a new *gerut* (ritual conversion) would be required in our case as well. This is only *mi-de-rabbanan*, however, for psychological and symbolic reasons. I speak of the basic law, from a purely formal point of view.

34. It was, of course, reenacted – independently, and yet, as part of a continuum – with the other *avot*.

35. Bereshit 17:8.

36. Hilkhot Sanhedrin 4:6.

37. For a lengthy and more general discussion of this point along similar lines, see *Kaftor va-Ferah*, chap. 10.

38. The first point, that the obligation remains, is certain. The second, that reentry would not necessitate *gerut*, is open to question. One might argue that even for one who is endowed with *shem Yisrael*, the recovery of *kedushat Yisrael* requires full *gerut*. It may also be contended that *gerut* would not be required, but only because the return to the fold would retroactively cancel the earlier renunciation.

39. From a moral point of view, the father is far more liable, as he is the culpable one. He would be the more severely judged, while the son would have full sympathy (see Rambam, Hilkhot Mamrim 3:3). However, the loss of *kedushat Yisrael* here is not so much a penalty, but simply the reflection of the objective situation that one has cut personal and emotional ties with *Knesset Yisrael*. This situation obtains in the child's case more than in the father's. For the same reason, even if environmental influences were the cause of conversion, it would make no difference in determining the convert's status. The fact remains the same, although our judgment of the worth of the agent would be changed considerably.

40. The gemara's citation of the text concerning begetting alien children may be variously understood. The gemara may be saying that the begetting of alien children (i.e., uprooting oneself from Jewry so completely that one's children don't even know they are Jewish) is itself an apostasy which causes the loss of Jewish status. In this case, the gemara's principle would apply to the father. However, the gemara may only be inferring from the use of the epithet "alien" that the children in this situation really are aliens and not Jews. In this case, it is possible to assume that the father remains a Jew.

41. See his *Conversion: The Old and the New in Religion from Alexander the Great to Augustine of Hippo* (Oxford, 1933).

42. "St. Augustine and His Age," in *Saint Augustine* (New York: Meridian, 1957), p. 47.

43. This is the generally accepted view, largely on the basis of the text cited in Yevamot 17a, 23a, and elsewhere. Some, however, require that both parents be Jewish; see Rashi, Yevamot 23a, and Tosafot, Kiddushin 76b.

44. The contention advanced by writers like Leslie Fiedler that "the essential nature of Jewishness is to be alienated, to be an exile, to be outsiders" (*New York Times,* June 19, 1963, p. 5) is completely untenable. It presents a wholly negative conception of *Knesset Yisrael* and rests, first, on a total misunderstanding of the nature of Jewry, and second, on an acceptance of Diaspora existence as the norm of Jewish life. Our critics understood us much better.

45. Zekharyah 14:9. Cf. Rashi, Shemot 17:16, 46.

46. The ideal of ultimate universality does not preclude the possibility that the special historical role of *Knesset Yisrael* will have metahistorical implications, so that it will also occupy a unique eschatological position. Universality, again, does not mean uniformity.

47. A full analysis of the concept of chosenness would require discussion of three elements: (1) the very notion of a limited group, (2) the special character of that group, and (3) the implications and consequences of being chosen. I discuss only the first.

48. Theoretically, such an extreme universalism could perhaps be reconciled with the concept of prophetic revelation, if one assumed that the revelation was sufficiently widespread and open to all. Only with difficulty, however, and practically, has the concept of special revelation gone hand in hand with the idea of a special religious corpus.

49. Classical formulations of this position may be found in the last book of Hooker's *Ecclesiastical Polity* (London, 1597) and in Coleridge's *The Constitution of Church and State* (London, 1830). Ultimately, this view rests on the distinction, touched on by Hooker and fully developed by Coleridge, between an ideal universal church including all true believers but having no visible form and a real national church organized like any political society and including all professed believers.

50. Going furthest in the direction of particularism is the type of church-state so prevalent in primitive societies and so aptly described in Christopher Dawson's *Religion and Culture* (London, 1949). However, this conception derives from placing a limitation not only upon the human but upon the divine: the notion of a local deity. Hence, it hardly merits consideration.

51. Keritot 9a.

52. Ernest Renan, "Qu'est-ce qu'une nation?" in *Discours et conférences*, in *Oeuvres complètes*, ed. Henriette Psichari (Paris, n.d.), vol. 1, pp. 903–904.

53. "Christianity and Nationality," in *Church, State, and Education,* American ed. (Ann Arbor, 1957), p. 136.

54. John E.E.D. Acton, "Nationality," in *Essays on Freedom and Power*, ed. G. Himmelfarb (New York, 1955), p. 164. The Burkean passage alluded to is from "Remarks on the Policy of the Allies," but the underlying concept is a recurrent theme, seen in both the *Reflections* and, especially, in Burke's *Appeal from the New to the Old Whigs.*

55. See, for instance, Horayot 3a, and Rambam, *Perush Ha-Mishnayot,* Bekorot 4:3. See also

my remarks in "Be-Inyan Semihah be-Eretz Yisrael u-ve-Hutz la-Aretz," *Bet Yizhak*, 5719, pp. 89–98.

56. Devarim 29:14.

57. It is for this reason that each of them is individually mentioned in the Shemoneh Esreh; see Pesahim 117b. That Jacob's children were the transitional figures in the shift from individual to communal religious life is reflected in the fact that they are enumerated twice in the Torah, once (Bereshit 46:8–27) as individuals (and hence their children are also enumerated) and once (Shemot 1:1–3) as heads of the future community. See also Rambam, Avodat Kokhavim 1:3.

58. Yevamot 47b. See also Rambam, Hilkhot Issurei Bi'ah 14:1–2.

59. Preface to *Androcles and the Lion*.

60. Yerushalmi, Bikkurim 4:3. The phrase is from Bereshit 17:5.

61. Shabbat 146a.

62. *Teshuvot Ha-Rambam*, ed. J. Blau (Jerusalem, 1960), p. 293. In the last sentence, some texts read, "for the Torah was given to us and to converts alike."

63. *Torat Kohanim* 2 (on Vayikra 1:2).

Chapter 4

The Parameters of Tolerance

Toleration in Jewish tradition is, at once, an easy and a difficult topic. Its exposition and analysis is, *prima facie,* simple, insofar as the obviously relevant sources are relatively accessible and straightforward. On the other hand, it poses formidable difficulty inasmuch as it elicits mixed and charged emotions. Compelling recognition that, at the very least, our pluralistic society admits of no alternative jostles with the gnawing intuition that perhaps we are inconsonant with both the spirit and the letter of *yahadut.* The result is often ambivalence, which oscillates between rigidity and apologetics.

Admittedly, the ambivalence is not confined to the Jewish sphere. While the Western mind regards toleration as an indispensable *modus vivendi,* it recoils somewhat from its substantive spiritual content. From a liberal perspective, the term reeks of supercilious condescension. To the passionately principled, on the other hand, it evokes associations of Westminster in 1689, weary of internecine strife, enacting legislation in the shadow of Locke's tepid latitudinarianism; of accommodation reached not through conviction but in its spite and in its absence. Even as we eschew conflict, we are impressed by the manliness of Dr. Johnson's assertion to Boswell, that "every man has a right to utter what he thinks truth, and every other man has a right to knock him down for it: Martyrdom is the test."[1] We espouse civil discourse and "sweet reasonableness;" and yet part

This paper was delivered at the Orthodox Forum 1997 and published in *Tolerance, Dissent, and Democracy: Philosophical, Historical, and Halakhic Perspectives,* ed. Moshe Sokol (Northvale, NJ; Jason Aronson, 2002).

of us appreciates the "real vital interest in literature." T.E. Hulme admired
the spirited riot which ensued when a Parisian lecturer made some dis-
paraging remarks about Racine. "These people interrupted," Hulme noted,
"because the classical ideal is a living thing to them and Racine is the great
classic. That is what I call a real vital interest in literature."[2] And we, for
our part, concomitantly wonder how much of the eagerness to live and
let live derives from the desiccation of commitment.

Unquestionably, however, the Jewish component exacerbates the
issue. As critics have often charged, a measure of intolerance is endemic
to *Yahadut* and we should acknowledge this candidly. Its vital center is the
concept and reality of monotheism; and monotheism, almost by definition,
is exclusionary. As the literal iconoclasm ascribed by familiar midrashim to
Avraham Avinu manifests amply, this aspect characterized our inception,
and it is part of our eschatological vision. Thrice daily, a Jew prays that he
may live to see idolatry expunged and the world exclusively suffused with
faith in the *Ribbono shel Olam*:

עַל כֵּן נְקַוֶּה לְךָ ה' אֱ-לֹקֵינוּ לִרְאוֹת מְהֵרָה בְּתִפְאֶרֶת עֻזֶּךָ לְהַעֲבִיר גִּלּוּלִים מִן הָאָרֶץ
וְהָאֱלִילִים כָּרוֹת יִכָּרֵתוּן לְתַקֵּן עוֹלָם בְּמַלְכוּת שַׁ-דַּי וְכָל בְּנֵי בָשָׂר יִקְרְאוּ בִשְׁמֶךָ לְהַפְנוֹת
אֵלֶיךָ כָּל רִשְׁעֵי אָרֶץ יַכִּירוּ וְיֵדְעוּ כָּל יוֹשְׁבֵי תֵבֵל כִּי לְךָ תִּכְרַע כָּל בֶּרֶךְ תִּשָּׁבַע כָּל לָשׁוֹן לְפָנֶיךָ
ה' אֱ-לֹקֵינוּ כֻלָּם יִכְרְעוּ וְיִפֹּלוּ וְלִכְבוֹד שִׁמְךָ יְקָר יִתֵּנוּ וִיקַבְּלוּ כֻלָּם אֶת עוֹל מַלְכוּתֶךָ
וְתִמְלֹךְ עֲלֵיהֶם מְהֵרָה לְעוֹלָם וָעֶד.

Therefore, we put our hope in you, Lord our God, that we may soon see Your
mighty splendor, to remove detestable idolatry from the earth, and false gods
will be cut off, to perfect the universe through the Almighty's sovereignty.
Then all humanity will call upon Your name, to turn all the Earth's wicked
toward You. All the world's inhabitants will recognize and know that to You
every knee should bend, every tongue should swear [allegiance]. Before you,
Lord, our God, they will bend every knee and cast themselves down and to
the glory of Your name they will render homage, and they will all accept
upon themselves the yoke of Your kingship that you may reign over them
eternally.

On Rosh Hashanah and Yom Kippur, the theme is honed yet further,
as the aspiration is extended to every sentient being and specific reference
is made to the God of Israel:

והופע בהדר גאון עוזך על כל יושבי תבל ארצך וידע כל פעול כי אתה פעלתו ויבין כל
יצור כי אתה יצרתו ויאמר כל אשר נשמה באפו ה' א-לקי ישראל מלך ומלכותו בכל
משלה.

Shine forth in your splendid majesty over all the inhabitants of Your world.
May every existing being know that You have made it; may every creature
realize that you have created it; may every breathing thing proclaim: "The
Lord, God of Israel is King and his kingdom rules over all."

In and of themselves, such supplications need not preclude toleration.
Let us bear in mind that toleration is not to be equated with pluralism.
Indeed, in a sense, it is its very antithesis.[3] Full-blown religious pluralism
acknowledges the radical legitimacy of conflicting faith commitments.
As such, it need not, it cannot, "tolerate" them. To tolerate is to suffer the
pressure of what is not only different but, by my lights, thoroughly erroneous; and to refrain, nonetheless, from the exercise of power to coerce
its devotees to cease and desist. "We cannot, properly speaking," Susan
Mendus has rightly asserted, "be said to tolerate things which we welcome,
or endorse, or find attractive;"[4] nor, one might add, things we recognize as
morally and metaphysically valid. It is precisely rigorous monism which
is challenged to tolerate; and its devotees can, in theory, respond to the
challenge by averring that conviction that freely willed sin ought not be
repressed is fully consonant with the credal hope that the deviant and the
erring, in due time and of their own accord, will see the light. Nevertheless,
historically and halakhically, *avodah zarah* has indeed not been tolerated;
and this critical fact casts a long shadow over any discussion of the limits
of toleration within Jewish tradition.

Difficult or easy, the topic can be addressed with reference to several
contexts. My instinctive predilection is of course to deal with it, first, as a
halakhic issue; but this is, itself, multifaceted. Halakhah is, preeminently, a
religio-legal order, and, as such, includes not only norms but varied sanctions for their violators and formal mechanisms for their implementation.
Consequently, it obviously does not assent to recalcitrance or tolerate disobedience. In this respect, it is no different from any legal system. Its canons
are of course fairly comprehensive and some of them relate to domains

which, in a religiously neutral polity, would be regarded as the province of private conscience. Given, however, the cardinal assumption of a community with a definitive spiritual character, the institution of sanctions in order to ensure its perpetuation is not distinctive. Civil libertarians rankle at the restriction of personal freedom, but most of them acknowledge the justice of contemporary welfare state legislation, with some trade-off of liberty for equality, as opposed to nineteenth-century laissez-faire enterprise. In any event, while their states exercise toleration with respect to the religious sphere, which is often marginal to their security and existence, they have few compunctions about recourse to restrictive coercion in sociopolitical areas which they regard as critical.[5]

Just how far coercive religious pressure can or should be exerted in the modern era, given a predominantly secular, and hence resistant, population, is of course questionable. It is certainly arguable that, under the circumstances, it is not only counter-productive but spiritually wrong. One might note – as, on occasion, had *mori ve-rabbi*, Rav Ahron Soloveichik זצ״ל – that the Rambam ascribed resort to force to the *melekh ha-mashiah* who, being steeped in Torah and profoundly engaged by it, "will compel all of Israel to walk in the path [of Torah] and reinforce the breaches [in its observance],"[6] possibly intimating that such a course is not currently practicable or advisable in a pre-Messianic era. There is, however, no blurring the fact that, in a halakhic *polis*, comprised of a fundamentally committed constituency, toleration, as popularly conceived, would indeed be circumscribed. The limits might not be as narrow as some fear and other desire. While, in principle, "the enforcement of morals" is certainly within the purview of a *bet din* – indeed, the Rambam[7] cited this function as the primary reason for its establishment – it could presumably decide that, in a specific sociocultural context, restraint in recourse to its authority would be prudentially and spiritually preferable to its maximal exercise. Or again, nothing would preclude a dissenting opponent of the Sanhedrin from embarking upon a lecture tour to convince the populace of its waywardness or error.[8] Nevertheless, it seems clear that, in a purely halakhic state, civil liberties would, in practice, fall short of the standard currently prevalent in most liberal democracies, and that sanctions generally abjured by them would, in all likelihood, exist.

The sanctions vary in character and purpose. They may serve as *ante facto* coercive pressure or *post facto* punishment, range from the corporal to the monetary, and include modes of anathema and ostracism. The latter are not popular with enlightened penologists, and their application was recently excoriated by the Israeli Supreme Court. I must confess that, from my own perspective, I am thoroughly baffled by the criticism. I find excommunication far more humane than prolonged incarceration, and, in a compact and largely homogeneous community, it is probably far more effective. Within the modern setting, typified by diversity and mobility, *niduy* has admittedly been robbed of much of its force, and *batei din* have thus lost a valuable tool. Whatever the details, however, the underlying principle is clear and, for our purposes, it is the common denominator which is relevant.

The degree of rigor inherent in the fabric of the halakhic social order, as part of its woof and warp, is one measure of the limits of toleration. It is not, however, the sole measure – and perhaps not the primary. No less significant is the attitude – on the part of a community or of individuals, and beyond the pale of formal sanction – which the tradition enables, encourages, or even mandates, with respect to deviationists. Does it foster, practically and emotionally, rapprochement or reproach, understanding or rejection? Does it engender conciliation or confrontation? Obviously, the tradition is not univocal on this matter, and it would be banal to seek a definitive yes or no response to such questions. There is much to be learned, however, from sharpening the major issues and identifying dominant strains.

Such a discussion would be particularly valuable for us because it is this aspect which is most relevant, contemporaneously. Whether in Israel or in the Diaspora, the phalanx of *batei din* implementing and imposing Jewish law and order, which was still fairly widespread in the pre-modern era, is now essentially inoperative; and for self-evident reasons. At the level of public policy and private conduct, however, debate over this general

issue and many of its specific manifestations, is both vibrant and vehement. Given disagreement and even delegitimization, a broad spectrum
of responses, ranging from denunciatory vendetta to genuine respect, is
open; and the limits of toleration can be analyzed with respect to it.

Presumably, the issue confronts us most sharply in dealing with the
wholly uncommitted whether *l'teiavon* or *l'hakh'is*, running the gamut
from virulent opponents through the apathetically indifferent to the
sympathetic and yet non-observant. However, as this question was dealt
with extensively in a previous Orthodox Forum, and as the papers presented therein were subsequently published,[9] I shall narrow my horizon
here today and focus upon intramural toleration, upon relation to those
who position themselves within tradition and yet are regarded by others
as aberrant, if not marginal. These may be movements or individuals,
motivated by ideology, impelled by iconoclasm, or animated by the quest
for mere convenience. Their hallmark is nonconformity, on the one hand,
and the claim to full legitimacy and equal authenticity, on the other; and it
is to this claim that the bar of tradition, whether conceived as an abstract
corpus or as a sociological reality, addresses itself.

Divergence – the term lies somewhere between deviation and diversity – may be manifested as regards either conduct or conviction; and so,
accordingly, toleration or its absence. With respect to both, the question of
toleration and its limits is dual. At one plane, a tolerant mindset impacts
upon definition of the norm and its parameters. At another, it limits attitudes towards those who deviate from it. As I have already suggested, from
a purely logical standpoint, the first element should be wholly out of court.
Theoretically, interpretive flexibility, reflected in sweeping application of
eilu v'eilu divrei elokim hayim, need not entail compassionate understanding of whatever lies, as something must, beyond the pale of *eilu v'eilu*. One
may be a fiery zealot, categorically condemning all modes of deviation,
and yet a halakhic and theological liberal, enlarging the bounds of legitimate inquiry. Conversely, one may be rigorously stringent in defining the
normative demands of tradition and yet, ideologically and interperson-
ally, accepting and receptive when relating to those unwilling or unable
to accept its full mandate. The width of the playing field bears no relation

to the consequences of being off-side. Presumably, the substantive content of Torah and its seventy aspects is to be determined by hermeneutic and analytic principles of exegesis, to which the philosophy and practice of toleration bear no relation.

Psychologically, however, the two are indeed often closely bound. In part, there may be correlation at the level of personality. The same rigor which manifests itself in interpretation or impels a given axiological balance may be similarly reflected in relating to others. And in part, to the extent that stringency is grounded in passionate commitment to ritual values, response to erosion of those values, unless counterbalanced by other factors, may be painfully aggravated. Were this, primarily, a historical and empirical survey, I have no doubt that we would find a significant correlation; and, even in an essentially analytic discussion, this factor cannot be wholly ignored.

The linchpin of the discussion is the *mizvah* of *tokhahah*, variously interpreted (the range is illuminating) as "reproach" or "convincing." Its source is in the *pasuk* in Vayikra, "You shall not hate your brother in your heart, You shall surely rebuke your neighbor, and you shall not bear sin because of him" (19:17). At one plane, this injunction can be restricted to the interpersonal sphere, as an exhortation to clear the air through frank discussion rather than letting tension fester. It was in this vein that the Rashbam, partly in light of the opening admonition, interpreted the *pasuk*: "Do not hate him in your heart, rather rebuke him for what he has done and as a result there will be peace." The Ramban likewise elaborates upon this theme:

והנכון בעיני כי הוכח תוכיח כמו והוכיח אברהם את אבימלך ויאמר הכתוב אל תשנא את אחיך בלבבך בעשותו לך שלא כרצונך אבל תוכיחהו מדוע ככה עשית עמדי ולא תשא עליו חטא לכסות שנאתו בלבך ולא תגיד לו כי בהוכיחך אותו יתנצל לך או ישוב ויתודה על חטאו ותכפר לו.

The correct interpretation appears to me to be that the expression "you shall surely rebuke" is similar to [the phrase] "And Abraham reproved Avimelekh" [Ber. 21:25]. The verse here is stating: "Do not hate your brother in your heart when he does something against your will, but instead you are to reprove him, saying, 'Why did you this to me'? And you will not bear sin because of him by covering up your hatred of him in your heart and not telling him, for when you will reprove him, he will justify himself before you [so that you will have no cause to hate him] or he will regret his action, and you will forgive him."

On this reading, the verse bears no relation to response to objectionable conduct and is irrelevant to our topic. However, as the Ramban of course knew, Hazal's prevalent halakhic interpretation does connect the *pasuk* to our theme; and he himself opens his comment on this note:

ואמר הוכח תוכיח את עמיתך מצוה אחרת ללמדו תוכחות מוסר ולא תשא עליו חטא שיהיה עליך אשם כאשר יחטא ולא הוכחת אותו ולזה יטה לשון אונקלוס שאמר ולא תקבל על דליה חובא שלא תקבל אתה עונש בחטא שלו.

And it states, "You shall surely rebuke your neighbor." This constitutes another commandment, [that is] to instruct him [by] moral remonstrance. "And you shall not bear sin because of him", for you will bear guilt because of his transgression if he does sin and you have not rebuked him, and to this [interpretation] Onkelos leans in that he states, "Do not receive punishment on his account", that you should not receive a punishment because of his transgression.

It is this understanding which is familiar from the *Sifra*, the gemara, Rishonim and *poskim*; and it is this which has become imprinted upon the popular mind. On this view, a critical response is not only sanctioned but mandated, and silence renders the observer an accessory after the fact, fully liable for his acquiescence.

What, one asks, are we charged to reprove? The Ramban speaks of sinful conduct, generally, "for you will bear guilt because of his transgression if he does sin and you do not rebuke him," without distinguishing between major infractions and peccadillos. The Rambam, however, apparently goes much further. In postulating the *mizvah*, he writes:

הרואה חבירו שחטא או שהלך בדרך לא טובה מצוה להחזירו למוטב ולהודיעו שהוא חוטא על עצמו במעשיו הרעים שנאמר הוכח תוכיח את עמיתך (דעות, ו:ז).

It is a *mizvah* for a person who sees that his fellow Jew has sinned or is following an improper path [to attempt] to correct his behavior and to inform him that he is causing himself a loss by his evil deeds as the [verse] states, "You shall surely rebuke your neighbor" (De'ot 6:7).

The stimulus need not be a specific wrong. The amorphous pursuit of a vaguely defined "path which is not good" suffices. Many may find this startling and perhaps alarming, but the formulation is clearly based upon two complementary gemarot. In the locus classicus of discussion of *tokhahah* in Arakhin, we read:

מנין לרואה בחבירו דבר מגונה שחייב להוכיחו שנאמר הוכח (טז:)

From where do we know that if someone sees an ugly act (*davar meguneh*) committed by his friend that he is obligated to rebuke him as it says: "You shall surely rebuke" (16b).

Whatever the exact position of *davar meguneh* on the continuum of sin and virtue, it certainly is not confined to outright halakhic violations.

The point is reinforced by an analogous citation in Berakhot, which, in addition, provides an illustrative example. Commenting upon Eli's remonstrance to Hannah, "Until when shall you continue to be drunk; remove your wine from yourself," Rav Eleazar observes:

מכאן לרואה בחבירו דבר שאינו הגון צריך להוכיחו (לא:)

From here we derive that if one sees something improper (*davar she-eino hagun*) in his friend he must rebuke him (31b).

Here, instead of *davar meguneh* we have the even blander *davar she-eino hagun* and the instance cited, mild intoxication (had Hannah appeared to be thoroughly stoned, others would presumably have ushered her out of the portal to the *heikhal*) while constituting objectionable asocial behavior, entails no explicit halakhic infraction. The message with respect to the imperative of *tokhahah* is thus sharp and clear.

Tosafot mutes it somewhat by evidently distinguishing between the two texts. Commenting upon the phrase *davar she-eino hagun*, they explain:

פירוש אע״ג דליכא איסורא דאורייתא דאי איכא איסורא דאורייתא פשיטא הוכח תוכיח כתיב.[10]

Even though there is no violation of a biblical commandment, for if there is a violation of a biblical commandment it is obvious, for it is written, "You shall surely rebuke."

Presumably, they understood that Rav Eleazar was not positioning a formal halakhic demand, subsumed under the obligation of *tokhahah*, but, limiting himself to *zarikh* rather than *hayyav*, was simply counseling what a person ought to do. On this view, *davar meguneh*, with reference to which the gemara cites the *pasuk*, evidently does refer to an explicit halakhic violation – and perhaps to a *d'oraitha* violation, to boot. Moreover, given the distinction, it is conceivable that the substance of the response may differ, respectively, and not only the degree of obligation. A *davar meguneh* might elicit full-blown reproach, whereas for a *davar she-eino hagun* a mild rebuke could suffice.

Tosafot's distinction is possibly supported by the juxtaposition of *zarikh* and *hayyav*, on the one hand, but strained as regards the import of *meguneh*, on the other. The Rambam evidently rejected it, however; hence, the inclusion of "following an improper path" (*holeikh be-derekh lo tovah*) as a cause for *tokhahah*. The implications for tolerance are clear. Individualists would no doubt bridle even at the possibly blander response called for by Tosafot's view; all the more so, however, with regard to the more intrusive procedure mandated by the Rambam.

And indeed there may be room for concern. So sweeping a term as *derekh lo tovah* could be manipulated into invasive rejection of all modes of nonconformity. On the face of it, one would obviously maintain a differentiation between social and moral deviation. In practice, however, the line is often blurred. Mores do not exist in a vacuum, and inherently innocent details of appearance or conduct can bespeak fealty to a problematic culture or counterculture. The habit doth indeed oft not only proclaim the man but defines him. Traditional educational institutions grapple with this issue continually; and justifiably. Within a given context, some actions are defined by their associations. Rav Yaakov Kamenetsky, זצ"ל, once remarked to me that while, retrospectively, he couldn't understand why, he clearly recalls that when he had learned at the yeshiva in Slobodka, rowing was regarded askance. I presume that, at the time, any talmid observed in a scull would have been called in for a reproachful chat. But can we readily transfer such an approach to society at large? And can we ignore the danger that, in the name of quasi-religious vigilance, individual initiative will be stifled? At the very least, we need pause for thought.

The question is exacerbated if we consider the full potential scope of *tokhahah*, on the one hand, and its possible force, on the other. The term *derekh*, as the Rav, זצ״ל, once emphasized in an analogous connection, need not refer to objectionable actions *per se* but to their matrix – the orientation, context, lifestyle and attitude within which they gestate and out of which they spring. Hence, in his *Avodat Ha-melekh*,[11] Rav Menachem Krakowsky suggests that *derekh lo tovah* may be understood as referring to *deʾot nifsadot* and he refers us to a passage in Hilkhot Teshuvah:

אל תאמר שאין תשובה אלא מעבירות שיש בהן מעשה כגון זנות וגזל וגניבה אלא כשם שצריך אדם לשוב מאלו הוא צריך לחפש בדעות רעות שיש לו ולשוב מן הכעס ומן האיבה ומן הקנאה ומן ההתול ומרדיפת הממון והכבוד ומרדיפת המאכלות וכיוצא בהן מן הכל צריך לחזור בתשובה ואלו העונות קשים מאותן שיש בהן מעשה שבזמן שאדם נשקע באלו קשה הוא לפרוש מהם וכן הוא אומר יעזוב רשע וגו׳ (ז:ג)

A person should not think that repentance is only necessary for those sins that involve deeds such as illicit sexual behavior, robbery, or theft. Rather, just as a person is obligated to repent from these, similarly, he must search after the evil qualities that he has. He must repent from anger, hatred, envy, frivolity, the pursuit of money and honor, the pursuit of gluttony, and the like. He must repent for all of these. These sins are more difficult [to repent from] than those that involve deeds, for when a person is immersed in these, it is more difficult for him to separate himself. And thus does it say [Isaiah 55:7], "May the wicked abandon their paths and the crooked man his designs." (7:3)

The implications for the range of *tokhahah* are self-evident. As his citation indicates, the *deʾot* noted by *Avodat Ha-Melekh* are in line with the Rambam's own usage – essentially, character traits. Obviously, however, *derekh lo tovah* could also encompass *emunot ve-deʾot* in the popular sense of the term; and this opens up entirely new vistas for vigilance and reprimand. Whatever we think of the much-belabored place of dogma in *Yahadut*, it clearly has a place. As such, it can be the source of personal aberration no less than communal polemic; and hence, a further test of the limits of toleration. Again, the issue is not where one draws the line of catechetical rectitude, of what one may or must affirm with respect to

Scriptural interpretation, metaphysical speculation, or historical inquiry. The issue is rather how one relates to those who have crossed it. Here, too, the imperative of *tokhahah* is presumably in full sway; and the question of its relation to toleration confronts us squarely.

Consideration of the mode of *tokhahah* sharpens the matter further. "How far does the obligation of reproof go?" the gemara asks, and it cites three conflicting views:

רב אמר עד הכאה ושמואל אמר עד קללה ורבי יוחנן אמר עד נזיפה כתנאי רבי אליעזר
אומר עד הכאה רבי יהושע אומר עד קללה בן עזאי אומר עד נזיפה (ערכין טז:)

> Rav says until the point of striking, Shmuel says until the point of cursing. Rav Yohanan says until the point of consternation. [This is] like the debate of the Tanaim: R. Eliezer says until the point of striking, R. Yehoshua says until the point of cursing, Ben Azai says until the point of consternation (Arakhin 16b).

Reproach which verges on eliciting such vehement reactions (I assume the prevalent view that the gemara speaks of reaction of the reproached and not, as some would have it,[12] of the means employed by the critic) must be cutting indeed; and yet, it is mandated nonetheless. Elsewhere, a far more restrained approach is counseled. "Said R. Il'a in the name of R. Elazar the son of R. Shimon," the gemara quotes in Yevamot (65b):

כשם שמצוה על אדם לומר דבר הנשמע כך מצוה על אדם שלא לומר דבר שאינו נשמע
רבי אבא אמר חובה שנאמר אל תוכח לץ פן ישנאך הוכח לחכם ויאהבך (סה:)

> As one is commanded to say that which will be obeyed so too one is commanded not to say that which will not be obeyed. R. Abba says it [i.e. not rebuking one who will not listen] is a duty, for it says in Scripture, "Reprove not a scorner lest he hate you; reprove a wise man and he will love you."

This appears to contradict the phalanx of views expressed in Arakhin, and various suggestions have been advanced to reconcile the texts. In reality, however, there need be no contradiction, as they address themselves to different issues. In Arakhin, the gemara defines the parameters of the obligation to rebuke: to what extent should a person be commanded to risk retribution in order to enhance his fellow's spiritual welfare. In Yevamot, it offers pragmatic advice as to how counsel is best proffered.

The limitation is imposed, however, with an eye to ensuring the effectiveness of the *tokhahah*, not in order to safeguard the privacy of its object. In theory, if it were reasonably certain that a reproach which would stimulate initial resistance bordering on violence would lead its listener to internalize the critique and mend his ways, one would be enjoined to express it, the immediate reaction to intrusion notwithstanding.[13] Our perception of the scope of *tokhahah* is thus heightened, and awareness concerning the limits of toleration is sharpened.

These limits are seemingly likewise notable with respect to a kindred phenomenon, protesting or *meha'ah*. Hazal stress the need to speak out against all forms of objectionable behavior in many contexts. The collective punishment implicit in *arevut*, "and they shall stumble one upon another – this teaches us that all Israel is responsible one for another," they ascribed to the general failure to protest – "that they had opportunity to protest and they did not" (Shevuot 39b). One is held liable, as a silent partner of sorts, in direct proportion to his ability to influence by protest.

כל מי שאפשר למחות לאנשי ביתו ולא מיחה נתפס על אנשי ביתו באנשי עירו נתפס
על אנשי עירו בכל העולם כולו נתפס על כל העולם כולו (שבת נד:)

Whoever can protest to his household members [to prevent them from sin-ning] and does not do so, is seized [punished] for their sins. Whoever can protest to his fellow citizens and does not, is seized for their sins. Whoever can protest to the whole world, is seized for the whole world (Shabbat 54b).

Moreover, as some rishonim noted, the admonition against express-ing a rejected *davar she-eino nishma* is wholly absent here, as evidenced from an interchange cited in the gemara in Shabbat:

א"ל ר' זירא לר' סימון לוכחינהו מר להני דבי ריש גלותא א"ל לא מקבלי מינאי א"ל
אע"ג דלא מקבלי לוכחינהו מר (נה.)

R. Zeira said to R. Simon, "Let the Master rebuke the members of the Resh Galuta's house." He replied, "They will not accept it from me." He responded, "Even though they do not accept it, yet the Master should rebuke them" (55a).

Substantively, *meha'ah* differs from *tokhahah* fundamentally. The latter is oriented to its object. As the context of the *pesukim* indicates amply, it is grounded in concern for him and a desire to ensure his spiritual well-being. As we are commanded to enhance our fellow's *hayyei sha'ah,* so are we enjoined to bear responsibility for his *hayyei olam.* Hence, where *tokhahah* will not result in the desired effect, and might even be counterproductive, it is best foregone. *Meha'ah,* by contrast is publicly oriented. It is part of an ongoing struggle for communal spiritual integrity, an initiative through which one not only dissociates from wrong but strives to prevent, or, minimally, to stifle and counterbalance, its impact. Consequently, the restrictive term, *amitekha,* which singles out a spiritual confrere, "a member of the nation who shares in your observance of Torah and *mizvot,*" for spiritual remedy of *tokhahah,* has no bearing upon *meha'ah* which is mandated by an event rather than by its agent. Hence, likewise, the openness of the miscreant to corrective protest is of little moment.

Given the distinction, the relevance of *meha'ah* to toleration may be relatively less, inasmuch as its individual object is not the primary focus. Nevertheless, depending upon its thrust and substance, protest, too, can impact severely. *C'est le ton qui fait la musique.* Vigorous public opposition can be variously inhibiting and punitive to the point of persecution; and I presume there is no need to adduce example, historical or contemporary. Vociferous rejoinder is often intended to silence more than to rebut. *Meha'ah,* too, then, beyond delegitimizing outright deviation – at times, an unavoidable necessity – can, in marginal instances, infringe upon the right or the ability to act or speak; and the question of the limits of toleration therefore bears upon it as well.

For many committed Jews, there is no real problem. Quite apart from the rigors of certain sources and *halakhot* governing relations to the wholly recalcitrant, the material we have surveyed regarding interaction with *amitekha* seems, to them, to point a clear direction. They would contend that the initiative of *batei din zedek,* at the institutional plane, and a plethora of remonstrance and protest, at the individual plane, effectively neutralize the standing of toleration as a desideratum. At most, it may be countenanced and even encouraged as a matter of practical necessity, in order to avoid bloodletting internecine strife – particularly, when *anshei shlomeinu* do not have the upper hand. The notion that there may be genuine positive content is out of court, however; and, these proponents argue, toleration should be recognized for what it is – an alien import from modern Western culture.

That the main thrust of Jewish tradition, in this respect, runs counter to modern culture goes without saying. The inviolable sanctity of private conscience is one of the cardinal tenets of liberal faith, secular or religious. In practice, this translates into great sensitivity about interpersonal criticism, as regards either giving or receiving. Many are open to collective reproach, especially if its source is an authority figure publicly or professionally empowered to express it. Very few, however, are genuinely open to even constructive criticism from peers. Whereas Halakhah mandates *tokhahah* even with respect to relative strangers, most of us are reluctant to hear it even from close friends – or, as some would have it, particularly from close friends. Looking around us, we can only conclude that if, indeed, "rebuke the wise man for he will love you," the wise are currently in very short supply.

This reluctance derives, in part, from social theory and reality, on the one hand, and from Protestant individualism, on the other. Divided, ideologically, between atomic and organic conception of society, most Western democracies tilt, in practice, to the former. The loss of community and the desiccation of roots decried by so many have driven home the sense that, at the plane of moral and religious decision, each man indeed is an island unto himself. And, on the theological side, the motto of personal grace and responsibility emblazoned by certain strains of the early Reformation, has left its mark. Not all modernists thirst for the anonymity glorified in Harvey Cox's *The Secular City*, but few would prefer the critical scrutiny of the Reverend Dimmesdale's Salem.

That much of this conflicts with halakhic sensibility – grounded in an organic view of *knesset Yisrael*, oriented to compact kehillot, and suffused with a sense of communal identity and collective responsibility – is, I repeat, a truism. Nevertheless, for many committed halakhic Jews – surely, for those likely to be reading these lines – the question of toleration and its limits is very real. Moreover, they are convinced, although opponents would contend this was sheer delusion, that the question does not arise from the engrafting of a secular transplant upon a traditional trunk, but from an internal tension within *Yahadut* proper.

For there are genuine concerns on both sides of the issue; and, hence, not just bifurcated centrists, caught between conflicting loyalties, but an inner dialectic between opposing axiological poles. On the one hand, within a deeply committed community, powerfully animated by a sense of both identity and destiny, the urge to impart or even impose normative values is strong. The impulse is dual. At one plane, it is rooted in confraternal concern for the well-being of others. To the liberal ear, this motif sounds almost inquisitional – not only paternalistic but patronizing, a clear expression of what Steven Schwarzschild once called "the imperialism of the soul." And yet, at its purest, it springs not from the quest for power but from the conjunction of passionate conviction of the objective truth of one's own lights with deep-seated desire to enhance the eternal welfare of others. Can one who truly believes and truly cares remain serenely apathetic to the most critical interests of his fellow? And even if he can, may he? The *arevut* by which we are bound is not to some collective abstraction but vis-à-vis each and every individual Jew.

וכשלו איש באחיו איש בעון אחיו מלמד שכל ישראל ערבין זה בזה.

"They will stumble one upon another" – each as a result of the sin of the other; this teaches us that all Israel is responsible one for the other."

Moreover, fealty to that *arevut* is not merely a duty extraneous to one's own religious life. To the extent that one is oblivious to others' halakhic observance, his own *kiyyum ha-mizvah* is imperfect, even if he has, technically, performed it flawlessly. Commenting upon the gemara's statement [regarding the blessings and curses on Mt. Eival and Mt. Gerizim], "There was a blessing in general, there was a blessing in particular, likewise there was a curse in general, there was a curse in particular," Rashi explains:

כל המצות כולן טעונות ארבעה אלה ולמדתם אותם ושמרתם לעשותם וכתיב ולמדתם
אותם את בניכם וגו' הרי כאן ארבע מצות לכל מצוה (סוטה לז.)

All the commandments contain these four elements, "you shall teach them and you shall keep and observe them", and it states "you shall teach them to your children.".... We therefore have four commands for each command-ment. (Sotah 37a)

At a second plane, the concern is collective. Perceiving himself, existentially, as part of an organic "community of the committed," rooted in a covenantal past and animated by a millennial vision, a believing Jew yearns and strives for the realization of what is at once both personal and national destiny. He intuits that, to this end, a determined sense of common purpose, bonded by an overarching identity, is essential. Consequently, he views askance whatever he perceives as eroding that bond.

These are genuine concerns but they are counterbalanced by equally valid considerations. Quite apart from the subjective spiritual dangers which lurk in intolerance and its concomitant negative emotions, external constraint impeding the freely willed growth of human personality is an affront to *kevod ha-beriyot* and, as such, religiously objectionable. Personal freedom, engaged and challenged at every turn, is the linchpin of Halakhah; and it lies at the heart of our conception of human nature, as fact and as ideal. *Zelem E-lohim,* invested with both dignity and sanctity, is grounded upon individuality, and entails, optimally, the capacity for limning its own specific contours and developing its own direction. In this respect, even the moral aspect of freedom is tinged with religious content. The religious significance of freedom focuses, however, upon the fact that *avodat Hashem, per se,* is ideally, freely willed. *Yahadut,* of course, rejects radical autonomy and demands submissive subjugation; but that is itself to be a freely chosen forswearing of freedom which, in turn, issues in the higher freedom of the *ben horin she-oseik ba-Torah.* Hazal went so far as to find even the original *matan Torah* flawed because, under the impact of awesome revelation, refusal was not a live option.[14] How much less worthy, then, is religious conformity imposed by societal pressures.[15]

Finally, intolerance exacts a communal price as well. Mistrust and recrimination are a social cancer. They both infect interpersonal relations and poison the body politic. As mutual respect is the basis upon which a vibrant community thrives, so mutual suspicion is its bane; and, once impaired, trust is not easily restored. When Hazal instituted various *halakhot – mipnei haheshad*, they did so not solely in order to safeguard personal reputation by preemptive suspicion but in order to enhance a healthy social climate, as well.

Pitting conflicting values against each other, the question of toleration thus induces spiritual tension. This tension is of course not peculiar to *Yahadut*. It is characteristic of any culture which cherishes both a definitive axiological commitment and the creative human spirit, and hence strives to navigate between the Scylla and Charybdis of aimless meandering and atrophying repression; and immanently so. To the extent, however, that each pole is significantly emphasized, the dichotomy is sharpened. This is very much the case with Jewish tradition, and its view of the limits of toleration needs to be seen from this perspective.

In practice, this has allowed, as regards both state and society, for a measure of toleration, albeit surely less than civil libertarians would wish. From their perspective, *meha'ah*, particularly when focused upon judgment rather than values, is fundamentally acceptable, but *tokhahah* problematic. Remonstrance they could regard as simply taking a stand on the issue, but reprimand, as a mode of pressure upon the individual, would be unacceptable. With respect to it, they are inclined to assume a stance analogous to that adopted in Mill's *On Liberty* with regard to state interference in personal life: It may be sanctioned when the public interest or the well-being of others is in danger but not when only personal morals are at stake.

That surely has not been the traditional Jewish position, however. Historically, *tokhahah*, running the gamut from suasion to pressure, not to mention possible legal sanctions, has been encouraged. Burke's sense that in order for evil to triumph it is sufficient that enough good men stand by idly and do nothing has been pervasive. In numerous communities, a *maggid meshorim* and/or *moreh zedek* was specifically engaged to press for improved public rectitude; and, particularly within smaller and relatively homogeneous settings, he could be most effective. This is not fully palatable to the liberal ear, for which such a post has totalitarian associations, but that ought not obscure the fact. Moreover, private *tokhahah* has been generally encouraged – albeit, admittedly, to varying degrees in different contexts. To the extent that conduct and thought have thus become the object of critical scrutiny and response, toleration has indeed often been circumscribed.

This has been particularly exemplified with respect to the sensitive area of *emunot v'de'ot*. As has been often noted, the topic was relatively low-key in Hazal, apart from the outright schism of Sadduceanism, but subsequently attained considerable prominence; and controversies concerning either specific issues or broad orientations, even within the committed camp, have generated much heat. The *Moreh Nevukhim*, *hasidut*, and Rav Menasheh of Ilye are cases in point; and they could be multiplied manifold. The issues are not necessarily halakhic. *Mori ve-rabbi*, Rav Hutner, זצ"ל, is reported to have asserted that apikorsut was not so much an averah as a disease; and I might add, the delicate nuances of quasi-dogmatic affirmation *a fortiori*. That has hardly encouraged toleration, however; and, given the general history of dogmatics, this should not surprise us. During the modern era, moreover, the divisive concern with ideology has only accelerated. Questionable assertions which could have been blandly ignored when the religious bedrock of the community was solid become flashpoints when its basic commitment has been fractured and heterodoxy in thought and practice abounds. The resultant quest for purity may thus encourage a more restrictive climate.

Nevertheless, historically and contemporaneously, there are countervailing elements which serve to balance the picture somewhat, so that the drive for integrity is tempered by respect for personal aspiration. In one sense, it is reflected in the specifics of *hilkhot tokhahah* proper. Expanding upon the injunction, "And you shall not bear sin because of him," Hazal explain: "I might think that [the obligation to rebuke holds] even if his face changes color [in shame – *panav mishtanim*], we thus are taught, 'and you shall not bear sin because of him.'" It should be emphasized that the formulation defines the *mizvah*. If, in the course of instructive reproach, one unnecessarily embarrasses his fellow, it is not as if the performance of the *mizvah* has been twinned with a violation. Inasmuch as the proper technique has been ignored, one has not fulfilled a *mizvah* at all.

Hence, Hazal were keenly mindful of the difficulty of imparting *tokhahah* properly. Immediately after the admonition regarding *panav mishtanim*, the gemara quotes Rabbi Tarfon's assertion, "I would be surprised [to find] if in this generation there is someone who accepts rebuke. If one says to a person: 'Remove the small stick from between your eyes,' he responds back, 'Remove the beam from between your eyes';" and this is countered by Rabbi Eleazar ben Azaryah's complementary statement, "I would be surprised [to find] if there is anyone in this generation who knows how to offer rebuke" (Arakhin 16b). As the conjunction of these rhetorical speculations with the preceding citation clearly implies, at issue is not only the pragmatic efficacy of flawed *tokhahah* but its morality.

A second balancing factor derives from a more general injunction, the *mizvah* of *be'tzedek tishpot amitekha*. In one sense, this refers to judicial proceedings;[16] in another, to interpersonal evaluation: "Judge every man favorably" (*Torat Kohanim*, Kedoshim 19, 15). The latter, classified by the She'iltot[17] as an independent *mizvah*, relates, in part, to charitable judgment of events and their circumstances; and it in this sense that the gemara in Shabbat (127a–b) elaborates upon it. However, it is no less concerned with perceiving motivation; and, in our context, this is the critical factor. The impulse to toleration stimulates favorable evaluation, and that, in turn, induces toleration. Again, this is not quite what the thoroughgoing liberal desires. From his vantage point, the question is not the quality of judgment but whether one should be judging at all. And indeed, in many contexts, if shorn of relativism and determinism, a non-judgmental stance has much to commend it. In some, however, if standards are to be maintained, it is essential. To Madame de Stael's familiar observation, that we forgive whatever we really understand, her descendant, the Duke de Broglie, rejoined: "Beware of too much explaining, lest we end by too much excusing."[18]

A third factor is of broad scope but, with reference to our issue, of particular relevance to the modern era. Human nature being what it is, reproach was presumably never ordinarily heeded with glee. Within a liberal context, however, upon this natural resistance a philosophic rationale has been superimposed, and it is entirely conceivable that its prevalence, even within our traditional circles, has injected an additional element into the balance. I refer of course to what Hillel designated as the most cardinal of moral – indeed, of Torah – principles:

דעלך סני לחברך לא תעביד זו היא כל התורה כולה ואידך פירושא הוא זיל גמור (שבת
לא.)

What is hateful to you, do not to your fellow. This is the entire Torah; the rest
is commentary. Go and learn! (Shabbat 31a).

To the not inconsiderable extent to which the ethic of private conscience has been subjectively internalized, the objective import of any
infringement upon it has been significantly altered. Constriction now
impacts more severely and is less consonant with the hegemony many
a potential contemporary arbiter of others' morals cherishes for himself.
Hence, insofar as *tokhahah* now often conflicts with *ve-ahavta le-rei'akha
kamokha*, the delicate balance between the current pros and cons of
toleration is measurably affected; and this, again, not out of pragmatic
prudence but, within the modern constellation, as a moral and halakhic
consideration.

The point is most telling with reference to a constituency which fundamentally negates the values in the name of which it is being castigated or
rejected. As I wrote in an analogous connection thirty years ago,[19] coercive
pressure, when oriented to the education of the person rather than to the
protection of the community, can only be justified – when its object subscribes, radically, to the system but has deviated within it. A cheat evades
taxes out of greed, but he knows he's in the wrong; and, when caught, curses
the IRS but, deep down, recognizes its authority. The situation of a modern
secularist vis-a-vis tradition is quite different, and modes of toleration or
rejection obviously need to take this element into account.

This factor is most relevant to relations toward the uncommitted,
which is not the primary focus of this presentation. However, it also bears
upon intramural interaction, within the camp of devotees of *Yahadut*, upon
whom the broader context impinges. Hazal taught us that "Before a blind
man you shall not place a stumbling block" – which Hazal took to include
spiritual, as well as physical, pitfalls – enjoins a father from striking his
adult son (Mo'ed Katan 17a), inasmuch as he thereby incites him to strike
back; and the same is true of strangers and of other provocations. In a
predominantly secular society, the definition of *davar she-eino nishma* is

drastically altered. Rav Zvi Yehuda Kook, זצ״ל, was wont to note that it was pointless to express *tokhahah* in a language foreign to its "auditor." The implications for toleration are self-evident. As the rationale for obtrusive pressure pales, the weight of counterpoised elements – respect for personality, the bond of fraternity, integrity of the spirit, not to mention the pragmatic quest for reciprocity – correspondingly increases.

To this, the Maharal, at the dawn of Jewish modernity, adds another element – the benefit, personal and forensic, of honest ideological debate. He quotes, approvingly, to this effect, from *Sefer Shamayim V'olam*, and goes on to expatiate on the theme:

וראוי מי שירצה לדון בדין האמת שלא יהיה מכעיס לבעל מחלוקתו... ולכך אין ראוי
להרחיק שום דבר המתנגד אל דעתו לאהבת החקירה והידיעה ובפרט אותו שלא כוון
לקנתר רק להגיד האמונה אשר אתו אף אם אם הדברים הם נגד אמונתו ודתו אין לומר אליו
אל תדבר ותסתום דברי פיך שא״כ לא יהיה בירור הדת... ולכך הראשונים ואף אם נמצא
דבר מה בספרים שהוא כנגד דתם לא היו המתנגדים דוחים דבר זה כי השכל מחייב
שלא יהיה מניעה מזה כלל ולסגור פיו של אדם בדבר שהוא מגיע אל הדת רק פתשגן
כתב הדת נתונה את הכל... ולא מצינו מעולם שיהיו מונעים ומוחים בדבר זה כלל ולא
היה כאן פוצה פה ומצפצף בדבר זה ("באר הגולה", באר השביעי)

It is proper for one who wants to arrive at a true judgment not to anger his opponent … therefore, out of love for deep investigation and arrival at true knowledge, it is improper to ignore opinions which differ from his own, especially those of one who does not intend to contend but simply to state his beliefs. Even if those beliefs differ from one's own beliefs and religious convictions, one should not say, "Do not speak! Stop up your words!" – for then religion will enjoy no true clarification…. Therefore, it was the practice of the Rishonim that even if they found something in a book which contradicted their religious convictions, they did not simply ignore it; for common sense requires that there be no limitation [of this sort of expression] and no closing of the mouth of one who is attempting to arrive at religious truth. A copy of the religious manifesto is distributed to all…. We never find them limiting this or preventing it at all; there was not a chirp of opposition in this matter.[20]

As a descriptive summary of the course of past debate, or even as an accurate account of prevalent seventeenth-century practice, the passage is open to question. As an affirmation of a direction the Maharal sought to encourage, it stands in its own right.

I am not clear as to just how far the Maharal would have gone. Would he have espoused giving Wellhausen a serious hearing while learning Tanakh? Should unadulterated and unmodified Darwinism be respectfully included in discussion of religious anthropology? The specific instance the Maharal adduces is the deference accorded the concept of the eternity of the world in medieval philosophic discourse. I am skeptical, however, as to whether that doctrine was indeed the rough equivalent, for Rishonim, of radical Biblical criticism or the animal descent of man today; and, in this respect, the Rambam's[21] conditional readiness to accept the Aristotelian position on this issue, were he so convinced philosophically, is instructive.

However the Maharal's position be understood, I must freely confess that – if pressed, with an eye to practical implementation, for clear definition of the parameters of toleration – I should find myself hard put to formulate an adequate response. Nevertheless, some remarks about general guidelines may, in conclusion, be suggested.

At the coercive juridic plane, determination of what is enabled and what is restrained – whether as punishment, as deterrent, or out of concern for public spiritual well-being – should presumably be governed by formal halakhic principles. Specifically, we should assume a functional relation between the gravity of a course of action and its being tolerated. The darker the crime, the more heinous the sin, the starker the danger, as measured by halakhic categories – *d'oraitha* as opposed to *d'rabbanan,* and a subdivided spectrum with respect to each – the greater the likelihood that it will be subject, normatively, to restraint, *ante facto,* and recrimination, *post facto.* Likewise, as regards *tokhahah,* conceived as a duty, the halakhic status of its projected object may be viewed as governing the content and scope of the *mizvah.* Thus, the principle of "Leave Israel be; better that they sin unknowingly than knowingly" (Beizah 30a) is confined by many rishonim[22] to *d'rabbanan* violations or, at most, to *d'oraitha* injunctions not explicit in the Torah's text, and hence, on this view, of presumably lesser stature.[23] Inasmuch as both juridic and forensic restraint constitute formal halakhic initiatives, determination of toleration with respect to them can clearly be rule-oriented. Implementation obviously hinges upon fleshing out details of the relevant phenomena; but, at least, the operative principles are reasonably well-defined.

The situation is radically different, however, with respect to societal and/or personal toleration. At this plane, the halakhic standing of what or who is problematic is often murky, if not nil; nor, in its absence, do other categories suggest themselves as norms to provide directives for toleration. In this area, the only viable approach is predominantly contextual. Here, the character and scope of toleration are to be judged, prospectively, by their fruits – and this, with reference to the delicate balance of often con-flicting values, both theoretical and practical. The standard of what, and to what extent, is to be tolerated, is indeterminate, on the one hand, and the gauge by which any particular action or person might be evaluated is vaguely inchoate, on the other. One is then impelled to intuited contextual judgment, not by situationist ideology but out of sheer necessity.

The point may be readily exemplified with reference to a well-known gemara in Sanhedrin:

כך היו נקיי הדעת שבירושלים עושין לא היו חותמין על השטר אלא אם כן יודעין מי חותם עמהן ולא היו יושבין בדין אלא אם כן יודעין מי יושב עמהן ולא היו נכנסין בסעודה אלא אם כן יודעין מי מיסב עמהן

So did the *nekiyei hadaʿat* [the refined] of Jerusalem conduct themselves: They would not sign a document unless they knew who was signing along with them; they would not sit as judges unless they knew who sat with them; they would not sit to table unless they knew who dined with them (23a).

An earlier Gerer Rebbi – I believe the "Bet Yisrael" – is reported to have commented that these spiritual esthetes did not refuse to dine with unknown and, hence, possibly unsavory, colleagues; they only insisted on knowing with whom they were to associate. I presume, however, that the remark was only a half-earnest *bon mot*. What is certain, in any event, is that the practice described and the attitude it embodies prioritize caution over toleration. On the basis of the text, however, can anyone surmise just how far this sanitized concern was pressed? By which standard would the *nekiyei hadaʿat* have determined who was a worthy companion? Would it have mattered if the prospect knew he or she were under scrutiny, so that there might be possible umbrage? How much weight did they assign, given their presumed prominence, to the public ramifications of their discriminating nicety?[24]

These dilemmas are painfully familiar. In the public arena, American Jewry has been torn asunder for over a generation by issues of who sits with whom, of how to strike a balance between confraternity and concern over implicit legitimization of deviation; and, at the private plane, decisions over with whom to share a platform or a volume are a common occurrence. Probably few would emulate M.K. Benny Begin's practice of emblazoning this gemara from Sanhedrin on our desktop; but almost all are challenged by it to define the limits of our toleration.

The challenge is not only sociological but spiritual; and yet – and this is the point to be stressed – we have little recourse to formal categories, Halakhic or other, in coping with it. We are all familiar with the Rambam's detailed list of twenty-four grounds for official excommunication.[25] But we do not have – and, in all likelihood, cannot have – a *Shulhan Arukh* instructing us about social ostracism. We are impelled by a blend of sensitivity and judgment; and, in the spirit of *gadol shimushah yoter mi'limudah*, Hazal's aphoristic valuing of appreticeship as superior to abstract study, we are guided by precedent. Unquestionably, values are critical to molding responses. At bottom, however, the approach is contextual, flexible, and very much concerned with the bottom line.

It is not just that the object of prospective toleration, problematic conduct or person, obviously varies immeasurably. Other factors, relatively extraneous to an action or its agent, may figure prominently, as well. For better or for worse, a school's decision concerning the possible discharge of a wayward student is governed by educational ramifications for the entire institution no less than by the best interests and just deserts of the aberrant. Analogously, to take an example which has, sadly, confronted and divided several communities in recent years, how does one respond to a respected member of a shul who has treated his or her spouse shabbily? Surely, opting for compassionate understanding, benign neglect, stony distancing, or sharp censure, should be determined not only by interpersonal considerations but, equally, by ideological and axiological concerns over implicit and explicit public messages. Enabling a philanderer or a cheat to maintain his congregational standing, when it is clear that he would have fallen from grace had he abandoned kashrut, endorses a chilling ideological statement. And these messages – regarding power and responsibility, status and sensitivity, demarcation of the private and the public sectors, or, if you will, the relation between *bein adam l'havero* and *bein adam lamakom* – and the need to emit them, may vary significantly in different locales.

Contextual attention to results dictates rejection of the simplistic correlation – rightly prevalent at the juridic plane – that the grosser the violation, the sharper should be the response. History has amply demonstrated, in the spirit of "Something in its category destroys it; something outside its category does not destroy it" (Zevahim 3a), that the danger from proximate rivals, real or perceived, may exceed that from distant adversaries. The Torah world often feels more threatened, for instance, by the band ranging from right-wing Conservatism to left-wing Orthodoxy than by Reform Judaism, and toleration, or its absence, may be affected accordingly.

Indeed, in the sensitive area of *emunot v'de'ot,* the issues are frequently not halakhic at all. A case in point is the perception of personages regarded as links in the chain of tradition. With reference to Scripture, there is a quasi-halakhic component, as reflected in the statements of Rabbi Yonatan that whoever states, in accordance with literal textual readings, with respect to a number of biblical figures, that they had sinned *eino ella to'eh,* "is but in error."[26] Even here, we note that error rather than breach is cited; and, if one moves to later periods, the normative element is virtually vitiated. In the background, a long shadow is cast by the Rambam's assertion, frequently cited by the Rav, ל"צז, that not only whoever denies the validity of *Torah she'b'al peh* but also whoever is *makh'hish maggidehah* "whoever contravenes its transmitters"[27] is classified as an *apikoros.* Nevertheless, if one were to impugn the integrity of the Ramban, it would be difficult to pinpoint a technical Halakhic violation. Yet, the statement would, rightly, arouse passionate indignation; and the question of toleration would arise accordingly.

The absence of directives does not preclude the suggestion of guide-lines, and I should like, in closing, to offer several. The first, implicit in earlier remarks and related to the theme of flexibility, is the wisdom of maintaining, within the social and interpersonal realm proper, a broad and subtle range of responses. Toleration may involve active respect to the point of encouragement – in which case, perhaps, it oughtn't be called that at all; alternatively, it may, ideologically or pragmatically motivated, entail nothing more than benign neglect or passive aversion. And, of course, its contrary can run the reverse gamut, from mild rebuke to active resistance – falling short, to be sure, of legal prosecution, but potentially vehement, nonetheless. The point to be stressed is that only a broad range of options can maintain the critical proportion between the stimulus of provocation and sensible and sensitive reaction. Recent declines in toleration, among "politically correct" circles in America – so amply demonstrative of Milton's lament, "New presbyter is but old priest writ large" – and, under the impact of post-assassination security consciousness, in Israel, are perturbing not only because of the erosion of "traditions of civility" *per se*, but because of the heavy-handedness which has accompanied them.

Secondly, in cases of doubt as to where to draw the line, we ought generally counsel moderation. Presumably, where such doubt exists, no major clear and present danger to faith or mores is on the horizon. Con-sequently, if one is uncertain as to optimal balance, it is surely better to tilt toward tolerating too much than too little. With respect to the *mizvah* of *tokhahah,* Tosafot is of the opinion that if it is uncertain whether a given observation will be favorably received, it ought to be expressed, as it is only "in a matter where we are certain to be ignored that we consider it better that they transgress unknowingly."[28] With respect to sharper measures, however, doubt should restrain. The onus of resolution should clearly be upon those who wish to impose censure or restriction rather than upon those potentially subject to them. Above all, in weighing judgment – as, in confronting the issue of toleration, generally – let us be certain that we have considered the matter from the vantage point of the prospective pariah, and not only from that of his ostracizers. Empathy may not always be decisive, but it should, at the very least, be part of the process.

This is particularly true of the ideological realm. In the practical sphere, a committed individual or community may feel justified in exerting pressure upon a deviant adversary on the ground that the respective stakes are asymmetrical – on one side, hallowed principle, and on the other, mere convenience.[29] This facile dichotomy is not so readily applicable, however, with respect to *emunot v'deot,* where both sides may very well be animated by considerations of principle. The appeal to stringency, even where no narrow Halakhic issue is involved – "For matters of the permitted and the forbidden," as the Rambam emphasized,[30] "exclude matters of the distasteful, the desirable, and the beloved," so that the attainment of a higher standard is laudable as an aspect of what A.D. Lindsay called "the morality of aspiration" even when it is not enjoined as a matter of duty – does not ring equally true when addressed to one who has pitched his tent at a given point of the ideological spectrum out of passionately nuanced conviction. Hence, in this area, the need for caution and sensitivity is all the greater.

Moreover, where convictions are at stake, rejection or repression cause particular anguish. As the Rambam explained that "ruminations about sin are worse than sin,"[31] because sin grounded in thought is graver than that rooted in bestiality, as through the former, one "commits an act of disobedience through the nobler of his two parts,"[32] so the affront to personal dignity is more painfully experienced when thought is under siege. Admittedly, these considerations are somewhat muted by recognition that, from a public and educational standpoint, too, the dangers are graver. And yet, on balance, the conviction that, in doubt, too much toleration is better than too little, and that this guideline is particularly relevant to the world of ideas, is firm. And, while, one can never be wholly certain, I trust that it derives from fealty to the call of *be'tzedek tishpot amitekha* and *ve-ahavta le-rei'akha kamokha* rather from exposure to the tradition of Locke and Mill.

Thirdly, with respect to both the juridic and the social spheres, but especially as regards the latter, it behooves us to distinguish between two elements, perhaps best denominated, in modern usage, as toleration and tolerance, respectively. Through the seventeenth century, the terms were generally used interchangeably, and some current dictionaries still invoke one to define the other; but in many contemporary contexts, they are fundamentally different.[33] Tolerance denotes a mindset and an attitude, toleration a course of action; the former constitutes a quality of soul and spirit, the latter, a policy or a *modus operandi*. In practice, the two need not coincide. One may be open and understanding, personally and ideologically, with regard to that which, out of public and educational concern, he opposes vigorously. Conversely, one may be thoroughly repelled by what, for pragmatic or moral reasons, he refuses to restrain. If pressed to consider, for instance, the lives and thought of Rav Kook and the Rav, respectively, I believe, it would be fair to conclude that, while perhaps neither was thoroughly consistent, Rav Kook was, philosophically, far more tolerant but, as a public figure, tolerated less; the reverse was true of the Rav. In seeking to suggest parameters, we need to refer to both elements, but, obviously, the respective limits may vary.

These considerations will probably carry little weight with the thoroughgoing Western libertarian, for whom any constraint in the realm of the spirit, whether governmental repression or societal pressure is pure anathema. I hope, however, that they are consonant with overall Jewish tradition. That tradition has dealt with spiritual dangers as modern societies deal with physical threats; and hence, having rejected moral autonomy as a radical right, it has contended with toleration as an equipoise between liberty and security. It has recognized that toleration is, to a large extent, a function of openness; and openness, in turn, hinges upon several interrelated factors: the degree of conviction, the readiness to risk, the assessment of prospective danger. In the spirit of "Perhaps they shall cause you to sin to me," where conviction and concern run high, when the integrity of a community is perceived as endangered, toleration is limited. It is agreeable and human, psychologically and morally, to tolerate; but when *malkhut shamayim* is affected, necessity – designated by Milton as "the tyrant's plea," but surely not his alone – often dictates otherwise. We owe it to ourselves and especially to others, however, to assure that, where *u'viarta ha'ra mi'kirbekha* or *al tit'haber la'rasha* are invoked, it is indeed that concern – and not animus, envy, the penchant for domination, or the lust for power – which motivates restriction. In no area is there greater need to internalize and realize the dictum of the mishnah, "All your actions should be for the sake of heaven."

Notes

1. *Life of Samuel Johnson*, August 30, 1780.
2. From his essay, "Romanticism and Classicism" from *Speculations: Essays on Humanism and the Philosophy of Art* in W.J. Bate, ed., *Criticism: The Major Texts* (New York, 1952), p. 565.
3. See, however, the discussion of the relation between tolerance and pluralism, in Moshe Sokol's essay, "Theoretical Grounds for Tolerance in the Jewish Tradition," in a forthcoming volume of the Orthodox Forum, secs. 4 ff, and the literature cited there. Our different views concerning the possible link of toleration and pluralism significantly affected, I believe, the parameters of our respective presentations. Given my premise, the concept of *eilu v'eilu*, for instance, is logically tangential to our topic – although it may have psychological weight – inasmuch as controverting protagonists recognize, within the limits of legitimate *mahloket*, their adversary's right to hold opposing views. Admittedly, however, we here touch upon the delicate balance between holding that a given view is erroneous, while yet acknowledging that it is, substantively, a possible reading (in alternate terminology, a *hefza*) of Torah.
4. In Susan Mendus, ed., *Justifying Toleration: Conceptual and Historical Perspectives* (Cambridge, 1988), p. 3.
5. I received a glaring and rather ironic reminder of this phenomenon – at least, with reference to Israel – some months ago. After the uproar over the withdrawal of a dance troupe from a jubilee celebration because of alleged interference by religious groups with the planned repertoire, a session of the Knesset's committee on *hok-u-mishpat*, in which I was invited to participate, was held to discuss the issue and the parameters of artistic freedom. En route, I heard over the radio that a defendant was to face trial, and possible imprisonment, over having insulted a judge, thus defaming the legal system. At the session – at which every single participant, for whichever reason and of whatever religious orientation, argued against governmental censorship – I noted drily that, evidently, blaspheming against *malkhuta dishmaya* was to be countenanced but reviling *malkhuta d'ar'a* was criminal.
6. See MT Melakhim 1 1:4.
7. See *Sefer Hamizvot, Assei*, 176. Unquestionably, in certain areas – see, e.g., Yevamot 88b and Rambam, *Yom Tov* 6:21 – *bet din*'s role as the steward of a halakhic polity and custodian of some of its components, would preclude the flexibility here suggested. It could, however, exist in many others.
8. Some have assumed that the Rambam, *Mamrim* 3:7, held otherwise; but, it should be noted that the Rambam clearly restricts his formulation to special circumstance, *k'fi mah she-yireh lahem she-ha-davr tzarikh le-kakh*.

However, the right of dissent might be circumscribed in another vein. The context of *zaken mamreh* – only culpable if he acts upon his minority view or, rebelliously, issues a *pesak* countermanding the majority decision – is that of *mahloket* within the parameters of *eilu v'eilu*. The situation could presumably be different if the dissent challenged the consensus of tradition, beyond the pale of legitimate controversy.

9. See Jacob J. Schachter, ed., *Jewish Tradition and the Non-Traditional Jew* (Northvale, NJ: Jason Aronson, 1992).

10. Berakhot 31b, s.v. *davar*.

11. See the comment on *De'ot* 6, p. 58.

12. See the view of the Ramakh, cited in *Shittah Mekubezet, Baba Mezia* 1a.

13. See Nimukei Yosef, Yevamot 65b (21b, in the Rif), who suggests that the contradiction can be resolved by predicating that reproach should be attempted, at least, once – and this is the import of the gemara in Shabbat – but, unlike usual *tokhahah*, need not be repeated; and this, for two independent reasons: *Mishum d'ulay yishm'un oh mishum she-lo yihiyeh lahem pithon peh*. The distinction I have suggested is closer to the second but not identical with it.

14. See Shabbat 88a.

15. In his previously cited essay, Moshe Sokol suggests that the determinism of R. Zadok can serve as a basis for tolerance inasmuch as it relates all causality to God, and hence, implicitly, ascribes value to everything, so that nothing ought to be banished. Given the premises – that, to me, are, to say the least, highly problematic in character – the conclusion is tenable. There is no question, however, but that, on balance, it is the emphasis upon free will which sustains tolerance.

    See also Joseph Raz, "Autonomy, Toleration, and the Harm Principle," in *Justifying Toleration*, pp. 155–165, who stresses the place of autonomy as the basis of toleration. From a Jewish perspective, we ought to speak of freedom rather than of autonomy.

16. See Sanhedrin 3a and Rambam, Sanhedrin 2:10.

17. See *Sh'iltot d'Rabbi Ahai Gaon*, 40.

18. Cited by Lord Acton in his "Inaugural Lecture on the Study of History," in *Essays on Freedom and Power*, ed. G. Himmelfarb (New York, 1955), p. 51.

19. See my "Religion and State: The Case for Interaction," in this volume, chapter 1.

20. *Be'er Hagolah*, sec. 7. The Maharal may be understood as holding that opposing views should not be stifled either because, intrinsically, they may contain a kernel of truth, or because, instrumentally (as Mill and Newman were to contend later), their challenge may stimulate *berur hadat*, in the quest for the truth.

21. See *Moreh*, 2:25.

22. See Rosh, Bezah 4:2; Ran, Bezah 30a (16b in the Rif); *Shulhan Arukh* Orah Haym, 608:2, and *Bei'ur Halakkah*, ad loc.

23. See however, *Havot Yair*, 164, who includes the thirty-nine *melakhot* among those which are not explicit. Evidently, on his view, the relevant criterion is not the objective gravity of the violation but the degree to which its perpetrator should presumably be aware of its nature.

24. Sanhedrin 23a. It is noteworthy that this precaution was taken with respect to both halakhic

and neutral contexts. Narrowly speaking, *nekiyut hada'at* does not relate to toleration at all, as the issue is not simply forbearance but conjunctive cooperation. A genteel refusal to sit around a table with certain persons, in no way prevents them from setting their own tables. The distinction is both theoretically and practically important. It is, however, primarily relevant to the official and political sphere, and less so with respect to the societal. As regards the latter, some antithesis between toleration and boycott does manifestly exist.

25. See Talmud Torah 6:14, and the comments of *Avodat Ha-Melekh* thereon. To the best of my knowledge, the list has no source in Hazal. The gemara in Berakhot states, "Rabbi Joshua ben Levi said: In twenty-four instances does *bet din* excommunicate to protect the honor of a rabbi, and all of these are listed in the Mishnah" (19a), but only several are identified. Likewise, the Yerushalmi states, "For twenty-four things is excommunication imposed," but offers little detail.

26. See Shabbat 56a. For an interesting discussion of the substantive and educational thrust of Rabbi Yonatan's *memrot*, see the exchange between Yehuda Brandes and Yaakov Medan in *Megadim*, 26 (5756), pp. 107–134, and responses thereto in 28 (5758), 87–122.

27. See Teshuvah 3:8.

28. Baba Batra 60b, s.v. *mutav*.

29. It should be stressed, however, that, from a libertarian perspective, the pressure itself, irrespective of the original issue, constitutes a matter of principle.

30. *Perush Hamishnayot*, Sanhedrin 7:4.

31. Yoma 29a. The Rambam's understanding of the text, let alone his explanation, is quite novel. Conventionally, it is taken to mean that evil thoughts are more difficult to surmount, with no hint that they are inherently worse than action. Obviously, however, the Rambam's position has analogues in many traditions.

32. *Moreh* 3:8; in Pines' translation, p. 435.

33. The OED's definitions and citations clearly include some overlap, but also reflect differentiation. The primary modern sense for "tolerance" reads: "The action or practice of tolerating; toleration; the disposition to be patient with or indulgent to the opinions or practices of others; freedom from bigotry or undue severity in judging the conduct of others; forbearance; catholicity of spirit." The corresponding entry for "toleration" only reads: "The action or practice of tolerating or allowing what is not actually approved; forbearance; sufferance."

Chapter 5

The Duties of the Heart and Response to Suffering

Give or take a few hours, in Hazal's chronology,[1] the history of suffering is coeval with man himself. From the wrenching anguish primordially attendant upon the bitterest of bites to the immediately present distress of millions, human existence has been fraught with pain, sorrow, frustration – with no end until the millennium in sight.

That history has a dual aspect. It is, primarily, of course, an existential reality, but secondarily, it is a philosophic issue. As such, it has germinated differently in different traditions. In the world of general thought, it has been, with moral and psychological elements interlaced, a major crux of ethics. Obviously, however, in the religious orbit it has assumed additional dimensions. For many, foremost among these has been the attempt to understand and explain suffering as a metaphysical phenomenon; and, particularly, its reconciliation with faith in omniscient, omnipotent, and beneficent God. This concern has spawned the genre of theodicy, familiarly associated in Western literature with a number of major works: Aeschylus's *Prometheus Bound*, Boethius's *De Consolatione Philosophiae*, Milton's *Paradise Lost*, Leibniz's *Essais de Théodicée*, Pope's *Essay on Man*,

---

This paper was delivered at the Orthodox Forum 1995 and published in *Jewish Perspectives on the Experience of Suffering*, ed. Shalom Carmy (Northvale, NJ: Jason Aronson, 1999).

and Tennyson's *In Memoriam,* to cite just a few; but it obviously pervades so much also.

Not surprisingly, the same concern has found expression within *yahadut.* In the Bible, *kitvei ha-kodesh,* the *locus classicus* is, of course, the Book of Job. But the Ramban also regarded the question as the central topic of Kohelet;[2] and in his homiletic discourse upon that *sefer,* he listed other relevant scriptural texts. Hazal, for their part, ascribed concern with the issue to Mosheh Rabbenu, asserting that it was the thrust of the plea petitioned after the episode of the golden calf:

אמר לפניו רבונו של עולם מפני מה יש צדיק וטוב לו ויש צדיק ורע לו יש רשע וטוב לו ויש רשע ורע לו;

> "Show me now Thy ways" (Shemot 33:13). Mosheh said before Him: Lord of the Universe, why is it that some righteous men prosper and others are in adversity, some wicked men prosper and others are in adversity?[3]

And Hazal themselves confronted the question in typically scattered anecdotes and epigrams.

Nevertheless, I presume that we are inclined to acknowledge the justice of the Rav's generalization that Judaism has not confronted suffering primarily as a speculative matter. Rather, it has related to it as an existential and experiential reality, to be dealt with pragmatically and normatively. Response, not explanation, is focal. Its message, in sum, is: "Don't waste your passional experiences; utilize them; exploit them; let every passional experience become a point of departure for a higher and nobler life."[4]

It is against this background that I wish to consider the question put to me: how can and should the classic *hovot ha-levavot,* or duties of the heart (repentance, prayer, fasting, etc.), affect our response to suffering, evil, and disaster? This is, in a sense, not a single question but an entire phalanx: the product, crudely stated, of the multiple of the *hovot* by the varieties of calamity, doubled to encompass both the "can" and the "should." And yet there is a specific issue to be discussed, with respect to the full gamut. Read literally, the formulation evidently rests upon the implicit assumption that *hovot ha-levavot* – presumably, qua *hovot* – can and should have an impact upon our response to calamity. What remains to be analyzed is the modality.

I must confess, however, that I find this proposition far from self-evident. That a Jewish response to suffering can and ought to include elements like prayer and fasting goes without saying. But to what extent, if any, is their inclusion grounded upon their normative aspect? Most Rishonim held that as an obligation, the *mizvah* of *tefillah* (prayer) only has *d'rabbanan* status, probably even in times of distress.[5] *Ta'anit*, likewise, is designated as such by the Rambam: "From rabbinic tradition one must fast for every calamity that befalls the community till heaven brings compassion."[6] By contrast, *teshuvah* (repentance) is patently mandated *mi'd'oraita*. Should our responses to the question confronting us with regard to these specific *mizvot* be significantly different? Further, none of these *mizvot* is mandatory for a non-Jew. Would we consequently formulate for a Muslim or a Christian inquirer an answer very much at variance with what we develop for ourselves?

I am fully mindful of the weight Hazal assigned to the normative character of a spiritual datum. We are all familiar with the gemara that initially presents the popular view that freely willed voluntary action is more meritorious than its required counterpart, but then concludes by citing Rav Hanina's contrary position that "greater is the reward of those who, being enjoined, do [good deeds] than of those who, without being enjoined [but merely of their own free will], do [good deeds]."[7] This view has unquestionably been accepted as definitive, and is cited by Rishonim and *poskim* in various contexts and multiple applications, ranging from the central *mizvah* of *talmud Torah*[8] to the minutest *d'rabbanan*.

Nevertheless, my reservations about the significance of the normative aspect in our context remain. For one thing, to the best of my knowledge, Hazal nowhere prescribe the degree of the superiority ascribed to the *metzuvveh*, so it is difficult to determine how much weight should be assigned to this factor. Secondly, some Rishonim apparently assumed that a mandated act was not intrinsically more meritorious, but was only deemed greater because it was likely to be accompanied by keener anxiety, growing out of concern as to whether one has discharged one's duty properly, which in turn might ensure that the fulfillment meets a higher standard. As Tosafot puts it: "It seems that this is the reason: one who is commanded and performs good deeds is preferred because he is more concerned [about his performance] and more cautious lest he violate the commandment, than the one who is not enjoined, who has the freedom to opt out of the performance at will."[9]

The Ritva, for his part, focuses upon the merit deriving from the need of the commanded to overcome greater resistance: "Our teachers explained the reason for this: Satan [i.e., evil inclinations] tempts him when he is commanded, but not when he is not, and according to the effort is the reward."[10] Beyond these largely subjective considerations, I believe that the obligatory element with respect to our question, even in light of the interpretation ascribed to the Ramban – "The commandments are not for the benefit of God, who commanded them, but for our merit, and one who is commanded fulfills the decree of the King; thus his reward is much greater than that of the one who did not fulfill the decree of the King"[11] – is of little moment. The impact of *tefillah* or *teshuvah* upon our response to suffering derives, overwhelmingly, from their sheer existence as facets of our relation to the *Ribbono shel Olam,* from the bare fact that their respective gates have not been barred, from the access, and all that flows therefrom, to Him, that they represent. The critical element is the interrelation, at some stage and in some form, between human suffering and the presence of God. In this respect, the phenomenon of the capacity of the inner self to engage its Maker is crucial, but its duty to do so, at the level of formal *mizvot,* is not.

Turning, then, to our topic in its expanded version, with respect to *havayot* (experiences) rather than *hovot ha-levavot,* I would like to open the analysis by deviating from the formulation in yet another respect. We should, I believe, address ourselves not just to the response to suffering, but, more extensively, to the relation to it. In discriminating between various aspects, we need to discern not only different modes but distinctive phases. Response comes, logically – and, by and large, psychologically and tempo-rally as well – *post facto.* It constitutes, virtually by definition, an aftermath. The impact of inner religious sensibility upon the experience of suffering, however, also precedes and coincides with that suffereing. It might significantly condition not only *how* the sufferer feels but *what* he feels. That sensibility is not merely an instrument of subsequent understanding and emotional response but a prism through which calamity is initially perceived and possibly refracted. Indeed, beyond perception, it is not just an observer of suffering but the epicenter of its victimized object.

Hence, contrary to the impression conveyed by the itemized list of my assigned topic, the impact of *hovot ha-levavot* upon our relation to suffering is not confined to those that fundamentally are conceived as addressing themselves to it. Rather, it includes more comprehensive elements that are critical to the total development of a spiritual personality and its relation to its Creator. We have been set down in the "vale of soul-making," in Keats's phrase, confronted with the challenge of molding ourselves – and this without reference to its possibly also being a vale of tears. Clearly, however, the extent to which we have discharged our task conscientiously and creatively will significantly affect how suffering will be received, if and when it comes. Enthralled by *ahavat Hashem* (love of God), awed by *yirat Hashem* (fear of God), charged by faith (*emunah*), and suffused with trust (*bittahon*), an individual, steeled and illuminated, faces calamity quite differently from a vacuous colleague – and this, again, anterior to response at the plane of *ab initio* experience.

The point can be readily exemplified by reference to the apex of *hovot ha-levavot,* at least in Rabbenu Bahye's view. "Whatever has been earlier stated in this work about the duties of the heart, about virtues and spiritual nobility," he writes at the opening of his concluding chapter on *ahavat Hashem,* "are rungs and stages leading to this supreme object."[12] How, then, we ask ourselves, does this loftiest of *hovot* affect our response to suffering? On one plane, of course, it affects it directly. One facet of this *mizvah* refers, quite specifically, to disaster – indeed, to ultimate disaster. "'With all your soul' (*be-khol nafshekha,* Devarim 6:5)," we learn from the mishnah in Berakhot, "even though He takes your soul [life]. 'With all that is yours [*me'odkha*],' that is, whatever measure He metes out to you."[13]

In the ensuing gemara, Rabbi Akiva is cited as the source of this *derashah* and also as its exemplar:

בשעה שהוציאו את רבי עקיבא להריגה זמן קריאת שמע היה והיו סורקים את בשרו
במסרקות של ברזל והיה מקבל עליו עול מלכות שמים אמרו לו תלמידיו רבינו עד כאן
אמר להם כל ימי הייתי מצטער על פסוק זה בכל נפשך אפילו נוטל את נפשך אמרתי
מתי יבא לידי ואקיימנו ועכשיו שבא לידי לא אקיימנו –

When R. Akiva was taken out for execution, it was the hour for the recitation
of the Shema, and they combed his flesh with iron combs while he accepted
upon himself the yoke of the kingdom of heaven. His disciples said to him:
Our teacher, even to this point? He said to them: All my days I have been
troubled by this verse, "with all your soul," [which I interpret as] even if He
takes your soul. I said: When shall I have the opportunity of fulfilling this?
Now that I have the opportunity, shall I not fulfil it?"[14]

The self-evident question, "Such is Torah, and such is its reward!?" is
ascribed in the *baraita* to spectator ministering angels (*mal'akhei ha-sharet*)
rather than to the protagonist. Correspondingly, the *Sifre*, after citing the
substance of the mishnah, expands upon the theme:

וכן דוד הוא אומר כוס ישועות אשא ובשם ה׳ אקרא וכן איוב הוא אומר ה׳ נתן וה׳ לקח
יהי שם ה׳ מברך.

So said David: "I will lift up the cup of salvation, and call upon the name
of the Lord." So too said Job: "The Lord gave, and the Lord has taken away;
blessed be the name of the Lord."[15]

But is this direct reference the only aspect of *ahavah* that bears upon
response to suffering? Halakhically, the commandment of *ve-ahavta* is
multifaceted. The Netziv, in a celebrated *teshuvah* concerning "rightists"
and "leftists" in *Yahadut,* speaks of two components:

ראשית דבר, יש לדעת דבמ"ע ואהבת את ה׳ א־לקיך וגו׳ שאנו קוראים בכל יום נכלל
שני משמעות ושניהם מבוארים בפסקי הרמב"ם ז"ל, פי׳ אחד שימסור גופו ונפשו
וכל רצונו לרצון ה׳ ... פי׳ השני שיהא דבק במחשבתו ותשוקה להשיג רוה"ק בזמן
שהיה אפשר או עכ"פ הערה גבוהה למעלה למשכיל ובלשון לועז מכונה אהבה זו [די
ליבע].

To begin with, one should be aware that the positive commandment to love
God, which we read each day, includes two meanings, and both of them are
clarified in the Rambam's rulings. The first interpretation is that a person
should commit his body, soul, and all his will to the Will of God…. The

second interpretation is that one should cleave in his thought and desire to attain the Holy Spirit at the time when this is possible, or, in any event, the higher inspiration which is the state of the enlightened (in the vernacular called *die Liebe*)."[16]

However, in addition to the imperative to martyrdom and *amor Dei intellectualis* that he discerned, one could readily append at least four other elements: the constant and consuming passion, at once self-sacrificing and possessive, ascribed by the Rambam to the lovesick (*holat ahavah*) of Shir Ha-Shirim;[17] the impetus to *kiddush Hashem*, that the Name of Heaven be sanctified because of you enjoined by the gemara in Yoma;[18] contiguously, the charge of *kiruv* prescribed by the *Sifre*: "Make Him beloved to humanity, as did our father Avraham";[19] finally – and on the Ramban's view, perhaps one should say, primarily – the mandate to ground the totality of *avodat Hashem* (the service of God) in love:

וענין האהבה בארו אותו רבותינו והמפורש שבדבריהם מה שאמרו בספרי שמא תאמר הריני לומד תורה בשביל שאקרא חכם בשביל שאשב בישיבה בשביל שאאריך ימים בשביל שאזכה לעולם הבא ת״ל לאהבה וגו'.

The purport of love [of God] has been explained by our rabbis, most explicitly in the *Sifre*: "Perhaps you will say, I will study Torah in order that I be called wise, in order that I lead an academy, in order that I live long, or in order that I merit the world-to-come." Therefore Scripture says: "to love the Lord your God, etc."[20]

Does anyone imagine that this complex will barely influence response to suffering? Is it conceivable that the thirsting soul, aroused by passion or contemplation, will react to catastrophe no differently from the flaccid and the placid? Will a loving spirit's beatific joy leave no imprint in anticipation of crisis? Can one's yearning for eternity effect no change in one's perspective upon the temporal? Shall the egoist and the altruist, religiously speaking, share the same response to divinely inflicted calamity? Has consistent commitment to loving submissiveness no lasting and pervasive effect? If one has dedicated himself to inculcating *ahavat Hashem* in others – in the *Sifre*'s phrase, "like Avraham your father" – will not the emulation of that paragon of love extend to how one experiences tribulation?

The answer is self-evident. Moreover, a similar set of rhetorical questions could be composed with respect to other *hovot ha-levavot*. Contemplation of the created phenomenal world, the Rambam tells us, induces not only love but reverential fear:

וכשמחשב בדברים האלו עצמן מיד הוא נרתע לאחוריו ויפחד ויודע שהוא בריה קטנה שפלה אפלה עומדת בדעת קלה מעוטה לפני תמים דעות כמו שאמר דוד כי אראה שמיך מעשה אצבעותיך.

And when he ponders these very matters, he will recoil with fear, and realize that he is a small creature, lowly and obscure, endowed with slight and slender intelligence, standing in the presence of Him who is perfect in knowledge. And so David said: "When I consider Thy heavens, the work of Thy fingers" (Tehillim 8:4).[21]

Obviously, a sensibility imbued with consciousness of its relative vacuity will confront disaster, particularly insofar as it is regarded as divinely ordained, quite differently from one serenely confident of its own worth. The difference between Prometheus and Job, even in his more rebellious moods, does not focus upon respective arsenals of instruments specifically geared to coping with suffering and interpreting it. It derives, rather, from how each has been religiously conditioned by the totality of his spiritual experience. Or again, the *mizvah* of *devekut* (cleaving unto God) – assuming that it does not refer exclusively to *talmidei hakhamim* but relates, perhaps primarily and in accordance with the literal sense of the *pasuk*, to the *Ribbono shel Olam*[22] – will clearly instill, in those who seek to cleave to Him, a total relationship that will impinge upon the full range of their spiritual being.

Ahavah and *yirah* exemplify *hovot ha-levavot* that have an impact upon our response to suffering but are not primarily formulated with reference to it. Other *mizvot*, and especially those that have been singled out for my analysis, *are* so formulated. This group itself might be differentiated, however. Some of them can be envisioned as grounded existentially in suffering, but not as bound with it, normatively. Thus, the Torah clearly places *teshuvah* in the context of crisis – not only the intrinsic crisis of sin and consequent alienation from God but the external crisis that results therefrom. In the wake of varied calamities – exile, dispersion, bondage – physical and spiritual repentance is anticipated and demanded: "And you shall seek from there the Lord your God, and you shall find Him, if you seek Him with all your heart and with all your soul. When you are in distress, and all these things have come upon you, in the latter days, if you turn to the Lord your God, and are obedient to His voice" (Devarim 4:29–30). Yet obviously the obligation to repent is not conceived halakhically as a mode of responding to tribulation, and it is not confined to the disadvantaged. Sin requires *teshuvah*, and affluence or poverty, robust or failing health, is irrelevant. Some, however, might be more closely related. *Tefillah*, for instance, is conceivably mandated specifically as a result of *ba-tzar lekha* ("when you are distressed") and as a response to it. Thus, the Ramban, while generally inclined to reject the Rambam's inclusion of prayer as one of the biblically mandated *taryag mizvot*, concludes his animadversion with the partial concession that such a duty is to be confined, if at all, to moments of crisis:

ואם אולי יהיה מדרשם בתפילה עיקר מן התורה נמנה אותו במנינו של הרב ונאמר
שהיא מצוה לעת הצרות שנאמין שהוא יתברך ויתעלה שומע תפילה והוא המציל מן
הצרות בתפילה וצעקה.

> If perhaps their derivation is biblical, we will count it in the list of the Rav [Rambam], and say that it is a commandment at times of tribulation for one to believe that He, may He be blessed and exalted, hears prayer and it is He who saves us from trouble through prayer and crying out.[23]

The Rav, זצ"ל, contended on occasion that the Rambam, too, on a fundamental level, subscribed to this view. He suggested that although the Rambam posited daily *tefillah* as mandatory *mi'd'oraita*, this was only because he regarded the human condition, sans communication with the *Ribbono shel Olam*, as a perpetual crisis to be resolved only by turning to Him in prayer. Even if this view is rejected, there is no doubt but that the Rambam, too, acknowledged the category of a *mizvah* specifically geared to *ba-tsar lekha*. To this effect, his remarks at the beginning of Hilkhot Ta'aniyot are fully explicit. The preliminary caption reads: "One positive commandment, which is to cry out before God at any time of great trouble that befalls the community," while the more detailed body of the text proper opens:

מצות עשה מן התורה לזעוק ולהריע בחצוצרות על כל צרה שתבא על הצבור שנאמר
על הצר הצורר אתכם והרעותם בחצוצרות כלומר כל דבר שייצר לכם כגון בצורת ודבר
וארבה וכיוצא בהן זעקו עליהן והריעו.

A positive scriptural commandment prescribes prayer and the sounding of
an alarm with trumpets whenever trouble befalls the community. For when
Scripture says, "Against the adversary who oppresses you, then you shall
sound an alarm with the trumpets" (Bamidbar 10:9), the meaning is: "Cry
out in prayer and sound an alarm against whatsoever is oppressing you, be
it famine, pestilence, locusts, or the like."[24]

The apparent qualification limiting the *mizvah* to public disasters is significant,[25] but the principle that there is a *mizvah* whose very essence is defined as a response elicited by crisis and reactive to it is nevertheless clear.

Taken collectively, the *hovot ha-levavot* we have surveyed affect our relation to suffering in several ways, perhaps most easily distinguished by reference to the various stages previously cited. On a primary level, they may condition how suffering is initially experienced; on a second, how it is understood and interpreted; on yet a third, what ensues in its wake. With reference to the first, I believe, as already suggested, that the most critical *mizvot* are the more general ones: *ahavat Hashem, devekut, yirat Hashem.* Broadly speaking, these *mizvot* mold a person's fundamental experiential relation to the *Ribbono shel Olam,* and their influence upon response to suffering is itself multiplanar. In one sense, their ongoing and cumulative effect transforms the individual, independently considered. The vivifying power of cleaving to the *Ribbono shel Olam,* even in reverential awe, charges the human soul so that its reinforced spiritual and psychological fiber is better able to sustain adversity, no matter how acutely perceived.

Second, these *hovot ha-levavot* affect the perception proper. Religious and secular experiences of the same calamity may vary, not because the sufferers are different, but because the respective blows ultimately are not truly identical. *Sub specie aeternitatis,* the scope of suffering is circumscribed and its significance diminished, not because an opiate has diverted attention from it, but because living, in Milton's phrase, "as ever in my great Taskmaster's eye," perspectives and values are reoriented. Hazal were highly sensitive to human suffering, not hesitating to describe as *yissurim* what are, after all, only disruptive annoyances:

עד היכן תכלית יסורין אמר רבי אלעזר כל שארגו לו בגד ללבוש ואין מתקבל עליו מתקיף לה רבא זעירא ואיתימא רבי שמואל בר נחמני מזו גדולה מזו אמרו אפילו נתכוונו למזוג לו בחמין ומזגו לו בצונן בצונן ומזגו לו בחמין ואת אמרת כולי האי מר בריה דרבינא אמר אפילו נהפך לו חלוקו רבא ואיתימא רב חסדא ואיתימא רבי יצחק ואמרי לה במתניתא תנא אפילו הושיט ידו לכיס ליטול שלש ועלו בידו שתיים.

What is the measure of suffering? R. Eleazer said: If a man had a garment woven for him to wear and it does not fit him. Raba Zeira (others report, R. Samuel b. Nahmani) demurred to this: More than this has been said. Even if he was to be served hot, and it was served cold; or cold, and it was served hot! And you require so much? Mar the son of Ravina said: Even if his shirt got turned inside out. Raba (others report, R. Hisda; some, R. Isaac, or, as was taught in a *baraita*): Even if he put the hand into his pocket to take out three [coins] and he fetched only two.[26]

Nevertheless, the importance attached to a temporal value, and hence the dismay engendered by its loss, is patently a function of one's total spiritual context. Elaborating upon the prohibition of retributive revenge, the Rambam concludes: "One should rather practice forbearance in all worldly matters. For the intelligent realize that these are vain things and not worth taking vengeance for."[27] From a purely moral standpoint, the explanation is disappointing. The injunction would be more demanding and its observance more heroically imposing if one thought that temporal matters *were* worthy of being avenged. As a religious affirmation, however, the statement expresses a basic tenet, and its implications for evaluating the impact of *hovot ha-levavot* upon response to suffering are self-evident.

The point obviously needs to be examined in the broader context of the question of otherworldliness, a subject that lies well beyond the scope of this paper. A word may be said, however, with respect to our immediate focus, especially as regards *ahavat Hashem*. The relation between love of God and disdain for His creation may be reciprocal. On the one hand, contempt for the world may draw one to its Maker. Rabbenu Bahye explains the sequence of his work in light of this fact:

ועל כן הקדמנו שער הפרישות לשער הזה כי מן הנמנע ממנו שתתיישב אהבת הבורא
בלבנו עם התיישב אהבת העולם בנו. וכאשר יהיה לב המאמין ריק מאהבת העולם
ופנוי מתאוותיו מצד הכרה ובינה תתיישב אהבת הבורא בלבו ותהיה תקועה בנפשו
כפי היכספו לו והכרתו אותו כמו שנאמר אף ארח משפטיך ה' קוינוך לשמך ולזכרך
תאות נפש.

This is why we placed the chapter on abstinence before this one [on love of God], since it is impossible for the love of the Creator to be firmly established in our hearts if love of the world is fixed there. But when the believer's heart has been emptied of love of this world and freed from its lusts, as a result of perception and understanding, the love of God can be established in his heart and fixed in his soul, in accordance with his yearning for God and recognition of Him, as it is written: "Even in the path of Your judgments, O Lord, have we hoped for Your name, and Your memorial is the soul's desire" (Yeshayah 26:8).[28]

On the other hand – and this is the more common, and presumably the nobler, mystical route – love of God may lead to denigration of all else. It is this heightened sense of *ein od mi-levado* ("there is nothing but He") that, even in much milder form, can have some bearing upon response to suffering.

This is not to suggest, of course, that *ahavat Hashem,* properly realized, necessarily does or should lead to the degree of renunciation espoused by the Rambam's son, the Hasidei Ashkenaz, or even, for that matter, by the *Mesillat Yesharim.* That stance is not too prevalent in the modern world, not only on the popular level but on the philosophic. Clearly, the two most prominent *baalei mahshavah* of this century, Rav Kook and the Rav, זצ"ל, rejected it categorically. And by and large, the contemporary Torah community fully subscribes to the critique of both world-rejection and stoic apathy that the Ramban enunciates in his preface to *Torat Ha-Adam.*[29] As this very text illustrates amply, however, some diminution of the dimensions of tragedy not only can but should flow from religious commitment; in this sense, *ahavat Hashem* serves to ameliorate suffering.

This effect is heightened by an additional element. Irrespective of how suffering is perceived or evaluated, its impact can be cushioned by the compensatory import of one's relation to the *Ribbono shel Olam*. When Yirmiyahu sang, "God is my strength and my stronghold, and my refuge in the day of affliction" (Yirmiyahu 16:19), he celebrated not only the succor or even the solace he might hope to attain to overcome his troubles, but the sheer offsetting force of the relation proper.

Beyond experience, albeit, in a sense, interwoven with it, we move to the second phase: understanding and interpretation. The literature of the problem of pain is, of course, quite extensive, even within the bounds of our own Jewish world; here, I shall confine myself to its interaction with our specific theme. In this connection, we need to distinguish between two aspects: the ascription of suffering to its agent as an efficient cause, and the designation of its motive as a final cause. The first is mandated as a facet of *teshuvah* and, in effect, requires – unpalatable as this might be, theologically and philosophically, in other respects – that human suffering be traced to the initiative of the *Ribbono shel Olam*; or, failing that, to the untrammeled operation of other forces, natural or human, in the absence of His protective shield. The theme is familiar from many *pesukim*, but at the normative level is most succinctly set down by the Rambam:

ודבר זה מדרכי התשובה הוא שבזמן שתבוא צרה ויזעקו עליה ויריעו ידעו הכל שבגלל מעשיהם הרעים הורע להן ככתוב עונתיכם הטו וגו' וזה הוא שיגרום להסיר הצרה מעליהם. אבל אם לא יזעקו ולא יריעו אלא יאמרו דבר זה ממנהג עולם אירע לנו וצרה זו נקרה נקרית הרי זו דרך אכזריות וגורמת להם להדבק במעשיהם הרעים ותוסיף הצרה צרות אחרות הוא שכתוב בתורה והלכתם עמי בקרי והלכתי גם אני עמכם בחמת קרי כלומר כשאביא עליכם צרה כדי שתשובו אם תאמרו שהיא קרי אוסיף לכם חמת אותו קרי.

This is one of the ways of repentance, that when overtaken by trouble, the community cries out in prayer and sounds an alarm, then all must know that evil has come upon them as a consequence of their own evil deeds, and that their repentance will cause the trouble to be removed from them. But if they do not cry out in prayer and do not sound an alarm, but merely say that it is the way of the world for such a thing to happen to them, and that their trouble is a matter of pure chance, they have chosen a cruel way that will cause them to persevere in their evil deeds and thus bring additional troubles upon them. For when Scripture says: "If you will walk with Me by happenstance; then I will walk with you in furious happenstance" (Vayikra 26:27–28), the meaning is: If, when I bring trouble upon you in order to cause you to repent, you say that the trouble is purely accidental, then I will add to your trouble fury, to lead you to repent.[30]

The statement is made with respect to public calamity, to which it relates particularly; but the basic motif – that disaster should be attributed to divine intervention rather than to "natural" extremes, causal law, or indeterminate chance – applies to personal suffering as well.

To what extent the attribution is to be asserted presumably depends upon how the scope of *hashgahah peratit* (special providence) is defined. The more prevalent view is the more comprehensive: the notion, however reconciled with human freedom, that whatever befalls each and every individual, for good or for ill, is divinely ordained. Popular provenance aside, this view has apparent support in Hazal: "All is in the hands of heaven save for the fear of heaven."[31] The Rambam, to be sure, qualified the statement severely by contending that "all of man's actions are included in the fear of heaven."[32] The general interpretation is presumably quite sweeping, however; *ha-kol* is taken to include all that befalls every person and *yirat shamayim* to refer to the religious realm, narrowly defined. Thus Rav Hanina's statement, "One does not crook one's finger below unless it is proclaimed above,"[33] is understood both literally and comprehensively, with the attribution of misfortune to divine fiat a direct corollary.

Some of the Rishonim adopted a far more restrictive view, however, both the Rambam and the Ramban holding that only a select minority benefit from constant providential attention. Their reasons varied, as did the populations they singled out. The Rambam spoke of an intellectual elite that attained personal care by dint of individual effort that raised one's level of spirituality, so that one was now within range, as it were, of providence, and attuned to its wavelength. "The divine overflow that exists united to the human species, I mean the human intellect, is merely what exists as individual intellects.... Now if this is so, it follows necessarily according to what I have mentioned in the preceding chapter that when any human individual has obtained, because of the disposition of his matter and his training, a greater portion of this overflow than others, providence will of necessity watch more carefully over him than over others – if, that is to say, providence is, as I have mentioned, consequent upon the intellect.... As for the ignorant and disobedient, their state is despicable proportionately to their lack of this overflow, and they have been relegated to the rank of the individuals of all the other species of animals."[34]

The Ramban, on the other hand, regarded piety and righteousness as the definitive criteria; and he also appears to ascribe the special concern to divine, rather than human, initiative:

ירמוז כי ידיעת השם שהיא השגחתו בעולם השפל היא לשמור הכללים וגם בני האדם מונחים בו למקרים עד בא עת פקודתם אבל בחסידיו ישום אליו לבו לדעת אותו בפרט להיות שמירתו דבקה בו תמיד לא תפרד הידיעה והזכירה ממנו כלל כטעם לא יגרע מצדיק עיניו ובאו מזה פסוקים רבים כדכתיב הנה עין ה' אל יריאיו וזולת זה.

God's knowledge, which is synonymous with His providence in the lower world, is to preserve the species, and even human beings are subject to accident as long as they live. But He attends to the pious individually, to guard him always, His knowledge and remembrance of Him never departs as it says: "He withdraws not His eye from the righteous" (Iyov 36:7). There are many verses on this theme, as it is written: "Behold, the eye of the Eternal is toward them that fear Him" (Tehillim 33:18), and other verses besides.[35]

The common denominator, however, is that the concept and the reality of personal providence, as generally perceived, is significantly circumscribed.

Clearly, the degree of conviction with which a sufferer may attribute his travails to the *Ribbono shel Olam* will vary considerably, depending on his views with respect to this controversy. And yet the obligation to do so as a facet of *teshuvah* need not be linked to this debate. Even with the latter view, misfortune is not necessarily the hand of God. Assuredly, however, it might be, and one is fully obligated to take this possibility into account and to draw the inference. The attribution, of course, cannot partake of the nature of blame and concomitant anger. At that level, various *pesukim* clearly bar any causal link: "The foolishness of man perverts his way, and his heart frets against the Lord" (Mishlei 3:19). Or, even more explicitly:

"Out of the mouth of the most High do not both good and evil come? Why then does a living man complain, a man for the punishment of his sins?" (Eikha 3:38–39). On the level of interpretive reflection, however, the need to assume that one may have received a divine retributive message is clear, and, as the subsequent *pesukim* amplify, so is the recipient's need to repent: "Let us search and try our ways, and turn back to the Lord. Let us lift up our heart with our hands to God in the heavens" (Eikha 3:40–41).

Hazal took it as a matter of course that one should regard personal suffering in the context of one's relation to the *Ribbono shel Olam*. But as to conjecture concerning its substantive significance, they acknowledged considerable latitude. On one level, they encouraged responses that would question whether suffering was truly disastrous. They counseled raising the issue even with respect to the temporal pragmatic plane. Thus, in the wake of a statement from the school of Rabbi Akiva that a man should accustom himself to say, "Whatever the All-Merciful does is for good,"[36] the gemara narrates an incident in which Rabbi Akiva himself lost some favored possessions and, as a result, fortuitously, was saved from almost certain captivity. More commonly, however, the presumed benefit is projected as being deferred to the world-to-come. As even the most righteous may be liable for the slightest peccadillo, exacting punishment from them here redounds to their advantage, as they then have a clean slate, having paid their penance with mundane currency.

On the other hand, it is conceivable that affliction is undiluted punishment or that it is, however this elusive term is understood, *yissurim shel ahavah*. Perhaps that is precisely the point: the range of perception and interpretation. One can rule out neither the chastising rod nor the stroking palm, and hence none of the correlative emotions. Various possibilities are to be entertained and examined, with no assurance that the uncertainty will be resolved. The key, however, remains acceptance. *Ante facto,* the central tradition of *Yahadut* gives every license to fight off impending disaster. *Post facto,* it urges acknowledgment, as an expression of the divine will, of the very affliction to which the most heroic resistance previously had been sanctioned. A simple story in the gemara in Bava Kamma makes the point succinctly:

רב שמואל בר יהודה שכיבה ליה ברתא אמרו ליה רבנן לעולא קום ניזל לנינחמיה אמר
להו מאי אית לי גבי נחמתא דבבלאי דגידופא הוא דאמרי מאי אפשר למיעבד הא
אפשר למיעבד עבדי.

When R. Samuel b. Judah lost a daughter, the rabbis said to Ulla: Let us go and console him. But he answered them: What have I to do with the consolation of the Babylonians, which is [almost tantamount] to blasphemy? For they say, What could have been done?, which implies that were it possible to do anything, they would have done it.[37]

The implicit demand is imposing, indeed. Yet it is firmly ensconced in the *Shulhan Arukh*[38] and incumbent upon the ordinary Jew.

Clearly, both *teshuvah* and *tefillah* can, as well as should, affect our response to suffering, but in different ways. To begin with the former, its import is dual. As a *mizvah*, *teshuvah*, as we have seen, demands that a person regard his suffering as divinely imposed and, consequently, examine his life and reorient it:

אמר רבא ואיתימא רב חסדא אם רואה אדם שיסורין באין עליו יפשפש במעשיו שנאמר
נחפשה דרכינו ונחקרה פשפש ומצא יעשה תשובה שנאמר ונשובה עד ה'.

Raba (some report, R. Hisda) says: If a man sees that painful sufferings come upon him, let him examine his conduct. For it says: "Let us search and try out ways" (Eikhah 3:40). If he examines and finds [something objectionable], let him do *teshuvah* as it says: and turn back to the Lord.[39]

If the *heshbon ha-nefesh* (self-examination) does not uncover grievous sin, one should probe the possibility that his affliction is due to the failure to maximize his spiritual potential:

פשפש ולא מצא יתלה בבטול תורה שנאמר אשרי הגבר אשר תיסרנו י־ה ומתורתך
תלמדנו;

If he examined and found nothing, let him attribute it to the neglect of Torah study, for it says: "Happy is the man whom You, God, chastise, and teach him from Your Torah" (Tehillim 94:12).[40]

But Hazal regarded this, too, most seriously. Quite apart from any explicit *issur* (prohibition), the failure to seize spiritual opportunity reflects axiological vacuity and is expressive of disdain for ultimate values.

Expanding upon Rabbi Nehorai's comment upon the *pasuk*, "For he has scorned the word of God," (Bamidbar 15:27) the Rambam writes:

וכן כל שאפשר לו לעסוק בתורה ואינו עוסק או שקרא ושנה ופירש להבלי עולם והניח
תלמודו וזנחו הרי זה בכלל בוזה דבר ה'.

Similarly, anyone able to occupy himself with Torah study who does not, or who has studied and turned away to the vanities of the world, leaving behind his study and ignoring it, is included in the category of those who scorn the word of the Lord.[41]

This awareness, as an initial phase of *teshuvah*, is significant in its own right; indeed, the Torah refers to it at one point as an independent phenomenon:

וחרה אפי בו ביום ההוא ועזבתים והסתרתי פני מהם והיה לאכל ומצאהו רעות רבות
וצרות ואמר ביום ההוא על כי אין א-לקי בקרבי מצאני הרעות האלה.

Then my anger will burn against them on that day, and I will forsake them, and I will hide My face from them, and they shall be devoured, and many evils and troubles shall befall them; so that they will say on that day: Is it not because my God is not in my midst that these evils have found me?[42]

Obviously, however, the *mizvah* relates primarily to change that ensues from this awareness. In this respect, *teshuvah* lends a practical cast to response to suffering, whether at the level of action proper or, as its context, with respect to attitudes and priorities. Presumably, there might, and probably should, be some functional relation between the degree of suffering and prospective change. Radical suffering may raise the possibility of fundamental revision; moderate affliction, only minor alterations. The principle, however – at least, at the theoretical level – is clear.

From another perspective, however, *teshuvah*, as a phenomenon rather than qua *mizvah*, has a wholly different effect. It bears two primary aspects, recoil *from* and return *to*: "return from your evil ways" (Yehezkel 33:11), as opposed to "return, Israel, unto your God" (Hoshea 14:2). The first constitutes the "moral" element, broadly defined: the recognition of sin and its retrospective and prospective renunciation. The second is its "religious" component: the rehabilitation and restoration of one's relation to God. The latter entails not only repentance but redemption. As a process that intensifies and deepens the individual's link to the *Ribbono shel Olam*, it affects the whole of his being, having an impact, derivatively, upon his response to suffering as well. As previously noted, the whole range of *hovot ha-levavot – ahavat Hashem, yirah, devekut,* and others – that mold our relation to Him, influence our reaction to suffering at the primary level. Hence, insofar as *teshuvah* enriches one's total religious personality, it enhances one's capacity to cope with suffering and points the direction that such coping will take. In its wake, suffused with greater *emunah* (faith) and *bittahon* (trust), one is both better able to withstand suffering and more inclined to experience and interpret it within the matrix of religious existence.

I fully recognize the problematic character of this presentation. Preaching the gospel of the uses of adversity sounds at best idealistically utopian, and at worst, glibly insensitive; emphasizing the normative or positive aspects of response to suffering may convey a sense that profound human tragedy is being dispassionately and facilely dismissed. The modern reader, suffused with Dostoevski's perception that the whole literature of theodicy is not worth the searing pain of a single infant, is properly revolted by the faintest resemblance to cavalier insouciance. Moreover, this response is thoroughly Jewish. The significance that *Yahadut* ascribes to physical and psychological experience confers genuine import upon mundane suffering; hence, our response to others' pain as a concrete human reality is tempered accordingly.

I trust that the point is obvious, if not platitudinous. And yet the clear fact remains that, without being Pollyannish, and fully mindful of the depths of pain, *Yahadut* indeed points to suffering's value and encourages the sufferer to recognize that value. Whether as a vehicle of forgiveness – "One should rejoice more in chastisement than in prosperity, for if one is prosperous all his life, no sin of his will be forgiven. What brings him forgiveness of sins? Suffering" – or as a means of bonding with the *Ribbono shel Olam* – " 'Whom the Lord loves He chastises, even as a father the son in whom he delighteth' (Mishlei 3:12); what causes the son to be pleasing to his father? Suffering" – or as an expression of divine grace – "And you shall consider in thy heart that as a man chastens his son, so the Lord, thy God, chastens you" (Mishlei 8:5) – or as an instrument for conveying divine bounty – "Precious is suffering, for three good gifts coveted by all the nations of the world were given to Israel solely through suffering, and they are Torah, the Land of Israel, and the world to come"[43] – it is seen as having a potentially positive aspect, if one can respond to it properly.

This is not to suggest, of course, that one should, ascetically or masochistically, seek out some *felix culpa*:

ר' יודן בשם ר' אמי אמר אמרה כנסת ישראל לפני הקב"ה רבונו של עולם אף על פי שכתוב כי את אשר יאהב ה' יוכיח ה' אל באפך תוכיחני אף על פי שכתוב אשרי הגבר אשר תיסרנו י-ה אל בחמתך תיסרני.

R. Yudan said in the name of R. Ami: The congregation of Israel said to the Holy One, blessed be He: Lord of the Universe, even though the verse states, "God chastises those whom He loves," "Do not rebuke me in Your anger" (Tehillim 6:1). Even though the verse states, "Blessed is the man whom God chastises," "Do not chastise me in Your anger."[44]

On the personal level, likewise, Hazal recognized that even the greatest might very well prefer to forgo both pain and its lucrative aftermath. The *sugya* in Berakhot that deals with the value of *yissurim* concludes by citing several amoraim who, when asked, "Are your sufferings welcome to you?" responded, "Neither they, nor their reward."[45] And yet the central message obtains: if unsought adversity does strike, it should serve as a stimulus to a nobler and purer spiritual existence.

This sense is particularly relevant to what Hazal denominated *yissurim shel ahavah* (chastisements of love). According to one view, the term refers to suffering's modality, defining it as that which does not disrupt one's spiritual functioning, whether Talmud Torah or *tefillah*.[46] Presumably, however, the more prevalent view is that it refers to its impulse. Thus, Rava and/or Rav Hisda state that if, after introspective self-examination, one finds no failings to which to ascribe one's suffering, "it is known that these are chastisements of love. For it is said: 'For whom God loves. He corrects' (Mishlei 3:12)."[47] Just how this is to be perceived depends on how one resolves the issue of whether "there is death without sin, or suffering without iniquity."[48] In either view, however, these pangs are neither purely punitive nor merely an opportunity for accumulating points to be credited in the afterlife. They are inherently purgative, even if occasioned, as the Ramban held, by the need to remit sin and vouchsafe grace:

וכשאין בית המקדש קיים משלח עליהם יסורין למרק מהן אותן שגגות ולהתכפר ביסורין כדי להיותן נקיים לעוה"ב, כשם שהקרבנות אהבה וחמלה על ישראל ושקרבן תחת כנפי השכינה.

When the Temple no longer stands, He visits upon them suffering to scour them of those unintentional sins, and to atone through suffering so that they may be cleansed for the world-to-come. It is like the sacrifices which are love and compassion for Israel, bringing them under the wings of the Divine.[49]

For this effect to be attained fully, however, the sufferer, great as the pain may be, must perceive it clearly. No doubt the bare fact of privation may ennoble by changing perspectives and priorities and by purifying motivation. Yet the total impact is very much a function of the response.

Raba, in the name of R. Sahora, in the name of R. Huna, said: If the Holy One, blessed be He, is pleased with a man, He crushes him with painful suffering. For it is said: "And God was pleased to crush him by disease" (Yeshayahu 53:10). Is this so even if he did not accept them with love? Therefore it is said: "If his soul would offer itself in expiation" (ibid.) Just as the trespass offering must be brought willingly, so too must the suffering be endured willingly.[50]

In general terms, much the same as has been said of *teshuvah* could be said of *tefillah*, but its impact upon response to suffering also bears a distinctive stamp. At least three elements may be singled out. Most obviously, when confronted by crisis or in the midst of suffering, one prays for succor. Whatever idealistic philosophers may think, petition is, halakhically, the heart of prayer; as long as there is hope, one responds to suffering by asking that it be reversed or at least contained. Moreover, this is not merely an option but a duty. Heroic self-sufficiency is but an arrogant delusion. The awareness of dependence and the consequent cry for aid is, as the Maharal,[51] well before Schleiermacher, emphasized, the essence of *avodat Hashem*:

A song of ascents to David:
Lord, my heart is not haughty, nor my eyes lofty;
Nor do I exercise myself in great matters,
or in things too wondrous for me.
For I have been still and silent,
like a weaned child beside his mother:
Like a weaned child is my soul.
Let Israel hope in God from now and forever.[52]

Second, even if calamity already has struck, one looks to the *Ribbono shel Olam* for solace. In one sense, this, too, is petition. He is the ultimate comforter: "'I hoped for condolence and there was none, and for consolers and I did not find them,' (Tehillim 69:21). Said God: 'I am your consoler,'"[53] and one turns to Him with a plea for spiritual as well as for material sustenance. In another sense, one does not supplicate at all but simply leans upon Him, even while breaking down in tears. He is also the ultimate shoulder.

Finally, the suffering religious soul turns to the *Ribbono shel Olam* not only as *Avinu she-ba-Shamayim* (our heavenly Father) but as an *ah le-tzarah* (a brother in need), as, *salve reverentia,* a fellow sufferer. There is strength, there is comfort, in sheer commiseration, in the bare knowledge that somehow He, too, has been affected. This element is presumably most relevant to national calamities, inasmuch as these relate to the theme of *shekhinta be-galuta*: not the self-willed exile of "I am with him in distress" (Tehillim 90), but the enforced *galut* imposed, as it were, when the historical process goes awry. It also obtains, however, on the personal level:

אמר רבי מאיר בשעה שאדם מצטער שכינה מה לשון קלני אומרת קלני מראשי קלני מזרועי
אם כן המקום מצטער על דמן של רשעים שנשפך קל וחומר על דמן של צדיקים.

R. Meir said: When man suffers, what expression does the *Shekhinah* use? My head is too heavy for me; my arm is too heavy for me. And if God is so grieved over the blood of the wicked that is shed, how much more so over the blood of the righteous.[54]

Awareness of the divine anguish serves to ameliorate the human.

Confronting the *Ribbono shel Olam* in prayer, a sufferer thus is engaged in a highly complex relationship. On the one hand, it is presumably God who has smitten. On the other, it is to Him that one turns for help, whether for relief or comfort. And, finally, it is with Him whom one is conjoined in crisis, He participating in ours, and we, as it were, in His: "What of the father who banished his children, woe to the children who were banished from their father's table."[55] *K'lal Yisrael,* and, to a lesser extent, Reb Israel, are thus bound to their Master-Father-Lover in a covenant of suffering. Paradoxically, in our quest for comfort, we draw solace from the knowledge that, *mutatis mutandis,* He, too, is engaged in the quest, and with only partial success: "So long as the seed of Amalek exists, it is as if a corner of a garment covers the Face.... So long as the seed of Amalek is in the world, neither the Name nor the Throne is complete."[56]

In this vein, the Midrash perceives *hurban ha-bayit* (the destruction of the Temple) and the attendant national exile as no less a divine, than a human, calamity: "And when Judah and Benjamin went into exile, it is as though (*kivyakhol*) the Holy One, blessed be He, said: Woe is me for my breach" (Yirmeyahu 10:19).[57] Consequently, the *Ribbono shel Olam* is portrayed as bewailing the course of events:

ר' יצחק פתח (ירמיה ט) כי קול נהי נשמע מציון איך שודדנו ויש עצים בוכים ויש אבנים בוכות שאתה אומר כי קול נהי נשמע מציון אלא ממי שהוא משרה שכינתו בציון.

R. Isaac commenced: "For a sound of wailing is heard from Zion: How we are ruined!" (Yirmeyahu 9:19). Now can wood wail, can stones wail, that you should say, a sound of wailing is heard from Zion? Rather it is from the One whose Presence dwells in Zion.[58]

Even more audaciously, He is envisioned as seeking assistance from fellow mourners:

וכיון שגלו יהודה ובנימין כביכול אמר הקב"ה מעתה אין בי כח לקונן עליהם הה"ד (ירמיה ט) קראו למקוננות וגו' ותמהרנה ותשאנה עלינו נהי עליהם אין כתיב כאן אלא עלינו דידי ודידהון.[1]

And when Judah and Benjamin went into exile, it is as though the Holy One, blessed be He, said: I do not have the strength to lament for them, but

"Summon the dirge-singers, let them come; send for the skilled women, let them come. Let them quickly start a wailing for us" (Yirmeyahu 9:16–17). It does not say "for them" but "for us."[59]

And when well-intentioned *mal'akhei ha-sharet* (ministering angels) proffer consolation, it is spurned, as it evidently stems from failure to grasp the tragedy's scope and depth:

ובחורבן בית המקדש כתיב על כן אמרתי שעו מני אמרר בבכי אל תאיצו לנחמני אל
תאספו אין כתיב כאן אלא אל תאיצו אמר הקב"ה למלאכי השרת ניחומין אלו שאתם
אומרים לפני ניאוצין הן לי למה כי יום מהומה ומבוסה ומבוכה לה' א-לקים צ-באות
יום מעורבב יום דביזה יום דבכיה.

About the destruction of the Temple it is written: "Therefore, said I, turn away from me, I will weep bitterly, strain not (*al ta'itsu*) to comfort me" (Yishayah 22:4). It does not say here "do not gather together," but "strain not." The Holy One, blessed be He, said to the ministering angels, The words of comfort which you offer to Me are insults (*niutsin*) to Me. Why? "For it is a day of trouble, and of trampling and of perplexity for the Lord God of Hosts" (Yishayah 22:5); it is a day of confusion, a day of plunder, a day of weeping.[60]

For us, commiseration with His troubles supports us as we seek to transcend our own anguish. A neighbor of ours, Leib Rochman, who lived through the Holocaust and wrote about it, once was asked by a pseudo-philosopher guest where the *Ribbono shel Olam* had been at the time. Looking her straight in the eye, he responded calmly, *"Er iz geven mit unz"* (He was with us). And, as he repeated the story, one sensed how much the awareness of that presence had sustained him.

I write these lines with anxious trepidation. The anthropomorphic note is clear, and associative analogues with Christian, and even pagan, motifs are unquestionably troubling. The analogy is limited, for there is nothing here even faintly resembling expiatory sacrifice, and both the reality and the experience of presumed suffering are conceived within a wholly different context and in radically different categories; but nonetheless a growing malaise persists. I ask myself, timorously: how would the Rambam have responded to these speculations? I am afraid the answer to this rhetorical question is clear. And it is, I repeat, troubling.

Evidently, the compiler of Eikha Rabbati was not oblivious to these concerns; he took care to parry them. The familiar modifying *kivyakhol* appears in several of the texts cited, and a fuller qualification appears in another. After portraying the responses of the resurrected Mosheh Rabbenu and the *avot* to the carnage of the *hurban,* the Midrash presents its impact upon the *Ribbono shel Olam* Himself:

כיון שראה אותם הקב"ה מיד ויקרא ה' א-לקים צ-באות ביום ההוא לבכי ולמספד
ולקרחה ולחגור שק ואלמלא מקרא כתוב אי אפשר לאומרו והיו בוכין והולכין משער
זה לשער זה כאדם שמתו מוטל לפניו והיה הקב"ה סופד ואומר אוי לו למלך שבקטנותו
הצליח ובזקנותו לא הצליח.

> When the Holy One, blessed be He, saw them, forthwith: "And in that day did the Lord, the God of Hosts, call to weeping and to lamentation, and to baldness, and to girding with sackcloth." Had the verse not been written, one could not have stated it. And they went weeping from this gate to that, like a man whose deceased lies before him, and the Holy One, blessed be He, wept, lamenting, Woe for a king who prospers in his youth and not in his old age.[61]

"Had the verse not been written, one could not have stated it." This formulation encapsulates both ambivalence about the comment and determination – in a sense, under the imprimatur of the *pasuk,* and yet, essentially, through the initiative of the homilist who imposed this interpretation upon it – to present it nonetheless.

Still, the chasm between these caveats and the doctrine of negative attributes is wide and deep. Confronted by the polarities of the issue and animated by fealty to a range of sources, we find ourselves on the horns of a dilemma; at some point, we need to pitch our tent. After the dialectic between transcendence and immanence has been honed, and our sensitivity to the *va-yered* that stops short on the symbolic plane of ten *tefahim* having been refined,[62] we still must choose, on the philosophic as well as on the literary level, between the graphic vividness of midrashic theology and the rarefied purity of the Rambam's.[63]

Generally speaking, as the Rav, זצ"ל, once noted in an analogous connection, *Knesset Yisrael* has chosen for Midrash and against the *Moreh.*[64]

On the popular level, this choice has no doubt often derived from weakness, the result of the inability to scale the heights of theological inquiry and perception and to confront its implications. However, it can be grounded equally in strength: in tensile religious sensibility and in the conviction that the language of *kitvei ha-kodesh* and Hazal clearly dictates this option. For those who face the dilemma squarely (most, of course, are simply swept along by instinctive inclinations or societal norms), resolution is not easy. It is accompanied by awareness that we are all wide of the mark, doomed to misapprehend and therefore, to some extent, to misserve Him whom to know and serve is the alpha and the omega of our existence. Precisely, however, because a measure of failure is endemic and inevitable, it can be regarded, in the spirit of *lo nittena Torah le-mal'akhei ha-sharet* ("the Torah was not given to angels"), with a degree of acceptance, if not equanimity. We are charged to transcend crudity and purify religious sensibility, and heaven forfend that we relax our efforts. But the mandate has its limits, not because, on the personal level, these might prove counterproductive, but inasmuch as purported purification might falsify reality.

At stake is not just the prospect of desiccated experience or truncated imagination. From the perspective of *baalei ha-midrash* and *hakhmei ha-kabbalah*, the exaggeration of transcendence distorts objective truth with respect to the nature of divine revelation and engagement. In perceiving and defining what we understand by immanent *Shekhinah*, we can err on either side.

The relevance of this excursus to the theme of suffering's relation to the *Ribbono shel Olam* should be self-evident. The point is crystallized, however, in a well-known, albeit admittedly enigmatic, gemara in Hagigah. Referring to a *pasuk* in Jeremiah (13:17) – "But if you will not hear it, my soul shall weep in secret for your pride" – the gemara comments:

ומי איכא בכיה קמיה הקב"ה והאמר רב פפא אין עציבות לפני הקב"ה שנאמר הוד והדר לפניו עוז וחדוה במקומו לא קשיא הא בבתי גואי הא בבתי בראי ובבתי בראי לא והא כתיב ויקרא ה' א־לקים צב־אות ביום ההוא לבכי ולמספד ולקרחה ולחגור שק שאני חרבן בית המקדש דאפילו מלאכי שלום בכו שנאמר הן אראלם צעקו חוצה מלאכי שלום מר יבכיון.

But is there any weeping in the presence of the Holy One, blessed be He? Did not R. Papa say: There is no grief in the presence of the Holy One, blessed be He; for it is written: "Honor and majesty are before Him; strength and beauty are in His sanctuary!" (Tehillim 96:6)? There is no contradiction; the one case [refers to] the inner chambers, the other case [refers to] the outer chambers. But it is written: "And in that day did the Lord, the God of Hosts, call to weeping and to lamentation, and to baldness, and to girding with sackcloth!" (Yishayah 22:12). The destruction of the Temple is different, for even the angels of peace wept [over it]; for it is written: "Behold, for their altar they cried without; the angels of peace wept bitterly" (Yishayah 33:7).[65]

The cryptic responses are obviously open to varied interpretations. But the tenor and thrust of the passage are perfectly clear.

The Maharal took note of this and sought both to elucidate and to qualify the gemara:

והתמיה בזה כמו בראשונים דלא שייך בכיה אצלו ותשובה זה כבראשונה שאין הדברים נאמרו אצל הש"י מצד עצמו רק שהש"י נמצא אצל המקבלים בבלתי רצון ואינו נמצא להם בשלימות כבודו שכאשר ישראל אינם בשלימות והם בחסרון כאשר הם בגלות וכך נמצא השם יתברך לעולם כמו שהתבאר למעלה שהש"י נמצא אל העולם כאשר הוא המקבל ואין להכפיל הדברים.

It is puzzling, as in the earlier cases, for there is no weeping with regard to Him. The answer is that before, the discussion was not about God in Himself, only that God's Glory is imperfectly present to the recipients. For when Israel is imperfect and deficient, when they are in exile, so is God present to the world, as was explained before that God is present to the world according to the recipient.[66]

To this deflection of the wail from the Creator to the creature one can fully subscribe at some level. That His quintessential being is wholly immutable is beyond question, and at most we can speak of an impact upon His interactive relation to the world. The point is, however, that this impact is no mirage, that the effect upon the *Ribbono shel Olam*'s manifest presence is genuine, and, hence, that the grief Hazal daringly attributed to Him is both real and related to an objective correlative.

Throughout this presentation, I have spoken of response to suffering primarily with respect to its victim. In drawing to a close, I would like to touch, however briefly, upon response at the level of *hovot ha-levavot* to the suffering of others. Broadly speaking, we are doubly engaged. On one level, we react as outsiders, almost as angels are envisioned in numerous midrashim as reacting. This response is itself dual. There is, first, the philosophical and theological issue of the sheer existence of evil and suffering, whatever their locus.

In addition, we are also engaged emotionally, commiserating – be it as outsiders – with the pain of others. Among the *hovot ha-levavot*, this empathy relates at the very least to *tefillah*. In this context, prayer more likely will be almost exclusively a plea for succor; but even as such, its significance is considerable.

The primary impact of *hovot ha-levavot* upon our relation to the suffering of others is felt, however, insofar as the suffering becomes, in some sense and on some level, our own. From a purely moral standpoint, this degree of empathy is desirable in itself, as a reflection of the ability to transcend egocentrism and weave an element of fellowship, community, or universality into the fabric of personal identity. Donne's affirmation that "No man is an island, entire of itself; every man is a piece of the continent, a part of the main; if a clod be washed away by the sea, Europe is the less, as well as if a promontory were;… any man's death diminishes me, because I am involved in mankind"[67] is both a statement of fact and an imperative demand. Possibly, its very scope is self-defeating; so comprehensive an identity is difficult to sustain. On the national level, however, such a sensibility is both requisite and possible, and readers of *Kol Dodi Dofek* will recall the metaphor of the two-headed Jew, both of whose heads scream when either is scalded.[68]

This sense bears directly upon response to a fellow Jew's suffering, and all the more so to response to a calamity that strikes *Knesset Yisrael*, collectively. There is a significant difference between these situations, as in one case we deal with a parallel, albeit intersecting, entity and in the other with an encompassing context. The element of enlarged identity is, however, common to both, and we can deal accordingly with the role of *hovot ha-levavot* in our response to suffering with respect to both.

In this connection, I believe we should distinguish between recourse to *tefillah* and to *teshuvah*. As regards the former, all three aspects that were discussed above with respect to personal suffering – the quest for help, a shoulder to cry on, and a covenant of anguish – are very much in order. Moreover, there exists a reciprocal relation between prayer for others and interaction with them. On the one hand, one prays not only out of a religious imperative, inasmuch as "if one is in a position to pray on behalf of his fellow and does not do so, he is called a sinner,"[69] but out of empathetic identification; on the other hand, the process of *bakkashat rahamim* itself reinforces the identification.

The situation is somewhat different, however, with regard to *teshuvah*, whether as interpretation or *tikkun*. In one sense, there ought to be no difference. The theoretical assumption that sin and punishment are related functionally applies to others no less than to oneself and to the extended self no less than to the limited. And yet, the expression of this assumption – or, beyond that, even its specific internalization – can be highly problematic, from both a religious and a moral perspective. We recoil instinctively from assertions regarding the causal nexus between sin and suffering. Such statements are, of course, central to the books of the Nevi'im, and they abound in Hazal as well. Nevertheless, contemporaneously, even as we do not deny any given possibility, to asseverate with assurance is out of the question. Such statements constitute the height of arrogance vis-à-vis the *Ribbono shel Olam* and invite Hazal's comment concerning Balaam: "Now, seeing that he did not even know the mind of his donkey, could he know the mind of the most high?"[70] Vis-à-vis one's fellow, they are both morally and halakhically reprehensible. Regarding Job's religiosity, Hazal entertained widely divergent views, with some perceiving him as rebellious and blasphemous.[71] None, however, challenged the assertion that his comforters' responses were, in effect, models of proscribed *ona'at devarim* (verbal oppressiveness): "One must not speak [to the sufferer] as his companions spoke to Job: 'Is not your reverence your confidence, and your hope the integrity of your ways? Remember, who ever perished, being innocent?' (Iyov 4:6)"[72] Consequently, while *yahadut* certainly espouses fundamental faith in the relation of sin and suffering, humility and sensitivity both demand that we desist from specific application; hence, continued adherence to the tenet remains more a facet of *emunah* than of *teshuvah*.

The point is perhaps more delicate with respect to communal calamities inasmuch as here the functional association has deeper roots, and the Rambam's emphasis upon proper interpretation as an element of *teshuvah* has greater imperative force. Here, too, however, the need for balancing humility and sensitivity against the impetus to *teshuvah* obtains. If one genuinely counts himself among the guilty, *u-mippenei hatta'enu* ("because of our sins were we exiled") can be a most positive response. However, at the point at which it begins to shade off into *u-mippenei hatta'ekha* ("your sins"), let us beware, all the more so today in the shadow of the most frightful *hester panim* (hiding of the divine face) and the awesome silence it imposes upon us.

The realm of *tikkun*, by contrast, is less problematic, except insofar as it is itself predicated upon the ascription of blame. Truly collective repentance, grounded upon truly collective acknowledgment of sin as a response to collective suffering, lies at the heart of our tradition. It has, moreover, a dual thrust. On one level, it is a means of averting threatened disaster and thus essentially conjoined with the aspect of *tefillah* that strives to nullify *ro'a ha-gezerah* (the evil decree). On another, it is a *post facto* response to suffering and serves as the basis for the spiritual regeneration of a chastised community. This takes place, moreover, on both the personal and the communal plane. When Nineveh was threatened with impending doom, its inhabitants responded with public fasting and prayer and with personal self-examination: "...and let them turn everyone from his evil way, and from the violence that is in their hands" (Yonah 3:8). All the more so in the case of a Jewish community, of which a higher standard is demanded, and which, at least in the Maharal's view, can be defined as more thoroughly organic. And unlike acknowledgment, with the possibility of concomitant finger-pointing, *tikkun* can be approached without self-righteousness and without recrimination in a forward-looking spirit rooted in commitment to both *avodat Hashem* and to *ahavat Yisrael*.

Nineveh reminds us symbolically of our relation to universal suffering, and most of us sorely need a reminder. The ethnic factor is of little moment on the philosophic level. In dealing with theodicy, whether Job was Jewish, Gentile, or fictional is wholly irrelevant. On the practical level, however, it is of considerable import. Up to a point, this is fully understandable humanly and also, from our perspective, morally. There is no gainsaying the fact, belabored by Max Weber, that Judaism espouses a double ethic. The Halakhah indeed champions a double standard grounded in recognition of *kedushat Yisrael* and the perception, of relevance to ideal Gentile morality as well, that intensive ethnocentric *hesed* is preferred to bland universalism. Yet the tendency, prevalent in much of the contemporary Torah world in Israel as well as in the Diaspora, of almost total obliviousness to non-Jewish suffering is shamefully deplorable. Surely Avraham Avinu and Mosheh Rabbenu felt and acted otherwise, and the intervening *mattan Torah* has not changed our obligation in this respect. Priorities certainly need to be maintained, as regards both practical and emotional engagement; but between that and complacent apathy there lies an enormous moral gap. Relation to enemies is a separate issue, with respect to which many of the biblical psalms are highly relevant; but the notion that only Jewish affliction is worthy of Jewish response needs to be excoriated and eradicated. In this respect, the Hafetz Hayyim's remark that if the Gentiles knew how much we pray for them on Rosh Hashanah, they would publish *mahzorim*, serves as an instructive guide.

In this respect, we need to redouble our educational efforts to integrate and inculcate the dual thrust of a most familiar text. In the Ashrei prayer, a double ethic, in effect, is ascribed to the *Ribbono shel Olam*. His mercy and bounty are described as universal: "God is good to all, and His mercy on all His creatures.... The eyes of all turn to You and You give them their nourishment in its time. You open Your hand and satisfy all living beings." At the same time, priority obtains and they are selective, as He is close to all who "call upon Him in truth," hears the cry and fulfills the desire of those "that fear Him," and securely guards "all them that love Him." Within our community, however, while the parochial element is expounded properly, the universal is often *sotto voce,* if not muted. When priority turns into apathy, we are witness to a moral and educational failure. Can we confidently assert that we are not at times more affected by the withering of favored ephemeral gourds than by the destruction of a metropolis "wherein are more than sixscore thousand persons that cannot discern between their right and left hands, and also much cattle" (Yonah 4:11)?

In conclusion, I return to the sinking feeling that much of what has been said here may fall upon deaf ears. In a scientific age, any linkage of suffering to sin, even as an instrument of repentance, may seem both hollow and naive; any attempt to cry up the purgative nature of suffering may be viewed, especially after the Holocaust, as trite, platitudinous, and – what is worst – callous. Many now will have no truck with the uses of adversity and brand references to the crucible of pain as insensitive.

I can understand this reaction, and indeed, up to a point, share it. But only up to a point. Ultimately, there is no denying the fact that, dissonant as these responses are to many modern ears, they are of the essence of *Yahadut*'s traditional reaction to suffering on the speculative, pragmatic, or therapeutic level. That they sound empty or unpalatable to some brings us back to a central point. Response to suffering cannot be divorced from the totality of religious experience, and the ability to integrate religious solutions is a function of the totality of faith and commitment. But that is precisely the Achilles' heel of modern man and of many a contemporary Jew, to the extent to which he has hitched his wagon to modernity, to a world in which, as Matthew Arnold lamented, "the sea of faith" no longer being full, there is

> Nor certitude, nor peace, nor help for pain;
> And we are here as on a darkling plain
> Swept with confused alarms of struggle and flight,
> Where ignorant armies clash by night.[73]

In such a context, the key to confronting suffering in a Jewish way lies beyond formulae related to the realm of suffering. It entails reaffirmation of one's fundamental *Yahadut*.

Notes

1. See Sanhedrin 38.
2. See his "Sermon on Kohelet," in *Kitvei Ramban*, ed. C. Chavel (Jerusalem, 1963), 1:193–199.
3. Berakhot 7a.
4. The citation is from a summary remark made at the conclusion of a discussion following his lecture on "Mental Health and Halakhah" at a symposium of the National Institute of Mental Health in 1961. In the opening section of *Kol Dodi Dofek*, the Rav relates this theme to the distinction between men of the covenants of fate (*goral*) and of destiny (*ye'ud*) and their respective responses to suffering. Of the latter, he writes: "His approach is halakhic – moral – and is lacking any metaphysical – speculative – note." *Divrei Hagut ve-Ha-Arakha* (Jerusalem, 1982), p. 12. As a summary of the attitude of *yahadut* in general, however, this strikes me as overly sweeping.
5. See *Sha'agat Aryeh*, 14; *Mishkenot Yaakov*, 90.
6. Hilkhot Ta'aniyot 1:4.
7. Bava Kamma 87a.
8. See Rambam, Hilkhot Talmud Torah 1:13.
9. Kiddushin 31a, s.v. *gadol*.
10. *Hiddushei Ha-Ritva*, Kiddushin 31a.
11. *Hiddushei Ha-Ramban*, Kiddushin 31a.
12. *Sha'ar Ahavat Hashem*, introduction; based on Ibn Tibbon's translation.
13. Berakhot 54a.
14. Ibid. 61b.
15. Va-Ethannan, sec. 7; on Devarim 6:5.
16. *Meshiv Davar* 1:44.
17. See Hilkhot Teshuvah 10:3.
18. See Yoma 86a.
19. Ibid.
20. Devarim 6:5. Cf. Nedarim 62a, and Rambam, Hilkhot Teshuvah 10:1–5. The Rambam speaks of pure moral idealism, "doing what is true because it is true," and religious idealism grounded in the love of God. The two are not necessarily identical.
21. Hilkhot Yesodei Ha-Torah 2:2.
22. The Rambam, in Hilkhot De'ot 6:2, in light of the gemara in Ketubbot 111b, refers only to the former: "the positive commandment to cleave unto scholars and their disciples in order to learn from their actions." However, Ibn Ezra and the Ramban interpret the *pasuk* with respect to God, and the Ramban links the *mizvah* to *ahavat Hashem*, which it amplifies and intensifies.
23. *Hassagot* on *Sefer Ha-Mizvot*, Asseh 5. It is noteworthy that the Ramban speaks of a duty to believe that *tefillah* is efficacious rather than of a duty to pray.
24. Hilkhot Ta'aniyot 1:1. As in parallel instances, the relation of the caption, in which, despite the source in Bamidbar, no mention is made of *hatzotzrot*, to the body of the *halakhot* bears

examination. Presumably, the caption refers to the quintessential *kiyyum,* the text to the mode of fulfillment.

25. Later, in 1:9, the Rambam also speaks of fasting and praying with regard to an individual's crisis. But this may only be only *mi-d'rabbanan.* See also *Kol Dodi Dofek,* 14 n.

26. Arakhin 16b.

27. Hilkhot De'ot 7:7.

28. *Sha'ar Ahavat Hashem,* introd. Cf. Rambam, Hilkhot Teshuvah 10:6 and *Guide* 3:51, where the same point is made, but with a less conative and more intellectual cast.

29. See especially the conclusion, in *Kitvei Ramban,* 2:13–14.

30. Hilkhot Ta'aniyot 1:2–3.

31. Berakhot 33b.

32. *Teshuvot Ha-Rambam,* ed. J. Blau, 714.

33. Hullin 7b.

34. *Guide,* trans. S. Pines, 3:18, 473. Initially, the Rambam only speaks of a functional ratio, but given his general orientation, the concluding statement about "the ignorant and the disobedient" probably leaves only a minority under any personal providence whatsoever.

35. Bereshit 18:19. I once asked *mori ve-rabbi,* Rav Hutner, זצ"ל, about this passage, and he categorically refused to take it at face value, arguing that leaving some to the vagaries of accident did not denote an absence of *hashgahah* but rather was a mode of its operation. The suggestion is striking but does not bear upon our discussion.

36. Berakhot 60b; see Maharal, *Netivot Olam, Netiv Ahavat Hashem,* chap. 1.

37. Bava Kamma 38a.

38. See Rema, Yoreh De'ah 376:2.

39. Berakhot 5a.

40. Loc. cit. Rava speaks of *bittul Torah* specifically, but the Ramban (see *Torat Ha-Adam,* in *Kitvei Ramban,* 2:270) explains that a far broader range is intended.

41. Hilkhot Talmud Torah 3:13.

42. Devarim 31:17. In the context of the *pasuk,* the phrase "God is not in my midst" probably means that "He has deserted me" rather than vice versa. Even with this view, however, the implicit recognition that the desertion is attributable to sin constitutes an aspect of *teshuvah.* Thus was it understood by the Ramban, ad loc.: "This is not a full confession like 'they shall confess their iniquity' (Vayikra 26:40), but it is reflection and regret. They will regret their iniquity and recognize that they are guilty."

43. *Sifre,* Va-Ethannan, sec. 7.

44. Midrash Tehillim 6:3.

45. Berakhot 5b.

46. Ibid. 5a.

47. Loc. cit.

48. Shabbat 55a. The gemara resolves that even the innocent die, but adduces no proof with regard to *yissurim.* The Rambam (*Guide* 3:17 and 3:24) and the Ramban (*Kitvei Ramban* 1:199 and 2:

271–274) cite the issue as a matter of debate among Hazal, but both are inclined to accept the view that there is no suffering without sin.

49. *Kitvei Ramban* 2:270. Elsewhere, he seems to ascribe a semi-mystical quality to such suffering. Cf. Maharal, *Netivot Olam, Netiv Ha-Yissurim,* chaps. 1–2.

50. Berakhot 5a.

51. See *Netivot Olam, Netiv ha-Avodah,* chap. 2.

52. Tehillim 131.

53. *Yalkut Shimoni* 474, on Yeshayah 51:1.

54. Sanhedrin 46a.

55. Berakhot 3a.

56. Midrash Tanhuma, Ki Tetse 11.

57. Eikha Rabbati, Petihta 2.

58. Ibid. 8.

59. Loc. cit.

60. Eikha Rabbati, Petihta 24. In the *pesukim* cited from Yeshayah 22:4–5, the *peshat* refers to troubles God causes to others, and not to His own.

61. Loc. cit.

62. See Sukkah 4b.

63. With respect to the Rambam, see Simon Rawidowicz, *Iyyunim be-Mahshevet Yisrael* (Jerusalem, 1969), pp. 171–233.

64. See, with reference to the controversy over reciting *piyyutim,* his comments in *Ish Ha-Halakhah, Galuy ve-Nistar* (Jerusalem, 5739), p. 56.

65. Hagigah 5b. In the context of the *pasuk* cited, the call to weeping might refer to the cries of others rather than those of the *Ribbono shel Olam.* As the link to *tivke nafshi* ("My soul weeps") amply indicates, however, Hazal here clearly did ascribe it to Him.

66. *Be'er Ha-Golah,* chap. 4 (London, 1964), pp. 66–67.

67. Donne, *Devotions upon Emergent Occasions,* 17.

68. See *Kol Dodi Dofek,* pp. 35–36.

69. Berakhot 12b.

70. Sanhedrin 105b.

71. See Bava Batra 15b–16b.

72. Bava Metzia 58b.

73. Arnold, "Dover Beach," stanzas 3–4.

Chapter 6

Prayer on Shabbat

Whatever image one may have of Shabbat, prayer looms large as one of its components. On weekdays, its value and obligation notwithstanding, prayer is peripheral in terms of time spent and energy engaged; a prelude, intermission, and coda – but not the heart of the day. On Shabbat, however, it is central. In this country, the contrast may be exaggerated due to lax shul attendance during the week (a phenomenon already prevalent in classical Babylonia)[1] and Shabbat services lengthier than those familiar to our forebears in Europe or our contemporaries in Israel. The essential contrast is long-standing, however – and not surprising. The leisure afforded by the day of rest, and its inherently spiritual character, render the centrality of Shabbat prayer perfectly natural.

It may come as a rude shock, therefore, to discover that the very possibility of Shabbat prayer poses something of a problem. The term *tefillah*, "prayer," is generally used in two ways. In its broader, more popular sense, it refers to all forms of verbal worship,[2] ranging from the reading of Hallel or Shema to the recitation of assorted *berakhot*. In the more technical sense, however, the sense that generally prevails in the gemara or the Rambam, for instance, the term denotes the Shemoneh Esreh. The essence of this

---

This paper was written in the context of a projected collaborative volume on prayer, under the auspicies of Yeshiva University, in the mid-1960s. The volume never came to fruition, but the paper was subsequently published, with some changes and in Hebrew translation, in *Siʾah Yizhak* (Jerusalem, 1978).

prayer, in turn, is the central, petitional section, for which the first and last three *berakhot* provide an overture and postscript as a framework. In fact, the term *tefillah* (or the equivalent verb) is sometimes reserved for this section exclusively: "R. Simlai said: One should always first set forth God's praises" – referring, as Rashi explains, to the first three blessings of the Shemoneh Esreh[3] – "and then let him pray (*yitpallel*)."[4]

Petition and Shabbat do not mix readily, however. Petition springs from a sense of need, if not frustration. It is rooted in anxiety about one's ability – or inability – to keep the wolf from the door or society in balance. It solicits divine aid for one's pursuit of the aggressive quest to enlarge the bounds of individual and collective empire. Shabbat strikes a totally different note. Its primary motifs are serenity and surcease, respite from strife and striving. It bespeaks contentment rather than frustration, security rather than need.

Man as petitioner is dominated by a sense of helplessness. Naked to the universe, alternately broken reed and aspiring shoot, he pleads, not for assistance and sustenance alone, but for the very maintenance of his physical and spiritual existence. The supplicant is man in crisis. The Shabbat celebrant, by contrast, is man relaxed. Uncoiled, he basks in the aura of a time to which care seems wholly antithetical.

Grounded in covenant, the day focuses on the Jew's joining in God's rest rather than on the abyss between them. Through its appreciation and observance, the rabbis tell us, one is regarded "as having become God's partner in primal creation."[5] Correspondingly, its associations are largely sweetness and light. Bialik's sentimental portrayals, invariably dominated by the candles Dov Sadan has pinpointed as a central image in his poetry, or the lachrymose reminiscences of Grade's *Die Mama's Shabbosim,* may strike us as romanticized bathos; but they tap a popular conception, one which is not without halakhic foundation. Obviously, however, the consonance of this conception with the mood indigenous to petitional prayer is, to say the least, problematic.

Moreover, the incompatibility of Shabbat and petition is not just a matter of psychological nicety. It is the subject of explicit halakhic proscription. The anonymous mishnah in Ta'anit implies as much when it lists potentially calamitous situations – "a town surrounded by [attacking] Gentiles or a river [i.e., a flood], a ship foundering at sea – over whose fate we exclaim on Shabbat."[6] Rabbi Yose is fully explicit, however, challenging this ruling with the statement that exclamation is permitted "for [securing] aid but not for outcry."[7] Both evidently agree, however, that, barring such emergencies, petitions are forbidden on Shabbat. The Rambam cites the prohibition in no less than four different contexts, the fullest coming near the end of Hilkhot Shabbat: "It is forbidden to fast, to cry out, to plead, or to beg mercy on Shabbat; and even with respect to one of those calamities over which the public fasts and exclaims, we neither fast nor exclaim on Shabbat."[8]

The relevance of these citations may be challenged on the ground that they deal with a very special kind of petition, intense in character and public in scope. An outcry welling up in response to a crisis clearly breaches Shabbat's relaxed mood far more than the muted plaint of an ordinary petition. Most likely, some such distinction was assumed by, among others, Rav Saadia Gaon. In his siddur, he includes two lengthy prayers for use by anyone who wishes to add to the standard Shemoneh Esreh but is incapable of composing a proper original prayer. In describing these prayers, he notes: "One of them I have made stronger and more forceful than the other, with the milder for Shabbat, festivals, and days of joy, and the stronger and tougher for fast-days and the like."[9] Even the milder prayer, however, while predominantly one of praise and thanksgiving, includes numerous petitions. In tone and substance, it is certainly no less plaintive than the standard Shemoneh Esreh, whose pleas it often parallels.

> May it be Thy will, O Lord our God, that Thou shalt remit all our transgressions, absolve us from our evils, and forgive our sins.... For Thy sake, we plead, accept us and vouchsafe our repentance. Cleanse us from our transgressions and purify us from our sins.... And may Thou heal our wounds and save us from our enemies' grasp.... And may Thou gather the remnants of Thy flock from all the places to which they have been scattered and return Israel to its home.[10]

As Rav Saadia's prefatory note suggests, these petitions are deemed proper for Shabbat because they are relatively mild – presumably less intense and less public than the crisis-oriented outcry proscribed by the mishnah.

Nevertheless, we encounter a similar prohibition elsewhere in a text explicitly dealing with ordinary and private petitions. Says the Yerushalmi:

> We have learned: It is forbidden for one to demand his needs on Shabbat. Rav Ze'ira asked Rav Hiyya b. Ba: What about saying, "Shepherd us, support us"? That, he replied, is the standard text.[11]

As is clearly implied by the question raised about phrases drawn from the Birkat Ha-Mazon,[12] this prohibition evidently includes petitions that are not crisis-induced. The Rambam evidently assumed likewise, as he cites the impossibility of uttering the necessary prayer-pleas as a reason for postponing the *hakhel* convocation, if its designated date occurred on Shabbat.[13] Consequently, the character – in a sense, the very possibility – of Shabbat prayer once again becomes problematic.

The Yerushalmi's prohibition was widely noted by the Rishonim, and a number of them cited it to explain why there is, in fact, less prayer on Shabbat. Lest this sound surprising, it should be pointed out that the presumed plenitude of Shabbat prayer is, in a sense, deceptive. Of course, we stay in shul much longer. Primarily, however, the additional time is devoted to other matters – particularly to the Torah reading and its interpretation – rather than to prayer proper. Moreover, most of the actual textual increments postdate Hazal. The practice of adding chapters of Tehillim to Pesukei de-Zimra evidently stems from the Geonim, while almost the whole of Kabbalat Shabbat is a sixteenth-century accretion.[14] The backbone of the davening – the Shema and its *berakhot* and the Shemoneh Esreh – is not expanded.[15] On the contrary, the *Tefillah*, in the narrower sense of the term, is considerably shorter. Instead of the standard eighteen or nineteen weekday *berakhot*, the Shemoneh Esreh (now somewhat misnamed, of course) on Shabbat consists of only seven, the thirteen intermediate petitions having been replaced by a single *berakhah*. The gemara in Berakhot ascribes the abbreviation to deference to Shabbat and its observance. In explaining why someone who erroneously begins to recite a weekday *berakhah* on Shabbat should conclude it, whereas someone who reminds himself in mid-*berakhah* that he has already davened should stop at once, it notes that the two cases are not comparable: "There [i.e., in the former instance] the person is essentially obligated, and it is the rabbis, out of deference to Shabbat, who have refrained from imposing upon him. Here, however, he has already prayed."[16] Nevertheless, several Rishonim cited the Yerushalmi as an alternative interpretation. A passage in *Siddur Rashi* is typical:

> Our rabbis taught: Why do we recite eighteen *berakhot* on weekdays, whereas on Shabbat, when we are at leisure, we only recite seven? Why not recite eighteen on Shabbat? Rav Huna said: Because it is forbidden [for one] to demand his needs on Shabbat.[17]

The Rambam, while he does not allude to the Yerushalmi directly, offers the same explanation. Responding to a question concerning Rav Saadia's aforementioned prayers, he firmly rejects incorporating them in Shabbat prayer; and in so doing he explains its limits:

> And [as regards] all these pleas, petitions, and prayers, well-known as compositions of the Geonim and the *paytanim*, it is absolutely forbidden to say any part of them, whether for an individual or for the public, whether on Shabbat or on a festival. For the sages insisted upon not saying the slightest thing of this sort on Shabbat. And they said: It is Shabbat, to be devoid of outcry, with cure soon to come, as His mercies are great[18] – and this by way of statement, not by way of plea. It is because of this that the middle *berakhot* of the Shemoneh Esreh were omitted, as they are all petitions. This is something that will not be mistaken by any person who is a *talmid hakham* if it is called to his attention, and will only be denied by one who rejects what is obviously apparent. And as prayer is very worthy service, so too the fulfillment of His commandment, may He be exalted, to honor days He has honored, that they may be maintained as He has ordained, is the most worthy service. This means that Shabbat is for rest and festivals for joy – not to make them days of fasting, weeping, and outcry, nor for saying on them anything but matters whose recitation is appropriate to the mood we have described.[19]

Rav Saadia presumably held that the Bavli's statement implied a rejection of the Yerushalmi's position. On its view, we are excused but not prohibited from presenting weekday petitions on Shabbat.[20] The Rambam, in effect, reverses the process, ignoring the gemara's apparent rationale. In Mishneh Torah, he cites the Halakhah grounded upon it, i.e., that one should conclude a weekday petitional *berakhah* mistakenly begun on Shabbat. However, this decision can be maintained even in the face of the Yerushalmi's prohibition. While ideally speaking, one ought not to present certain pleas on Shabbat, the Shabbat petitioner may nonetheless be distinguished from a person who has already davened. At the moment of error, the former is still, as regards the *mizvah* of *tefillah*, a normative being; and while his particular prayer may be inconsonant with, even offensive to, the mood of Shabbat, it remains a response to the duty of prayer. Regrettable from one perspective, it fulfills a command from another. Hence, one who has already begun the *berakhah* is urged, after the fact, to conclude it, as it will not constitute a *berakhah* in vain. However, one who has already prayed lies beyond the pale of duty entirely, and unless he resorts to the procedure for voluntary prayer (i.e., by adding an original element), he cannot present normative *tefillah*.[21] He is therefore enjoined from continuing, since even as a fait accompli, his *berakhah* would indeed be in vain. Thus, while the Rambam cited the gemara's ruling, he was not logically bound to assume either the explanation for the curtailment of the Shemoneh Esreh or the license for Shabbat petition that one might, *prima facie*, regard as implicit in it. Relying on other sources, and possibly interpreting the gemara in their light, he therefore ruled, firmly and consistently, against offering the weekday Shemoneh Esreh or its equivalent on Shabbat.[22]

Still other Rishonim linked the two texts, regarding the Yerushalmi's prescription as the basis of the gemara's statement. Thus, the Provençal *Sefer Ha-Manhig* quotes the latter and, before presenting and rejecting the more literal interpretation, explicates it in the light of the Yerushalmi:

> "Out of deference to Shabbat, the rabbis have refrained from imposing upon him [i.e., the *mitpallel*]": To wit, that he should not be pained. Since if he has a sick person [at home], he mentions this in the *berakhah* "Heal us," therefore we only recite seven *berakhot* on Shabbat, as it is forbidden for a person to demand his needs on Shabbat. Others explain [that it is] because, on Shabbat, people come [to shul] early and leave early,[23] and one who is detained

due to the Shemoneh Esreh will be upset. This does not seem [correct] at all, however, but rather [it is] as we have explained.[24]

Be this as it may, the notion that prayer must be restricted on Shabbat is clearly deep-rooted.

While grounding themselves upon the Yerushalmi, these Rishonim did not eliminate Shabbat petition. They only explained its abbreviation. The Rabad went a step further. Commenting upon Rav Yohanan's dictum that one may voluntarily pray more than thrice daily,[25] he argues that this license only applies to weekdays; and in the course of presenting this argument, he draws a sharp distinction between daily and Shabbat prayer:

> Rav Yohanan only said, Would that one could daven all day, with reference to the Shemoneh Esreh, which is a prayer of plea and petition – with the proviso that he [the *mitpallel*] pause between them [the recitations of the Shemoneh Esreh], so that his mind can clear and he can focus his attention to plead [again] for mercy. However, with respect to the prayers of Shabbat and Yom Tov, which are purely thanksgiving, Rav Yohanan said nothing. If one were to thank and then thank again, the [latter] *berakhot* would be in vain, as would be the case with the morning or evening *berakhot* of the Shema, those over *mizvot* or fruit, and the like.[26]

On this view, Shabbat banishes anxiety and crisis entirely. We ask for nothing because we lack nothing. Man in need – incarcerated, Jonah-like, within the bowels of an indifferent universe, dangling, impotent and terrified, over the abyss of nothingness – is no more. Normatively speaking, Shabbat knows only the relaxed, contented, redeemed Jew. Its prayers – devoid of petition, devoted to thanksgiving and praise – both reflect and express his mood. It is all so symbolically idyllic as to be almost transhistorical.

In fact, some Rishonim explicitly discuss Shabbat prayer in quasi-eschatological terms. Thus, the *Shibbolei Ha-Leket* employs the analogy to explain why Mizmor le-Todah, the brief "Psalm of Thanksgiving,"[27] should be recited on Shabbat. He notes that Rashi – in this case, the precursor of our present practice – ruled that it should only be said on weekdays, inasmuch as he associated it with the *korban todah* (thanksgiving sacrifice),[28] which, since it never has a fixed date,[29] may not be offered on Shabbat. On the contrary, the *Shibbolei Ha-Leket* contends, it should be recited only on Shabbat, "as it is a day of thanksgiving;" and he buttresses this view by quoting and then applying a midrash:

> At the millennium all sacrifices shall lapse, but the thanksgiving sacrifice shall remain; all prayers are destined to lapse, but thanksgiving prayer shall remain. And thus has David said: "Upon me are Thy vows, O God; I shall render *todot* unto Thee."[30] It does not say *todah* but *todot*:[31] [both] thanksgiving prayer and sacrifice.[32]

"And Shabbat," he concludes, "is a day of rest, paradigmatic of the millennium."[33]

To many Rishonim, however, such semi-millennial discourse – and the concomitant rejection of all Shabbat petitions – would no doubt have seemed somewhat heady. They do not, at any rate, make the Rabad's point; and a number of them obviously dismissed it. Thus, some permitted repeated prayer on Shabbat as on weekdays,[34] while others rejected it on different grounds.[35] Nor should such opposition surprise us. The fact is, of course, that even on Shabbat the Jew remains very much in want. Regardless of its substantive and symbolic value, Shabbat cannot catapult the Jew beyond need. And this, not because so few of us, lamentably, realize its full potential. It is simply because no matter how great its redemptive capacity, nothing can alter the fact that man is indigenously destitute. Moreover, the awareness of dependence is, as Schleiermacher emphasized, central to religious experience; and it is particularly relevant to prayer. As Maharal put it:

> For the prayer that a person prays to God indicates that the person is dependent upon Him, needs Him, and has no existence without Him…. It is for this reason that prayer constitutes service (*avodah*) of God, while fear of Him does not. It is not called service because it does not indicate that a person is dependent upon Him.[36]

Hence, Shabbat or no, prayer without petition is inconceivable. Man's metaphysical condition precludes it.

For these Rishonim, then, the reconciliation of the Yerushalmi's prohibition with the very essence of prayer remains a problem – not, to be sure, whether to petition but how and for what. This, in turn, raises several specific questions. First, why should petition be proscribed at all? The Rishonim advanced two explanations. One, exemplified by the passage I have quoted from *Siddur Rashi,* is that the recitation of *berakhot* dealing with various needs may lead the *mitpallel* to reflect upon his own troubles in these areas and, in consequence, to feel anguish.

On this view, it is not the recitation *per se* which is objectionable but the anxiety stimulated by it. A passage in *Ohel Mo'ed,* a fourteenth-century compendium, suggests otherwise, however: "A person should not discuss his affairs on Shabbat; rather, his discourse should be about Torah. Likewise, it is forbidden [for one] to demand his needs on Shabbat."[37] The context clearly indicates that the recitation proper, as an expression of secular concerns, is proscribed – evidently subsumed under the general prohibition against conducting or discussing mundane business on Shabbat.[38] This would also appear to be the import of the Yerushalmi's statement that "as it is forbidden to do work before *Havdalah,* so is it forbidden for a person to demand his needs before *Havdalah,*"[39] the equation seemingly suggesting an intrinsic desecration in both cases. Interestingly, both reasons, albeit somewhat run together, are cited by the Midrash Tanhuma.

> We do not recite [the] eighteen [*berakhot*] on Shabbat, for if one should have a sick person at home, he will be minded [of this] at "the healer of the sick of His people, Israel," and will be pained. Shabbat, however, was given to Israel for sanctity, for enjoyment, and for rest – not for pain. Therefore, one [only] prays the first three and last three [*berakhot*] and that concerning rest in the middle. And therefore, David said: "Seven on this day have I praised Thee."[40] These are the seven *berakhot* we recite on Shabbat, the special day of rest which is unique, as it is written: "Remember the Shabbat day to render it holy"[41] through every means, even by [refraining] from pursuing thy business and speaking thereof.[42]

The respective reasons have clear implications for a second question: the scope of the prohibition. The adherents of neither reject petition categorically. However, they would presumably define its limits differently – the one in terms of anxiety stimulation, the other in terms of subject-matter. Thus, if secularity is the sore spot, those *berakhot* of the Shemoneh Esreh that deal with spiritual concerns should be unobjectionable. The *Ohel Mo'ed* actually assumed this position:

> Although it is forbidden [for one] to demand his needs on Shabbat – i.e., that he should demand his economic needs – it is permissible to plead for mercy, e.g., "Lead us back in perfect repentance," and the like. This is why they said, "It is forbidden [for one] to demand his needs," and did not say, "It is forbidden to plead for mercy."[43]

Given Rashi's explanation, however, we ought not to distinguish; and, in fact, he did not. Both *Siddur Rashi* and the cognate *Mahzor Vitry* list "spiritual" *berakhot*, concerning intelligence and penitence, among those to be shunned on Shabbat.[44]

On the other hand, Rashi's position might conceivably allow for a measure of petition in circumstances unlikely to induce anxiety. Such a distinction seems, in any event, to emerge from the likeliest interpretation of the Yerushalmi's enigmatic conclusion. It will be recalled that Rav Ze'ira had raised a question about certain petitional phases in Birkat Ha-Mazon, and that he was met with the rejoinder that these were just standard texts. The difficulty is obvious; on the whole, the Shemoneh Esreh is now equally standard. However we resolve this crux, the implication of the reply is clear: the prohibition against petition is a function of tone and context. This can obviously be better understood along Rashi's lines.[45]

The specific import of this point and likewise, therefore, the precise scope of the prohibition are somewhat elusive, however. Unfortunately, the Rishonim, by and large, wrestled with the problem on an ad hoc basis, producing a variety of specific judgments but rarely any definitive criteria. Some attempted to tread a very fine line. Rabbenu Yom Tov, for instance, objected to *rahem*, "pity [us]," but accepted *nahem*, generally interpreted as "console [us]," but which he felt could be construed reflexively as "reverse [Thyself]" regarding any projected misfortune.[46] R. Yehudah Sir Leon, on the other hand, argued that the difference, if any, was minuscule; and he was inclined to accept either so long as it was part of the standard text of Birkat Ha-Mazon.[47]

Another group, led by Rav Asher of Lunel,[48] evidently distinguished between the plea for wisdom and all others, including such spiritual requests as penitence or forgiveness. In discussing the issue of completing a weekday *berakhah* erroneously begun on Shabbat, he states that the gemara's ruling (that the *berakhah* be completed) should be confined to the first petition, for wisdom and intelligence. As the Meiri noted,[49] the sanction for this position is probably Rabbi Yehudah Ha-Nasi's statement, cited by the Yerushalmi: "I wonder how they [i.e., the rabbis] eliminated [the *berakhah* of] 'the bestower of wisdom' on the Shabbat. Without wisdom, whence prayer?"[50] Its rationale, however, is clearly that all the other *berakhot* were eliminated as being both burdensome and objectionable, this one only as an onus. Most Rishonim apparently saw no basis for the distinction, however, and they rejected this ruling.

Another disagreement is reflected in a responsum cited by the *Or Zarua*. Rav Yehudah b. Kalonymos inquired of Rabbenu Ephraim about the propriety of saying on Shabbat the passage that begins, "My God, keep my tongue from evil," a prayer initially recited as a personal addendum by Ravina's son, Mar, but later customarily adopted as the conclusion of the standard Shemoneh Esreh. He writes:

> As regards [the *berakhah* of] "grant peace," there is no problem. It is the standard text, as the Yerushalmi says with respect to "shepherd us, support us." But "my God, keep," which an amora was wont to say after his prayer and [to which] people have likewise become accustomed: who has fixed and ordained it in prayer, that it too should be said on Shabbat?[51]

Rabbenu Ephraim replied:

> You could similarly ask whether it is proper to elaborate on Shabbat, "May the All-merciful preserve us from the straits of poverty and avenge the vengeance of His servants' blood."[52] None of this was ordained by the rabbis to be said. What, then, can you respond? That since the commonalty instituted and made it customary to say it, there is no ground for concern. Here, too, it is no different.[53]

In a sense, this begs the question, but the difference in approach is clear. Whereas Rav Yehudah thought in terms of formal authorization, Rabbenu Ephraim answered that it was not a matter of dispensation at all. Anything that is, in effect, recited by way of conformity with a general routine rather than as a personal plea does not come under the prohibition. Presumably, in such a case – and here we come back to Rashi's reasoning – the emotional charge of a petition is ordinarily insufficient to disrupt the Shabbat mood.

The example adduced by Rabbenu Ephraim could be easily multiplied. The Mi Sheberakh regularly proclaimed for a person who has been called up to the Torah includes the sentence, "May the Holy One, blessed be He, guard him and preserve him from all trouble or sorrow and from every plague or illness, and bestow blessing and success upon all his activities"; Yekum Purkan[54] opens with the wish, "May there issue from Heaven redemption, grace, kindness, mercy, long life, ample sustenance, divine support, and supernal light," as well as vibrant and Torah-studying children, for the leaders and the members of the community; and the *Mahzor Vitry* records the practice of reciting, during Minhah on Shabbat, a series of prayers, each beginning with the words *yehi ratzon* ("may it be Thy will"), that express hopes that God may "have mercy upon our remnant and avert from us any destroyer or plague" or pity and redeem "our brethren who are impounded in trouble or captivity."[55]

Possibly, Rabbenu Ephraim fastened upon Ha-Rahaman for evidence rather than upon these instances because of a point cited in their defense by the *Sefer Ha-Ittim*. While himself critical of reciting either Yekum Purkan or Mi Sheberakh, he records that apologists have contended that the rabbis only proscribed prayers that can be regarded as fixed institutions, "but things that are incidental, such as these which these [hazanim] practice, are permitted."[56] This license may very well not apply to Ha-Rahaman, regularly recited as part of Birkat Ha-Mazon. Yet even this is not necessarily relevant to Rav Yehudah's question. The passages I have mentioned, Ha-Rahaman included, all express hopes rather than pleas. While perhaps ultimately petitional in purpose, they are purely optative in tone and form. The point Rav Yehudah raised, however, concerned a truly suppliant prayer; and any comparison is obviously open to challenge.

The general scope of the prohibition, although not Rav Yehudah's specific problem, may be further clarified by another distinction between the Shemoneh Esreh and other prayers. Rav Yehudah clearly assumed the license of standardization applied to the Shemoneh Esreh no less than to other texts. It was for this reason, it may be recalled, that he set his mind at ease concerning the concluding *berakhah* of Sim Shalom.[57] However, one can readily make a distinction. Birkat Ha-Mazon, for instance, may contain petitional lines, but its essence is clearly praise and thanksgiving. The Torah defines the *mizvah* as "blessing" God, and it is to this end that Birkat Ha-Mazon is overwhelmingly devoted. Hence, it does not, as a unit, pose any problem on Shabbat. Of course, were an individual, out of genuine financial concern, to interweave pleas for economic succor, he would violate the prohibition against "demanding one's needs." However, if he is routinely reciting a standard text, there is no violation, inasmuch as neither the overall stance nor any of the particular statements bespeak distress. As regards the Shemoneh Esreh, however, distress and outcry are the core. Anguish is its middle name. It is, quintessentially, "a prayer of the afflicted when he breaks down and before the Lord pours out his plaint."[58] Plea is the fundamental stance – again, not because the urge cannot be resisted, but as the *mizvah*'s normative essence. As regards Shabbat, therefore, the fact that the petitions of the Shemoneh Esreh are standard texts may be to no avail. Uttered in a pleading stance, they are, *ipso facto*, full-blooded pleas. If one enunciates them by rote, as we frequently do, he has not just sloughed over an embarrassing line but neglected his central duty. To avoid the Shabbat problem by recommending routine reading would be to mandate failure. In this case, revision of the texts was the only alternative.[59]

This point emerges quite clearly from the fullest single treatment by a Rishon of the Yerushalmi's prohibition. It occurs in the concluding chapter of *Magen Avot*, a small work written by the Meiri in defense of Provençal customs against criticisms leveled by students of the Ramban. One of their targets was the practice of saying Avinu Malkeinu (a series of pleas, each beginning "Our Father, our King") on the Shabbat between Rosh Hashanah and Yom Kippur. "They cry out against us," writes the Meiri, "[asking,] How do you pray on Shabbat prayers demanding a person's needs, since Shabbat was not ordained for prayer of demanding needs but for prayer of praise and thanksgiving or the sanctification of the Shabbat day and its remembrance?"

In defense, he advances three contentions. First, the High Holiday period is an exception. Second, public needs are different; and many Geonim "sanction the mention of public needs in prayer even on Shabbat."[60] Third, the crucial factor is the overall character of a prayer. In this case, "Everything is incidental to the essential point, which is repentance, submission of the will, total commitment to God, and praise and thanksgiving." As a basis for his last position, he cites the Yerushalmi's reply concerning standard texts; and he argues, further, that it explains the inclusion of numerous petitions in the Ha-Rahaman at the end of Birkat Ha-Mazon – precisely the point raised by Rabbenu Ephraim. It would be inconceivable, in contrast, to present such petitions in the form or context of the *berakhot* of "the Shemoneh Esreh, all of which are primarily directed at demanding needs and were instituted for that purpose."[61] Consequently, he concludes, the practice of reciting Avinu Malkeinu on Shabbat may be upheld even if the inclusion of the identical phrases in the Shemoneh Esreh were to be categorically rejected.

The Meiri's formulation speaks for itself. I would merely add that even his critics might very well acknowledge his principle, rejecting only its specific application. That application does, in fact, pose some difficulty. Even a cursory reading of Avinu Malkeinu reveals that it is primarily devoted to petition – much of it to anguished petition. It is perhaps noteworthy that, in his final comment, the Meiri verges on falling back upon a largely contextual approach: "This custom appears proper and acceptable to us. We see no trace of violation in it – and 'God desires the heart.'"[62] The concluding citation seems to reflect a concession that, on the basis of formal criteria, Shabbat recitation of Avinu Malkeinu is perhaps indefensible after all. It can only be saved by recourse to a more tenuous contextual criterion. Such an approach points in the general direction of the *Ohel Mo'ed*, only with an added twist. Overall posture substitutes for specific content as the definitive factor. One still draws a line between homocentric and theocentric petitions; but the issue is not so much subject-matter as a spiritual focus – the welfare of man or the service of God. Barring this approach, however, Avinu Malkeinu could be banned even if we recognized the previous distinction between, say, Birkat Ha-Mazon and the Shemoneh Esreh. It is, therefore, entirely possible that the Ramban's disciples, too, may have subscribed to this distinction in principle.

On an admittedly conjectural plane, one may detect a trace of this position in the Rambam. In discussing the addenda following the Shemoneh Esreh, he indicates that Nefillat Appayim is omitted on Shabbat and Yom Tov.[63] This is nowhere explicitly mentioned in the gemara. Rishonim noted, however, that it was clearly implicit in the account of the celebrated incident involving Rabbi Eliezer and his wife, recorded in Bava Metzia.[64] The reason seems fairly obvious. Defined as Tahanunim,[65] i.e., "pleas," Nefillat Appayim is clearly out of court on Shabbat. One is puzzled, however, by a comment the Rambam makes later in the same Halakhah. "And Kedushah and Tahanunim" – he is referring to Uva le-Tziyyon – "are not said after the Shaharit prayer as on other days, but one says it before the Minhah prayer."[66] This is familiar, as it corresponds with our present practice. The question is obvious, however. If Uva Le-Tziyyon is proscribed as Tahanunim, why is it said at Minhah? And if not – being, let us say, less plaintive than the Tahanun said during Nefillat Appayim – why shift its position?

In light of the Meiri's distinction, a possible solution suggests itself. The Tahanunim following the Shemoneh Esreh are, in effect, an extension of it. They may be said differently – while sitting and with no *berakhah* form, for instance – and are not an integral part of the Shemoneh Esreh in quite the same sense as those added before the *mitpallel* has "uprooted his legs." Nevertheless, they are part of a single complex.[67] Before the Shemoneh Esreh, however, Uva le-Tziyyon serves in a wholly different capacity. Like Ashrei it helps set the stage for the Shemoneh Esreh, without being an integral part of it.[68] Hence, the same pleas that could not be presented on Shabbat after Shaharit – the license of "standard text" not being applicable to the Shemoneh Esreh or its extension – could be recited as a prelude to Minhah.

We have encountered, then, several theoretical modes to resolve or modify the antithesis between Shabbat and petitions: (1) Only extraordinary crisis-induced outcries are prohibited. (2) Standard texts are permissible. Given these views, regular weekday prayer (with adequate provision for mention of the day's uniqueness) would originally have been permissible but unnecessary – although now that Hazal have composed different *tefillot* for Shabbat, one should, optimally and initially, observe their precept. Others have suggested that pleas for (3) spiritual or (4) communal needs are permissible, in which case much of weekday prayer remains objectionable; still others, that (5) incidental petition was licit; while (6) the Rabad insists that there can be no reconciliation. We now turn to examine the Shabbat prayers, considering these positions – all but the first two, for which there is no problem – inductively, in the light of what we actually say.

The primary touchstone is clearly the Shemoneh Esreh, especially the core of the middle *berakhah*, the concluding paragraph common to every Shabbat Shemoneh Esreh.

The paragraph opens with a vocative address, "Our God, and the God of our fathers," followed by a series of summary pleas: "Favor[69] our rest; sanctify us through Thy commandments, and place our portion in Thy Torah; sate us with Thy bounty, and rejoice us with Thy salvation; and purify our heart to serve Thee in truth." It draws to a close by returning, this time more fully, to the theme of Shabbat: "And endow us, Lord our God, in love and favor, with the Shabbat of Thy holiness, and Israel, who hallow Thy name, shall rest[70] upon it." Finally, the *berakhah* concludes in the standard form: "Blessed art Thou, O Lord, who sanctifies the Shabbat."

On the face of it, this is petition pure and simple. It is hardly surprising that the gemara in Pesahim explicitly describes the passage as *rahami*, "mercy-pleas."[71] One is at a loss to understand it in light of the Rabad's position – and vice-versa. I can only suggest that for the Rabad, petition is defined by a psychological, rather than a grammatical, mood. A statement may be in the imperative and yet, for halakhic purposes, constitute neither a plea nor a demand. These are molded by tone and timbre, with urgency and persistence the critical factors. Given a measure of detachment, even apparent petitions may be defused to the point of being considered, in effect, "praise and thanksgiving."

Support for this distinction might be drawn from an analogue – again the last unit of the Shemoneh Esreh. Its three *berakhot*, too, should contain no petition; and yet it opens with an imperative – in fact, with the very same word, *retzei* ("favor"), as our *berakhah*. Evidently the form does not, *ipso facto*, constitute halakhic petition. Moreover, in daily prayer, the character of this distinction is accented by the proximity of Retzei to its immediate predecessor, Shema Koleinu ("hear our voice"). The latter, a comprehensive plea for acceptance of our prayers and response to them, would seem to render superfluous the opening of Retzei – "Favor, Lord our God, Thy people Israel and its prayer." Obviously, however, Hazal saw no redundancy – nor is there any. While their specific contents overlap, the tone and spirit of the respective *berakhot* differ markedly. As part of the petitional core of the Shemoneh Esreh, Shema Koleinu presents a plea that is not only fuller but incomparably more urgent than its counterpart in Retzei: "Hear our voice, Lord our God, pity and have mercy upon us, and accept our prayer with mercy and favor. For Thou art God, who hearkens to prayers and pleas, and do not, O our King, return us from Thee empty-handed."

Never is the *mitpallel* more on his figurative hands and knees than in these lines. It comes as no surprise that they figure prominently in Selihot or that any variety of pleas may be appended to them.[72] Retzei, by contrast, is pervaded by a recessional aura. It is the statement of a votary, who, in the process of gracious withdrawal, retrospectively regards his offering and expresses the desire – both hope and plea – that it will be favorably received. The suppliant-turned-observer mops his brow and, psychologically speaking, begins to tiptoe backward. As he proceeds, hope and plea turn into conviction, and he thanks God for favors past, present, and future – for the hearing accorded previous prayers and the anticipated fulfillment of this one. In this context, the use of the imperative form is consistent with a prevalently optative and appreciative mood. Grammar aside, the dominant motif is gratitude.

We have here, therefore, an apparent parallel for the Rabad's conception of Shabbat prayer: the substance of thanksgiving couched in the language of demand. And yet, the analogy is open to challenge. There is nothing recessional about the Retzei of the Shabbat Shemoneh Esreh. Coming at the middle rather than toward the conclusion of prayer, it seems more petition than either implicit gratitude or yearning for acceptance. Furthermore, the character of the *berakhah* is underscored by the catalogue of pleas incorporated within it. Comparison with the final *berakhot* of the Shemoneh Esreh consequently offers only minimal support for the Rabad's position, and one must still contend with the gemara in Pesahim. In the final analysis, therefore, his position remains puzzling.

With respect to the other Rishonim, the problem is less severe. The desiderata requested are obviously of a spiritual character. Even the terms *tuvekha* ("Thy bounty") and *yeshuatekha* ("Thy salvation"), which admittedly sometimes refer to material goods, appear to me to have here, as they often do in Tanakh, clear spiritual import.[73] Given the *Ohel Mo'ed's* position that all spiritual petitions are permissible, the text poses no problem at all.[74] It can likewise be readily understood in light of Rav Asher of Lunel's view. While he rejected even petitions for penitence and forgiveness, only sanctioning a plea for wisdom, it seems clear that our passage is comparable to the latter. The difference between asking for wisdom and asking for penitence is presumably that we ordinarily ask for the first within a perfectly lucid and stable context, but implore for the second against a background of sin, anguish, and remorse. One plea is the corollary of healthy-mindedness, the other an outgrowth of soul-sickness. Without question, the petitions presented in our passage resemble the quest for intelligence far more than the drive for repentance. They all grow out of an aspiration to soar aloft rather than a desire to escape the lower depths.

On Rashi's view, that even the plea for wisdom is proscribed in the Shemoneh Esreh, however, we evidently do have a problem. What, after all, is the distinction between "Place our portion in Thy Torah" and "Vouchsafe us from Thee wisdom, understanding, and insight"? Textually and thematically, hardly enough to matter. Contextually, however, there is an important difference. The latter is the core of an independent *berakhah* specifically devoted to pleading for wisdom. The former is incorporated within a *berakhah* celebrating Shabbat and expressing the hope that God may regard our observance of it graciously and provide us with the wherewithal for its full realization. During the week, intelligence *per se* is solicited, the attention of the petitioner riveted upon his intellectual needs. On Shabbat, we ask for Torah – or bounty or salvation – as a vehicle for fulfilling the day. In the one case, the focus of our plea is reason – or repentance or redemption or justice. In the other case, it is Shabbat. For Rashi, this distinction may very well be decisive. Even if all petitions be prohibited on Shabbat, it seems inconceivable that we should be enjoined from pleading for the acceptance of our proffered rest or the bestowal of means for its optimal attainment. When petition becomes part of our striving for Shabbat, it can hardly be proscribed as an obstacle to its observance.

On Shabbat, then, we do not escape either the state or the sense of need. That would deny our creaturely humanity. We do, however, reorient our needs. As regards prayer, they are reduced to one: Shabbat. We plead for nothing else. The central plea has many tributaries, but we ply them only from the perspective of the main stream. Striving through prayer toward maximal realization of the day's sanctity, we thus assert both our weakness and our strength – the inability to go it alone, and the capacity for spiritual flight.

Notes

1. See Shabbat 24b, Rashi, s.v. *mishum*.
2. All prayer must be verbal. Whether it must be oral is a matter of dispute, however; see Berakhot 20b and *Magen Avraham* 101:2.
3. S.v. *yesader.* This also seems to have been the Rambam's interpretation; see Hilkhot *Tefillah* 1:2. In *Siddur Rashi*, however, the praise is taken as referring to Pesukei de-Zimra; see 6, p. 6. This was the prevalent view among the Geonim; see *Otzar Ha-Geonim*, Berakhot, pp. 76–77.
4. Avodah Zarah 7b.
5. Shabbat 119b. Interestingly, the *Orhot Hayyim* (Erev Shabbat, 10; p. 136) was somewhat scandalized by the literal sense of the passage and attempted to reinterpret it.
6. Ta'anit 3:7, 19a. The mishnah uses the term *matri'in*, literally "sound forth," which, as in the Tanakh, could refer to either verbal or instrumental exclamation (i.e., through blowing shofar). The gemara considers both alternatives but concludes that prayer must be intended; see Ta'anit 14a.
7. Ibid.
8. Hilkhot Shabbat 30:12. The Rambam goes on to list the exceptions cited in the mishnah. Whether

he accepted Rabbi Yose's or the preceding position is problematic, however. Cf. his commentary on the mishnah here and the other references in Mishneh Torah, Hilkhot Shabbat 2:24, Hilkhot Ta'aniyot 1:6, and Hilkhot Hagigah 3:7. See also *Lehem Mishneh*, Ta'aniyot 1:1 and 1:6.

9. Siddur Rav Saadia Gaon, p. 46.

10. Ibid., pp. 61–63.

11. Shabbat 15:3, 78b.

12. Extant texts of the Yerushalmi only include the two phrases cited, and the passage is quoted in this form by the *Or Zaru'a*, II, 89:7. However, some Rishonim quote it as including the phrase "feed us," which appears in our text; see, e.g., Tosafot, Berakhot 48b, s.v. *mathil*, and *Roke'ah*, 337. I do not know whether they had a variant reading or adapted the Yerushalmi's question to their own version of Birkat Ha-Mazon. The Rambam's text of the latter omits the whole sequence; but inasmuch as it seems to derive from no other "standard text," Hazal evidently did recite it.

13. Hagigah 3:7. The convocation was held on the Temple Mount once every seven years during Sukkot; see Devarim 31:10–13. It should be noted that the prayers involved, while not crisis-induced, were both public and, by dint of the rarity of the occasion, quite special.

   Other Rishonim gave different reasons for the postponement. See Rabad, ad loc., and Rashi, Megillah 5a, s.v. *va-hagigah*.

14. In the practice of the Rishonim, only Mizmor Shir le-Yom Ha-Shabbat, at most, was recited.

15. E-l Adon is an exception, but a minor one.

16. Berakhot 21a.

17. *Siddur Rashi* 515, pp. 257–258. The fourteenth-century Provençal compendium, *Orhot Hayyim*, cites, without ascription, the reasons adduced in the Bavli and the Yerushalmi, as alternative interpretations: "And we do not petition for needs on Shabbat, lest one be saddened then, and it is forbidden for a person to be sad on [Shabbat]. And some say that we do not recite them [petitions] because of imposition upon the public." *Seder Tefillat Erev Shabbat*, 1.

18. See Shabbat 12a.

19. *Teshuvot Ha-Rambam*, ed. J. Blau, 208, pp. 369–370.

20. This was also clearly assumed by Tosafot, Berakhot 26b, s.v. *ta'ah*. See also the eighteenth-century *She'eylot U-Teshuvot Shevut Yaakov* 3:31, who, in the course of a discussion concerning the issue raised by a number of Aharonim, as to whether *Kiddush Ha-Levanah* may be recited on Friday night, likewise rejects the Yerushalmi's prohibition of Shabbat petitions. In doing so, he cites, *inter alia*, another passage from the Yerushalmi, from which it would appear that Musaf consists of the recitation of the full text of the Shemoneh Esreh, with the added insertion of a passage concerning Shabbat, and not, as is our custom, of a wholly different text of seven *berakhot*. However, Tosafot, Berakhot 21b, s.v. *ad*, understood this passage as only referring to the weekday Musaf, such as that of Rosh Hodesh or Hol Hamo'ed.

21. See Berakhot 21a and 31a and Rishonim, ad loc. The question of the relation of duty to prayer and the possibility of voluntary prayer require much fuller discussion in their own right. They touch upon the issue of freedom and formalism in prayer, which, in turn, has implications for

other areas of Halakhah. These lie beyond my immediate scope, however. Here I would only point out that in the case at hand, the *mitpallel* must break off and cannot continue even if he should add an original element. Inasmuch as he began his Shemoneh Esreh as a mandatory prayer, most Rishonim hold that he cannot alter its character in midstream. See *Otzar Ha-Geonim*, Berakhot, p. 51; *Rif*, Berakhot 21a and the comment of *Talmidei Rabbenu Yonah* thereon; but cf. *Hiddushei Rabbenu Hayyim Halevi, Tefillah* 10:6.

22. This interpretation is only feasible according to the standard text of the gemara, which states that on Shabbat, *gavra bar hiyuva*, "the person is under obligation," but is relieved of it out of deference to Shabbat. However, the Rif and several other Rishonim read *dibedin hu d'iboye lei letzeluye shemoneh esreh*, "that, by right, he ought to have prayed eighteen." This shifts the focus from the general status of the *mitpallel* to the specific situation at hand; and it would seem to render the interpretation I have suggested inadmissible. Rav Hai, who may, however, be paraphrasing rather than quoting, has *demin dina bar hova hu*, "that by right he is under obligation," which would also preclude my suggestion; see *Otzar Ha-Geonim*, loc. cit.

23. See Megillah 23a.

24. Hilkhot Shabbat 11, p. 39.

25. See Berakhot 21a.

26. *Hassagot* on the Rambam, *Tefillah* 1:9. To the best of my knowledge, there is no source for the proviso regarding a pause. Its rationale may be grounded in the need for an innovation that would require a fresh approach and the opportunity to collect one's thoughts anew. It may also derive from a sense that if one arrogates to himself the right and the distinction of additional prayer, he should be doubly sure of his spiritual footing. Emulation of the "early hasidim" who paused at length before prayer (see Berakhot 30b) would be a good start. Cf. the Rosh's comment that one should only undertake voluntary prayer if fully confident of maximal concentration. Otherwise, one is subject to the strictures of the *pasuk* in Yeshayahu 1:11, "To what purpose is the multitude of your sacrifices unto Me?" See his *Teshuvot* 4:13.

27. These are the opening words of Tehillim 100.

28. See Rashi's commentary on Tehillim 100:1.

29. Only such sacrifices would be offered on Shabbat; see Temurah 14a.

30. Tehillim 56:13.

31. I.e., in the plural.

32. The midrash is quoted, with minor variations, from *Midrash Shohar Tov*, Psalm 100; Buber's ed. p. 426. Cf. Psalm 56; p. 295.

33. *Shibbolei Ha-Leket*, 76; p. 55.

34. E.g., Rav Hai Gaon, in *Otzar Ha-Geonim*, Berakhot, pp. 50–51; Rif, Berakhot 21a; Rambam, *Tefillah* 1:9.

35. E.g., "one of the Geonim" cited by the Rambam, loc. cit.; a view cited by the Rosh, Berakhot 3: 15. It might be noted that *Talmidei Rabbenu Yonah*, on the other hand, accepted the Rabad's basic premise but held that his conclusion may possibly be rejected "because, inasmuch as it [Shabbat prayer] was instituted vis-à-vis the prayer of the Shemoneh Esreh, which is a plea,

with respect to this [question], we treat it as a plea." Commentary on the Rif, Berakhot 21a, s.v. *ve-yesh*.

36. *Netivot Olam*, Netiv Ha-Avodah, chap. 2. Cf. Rav Saadia's preface to his Siddur, p. 9. The emphasis upon petition in prayer runs counter to a powerful and historically persistent philosophic current which has often rejected petition as either futile or self-centered. It is, however, from time immemorial, grounded in human experience; and it is clearly fundamental to Jewish thought, which is less interested in having us play the idealistic, self-sacrificing hero than in our recognizing the limits of our existential situation and responding to them. So long as a man wants and needs to live, he must, in honesty and humility, place petition at the heart of his prayers.

37. *Sha'ar Ha-Shabbat* 1:4; p. 38b.

38. See Yeshayahu 58:13, Shabbat 150–151, and Bezah 36b.

39. Berakhot 5:2; p. 39b. The implicit equation is even more strongly suggested by a variant reading cited by the Rashba. The standard text reads *la'assot melakhah* and *litvo'a tzerakhav* for the respective prohibitions. The Rashba, however, cites *la'asot hafazav* and *litvo'a hafazav*, i.e., to be engaged in or to press his affairs, respectively; see his *Teshuvot* 1:739. Cf. also Rav Yizhak ibn Giyyat, *Sha'arei Simhah*, p. 17a.

40. Tehillim 119:164. The midrash evidently stresses the definite article included in *ba-yom*, "on the day," as the basis for referring the *pasuk* to Shabbat. This view was also assumed by the *Mahzor Vitry* 134. p. 106. The more common interpretation, however, is "seven times daily." In this sense, it was cited by the Yerushalmi (Berakhot 1:5; p. 9a), often cited by Rishonim, as a hint of the number of *berakhot* recited daily in conjunction with the Shema.

41. Shemot 20:8.

42. *Midrash Tanhuma*, Vayera 1. This segment does not appear in Buber's edition.

It might be added that a statement by Rav Hai Gaon in a responsum suggests a third interpretation. After quoting the gemara concerning the reduction from eighteen to seven *berakhot* out of deference to Shabbat, he concludes: "And we do not ask for *hol* [secular and/or weekday] matters that are needed for *hol* [the weekdays] on Shabbat." *Otzar Ha-Geonim*, Berakhot 21a, p. 51. This sequence appears to assume the *Sefer Ha-Manhig*'s interpretation of the gemara. The passage also seems to follow the general thrust of the *Ohel Mo'ed*'s position – but with a difference. Rav Hai emphasizes the fact that one is anticipating his weekday needs, which it is forbidden to prepare on Shabbat, as much as the secular content of his prayer. However, inasmuch as this view is barely hinted at, and the term *hol* is a bit ambiguous, I have not treated it as a full-blown alternative interpretation.

43. *Sha'ar Ha-Shabbat* 1:4; p. 38b. The example cited is the second petitional *berakhah* of the weekday Shemoneh Esreh.

44. *Siddur Rashi* 515, p. 258; *Mahzor Vitry* 140; p. 110.

45. The *Ohel Mo'ed* does cite the Yerushalmi's conclusion, however.

46. Cited in *Tosafot Rav Yehudah Hasid* (= Tosafot Rav Yehudah Sir Leon, according to Rabbi M.Y. Blau, *Shitot Rishonim* on Bava Metzia, introduction), in *Berakhah Meshuleshet*, Berakhot 48b. s.v. *uve-shabbat*. Cf. Tosafot, Berakhot 48b, s.v. *mat'hil*. The view that *nahem* or *nahamenu* should

supplant *rahem* on Shabbat was held by many Rishonim, and is most prominently identified with the Rif, Berakhot 48b. However, the Rif does not explain the change; and it is possible that it is grounded upon a positive desire to seek comfort rather than upon any prohibition against pleading for pity. See also *Be'urei Ha-Gra,* Orah Hayyim 188:4, where the Gaon of Vilna suggests a kabbalistic basis for the distinction.

47. Loc. cit.

48. Quoted by the Rosh, Berakhot 3:17.

49. Hiddushei Ha-Meiri, Berakhot 21a.

50. Berakhot 5:2, p. 39b. Cf. *Bayit Hadash* on *Tur,* Orah Hayyim 268. See Berakhot 17a.

51. *Or Zarua,* II, 89:3.

52. These were probably two separate petitions, each beginning, like many others widely recited at the conclusion of Birkat Ha-Mazon today, with the formula "May the All-merciful . . ."

53. Loc. cit.

54. An Aramaic prayer, presumably dating from the Geonic period. It is recited between the Keriat ha-Torah and Musaf

55. *Mahzor Vitry* 199, p. 179. This series, with some variations, is recited to this day, but only on Monday and Thursday mornings. One variant is particularly noteworthy. In our version, the last paragraph ("Our brethren...") is written in the third person. In the *Mahzor Vitry*'s version, it is addressed to these brethren, the second-person *aleikhem* substituting for *aleihem,* and thus assumes a radically different interpersonal character.

56. Sefer Ha-Ittim, p. 280.

57. It might be noted that at least one later authority assumed likewise. The author of *Penei Mosheh,* in his standard commentary upon the Yerushalmi, explains that its prohibition against Shabbat petitions refers to personal increments added at the conclusion of the Shemoneh Esreh; see Shabbat 15:3. He evidently considered recitation of the main body permissible, presumably because it is a standard text. Of course, on this view, any discussion of the problem of Shabbat petition becomes, in practical terms, much less relevant.

58. Tehillim 102:1.

59. This distinction applies most readily to the middle portion of the Shemoneh Esreh. The status of the first three and last three *berakhot,* defined, respectively, as praise and thanksgiving, might be argued. They could conceivably be compared to Birkat Ha-Mazon and the like; or it may be contended that all of the Shemoneh Esreh should be regarded as an integral complex. The fundamental stance of the *mitpallel* is that of a petitioner throughout. Even segments which do not plead explicitly are part of an overall entreaty and help to frame the pleas. However, these *berakhot* pose no specific Shabbat problem in any case, as one is generally forbidden to "demand his needs" in these sections even on weekdays; see Berakhot 34a. The definition of the phrase, however, may vary with regard to the respective injunctions. Be this as it may, Rav Yehudah's specific question concerning *E-lohai nezor* remains untouched by this distinction, as such increments are defined as *tahanunim* ("mercy-pleas"); see Berakhot 29b and 31a.

60. As formulated by the Meiri, this dispensation applies even to the Shemoneh Esreh. However,

I am aware of no source in the Geonim for such license. Many of them distinguish between private and public needs with respect to the prohibition against petitions in the first and last three *berakhot* of the Shemoneh Esreh; and it was on this basis that they sanctioned the inserts we add during Asseret Yemei Teshuvah (see *Otzar Ha-Geonim*, Berakhot, pp. 80–82). There is, however, a great difference between that prohibition and the ban against Shabbat petitions, simply because their grounds are radically different. The former is based on the implied arrogance in pushing one's demands before paying due homage or without expressing proper appreciation. Hence, the fact that one pleads for communal rather than personal needs may be very material. The latter, however, derives from the inherent dissonance of the themes with the day's mood, a factor essentially untouched by the public character of the plea. While this undercuts the first *issur*, it can at most only override the second. The Meiri first cites the Geonic view concerning the first and last three *berakhot* and then continues with the line I have quoted, possibly arguing from one to the other. Any such analogy would present a problem, however; and he does seem to be citing a dispensation regarding Shabbat specifically.

It is true that the Geonim sanctioned inserting the High Holiday increments even on Shabbat. However, this could be explained by the exceptional nature of the period – the Meiri's first point – and provides no basis for an independent argument. Perhaps the Meiri was relying upon the example set by Rav Saadia's widely accepted prayer, as well as upon those of other *paytanim*, as constituting, in effect, a geonic source for the distinction. As I have already indicated, however, Rav Saadia may well have approached the whole problem differently, in a way that might leave a crisis-oriented Avinu Malkeinu very much under a cloud.

The exception of public needs raises an obvious question: all of the Shemoneh Esreh deals with them and should therefore be permitted. The Meiri goes on to consider this objection, arguing, in effect, that the Shemoneh Esreh is primarily a private plea in plural form, whereas Avinu Malkeinu is a genuinely public petition.

61. *Magen Avot* (Jerusalem, 1958), chap. 24, pp. 157–158.
62. Loc. cit. The concluding quotation is from Sanhedrin 106b.
63. See Hilkhot *Tefillah* 9:13.
64. See Bava Metzia 59b and *Hiddushei Ha-Ritva* ad loc.
65. See Mishneh Torah, Hilkhot *Tefillah* 9:5–6.
66. Ibid. 9:13.
67. This relation is suggested by the view of many Rishonim that, as the *Orhot Hayyim* put it, "One should not talk between *tefillah* and *tehinnah* as it is all like one long *tefillah*" (quoted in *Bet Yosef*, Orah Hayyim 131; I have been unable to find this in the original). This statement refers to Nefillat Appayim and not to Uva le-Tziyyon. However, given the Rambam's description of the latter, the same principle may apply, even if this particular detail – which the Rambam does not mention – may also be indicative of this relation, although admittedly some Rishonim explained it otherwise.
68. See Berakhot 31a, Tosafot, s.v. *rabbanan*.
69. The opening verb, *retzei*, translated here as "favor," has multiple meanings. The most literal is

"desire" – clearly inadmissible, in its narrow sense, with reference to God. With reference to worship, the word generally denotes acceptance with grace. It is most frequently applied to sacrifice; and, with respect to prayer, usually in contexts in which its relation to sacrifice is emphasized.

70. The future form, *ve-yanuhu,* has both optative and indicative meaning.

71. Pesahim 117b.

72. See Berakhot 31a.

73. See, e.g., for *tuv*: Shemot 33:19; Tehillim 27:13, 31:20, 65:5; for *yeshuah*: Yeshayahu 12:2, 33:6; Tehillim 3:3, 62:2, 119:155, 166, 174. *Yeshuah* has far stronger materialist overtones, connoting personal survival or social and political regeneration, than the corresponding English term "salvation." In Christian contexts particularly, the latter has a far narrower scope.

74. A suggestion that this passage was intended as a summary of the usual weekday petitions strikes me as ingenious but nevertheless wrong as regards primary denotation. At the level of overtone and allusion, however, the parallel is suggestive. See Yaakov Rothschild, "*Tefillot* Sheva shel Yom Ha-Shabbat," in *Tefillah,* ed. H. Hamiel, *Ma'ayanot* 8 (Jerusalem, 1964), p. 183.

Chapter 7

Thoughts About Shemittah

As is the case whenever the seventh year rolls around, people are preoccupied with the subject of shemittah. Books about it are being published,
we are almost inundated with articles, and lecturers throughout Israel are
giving talks on shemittah. All these authors and lecturers, whether discussing the relevant laws or explaining the reasons for the *mizvot* involved or
developing some philosophical aspect of the topic, are toiling for the sake
of Torah, and they are to be encouraged. But the true nature of shemittah
remains a deep secret. The simple fact is that the shemittah year of 5733
constitutes a halakhic tragedy. It is not pleasant to hear this – and even less
pleasant to say it – but it is the cold, bitter truth, and there is no escaping
it except through deception.

But, you ask, what does it mean to call something a halakhic tragedy?
You spend most of your time studying Halakhah, and once in a while I lecture to you about tragedies of different kinds, but you still don't understand
the nature of this hybrid. In order to explain what I mean, I will have to
say a few words about tragic thought – or, to be more precise, about the
tragic viewpoint in general.

Mundane reality may be looked at in countless ways. Every thinking
person has his own viewpoint, but basically there are two fundamental

This article originally appeared in Hebrew in *Alon Shevut* during the shemittah year
of 5733 (1972–73), and was translated with a postscript for the Yeshivat Har Etzion
dinner journal in 5754 (1994).

viewpoints – the lyrical and the tragic. The lyrical viewpoint is, first and foremost, uniform. The lyric poet, with the clarity of his perception, expresses an experience clearly and fully. He looks in only one direction, and even if he does see a variegated reality, it is likely to be harmonious. He tends to see the universe as an organic whole, with light flooding it from one end to the other, and with a comprehensive purpose activating it. Most likely, although this is not essential, his view is optimistic. But that is not the main point. The central point is that the experience is treated as having a clear nature, and thus the requisite response is also unambiguous. Again, this is not because the poet is unaware of the existence of contradictory phenomena. A sonnet saturated with youthful love may be followed by a plaintive elegy. Yesterday we feasted with the winners, and today we will mourn with the losers – but not at the same time. According to the lyrical conception, every poem is separate. And poetry reflects a reality that is not seen as full of conflicts and contradictions, but as uniform, or, at most, composed of parallel tracks and separate compartments.

In contrast, the experience of conflict and contradiction constitutes the focus of the tragic view. Ruin and loss – the popular sense of tragedy – are no more than the outcome of a process accompanied throughout by a tragic undercurrent: a torn, divided life in which the individual is influenced by a variety of factors and simultaneously has to face conflicting demands. It is drama that constitutes the natural expression of tragedy, as tragedy deals mainly with divisiveness and struggle, whether internal or external; and this confrontation is the cornerstone of the dramatic work. The tragic poet, for his part, does not emphasize the unity of reality. He sees it somewhere far-off, as a sublime but distant goal; but the immediate daily life he deals with is characterized by conflict. To the extent that the tragic poet or thinker confronts people as they really are, he sees them as divided beings, with contradictory aspirations and conflicting emotions. Each makes its claims on the individual's resources, and adjudicating these demands is a task not easily accomplished. In short, the tragic view sees life as a continual dialectical play, an arena of confrontation and controversy.

This dialectal process may – indeed, must – lead to personal growth and development, but along the way it claims its victims. Some of them are human beings, others are values. Unfortunately, the *mizvah* of shemittah is one of its victims. Obviously, the subject of shemittah is first and foremost a body of Halakhah covering several areas: prohibitions on work and the obligation to refrain from work, and thus analogous to those imposed by Shabbat; prohibitions regarding consumption of, and trade in, sabbatical produce, analogous to those affecting forbidden foods; acts befitting objects of *kedushah* and processing of the produce, as with *terumah* and *ma'aser sheni*. But the halakhic rules regarding shemittah reflect a multitude of values and serve to inculcate them in the body politic of *K'lal Yisrael*.

There is no need to investigate the purpose and intent of the *mizvot* related to shemittah; they are plain to see. At least three strains may be distinguished. As with the weekly Shabbat, the "Sabbath of the land" instills an awareness of God's absolute and exclusive ownership of the land and His authority over it. On the other hand, it liberates farmers from the drudgery of everyday chores in order to afford them time for the contemplation of eternal issues. It clips man's wings, yet enables him to fly. Third, it has a clear democratic strain; it provides equality for great and small. Where its produce is concerned, there are no rich and no poor ("Let the needy among your people eat of it"; Shemot 23:10); it all but elides the difference between man and beast ("and what they leave, let the wild beasts eat"; ibid.). The entire universe is invited to eat at the heavenly table ("but you may eat whatever the land will produce during its sabbath – you, your male and female slaves, the hired and bound laborers who live with you, and your cattle and the beasts in your land may eat of its yield"; Vayikra 25:6–7).

What remains for us today of this enchanting vision? Nothing but a hollow shell! The transition from an agricultural economy to an industrial one has taken most of the prohibitions of work off the agenda for nearly everyone. For most people, the situation is relatively convenient and also straightforward – they need not circumvent or distort the prohibitions; they are simply lucky enough not to confront them. However, as regards the prohibitions pertaining to consumption and the obligation to treat the produce of the shemittah year as *kedushah*, the situation is considerably more serious. What options are available to people who are anxious to observe the *kedushah* of shemittah with careful attention to all the details? They can rely on the legal fiction that – woe to the ears that hear this! – the fields of Eretz Yisrael, from Lebanon to Egypt and from the Mediterranean to the Jordan, have been sold or leased to non-Jews. I have no intention of questioning the halakhic validity of this sale, or the ability of a non-Jew's purchase to release the land from its *kedushah*. Let us assume that those who permitted this were correct in doing so; it is the phenomenon itself that we should examine.

Those who do not wish to rely on this *heter* have the option of going to the trouble of importing produce from abroad. If they are willing to rely on the ruling of the Bet Yosef that the *kedushah* of shemittah does not apply to produce grown by a non-Jew, even if the non-Jew's purchase cannot release the land from its *kedushah,* they may purchase produce from fields cultivated by Arabs. But what of this running to a lone fruit-and-vegetable seller in order to pay exorbitant prices for produce grown by non-Jews, when the people doing so are annoyed by the bother of the trip and the expense, on the one hand, and half-proud of themselves for their great righteousness, on the other? What has this to do with the biblical rule that "you may eat whatever the land produces during its sabbath"? Is there any recognizable connection between this (perhaps overweening) pride and the feeling of man's subservience and the Creator's supremacy that lies at the heart of the *mizvah* of shemittah, and is engendered by performing it? Among those who are punctilious about observing the prohibition on uncultivated produce, how many of them accept and live the shemittah year in simple joy, as opposed to the many who are waiting, with all but bated breath, for it to end?

I do not want to give the wrong impression; I am not criticizing those who rely on the *heter* of selling the land or the Chief Rabbinate for implementing it. If I were chief rabbi, I would most probably do the same. In practice, that is, as far as the general public is concerned, there is no viable alternative. It is true that there are a few isolated places where no agricultural labor is performed during shemittah, but these operations are successful precisely because they *are* isolated. At the moment, there is no solution on the horizon that will meet the requirements of the whole country, and there is no shemittah fund that could provide the needs of the entire state. On the other hand, I am not suggesting, God forbid, that we should ignore our halakhic obligations, however unpalatable they may seem to us. We understand our total responsibility for the fulfillment even of a *mizvah* that seems to have outlived its purpose. I insist on only one thing: that we should recognize the reality – and lament it.

The reality is that there is no practical solution that can quiet our consciences. When I am told that one of the honored rabbis of our generation demands that the people in his yeshiva rely on the *heter* in order to uproot any opposition to it in their hearts, I am absolutely amazed. While it is entirely possible to *accept* the *heter,* how can anyone *embrace* it? We take medicine – but without a *berakhah*. We must not be seduced into believing that the bone stuck in our throats is actually candy. Perhaps there is no alternative – but that is precisely the problem! That is the root of the halakhic tragedy. We are forced to choose between two values – the ideal that "the land shall have a sabbath of complete rest" (Vayikra 25:4), and the economic requirements of the state, whose existence also constitutes, to a great extent, a moral and pragmatic value. We are forced to sacrifice one for the other, but we mourn, with a divided heart, the very need to decide. We cannot fault the Chief Rabbinate for its decision, but as a result, shemittah has become a victim, and its total failure diminishes all of us.

The entire process was foreseen from the outset. Two different passages in the Torah warn us that the difficulties of observing shemittah may weaken our faith; and in both cases we have failed the test. In reference to the agricultural aspect of shemittah, the Torah warns: "And should you ask, 'What are we to eat in the seventh year, if we may neither sow nor gather in our crops?'" (Vayikra 25:20). In the end, we have been forced to rely on the *heter* of selling the land. In reference to the financial aspect of the shemittah, the Torah warns: "Beware lest you harbor the base thought, 'The seventh year, the year of remission, is approaching,' so that you are callous to your needy kinsman and give him nothing" (Devarim 15:9) – and we have recourse to the *prozbul*. Two *mizvot*, two purposes, two challenges, two tragedies.

Liberals often cite the establishment of the institution of the *prozbul* as an example of the Halakhah's ability to adapt to new circumstances. Every other day they point out Hillel's dynamic flexibility, as opposed to the supposedly fossilized conservatism of the later *poskim*. But truth will out. Anyone who considers the *prozbul* a victory worthy of celebration does not begin to understand Hillel's thinking. Do you think he was happy to circumvent a *mizvah*, even though he had all the authority in the world to do so? Did he not approach his task with a broken, despairing heart?

Hillel unfortunately found himself and his generation in a serious predicament. The Torah commands us to lend money, especially to the poor, but it also decrees that all debts must be remitted once in seven years so that everyone can start afresh; it even adds a warning that this provision should not make us unwilling to proffer loans. If Hillel's generation had been worthy, both of these goals would have been achieved. Those who needed it would have found the necessary resources, and the lenders would have learned, at least once in seven years, to relax – at least for a moment – the tight embrace in which they caress every penny as if it were the apple of their eye. But Hillel's generation was not worthy, and the possessors of wealth, who tend, like most of us, to be selective in their obedience to the warnings of the Torah, began to slam their doors in the faces of the poor.

In these urgent circumstances, faced with an ultimatum on the part of the lenders, Hillel decided – as he had, of course, full halakhic authority to do (see Gittin 36b) – that one value must be preferred over the other. Therefore, in order to prevent the lenders from shutting their doors to the borrowers, he decided to circumvent the financial aspect of the shemittah. But any sensitive student of the Halakhah can perceive how much it must have hurt him to do this. What price would Hillel not have been willing to pay in order to avoid being confronted by this cruel dilemma? He certainly did not celebrate this decision as a victory. When he observed the reality of the situation, he could have responded in only one way: "You have defeated me. Here I am, the representative of the Halakhah and of Tradition. I have succeeded in escaping the dilemma, but on another level I have been broken. Instead of preserving the *mizvah* and helping to enforce its observance, I have established a means of circumventing it."

This is our situation today, with respect to the agricultural aspect of the shemittah. In a formal sense, perhaps, all is well; but we are not fulfilling the *mizvah* of giving the land its "sabbath of complete rest." All of us – those who support and oppose the *heter* alike – are not so much observing the shemittah as avoiding its observance. I do not see any way to improve the situation in the foreseeable future. But at least, let us feel the pain of it, as Hillel did in his day. Since we have no choice, we will make use of all the *heterim* and other means of circumvention, and we will bow our heads before the sad reality. But we will not – nay! a thousands times not – make peace with it. We will admit our failure and regret it – and hope that God will provide what is missing.

POSTSCRIPT: 5754

As I reread the preceding article, three *shemittin* later, I naturally ask myself: What has changed in the interim? Very much – and very little. On the plane of consumption, the range and availability of options for those who, in some way, take shemittah into account when purchasing produce, have been radically transformed and widened. There has been an almost exponential growth of choice – in part, because of the increased sophistication of the Israeli economy, and, in particular, of its marketing sector, because of the patent upgrading of kashrut standards among the halakhically committed, in Israel as well as in the Diaspora. (Someone has remarked, quite aptly, that compared to previous generations, less kosher meat is now sold abroad, but more of what is sold is glatt; less matzah is sold, but more of what is sold is *shemurah*). And, in part, this increase is due to a heightened awareness of *shevi'it*.

Whatever the reason, the facts are clear. Twenty years ago, we had a sense of having to scrounge around. In our neighborhood of Katamon, much of whose populace is observant but not haredi, our only recourse was to several basement outlets, more hovels than stores, which peddled their meager wares at irregular hours. In some areas, the situation was better – but not in many and not by much. The overall sense was one of isolated pockets of suppliers – several stands in Mahaneh Yedudah, a number of stores in the vicinity of Geulah or Me'ah She'arim, and a few in Bayit Vegan or its counterparts – and all this in a market that was predominantly oblivious to the significance of the year, providing produce only to a stubborn minority that refused to rely on the *heter mekhirah* and thus sought out these purveyors.

Today, a relative cornucopia is within easy reach in almost every neighborhood of the city – and not just at selected greengrocers, but at numerous supermarkets. In many instances, the range of shemittah-denominated options offered by a single store is impressive. Cellophane-wrapped lettuce and cabbage grown on dirt-laden tables rather than on terra firma (not foolproof halakhically, but sanctioned by leading *poskim*) and tomatoes from the southern Aravah in the Negev (again, not beyond question, depending upon where one draws the halakhic boundaries of Eretz Yisrael, but relied upon by many) are sold alongside bountiful supplies of Arab fruits and vegetables or produce channeled through an *otzar bet din*. For us, it is absolutely painless. We phone in an order to the greengrocer in the market at *Bet Yisrael* from whom we buy regularly, and the delivery of quality produce is as prompt as in other years.

The practical benefits of this transformation are self-evident. There is, however, a spiritual profit as well. It makes it possible to follow one's halakhic conscience without the danger of lapsing into the unctuous self-righteousness, inwardly felt, that often accompanies the observance of higher religious standards at the cost of some measure of tribulation and perceived sacrifice. As opposed to a generation ago, when concern about *hadash* generally entailed storing a winter's supply of bread and hallah in freezers, the current ready availability of *yashan* products has effectively neutralized this factor with respect to one area of kashrut in the United States. The normalization of the produce supply has had a similar effect in regard to the *mizvah* of shemittah, at least in Eretz Yisrael.

So the scene has indeed changed. Moreover, to this factor may be added yet another consideration – the perception of the purchase of Arab produce, then and now. While the weight assigned to this factor is probably a function of one's political orientation, can anyone regard this option as he did before the intifada? On the other hand, the impact of an incipient peace process and its possible implications, both political and economic, also bears upon this issue.

And yet, fundamentally, relatively little has changed in regard to the halakhic tragedy of *shevi'it*. Awareness of the *mizvah* has been heightened; more and more observant Jews have been sensitized to it; and greater effort is expended in coping with the basic halakhic issues. Nevertheless, the essential reality remains. For most, shemittah exists, to the extent that it is experienced at all, more as a problem than as a value, as a *mizvah* that confronts us with the challenge to circumvent it more than with the impetus to implement it. To be sure, its impact upon producers – and I don't mean just neglected lawns – is more vivid than upon consumers; and of the latter, those who heed the view of R. Moshe di Trani (the Mabit), against that of the Bet Yosef, that the sanctity of *shevi'it* must be observed with regard to non-Jewish produce, are more affected than those who do not. And yet, the underlying fact is beyond challenge. Overwhelmingly, we have lost the vision, we have been left with an obstacle course – and that is hardly how we should strive to experience a halakhic lifestyle. Would we, for even a moment, countenance relating to our weekly Shabbat as we do to our septennial one?

In a more personal vein, what has changed – and it is at once very little and very much – is our response to the situation. I am not at all certain that I would instinctively write "Thoughts About Shemittah" today. This is not merely because, with advancing years, language becomes less malleable and precise expression more elusive, but simply because the pain is less acute. Three *shemittin* have served, if not as anesthetic, then, at least, as analgesic. It has all become so routine. From the abyss of our normalization, I look back with envy to the early years of the Yishuv, when the halakhic issues were thrashed out anew with every shemittah, in 5649 and again in 5656, when any ground was given grudgingly. I recall a time when Rav Kook's reservation, in the preface to *Shabbat Ha-Aretz*, that the *mekhirah* be confined to a critical *she'at ha-dehak,* had vital meaning.

Three *shemittin* later, that is perhaps the saddest change in this halakhic tragedy – the assuaged pain, the muted cry, the pallid response. Calling in the routinized order to the greengrocer, I – and I trust I am not alone – hear a prayer in my heart: "*Ribbono shel Olam*, אל תשליכנו מלפניך ורוח קדשך אל תקח ממני – Do not cast us out from before You, and do not remove from us Your holy spirit." Let us, at least, realize the ability to feel the loss, to commiserate with the Torah, bereft of the realization of so wondrous a *mizvah*. אל תשליכנו לעת זקנה – "Do not cast us out in our old age." Let not the passing years numb the pain or dull its expression. If we are indeed destined to be spectators – nay, in part, actors – in this halakhic tragedy, give us, at least, the power to recognize our role and to respond accordingly.

Chapter 8

Conversion: Birth and Judgment

The status of *gerut* as a subject of discussion and debate is not a recent phenomenon. For ages, indeed millennia, this topic has been implicated in a broad range of problems. Some authorities are disturbed by the option of *gerut per se*. This is especially so of those who stress the unique, inborn holiness that characterizes the Jew. To cite but a few instances, the ability of a non-Jew to convert precipitated a variety of difficulties and objections for Rabbi Yehudah Halevi, the Maharal of Prague, and the School of Habad.

Quite apart from this primary issue, however, the problems can be further subdivided. First, how is one to treat a candidate for Judaism? This question has practical consequences in determining the actual conversion process. Shall we pursue the proselyte or avoid him? Repel with the left hand while attracting with the right, or vice versa? Second, how should we relate to the *ger* after his conversion? Needless to say, the possibility of derision is out of the question; the Torah explicitly admonishes us: "And the *ger* you shall not deride nor oppress."[1] And the rabbis state: "He who derides the *ger* violates three negative commandments";[2] R. Eliezer the Great enumerates thirty-six distinct places, and according to one opinion, forty-six, where the Torah forewarns us to respect the *ger*.[3]

But beyond this, how to assess the nature of the *ger* and his integration

---

The Hebrew version of this article appeared in *Torah she-be'al Peh*, vol. 13 (5731). The English translation, prepared by Dr. Michael Berger, appeared in *Tradition* 23: 2 (1988).

into the Nation of Israel is unclear, and perhaps in dispute. Encouragement on the one hand and repulsion on the other; some esteem the *ger*, while others approach him with cautious apprehension.

However, the issue of relating to the *ger* is not the one I wish to address. My focus is on the process of *gerut,* the phenomenon in itself. If we wish to define and describe *gerut,* we will discover that its essence is in its being a turning point. The foundation of *gerut* is a radical transformation: an uprooting from one world to strike root in a different one.

This point specifically characterizes Jewish conversion and distinguishes it, historically, from parallel movements in the classical world. As Arthur Darby Nock emphasized, whereas adoption of one of the religions that dominated the Hellenistic world, such as Orphism or Mithraism, meant merely a supplement to the local tradition and not its total negation, Judaism (and, consequently, Christianity) presents conversion as a total metamorphosis. The *ger* is compelled to abandon his past background and enter the realm of his future, for commitment to Judaism is based on Elijah's question: "How much longer will you oscillate, wavering between two options?"[4] In the words of Nock, conversion demands "renunciation and a new beginning. What was required was not merely the acceptance of ritual, but rather a willful attachment to a theology; in a word, faith: a new life in a new nation."[5]

This should not cause surprise. *Gerut,* after all, embodies, nay constitutes, the forging of a covenant that is, by its very nature, exclusive: "...And the two of them made a covenant"[6] – to the exclusion of others. Nonetheless, the question still arises: What type of turning point? How does it take effect, and in what manner is it realized and manifested?

It seems to me that in *gerut,* both in the process and in the outcome, there exist two elements that are to some extent parallel, to some extent complementary, and to some extent contradictory.[7] On the one hand, *gerut* is grounded in a profound revolution. In its ideal form, its root is a longing for holiness, its core, desire for the Ein Sof, gravitation to a sublime and exalted ethic, striving for a world wholly good and wholly true. "David called himself a *ger,* as it is said:[8] 'I am a stranger (*ger*) in the land.'"[9] Of course, he was not a *ger* in the strict halakhic sense (although he was descended from proselytes); but in the realm of religious experience, he had penetrated the soul of the *ger* and related to it: "As a hart panting after water brooks, so my soul pants after You."[10] Here is the essence of *gerut*: a craving that dislodges one from the society of one's youth and finds expression in the overcoming of the confines of group and nation.

To be sure, the source and character of this element are apt to change. In certain cases, its essence is reaction to a sullied past, a renunciation of a life filled with iniquity or deprived of meaning and purpose. In this form, *gerut* is included in *teshuvah* (repentance); it is precipitated by regret over the past, abandonment of sin, and resolve for the future. At other times, the motive propelling the proselyte is the glow of the future, not the sordidness of the present. The potential *ger*, despite being in a setting that is not necessarily defiled, but merely defective, sees himself as isolated, "in a dry and thirsty land, without water." In his anguish he pleads: "O God, You are my God, earnestly I seek You: my soul thirsts for You, my flesh longs for You."[11] On the practical level, as the Rambam put it, the *ger* desires "to enter the covenant and to be absorbed under the divine aegis, and to accept for himself the yoke of the Torah."[12] But categorizing the different types of *gerut* is merely a matter of detail. The fundamental motive is one: a religious experience, a spiritual effervescence – sometimes feverish, ofttimes tranquil; in short, the birthpangs of a Jewish soul. This creation is private and personal – if you will, even subjective. Essentially, it is the *ger*'s intimacy with the Holy One. "The king has brought me into his chamber," and no stranger will trespass into the inner sanctum. Nothing is more a matter of the heart than *gerut*, and, in the channels of the heart, can there be room for external involvement?

This principle finds expression in a simple, yet famous, Halakhah: "A *ger* is like a newborn babe."[13] We customarily associate this statement with several laws: a *ger* is not aligned genealogically to his father, nor does he inherit from him (by biblical injunction); and, according to Resh Lakish, he does not fulfill the commandment to be fruitful and multiply through children born to him while he was a Gentile.[14] However, these are only consequences; it behooves us to understand and grasp the concept itself, in its literal context. The *ger* returns to the source, penetrating the secrets of ontological reality, and, while standing on the threshold of a new life, ruminates over the mystery of existence and is involved in a superior creation: he is born and gives birth at once.

The validity of this comparison is pronounced (albeit with an emphasis on the "converter" more than on the convert) in its aggadic formulations: "Whoever brings another person under the wings of the *Shekhinah* is considered as having created him, shaped him, and brought him into the world."[15] To be sure, this refers to the educator of a Jewish child, but how much the more does it apply to *gerut*. In the well-known words of the *Sifre* regarding Avraham our Patriarch: "And you shall love... like the love of humanity that Avraham your forefather had, as it is written: 'and the souls that they had acquired in Haran.' Now if all people united to create a small gnat and give it a soul, they would not succeed. What then does this verse mean? It teaches that Avraham was converting people and bringing them into the Jewish faith."[16] And in Bereshit Rabbah, the same passage concludes: "Rather, to teach us that one who brings the non-Jew closer to Judaism and converts him, it is as if he had created him."[17]

So far we have only been dealing with only one aspect of *gerut*: subjective and intimate, confined to the relationship of the *ger* to his Creator, centered around an internal experience and spiritual nascence, linked to *teshuvah*, which, in the Rambam's celebrated formulation, is also defined as a personal metamorphosis and new creation symbolized by birth ("And he alters his name, as if to say: I am another, and I am not the same person that committed those deeds").[18]

However, there is a second aspect to *gerut*: objective, formal, communal. If the *ger* is a partner in the dialogue taking place in the depths of his soul, he simultaneously becomes the subject of public assessment, participating – albeit, to be sure, not in an emotional vacuum – in a crystallized ceremony. Here, the emphasis is not upon process, including all the adventures and apprehension implied in the word, but on procedure. To his knocking on the door, he hears a response, to wit: Let us presume that your spiritual pilgrimage has prepared you sufficiently for *gerut*; but if you want to achieve it, you must follow these steps in order to be accepted.

This element, too, finds expression and symbolic representation in a Halakhah. "Rabbi Hiyya bar Abba said in the name of Rabbi Yohanan: A *ger* requires the presence of three people, for *mishpat* [judicial process] is written with reference to a *ger*."[19] For the same reason, since Halakhah deems *gerut* a form of legal procedure, conversion cannot take place at night;[20] and the Rambam saw this as the source of the gemara's prohibition against the *ger's* ritual immersion (*tevilah*) on a Sabbath or a holiday: "Since *gerut* requires a *bet din*, we immerse the *ger* neither on a Sabbath nor on a holiday nor at night; although if he was immersed, then he is a *ger*."[21] This is not merely a matter of supernumerary piety. In the opinion of some commentators, led by the Ramban,[22] *tevilah* at night is ineffective even *post factum*. Even according to the Rambam, we may assume, as did the *Maggid Mishneh*, that it is valid *a posteriori* only because, in certain cases, juridical procedures may be concluded at night.[23] This assumption is clearly borne out by the Rambam's formulation with respect to the need for three judges: "If he immersed privately, and converted with no witnesses, or even in front of two persons, he is not a *ger*."[24] Many Rishonim took issue with him on this point and sanctioned private *tevilah* – this, however, not because they valued the necessity of a *bet din* any less, but because they deemed a *bet din's* presence as mandatory only at the time that the *ger* accepts the normative onus of *mizvot*, and not during the immersion ceremony.[25] As for the requirement of having a *bet din* at one of the stages of *gerut*, all commentators – with the exception of one opinion quoted by Tosafot[26] – recognized it as indispensable; *gerut* consists of an actual *din*, a judge and his subject.

Between the elements of birth and adjudication, there are two distinctions that are completely separate from a logical standpoint – in fact, one could probably find one in the absence of the other – but that actually tend to arise concomitantly. Until now, I have accentuated one point, that of process – spiritual and private on the one hand, formal and communal on the other. Beyond this, however, the goal differs no less than the path. Birth emphasizes a spiritual creation; the legal aspect, a social affiliation. The potential *ger* appears on society's rostrum and presents himself as a candidate for citizenship in "the kingdom of priests and the holy nation," knocking not only on Heaven's door but also on the gates of *Knesset Yisrael*, the Jewish people. He is not content with being brought by the king into his chamber; the *ger* strives, as well, to "climb the date palm and take hold of its twigs."[27]

Our initial consideration of the two features of *gerut* certainly inclines us to see the yearning of the potential *ger* as the essence of *gerut*, and the judicial process as merely a validation, an endorsement. To a degree, this inclination is correct, but only to a degree. The legal aspect of *gerut* and the attachment to *Knesset Yisrael* involved in it are not solely an issue of a seal of approval. *Knesset Yisrael* does not merely mediate between the *ger* and the Almighty. She is a participant, and not just a broker; a concerned party, and not just an agent of God. In the encounter of the I and Thou that is established through *gerut*, the *ger* meets two Thous: The Lord of the Universe, and his nation, Israel. Not, God forbid, the latter alone; this would border on idolatry. Surely he confronts *Knesset Yisrael* solely in the light of its being "holy unto God, the first of His harvest." In this context, however, there is a very real encounter.

This point is reflected in the very procedures of *gerut*, especially as the Rambam delineated them:

> How are *gerim* accepted? When one comes from the Gentiles to be converted to Judaism, and [the *bet din*] finds no pretext [for his conversion], they say to him: "What has led you to such conversion? Don't you know that Israel is at present afflicted, oppressed, attacked, preyed upon, and that misfortunes befall her?" If he responds, "I know, and I am not worthy," they accept him immediately.[28]

The question arises: What is the nature of this declaration? It is mentioned in the gemara,[29] but there it can be understood as a part of the investigation to determine the sincerity of the *ger*. However, the Rambam here is explicitly dealing with the stage at which the *ger*'s sincerity has already been demonstrated. If so, why is this lengthy discourse needed?

Actually, the answer is quite simple. Let us ask ourselves what would happen if a potential *ger* were to declare himself ready to accept every one of the 613 commandments, committing himself to rigorous observance of the *mizvot*, minor as well as major, but refused to accept any sort of attachment to the nation, even the most minimal degree of allegiance. He does not wish to share in its present adversities, does not identify with its past, and does not yearn for its future. What is his status? We may answer unequivocally, on the basis of the Rambam's words in the *Hilkhot Tes-huvah*. Among the transgressors who, "for their tremendous wickedness and sinfulness," do not inherit a share in the world-to-come the Rambam counts "those who separate themselves from the ways of society." And characteristically he details:

> He who separates himself from the [Jewish] people, although he may never have violated a law, if he stands aloof from the community of Israel, and does not participate in their communal observances, or share in their calamities, or fast on their fasts, but instead goes his own way like any member of the local [non-Jewish] populace, as if he were not one of them: no share in the world-to-come awaits him.[30]

This being so, the verdict in our case is crystal-clear: there has not been a total, comprehensive acceptance of *ol mizvot*. The prospective *ger* has readily committed himself to the entire Torah, only excluding involvement in the community, but this exclusion is hardly a trivial matter.

In light of this decision, we no longer need to wonder about the declaration concerning Israel's situation at the *gerut*. It is not solely an inquest into the motivation for conversion. The declaration by the *bet din* is a stage in the fulfillment of *gerut per se* and relates to the commitment implicit in it.

In this context, the individual and the community encounter each other along a very wide front. The *ger* does not meet and identify with the present nation alone, but with its past and future as well. Once again, it is the Rambam who underscores this point. The Mishnah states:

> The *ger* must bring [his first fruits], but he does not utter [the accompanying declaration], for he cannot say "that God has sworn to our fathers to give us"; and if his mother was Jewish, he brings [the first fruits] and utters [the declaration]. And when [the *ger*] prays privately, he says "the Lord of Israel's forefathers"; and when he is in the synagogue, he says "the Lord of your forefathers."[31]

In contrast, the Rambam rules in accordance with the view of R. Yehudah in the Jerusalem Talmud:

The *ger* himself brings [the first fruits] and makes the declaration. Why?
[God said to Avraham:] "For I have made you a father unto a multitude of
nations": hitherto you were the father of Aram, and herewith you are the
father of all nations.[32]

And, in the Rambam's own words:

The *ger* brings [the first fruits] and makes the declaration, since it was spoken
to Avraham, "I have made you a father unto a multitude of nations"; here
he was made the patriarch of everyone in the world who [ever] becomes
Jewish.[33]

In this formulation, the opinion of R. Yehudah does not identify
the *ger* with a specific history, for it is possible to view the attachment
to Avraham as direct, exclusive of mediation through *Knesset Yisrael*.
If so, one may ask (as the Ramban already hinted),[34] that while the
mention of Avraham is understandable, how can a *ger* describe Yizhak
and Yaakov as his forefathers? The Rambam dealt with this issue in
his famous responsum to R. Ovadiah Ger Tzedek. He opens with an
explanation in keeping with the thrust of his words in the Mishneh
Torah:

The fundamental point here is that it was Avraham our father who instructed
the nation, enlightening them and informing them of the true faith, and
of God's unity and singularity. It was he who repudiated idol worship and
violated its worship, nullifying it, bringing many to accept God, teaching and
instructing them, commanding his sons and future descendants after him to
remain faithful to the Way of God, as it says in the Torah: "For I know him,
that he will command his children and his household after him, and they
shall keep the way of the Lord." Therefore all who embrace Judaism until the
end of all generations, and all who profess the unity of the Lord's Name as
is directed in the Torah, are like the pupils of Avraham of blessed memory
and are members of his household, all of them; it was he who brought them
to this positive juncture, and, as he did with the members of his own generation by dint of his skill at oratory and teaching, so he has reclaimed everyone
who will convert in the future, through the testament he left his children
and his descendants. As a result, Avraham our forefather was the father of
his legitimate progeny who follow the path forged by him, and he is also the
father of every *ger* who converts.

Up to this point, the Rambam has discussed the direct link to Avraham; on the basis of his thesis, he concludes:

> But [as for saying] "You [God] took us out of Egypt" or "[God] performed miracles for our ancestors," if you want to change the wording and say "You took Yisrael out of Egypt," or "the miracle You wrought for Israel," say it [however you please].

But then he goes a step further:

> And if you do not change [the wording], there is no loss whatsoever, for after having entered the Jewish fraternity and accepted Judaism, there is no difference between you and us, and all the miracles that were wrought were wrought for us and for you. This is Isaiah's intention in the verse: "Neither let the son of the stranger, that has joined himself to the Lord, speak, saying, 'The Lord has surely separated me from His people.'"[35] There is no difference or incongruity between you and us in any respect.[36]

The words are self-explanatory: in the aftermath of his admission into *Knesset Yisrael*, the *ger* identifies with its past, its triumphs as well as its failures, no less than he does with the present; with eschatological vision as with current vibrant reality. The *ger* is born both as a servant of God and as a citizen of the nation, and hence the appropriateness of a *bet din* to judge and accept him.

We can, if we wish, discern the duality of *gerut* reflected in various manifestations over the generations. If we focus on the process of *gerut*, we may note three prominent phases. The first is symbolized by Avraham Avinu. Avraham, our rabbis informed us, is called "the forerunner of *gerim*"[37] – and not merely in a symbolic sense. The Mekhilta describes Avraham's circumcision as an actual proselyte's berit milah, not only as a fulfillment of God's command.[38] Clearly, Avraham's *gerut* highlights the first aspect of *gerut*. It is an individual process in toto, for it is characterized by singularity. He is lonely by nature. "Avraham was a *yahid* – Avraham was singular," exclaims the gemara.[39] The significance of this quality is further stressed in the well-known adage by which Rabbi Yehudah interpreted Avraham's title *Ivri* – "the whole world on one side, and he alone on the other."[40] When was he more solitary than at his conversion? His *gerut* was conducted purely on the level of a direct attachment to the Creator, striving and yearning for the Absolute, and following a direct divine bidding: "And the Lord said to Avraham, 'And you shall observe My covenant, you and your descendants after you for all their generations.'"[41] This verse introduces the commandment of *milah,* but in its original context, it was an injunction for *gerut.* This *gerut* is exclusively birth, *it'aruta di-letata ve-it'aruta di-le'ela* – "arousal from below and arousal from above," but without brokers. Neither judge nor judicial procedure; only the birth of a world and the creation of a soul. It is epitomized in an interpretation by the Midrash Tanhuma on the verse "and I shall make you a great nation": "'I will transform you' is not the word chosen here, but 'make,' for I am creating in you a new person, similar to what is said: 'and God *made* the heavens, and God *made* the two lights.'"[42]

The second stage consists of a singular phenomenon: the period from the exodus from Egypt to the revelation at Sinai. Here, of course, the communal dimension of *gerut* was added: the Torah portrays the day of *mattan Torah* as a "Day of Assembly."[43] The meaning of that *gerut* is not exhausted merely in attachment to the Creator, but includes the formation of a "righteous nation that keeps faithfulness."[44] The legal charter, however, is missing. There is neither a judging nor a judged congregation; rather, a people standing together on the threshold of emergence into the world, and entering, without mediator or midwife, the world of eternal life as the lot of God's inheritance.

However, what transpired at Sinai was a unique event. From that time on, in the third stage, the *ger* requires both birth and *mishpat* in order to identify with *Knesset Yisrael* even as he clings to the Sovereign of the universe. Within this framework, although both components are compulsory, there may, in all likelihood, be certain cases wherein the social aspect is primary. If Avraham Avinu is the *ger* of birth par excellence, we may perceive another biblical convert as a prototype for a predominantly legal-social conversion. This element is symbolized by Ruth, not so much because of the emphasis upon formal procedure as because of the stress on interpersonal union as the impetus behind *gerut.* Doubtless, she unconditionally accepted upon herself the yoke of the Torah and *malkhut shamayim* – "and your God is my God." But from the biblical text it is quite clear, most significantly, that she was animated by love for Naomi, and through Naomi for all Israel: "And Ruth said. 'Entreat me not to leave you.' "[45] The source of the internal pressure is bared to all. This point is similarly stressed in what Boaz says. "And Boaz answered and said to her, 'It has been fully related to me, all that you have done to your mother-in-law since your husband's death: how you left your father, your mother, and the land of your birth, and went to a people unknown to you before.' " Only in the next sentence does he mention the purely spiritual element: "May God reward your deed, and may it be a full reward from God, the Lord of Israel, under whose wings you have come to seek refuge."[46]

Whatever the examples, the central fact for us today is that, since Sinai, there has been an intrinsic dualism in the framework of *gerut:* spiritual nativity as a servant of God on a certain level, together with standing for judgment as servant and peer.[47] The Halakhah insists upon both aspects. In keeping with the general spirit of Halakhah, the internal experience alone does not suffice. Contrary to the modern Zeitgeist, which tends to define religion as a purely subjective reality, Halakhah strives to interweave the external and the internal. Wary of founding the spiritual life upon castles in the air, Halakhah relies upon defined actions and firm limits – and demands them. Even in a nonsocial framework, Hazal assumed, almost axiomatically, the necessity of an objective act in *gerut.* "And [according to] Rabbi Yehoshua," asks the gemara, "where do we see that the matriarchs performed *tevilah*?" The answer is immediate: "It is dictated by logic: for in its absence, how could they have become Jewesses at all?"[48]

If this is the case with the matriarchs, then all the more so after the giving of the Torah, when *gerut* has assumed the added dimension of entrance into *Knesset Yisrael.* One need hardly stress, however, that integration into the nation, be it rooted in the most sublime self-dedication, is insufficient. *Gerut* means, first and foremost, a religious-spiritual turning. The procedure of *gerut* comes in the wake of such a transformation, but not in its stead. The conversion consists of formal stages, but they are not *pro forma.* Moreover, the Halakhah stresses the interlacing of this turning into the actual act of *gerut.* Acceptance of the laws must occur twice: once before the *tevilah,* at which time, according to the Rambam, the *bet din* discourses at length on the tenets of Judaism, "the unity of God and the prohibition against idolatry,"[49] and also informs the convert of some of the more lenient and more stringent commandments; and again during the *tevilah,* when "three stand over him and inform him of some of the lenient commandments and some of the strict commandments a second time while he stands in the water."[50] What is the nature of this second declaration? Are we worried that the *ger's* commitment has lapsed in so short a time? It is solely in order to weave the acceptance of the *mizvot* into the act of *tevilah,* to supply the *tevilah* with the specific character of a *tevilah* of *gerut,* to integrate the spiritual intent with the formal act.

It would be pleasant to assume that there is no conflict between these two themes; that the selfsame act effectively subsumes both domains. A single *tevilah* is doubly efficacious. It climaxes protracted spiritual birth, culminating in emergence into the Jewish world, and, as definitive judgment, confers citizenship of *Knesset Yisrael.* Thus it serves simultaneously as the apex of a spiritual pilgrimage and as the essence of a social quest.

This would be agreeable, but I doubt whether so flattering an assumption can be conscientiously maintained. We should not make light of the difference between these two factors. Each is distinct in its very essence: one rooted in nature, the other in legality. Of course, birth too, even in its biological form, constitutes a phenomenon that concerns Halakhah; it is defined and quantified: the emergence of most of the fetus, of its head, its forehead,[51] and, according to the Rambam, even of most of its forehead, is an actual halakhic measurement.[52] This, however, is nothing more than coincidental. Intrinsically, birth lies outside of the juridical field, except that the law must pass judgment upon it. *Gerut,* however, is actual *mishpat,* and here lies the duality. This duality may in fact become, especially in today's prevalent mood, antinomy – and not only according to the individualistic romantic view that stresses the contradiction between law and nature and emphasizes absolute privacy in the spiritual realm. Even a traditional sensibility appreciates the breaching of the sanctum when the *ger* bares his innermost soul *coram populo,* with three strangers present in the delivery room. Recognizing and valuing modesty, it encourages concealment over revelation. Itself a "spring shut up, a fountain sealed,"[53] it senses that the juridic presence and framework are likely to undermine the religious-aesthetic moment at that most sublime instant. The *ger* is eager to soar – and three judges clip his wings, subjecting him to their examination.[54] In candor, we must further admit that the combination of these two factors may produce paradoxical results. Suffused with an effervescence and longing that characterize the end of a lengthy internal struggle and a supreme purification, the *ger* may stand trial in front of judges (even laymen according to some)[55] possessing a routine if not indifferent religious sensibility. In his heart, burning fire; in theirs, perhaps dimming embers.

Nevertheless, the Halakhah insists on the need for birth and *mishpat* together, and with good reason. The duality of *gerut* is not an isolated fact. It is an inherent part of the fundamental duality of religious life in general. The life of the devout, both in its universal form and, to a sharper degree, in its specifically Jewish form, is also dual. On the one hand, it is purely the realm of the individual: the sanctum sanctorum, innermost of the innards. Within the man of faith, as Rav Soloveitchik stressed in his essay, loneliness reverberates.[56] His relation to the Creator takes place in intimacy. His ideal experience is, in the famous words of Plotinus, "the flight of the alone to the alone."[57] "Religion," said Whitehead, "is solitariness.... If you are never solitary, you are never religious."[58] But on the other hand, religion has always developed in a congregational setting. Its historical existence is dependent at every stride and step on communal ritual and shared faith. This cannot be explained solely in the manner of Durkheim and his school, who view society as the source of religion, in the sense that religion grows and develops only in response to social needs and demands, so that, in the final analysis, it is society itself that is served in one form or another.[59] This doctrine is open to criticism even from a purely sociological standpoint. I, for one – far from an expert in the field – am inclined to accept Malinowski's contention that Durkheim's approach ignores some important phenomena, and may even be based on a distorted sense of some fundamental concepts.[60] In any case, from a Jewish perspective, the issue is clear. Religion, as described by Durkheim, has been categorized halakhically: it is *avodah zarah*, idol worship, no less evident when the idol is the society or the state than when it is a statue or a graven image. However, the public dimension of religion relates even to proper piety and worship. Even the service of God, for its own sake, recognized as an independent goal, not adulterated as a means to the achievement of the demands of an apotheosized society, is rooted in the community as well as the individual. Herein lies the duality of religion: at once a personal and a social phenomenon.

This duality stems from man's complex situation and fate. Man has a relationship to eternity and to the temporal. Therefore, two obligations and two destinies confront him. One is self-improvement, a catharsis of the soul in preparation for encountering the Divine Presence in the world of beatitude. With this thought R. Moshe Hayyim Luzzatto opens his *Mesillat Yesharim*:

> The cornerstone of piety and the root of sincere service is the resolution by every man of his duty in life…. [F]or this reason man was put in this world, so that, taking advantage of the opportunities and faculties that come his way, he may reach the place destined for him, that is, the next world.

From this perspective, man has no interest in the society that will evolve from him and his progeny. "All generations," said the historian Ranke, "stand equidistant from eternity."[61]

Man, however, has a second mission. He is not only a creation of eternity but a child of history. Judaism specifically stressed this destiny. Greek philosophy, in general, minimized the importance of history. For Plato and his school, this world is nothing more than a meager shadow, a reflection of an image of the world of ideas which alone have true metaphysical permanence. To the Stoics, the annals of history are merely a repetitious cycle, barren of innovation. In contrast, Judaism insists that history is decisively important, its events effecting major changes, generating real turning points. For Judaism, history is a process with a beginning and end, spanning "world to world," from the specific moment of initial creation until the realization of the vision in which "God will be one and His Name one." Such a relationship mandates that man, who finds himself in the framework of history, bears an obligation toward it. However, every effort to discharge this obligation removes man from his domain of privacy, for the process of history is, by its very nature, collective. Therefore, insofar as religion seeks to hasten eschatological fulfillment directly – and how can it shirk such a responsibility? – it must necessarily infiltrate the life of the community.[62] From this perspective, society is not seen merely as an avenue or backdrop to the attainment of individual spiritual values. The group's life and progress are transformed into a field of operations for the individual, and into one of his destinies. "It is not incumbent upon him to finish the work," but the task is, nonetheless, his.

This duality – of private and communal life concomitantly, of simultaneous attachment to eternity and the temporal – is reflected in every person's life. We can, however, find an especially salient example in the lives of humanity's elect – the prophets. Who can match the prophet in striving for superior sanctity? Who, as much as he, yearns to be alone with his Maker? Who, like him, is lonely, "consecrating himself, separating himself from the popular course followed in darkness?"[63] Who, more than the prophet, is preoccupied with self-creation? "And when the spirit descends upon him, his soul mingles in the upper spheres of the angels called Ishim, and he is transformed into a different person, aware that he is no longer as he was, but, rather, elevated above all wise human beings, as is said to Saul: [64] 'and you will prophesy with them and become a different person.'"[65]

Is the prophet, then, detached from reality, indifferent to the course of human events? Not at all. On the contrary, Scripture portrays the prophet primarily as a fighter, a leader, as one who is concerned for his nation's fate and character. The flame that burns in his heart, shut up in his bones, turns into a fire that consumes wickedness, purifying the world. Again, who can match the prophet in becoming a partner to the Almighty not only in the act of Creation, but also in the fashioning of generations, in molding history as in shaping nature? But this activity forces him to abandon his solitude and join the life of his generation. God, claim the kabbalists, created the world by *tzimtzum* – withdrawal; man, on the contrary, can become God's partner in creation only through expansion.[66]

To this point, we have dealt with the duality of religious life in its universal context. However, in a Jewish context, the problem is even more acute. *Knesset Yisrael* is not merely a sociopolitical setting in which every individual strives to pave his own path to *Ha-Kadosh Barukh Hu*. Nor is it an embellished means, or fertile field, for the prodding of universal human history. It is defined as "a kingdom of priests and a holy nation,"[67] its whole being and autonomy depending upon its character as a people serving God. And we may underscore nation – not a chorus of individuals or an assembly of persons – but a nation: the people in its entirety.

In Halakhah, this point is emphasized in several spheres. Most important, of course, is the dictum that "all Israel are responsible for one other."[68] But the notion is reflected – and perhaps more noticeably – in other areas. Thus, the Ramban states that if *K'lal Yisrael* were to congregate at a specified time to bring a sacrifice in partnership, the sacrifice would not be a *korban tzibbur*, a public offering of all Israel, but a sacrifice of partners, for here they do not appear as a unitary group but as an assemblage of individuals.[69] Moreover, the character of full-fledged *tzibbur* is such that it transcends the confines of time and space. A later generation, suggests Rav Papa, may offer a bull for a transgression through ignorance (*par he'alem davar*) of an earlier generation, even if not one member of the generation that perpetrated the sin is still alive, "for there is no death for the *tzibbur*."[70] The Congregation of Israel, from the revelation at Sinai until the millennium, constitutes a single organic unit – at once metaphysical and social, if you will – that is destined to be "holy to the Lord, the first fruits of His produce."[71] "Not with our ancestors did God forge this covenant, but with us, today, here, all of us alive."[72] Not with our ancestors alone, adds Rashi.[73] For as much as the individual is embedded in *K'lal Yisrael* and does not just float upon it, the communal element assumes a significant role in his spiritual life, based both on the character of the nation and on his drawing closer to its future. This fact intensifies the duality in the life of the Jew.

Hence, the tension of the dialectic inherent in *gerut* is sharpened even further. A real gap exists between, for example, *gerut* and the parallel term "conversion," as understood by many Gentile scholars. Christian discussions describe a phenomenon totally different from the Jewish conception. In the most famous of these descriptions, two chapters devoted to the subject by William James in his *The Varieties of Religious Experience,*[74] we read page after page of delicate and sensitive analysis, yet sense that the subject is not *gerut* at all, but the psychology of *teshuvah*, repentance. Since, in fact, James promises a religion with pretensions to universality, there is no significant *religious* place for entry into a congregation or community; hence, there is hardly a difference between repentance and conversion. In Jewish *gerut, le-havdil,* the communal point is fundamental. For the *ger,* his day of entry into the covenant is, as for the whole nation at Sinai, "a day of Assembly."[75]

And so, I conclude with that with which I began: the problematic. We may not ignore the duality, even the antinomy, in *gerut.* It is not ours to resolve the issue, but to clarify it. We shall overcome it only insofar as we recognize it – being sensitive to it on the practical level, and pondering it on the theoretical plane; if we fuse empathy with elucidation. It is not for us to choose between the two factors, nor do we desire to do so – God forbid. Both are essential, but our obligation is to understand and balance their relationship. The tension within *gerut* exists, but, acknowledging its existence, we may be able to master it. When the *ger* grasps the scope and the complexity of his commitment, and the members of the *bet din* are attentively attuned to the possible stirrings of his heart, then, out of their mutual sensitivity to the majesty and the tones of the event, the gap will be bridged.

Proper understanding will only issue, however, if we place the matter in the proper framework: the duality in *gerut* is indispensable and dialectical. It is inherent in the nature of religious life in general both, in its universal form and, principally, within the structure of *Knesset Yisrael.* The dialectic that exists between the individual and the community in religious life is reflected in the duality of the *gerut* process, in which the two separate factors meet in mutual relationship. Insofar as a conflict exists between them, it does not stem from the blurring of terms and experiences, but is the result of the richness of Jewish life, with all its fertile consequences and variegated nature. The gate matches the home.

Notes

1. Shemot 22:20; compare ibid. 23:9 and Vayikra 19:33.
2. Bava Metzia 59b. See also the Rambam's *Sefer Ha-Mizvot,* the beginning of the ninth shoresh (in Rav Heller's edition, pp. 19–20), in which he explains, in light of his opinion of multiple warnings for one commandment, that the transgressor does not violate three actual negative commandments, but only one, which is merely "strengthened" by the repetition of the admonitions. But in the Mishneh Torah, Hilkhot Mekhirah 14:15–17, the Rambam sets down that one does literally transgress three negative commandments. However, his words there require further explanation in their own right, for it appears that in reference to a *ger* he ruled that all who vex the *ger* either verbally or financially violate both *issurim,* whereas for vexing a Jew he made a distinction between the two. See also the problem raised by the discussion in the gemara, ad loc. The commentators on the Mishneh Torah deal with this at length.
3. See Bava Metzia 59b and the sources cited in the notes of Rav Hayyim Heller on the *Sefer Ha-Mizvot,* loc. cit.
4. I Melakhim 18:21.
5. Arthur Darby Nock, *Conversion* (Oxford, 1933), p. 12.
6. Bereshit 21:27.
7. My approach here is phenomenological, and I am dealing with types. From a sociological standpoint, the issue must be dealt with quite differently, but the two approaches are not mutually exclusive.
8. Tehillim 119:19.
9. Mekhilta de-Rabbi Yishmael, *Mishpat*im, portion 18; in the Horowitz-Rabin edition, p. 312.
10. Tehillim 42:2. I quote the verse in light of the explanation of the words in the Targum: די מרגג, "that desires." The Septuagint translates likewise, and from there the Vulgate, *desiderat.* But Rashi accepted the interpretation of Dunash that the verb refers to the ram's cry; the *Midrash Shoher Tov,* following in the same vein, understood the whole psalm as placed in a time of exile and calamity.
11. Tehillim 63:2.
12. Hilkhot Issurei Bi'ah 13:4. His three-way division is of fundamental importance, but this is not the place to analyze it.
13. Yevamot 22a.
14. On genealogy, see Yevamot 22a and 97b; on inheritance, Kiddushin 17b; and concerning reproduction, Yevamot 62a. In the same vein, Rabbi Yohanan and Resh Lakish disagreed about whether the firstborn son of a *ger* born after his father's conversion is considered the firstborn for inheritance. Similarly, the halakhah is cited with respect to the acquittal of the *ger* for all his transgressions prior to his conversion; see Yevamot 48b and Sanhedrin 71b. The breadth of the halakhah as regards genealogy depends upon a dispute among the Rishonim as to whether a son of a *giyoret* (female proselyte), conceived and born after the conversion, is forbidden from marrying his mother's daughter, born prior to the mother's conversion, who herself converted

before the son's birth. Rashi is of the opinion that it is only forbidden by rabbinic injunction, since by Torah law he has no attachment to a daughter born as a non-Jew. However, Rabbenu David forbids it even according to the Torah, evidently assuming that *gerut* severs all relationships that exist at the time of the *gerut*, but does not totally discard the attachment of the *ger* to his family. See *Hiddushei Ha-Ran* on Sanhedrin 58a. s.v. *ger.*

15. *Tosefta* Horayot 2:7.

16. Va-ethanan, piska 32.

17. Portion 39:14; in the Theodor-Albeck edition, p. 379.

18. Hilkhot Teshuvah 2:4.

19. Yevamot 46b.

20. Ibid.

21. Hilkhot Issurei Bi'ah 13:6. The simplest understanding of the talmudic passage in Yevamot 46b bases the prohibition against immersion on Sabbath and holidays upon *tikkunei gavra*, improving the state of a person, similar to the prohibition against sprinkling water on the ritually unclean on Sabbaths and holidays (see Pesahim 65b). Apparently, it has no juridical basis. But the Rambam, perhaps because he understood that the gemara reversed itself at the end of its discussion, related *tevilah* back to juridical roots.

22. See *Hiddushei Ha-Ramban* on Yevamot 46b, where he deliberates the point but ultimately concludes that a second *tevilah* is required by day.

23. See Yevamot 104a and Sanhedrin 34b.

24. Hilkhot Issurei Bi'ah 13:7.

25. See Yevamot 45b, Tosafot, s.v. *mi.* According to their understanding of the text, that the *tevilah* of menstruants serves as the model for the *tevilah* of *gerim,* some basis for this opinion can be found in it. However, the Rambam understood that the *tevilah* of menstruants is nothing more than an indicator that the entire procedure of *gerut* has already taken place, as implied by his mentioning other indications as well ("a *giyoret* who has been seen practicing Jewish customs consistently," e.g., she immerses herself after her menstrual, cycle. she separates *terumah* from her dough, etc.; see Hilkhot Issurei Bi'ah 13:9); and according to this, the talmudic reference proves nothing.

26. Kiddushin 62b, Tosafot, s.v. *ger.* Rav Yizhak Alfasi (the Rif) on Yevamot 45b likewise distinguishes between *le-khat'hila* (the proper way of performing a commandment) and *di-avad.* In the opinion of the Tur (Yoreh De'ah 268), if one immersed in the presence of two judges, married a Jewish woman, and had a son, then the son would be a Jew, for the father's immersion was acceptable *di-avad.* According to this, the Rif's position corresponds to the opinion of Tosafot, and it was indeed interpreted as such by the *Shiltei Ha-Gibborim,* ad loc. However, close analysis of the Rif's wording indicates, *prima facie,* that he is discussing whether a different *gerut* had been performed prior to this one; he does not deal with *bet din* as validating the act of *gerut* in this *tevilah.* If so, then his opinion corresponds to that of the Rambam, who presumably based himself upon the Rif. See the *Bah,* sec. 268, who argues convincingly in this vein.

27. On these two sides of *gerut,* see the work of my master, Rav J.B. Soloveitchik, *Kol Dodi Dofek,*

in *Ish Ha-Emunah* (Jerusalem 1968), pp. 95–99, especially the footnotes. The Rav sees the two aspects of conversion as embodied in the two covenants that evolved from two historical events, the Exodus from Egypt and the Revelation at Sinai. The major thrust of this article is based on the essential cornerstone laid down in that work, but I will not go into the stages of *gerut* here.

A different interpretation of the character of circumcision and *tevilah* was suggested by Rav Yosef Engel in the *Gilyonei Ha-Shas,* Yevamot 46a. Compare also the *Milhamot Hashem* of the Ramban, Shabbat 135a.

28. Hilkhot Issurei Bi'ah 14:1.

29. Yevamot 47a.

30. Hilkhot Teshuvah 3:11. However, Rashi to Sanhedrin 47a, s.v. *mi-darkhei tzibbur,* explains, "such as an apostate." On the connection of the Rambam to this topic, see *Kol Dodi Dofek*, p. 96.

31. Bikkurim 1:4.

32. Ibid. But the *Tosefta* reads (Bikkurim 1:2): "Rabbi Yehudah says: All the *gerim* bring the first fruits but do not utter the declaration; the sons of Keni, Mosheh's father-in-law, bring the first fruits and utter the declaration." The issue was discussed by the Rishonim; see the sources cited in *Tosefta Ki-Peshutah* by Rabbi Saul Lieberman, pp. 823–825.

33. Hilkhot Bikkurim 4:3, 34. In his *hiddushim* to Bava Batra 81a.

35. Yeshayahu 56:3. The text reads, however, "shall surely separate me."

36. The Rambam's Responsa, Blau edition, no. 293; II:549. It is worth noting that according to his view, there may, *prima facie*, be a halakhic ramification. A *ger toshav* may trace himself to Avraham (and if we presume, as did the Ramban, loc. cit., that "the three patriarchs of the world were like Avraham," then he may trace himself to Yizhak and Yaakov as well), but he may not say "who took us out of Egypt."

37. Sukkah 49b.

38. See above, n. 6.

39. Sanhedrin 93a.

40. Bereshit Rabbah 42:13; in the Theodor-Albeck edition. p. 414.

41. Bereshit 17:9.

42. Lekh Lekha: Buber edition, p. 31.

43. Devarim 9:10.

44. Yeshayahu 26:2.

45. Ruth 1:16.

46. Ruth 2:11–12. Despite this emphasis, we need not be surprised that Ruth described and perhaps perceived herself as an alien (*nokhriyyah*). Even if we discount the possible explanation that the words apply only to her roots, and not to her present state, we may intuit that although she desired to identify with *Knesset Yisrael*, her social-personal integration was still incomplete. However, the famous description of Keats, who ruminates that the nightingale's is "Perhaps the self-same song that found a path / Through the sad heart of Ruth, when sick, for home, / She

stood in tears amid the alien corn" (*Ode to a Nightingale*, vv, 65–67) is purely conjectural and has no basis in the text.

47. Needless to say, in the preceding section I do not mean to suggest that changes occurred in the laws of *gerut*, but refer to changes in the atmosphere surrounding it, with varying emphases in specific cases and perhaps in specific periods.

48. Yevamot 46b. Rabbi Yehoshua holds that *tevilah* without *milah* is sufficient, *post facto*, for *gerut*.

49. Hilkhot Issurei Bi'ah 14:2. In the gemara (Yevamot 47a), only a description of the *mizvot* is mentioned. Presumably, theological rudiments were to be discussed during the course of the exposition; nevertheless, the Rambam's express reference is noteworthy.

50. Hilkhot Issurei Bi'ah 14:6; based on Yevamot 47b.

51. See Niddah 28a, Berakhot 46b,

52. Hilkhot Issurei Bi'ah 10:6. He refers there to a live fetus; with respect to a miscarriage, to exempt the child who follows from the title of firstborn, the Rambam required the whole forehead (Hilkhot Bekhorim 11:15). In the former case, the law of birth takes effect through the emergence of the head in its own right; hence, even most of the forehead, which is considered most of the head, is sufficient. In the latter case, since there is no person, the head is considered nothing more than the representative of most of the body, and most of the head no longer suffices (from Rav J.B. Soloveitchik).

53. Shir Ha-Shirim 4:12.

54. On the basis of his experience in dealing with *gerim*. Rabbi Ze'ev Gotthold has pointed out to me that many of them, facing a very confusing transitional period in their lives, derive spiritual support from the presence of the *bet din*. In his opinion, most *gerim* view it as supportive rather than as interference. Yet perhaps, ideally speaking, the contradiction persists, and I am inclined to assume that it is a factor in many specific instances.

55. See the opinion of Rabbi Netanel in the Tosafot, Kiddushin 62b, s.v. *ger*, and in the *Hiddushei Ha-Ramban* on Yevamot 46b. It should be pointed out that the term "laymen" in this context has a specific halakhic sense, referring to persons who have not been formally or technically ordained, and is not to be understood in its usual sense.

56. See above, n. 24.

57. *Enneads* 6:9.

58. Alfred North Whitehead, *Religion in the Making* (New York, 1927), p. 17.

59. See Émile Durkheim, *Les formes élémentaires de la vie religieuse* (Paris, 1912), passim.

60. See Bronistlaw Malinowski, *Magic, Science and Religion* (Garden City, NY, 1948), esp. pp. 54–60.

61. Quoted in Herbert Butterfield, *Christianity and History* (London, 1957), p. 89.

62. Of course, we may indirectly bring *ge'ulah* closer by serving God in the strictly private domain, for this brings in its wake an increase in divine assistance.

63. Hilkhot Yesodei ha-Torah 7:1.

64. 1 Shemuel 10:6.
65. Rambam, loc. cit.
66. From time to time, the prophet requires withdrawal in order to prepare himself for prophecy. But the fulfillment of his task necessarily demands expansion.
67. Shemot 19:6.
68. Shevuot 39a.
69. *Milhamot Hashem,* Berakhot, chap. 3. In his commentary on the Torah (Vayikra 1:2) he assumes that this is Rashi's opinion, but there, he himself leans toward assuming that "if the *tzibbur* desires to set aside funds for a voluntary sacrifice, and money is raised [for that purpose] as *shekalim* are similarly collected for daily and additional sacrifices, then this would be a *nidvat tzibbur.*"
70. Horayot 6a. After some discussion, the gemara reaches the conclusion that there is no source for this law and it is likely that one generation cannot atone for another unless some members of the earlier generation are still alive. This notwithstanding, the notion of a link between generations remains valid. Even according to the conclusion, it is not the individual persons remaining who sacrifice the atonement, but the whole *tzibbur.* The need for a remnant is just a stipulation required of a sacrifice for a transgression that there be present "offerers" who have a direct connection to the offering. In any case, the position that "there is no death in the *tzibbur*" has been already established. Thus, the Halakhah pertaining to a *hattat* (sin-offering) whose owners have died," i.e., that it cannot be offered or redeemed but must graze until it dies, does not apply to a *hattat tzibbur,* as its "owner" never dies. See Rambam, Hilkhot Pesulei ha-Muk-dashim 4:1.
71. Yirmiyahu 2:3.
72. Devarim 5:3.
73. Ibid.; see the two interpretations of Ibn Ezra ad loc.
74. See William James, *The Varieties of Religious Experience* (New York, 1902), chaps. 9–10. A similar bent is evident in some of those who followed James: e.g., A.C. Underwood, *Conversion: Christian and Non-Christian* (New York, 1925); W. Bryn Thomas, *The Psychology of Conversion* (London, 1935); Robert O. Ferm, *The Psychology of Christian Conversion* (Westwood, NY, 1959). To a degree, this notion is incorporated into a general emphasis on the subjective that is an outgrowth of dealing with the psychological side of the issue, and that is noticeable, in particular, among Protestant authors. However, it exists even among those whose bent lends more importance to the formal, objective points. e.g., Catholics. In a different sense, it is essential to Catholics even more than to Protestants, since universalism is at the core of Catholic theology.
75. The concept of a religious *tzibbur* as a distinct social, organic unit is not, of course, foreign to Christianity, and it served from its inception as one of the fundamental points in the formative molding of the Church as idea and institution. Moreover, another central dimension was added during the Protestant Reformation, as national churches evolved, at which time the concept actually served as a major bone of contention, especially in England. But this concept never

paralleled that of *Knesset Yisrael*, even during the Reformation. In the writings of the Anglican divine Richard Hooker (*Laws of Ecclesiastical Polity*, book 8), the idea of an *ecclesia* was, in essence, universal, and he sought primarily to search and find, within this framework, room for a national entity, despite its being, relatively speaking, an artificial unit.

On the other hand, in earlier societies, the interweaving of religion and nation, or of religion and city-state, was the norm, both encompassing the same group. But this is effective only in a polytheistic framework, wherein the idol and its worship were limited to a specific place and community, and bears no similarity whatsoever to our conception, which, in comparison with polytheism, is thoroughly universal.

Chapter 9

Patterns of Contemporary Jewish Self-Identification

A comprehensive treatment of the patterns of contemporary Jewish self-identification – or, to use the reflexive Hebrew term, *hizdahut* – must operate on two planes. There should, first, be a descriptive account of the manner in which, in current practice, Jews identify themselves. Second, inasmuch as behavioral patterns are obviously a function of one's interpretation of Jewishness, substantive and perhaps even prescriptive issues should be dealt with. By way of preface to my statement, however, I confess to a certain bias. While I do not intend to ignore the first aspect entirely, I do find myself driven by temperament, training, and conviction to focus upon the second. I do this not only because I am more at home with ideological, than sociological, categories, but because the analysis must be grounded upon awareness of the archetypal modes of *hizdahut*. From a traditional perspective, the constant element in Jewish identity far outweighs the contemporary, and this relation is, and should be, reflected in the processes and patterns of Jewish identification.

Substantively, *hizdahut* comprehends two distinct, if related, components. In one sense, it constitutes empathy and/or commitment. We identify with a person or a people by the vicarious sharing of experience; and we identify with a cause or a party insofar as we possess a sense of common

Reprinted from *World Jewry and the State of Israel,* ed. Moshe Davis (Jerusalem, 1977).

purpose. Thus, *hizdahut Yehudit* – Jewish self-identification – is understood as adherence to Jewish history and Jewish values: the existential sharing of past experience, present anxiety, and hope for the future; the acceptance, both intellectual and emotional, of a complex of norms and ideals.

Hizdahut is inherently relational. It is perceived as a positive stance vis-à-vis a given reality. There is, however, a second sense in which we neither align nor affiliate, but rather become the focus of a self-contained process. As the reflexive form of the term suggests, it denotes, above all, self-definition: identification not *with* but *as*. At this level, we are much less concerned with our stance toward others than with expressing the reality of our own being. To the extent that being is conceived in social categories, the relational aspect is never wholly absent. The quest for identity may very well lead to finding one's milieu. Nevertheless, there is a vast difference between personal definition and empathetic alliance.

MODES OF IDENTITY

Hizdahut Yehudit encompasses both aspects; and both are enjoined and/or reinforced by specific rabbinic sanctions. The need for empathy is stressed in a talmudic passage in which insensitivity to suffering is equated with *carpe-diem* hedonism. The rabbis taught, the Talmud declares in Ta'anit:

> When the community is in distress one should not say, "I will go home, eat and drink, and peace will be upon my soul." And if he does so, Scripture says of him: "And behold, joy and gladness, slaying oxen and killing sheep, eating flesh and drinking wine – 'let us eat and drink, for tomorrow we shall die'" (Yeshayah 22:13). Now, what are the words that follow this verse? "And the Lord of Hosts revealed Himself in mine ears. Surely this iniquity shall not be expiated by you till ye die." One should therefore afflict himself with the community, for thus we find that Moses afflicted himself out of sympathy with the community, as it is said: "But Moses's hands were heavy and they took a stone and put it under him, and he sat thereon" (Shemot 17:12). Now, did not Moses have a cushion or a pillow to sit upon? But Moses said to himself, "As Israel is in trouble, I will share it with them."[1]

Such empathy is simply an aspect of fundamental humanity; but to the extent that it is universal in character, it is devoid of any identifying force. In this case, however, as the allusion to Moses makes clear, there is a sensitivity to specifically Jewish suffering. This sensitivity, in turn, simply exemplifies, within a Jewish setting, a natural and universal element: affinity for our sociocultural and ethnic confreres. In part, however, it includes a particularly Jewish component. It is grounded in the sense of mutual responsibility mandated by a common covenantal commitment, thus constituting the positive root of that "double ethic" with which, not altogether without justice, Max Weber and others have charged us. The halakhic implications of this bond were formulated by the rabbis in strictly legalistic terms: *Kol Yisrael arevim zeh ba-zeh* ("All Jews are guarantors for each other").[2] However, beyond the liability of each Jew for the physical and spiritual welfare of every other Jew lies the dimension of love – that which, as Denis de Rougemont once observed, results not from two persons contemplating each other, but rather from looking together at a common object.

Sinai produced no social contract. The *Gemeinschaft* which in one sense constituted its basis, and in another its issue, derived, not from reciprocal fealty, but from the reality of the gestation of "a kingdom of priests and a holy nation" with whose members and aspirations we could identify and to whom we could belong.

The kinship implicit in common commitment goes far beyond affiliation. It is in the nature of a brother's concern rather than a stranger's sympathy. Empathy is more the result of felt identity than an alternative to it or to its dialectical pole. From this perspective, both types of *hizdahut* are clearly related; and yet, in at least one important respect, they are fundamentally different. Empathy is essentially expansive. It projects an individual from the confines of his own being into the human reality beyond; and, through a process of imaginative transference – that existence as "the Proteus of human intellect" which Hazlitt so admired in Shakespeare – enables the individual to identify with the joys and sorrows of his fellows.

Self-definition, by contrast, is inherently confining. As the term indicates, definition places bounds upon the individual, since he attains one identity at the cost of dissociation from others. At this level, *hizdahut* requires a choice between mutually exclusive options.

SINGULAR AND UNIQUE

The significance of this element is reinforced, for our purpose, by a specifically Jewish factor. Judaism's blending of universalism and particularism has always included a strong element of separatism and even exclusiveness. As both adherents and critics have noted, the concept of a *goy kadosh* – a holy and therefore different nation – or of "distinction between Israel and the nations" has been central to Jewish thought and life from the very beginning. The sense of being not only singular but unique has lent Jewish national consciousness a special dimension. "And who is like Your people, Israel, a single nation upon earth?" the Jew asks God rhetorically in his Sabbath-afternoon prayer; and the implicit reply helps mold his self-definition.

The modes of self-identification as well as their substance are clearly determined by individual perceptions of the content and meaning of Jewish identity. What does it mean, personally and collectively, to be a Jew? Is Jewishness an axiological or a sociopolitical category? Is its primary axis normative or cultural? Does it impose spiritual demands or merely provide a historical locus? Must it be religious, or can it be secular in character? The answers to these questions will determine the nature of one's *hizdahut*.

From my own halakhic perspective, the answers may seem fairly obvious; and yet we should beware of oversimplification. Ideally, Jewish existence is inextricably rooted in religious commitment. Nevertheless, the possibility of fragmentary Jewishness cannot be dismissed. The Halakhah allows for it, declaring that the secular Jew is "like a Gentile" for some purposes, whereas "a Jew, although he has sinned, remains a Jew."[3] The traditional Jew may be tempted to limit Jewish self-definition to spiritual commitment while relegating national *hizdahut* to empathy. However, such a view, comfortable as it may sometimes be, is simplistic. It is wrong, logically, because nationality is no less defining than religion; and it is wrong, morally and halakhically, because it understates and undercuts the bonds that link the secular and even the assimilated Jew to his fellows, and vice versa.

Notwithstanding the profound importance of ideological considerations, there is a point beyond which they should not be pressed. On the basis of pure ideology, I should feel much closer to Gilson than to Weizmann. Do I? Only the grossest misinterpretation of Jewish identity could lead to greater existential kinship with a Damascus qadi than with a Mapam kibbutznik.[4]

We should also beware of a second error: the facile assumption that, while empathy need not entail self-definition, the latter does include the former. This is not necessarily the case: a Jew may be conscious of his Jewishness and yet reject his patrimony. However, we should not dismiss this level of identification entirely. While full *hizdahut* embraces acceptance as well as awareness, even self-hatred reflects a sense, at times both profound and perverse, of one's roots. Blasphemy, Eliot often contended, is more religious than indifference.

PUBLIC DIMENSION

While identification is clearly a function of identity, the two are nevertheless distinct. The latter relates to essence and existence, the former to experience and expression. This distinction is relevant even to a discussion of the individual Jew *tout seul*. Primarily, however, it is reflected in his relation to others. While *hizdahut* may be a purely personal phenomenon, it generally includes, both consciously and unconsciously, a public dimension. Empathy and self-definition are communicated as well as felt. Moreover, the process of communication is dynamic, and the inner reality is modified by its expression.

This public identification is itself dual. In some respects it may be largely or even wholly involuntary, the inevitable result of simply living and being observed and classified by others. In a Jewish context, visible *hizdahut* is also a matter of conscious choice; and, as such, it is, like empathy, halakhically mandated: "Neither shall ye walk in their [the Egyptians' and the Canaanites'] statutes." This is elaborated by the rabbis and codified by Maimonides:

> We should not follow the customs of the Gentiles, nor imitate them in dress or in their way of trimming the hair, as it is said, "And you shall not walk in the customs of the nation which I have cast out before you" (Vayikra 20:23); "Neither shall you walk in their statutes" (ibid. 18:3); "Take heed to yourself

that you be not ensnared to follow them" (Devarim 12:30). These texts all refer to one theme and warn against imitating them. The Israelite shall, on the contrary, be distinguished from them and be recognizable by the way he dresses and in his other activities, just as he is distinguished from them by his knowledge and his principles. And thus it is said, "And I have set you apart from the peoples" (Vayikra 20:26).[5]

Put in these terms, the demand that one not only *be* but *appear to be* a Jew is largely inner-directed, as it serves to deepen personal identity. However, differentiation clearly has centrifugal significance. As an overt assertion of Jewish existence, it confronts the world with an implicit declaration of Jewish values and Jewish destiny. It reaffirms, publicly, the Jew's commitment to the God of Israel.

PATTERNS OF INDENTIFICATION

The specific patterns of *hizdahut Yehudit* may be divided into two broad categories, one consisting of fairly direct and even pragmatic activities, the other of predominantly symbolic elements, both cutting across the line between empathy and self-definition. Practical action ranges from support of Jewish causes, through adherence and affiliation, to commitment to Jewish culture and full halakhic living. Support may be moral or financial, political as well as philanthropic. Overt affiliation translates itself into membership in a *Hizdahut Yehudit*, a synagogue, or any other communal or fraternal organization, with widely divergent degrees of involvement. Finally, in a more private sphere, a sense of Jewishness finds expression in day-to-day personal behavior. Minimally, this entails marriage within the fold; maximally, the discipline of a comprehensive and intensive regimen of *mizvot*, some of which, as the Torah tells us, posit the sharpening of Jewish identity as their immediate rationale, but all of which collectively advance this aim in an ancillary way.

As for identification through symbolic elements, there were three which, according to a midrash, distinguished the children of Israel in Egypt: name, language, dress. Naturally, these elements differ in character. Nomenclature generally belongs to that group of relatively superficial and accidental (in the scholastic sense) badges that set apart a given referent.

Language, by contrast, is both the repository of past experience and the vehicle of present expression, in a symbolic order organically related to the collective reality it signifies. Dress, which for our purposes includes personal appearance, straddles the two. Nevertheless, each in its own way is a principal instrument of identification, its significance depending upon the degree of choice involved in its use. The halting Hebrew spoken by a Russian activist may reveal far more Jewish consciousness than the fluent Hebrew prattled by an Israeli youngster.

SOCIOPOLITICAL IMPACT

Thus far, I have made minimal reference to particular contexts, preferring to focus upon constant elements. It now remains to discuss some contemporary facets of our subject. The situation today is, for better or worse, significantly different from that which obtained for almost two millennia. The causes of this change are of two types. Some are attributable to the general course of modern history, and thus, as regards European or American Jewry, date back a century or two; others are the outgrowth of more strictly contemporary developments. The major changes in the fabric of Ashkenazi society, wrought by the transition from the medieval to the modern world, are too familiar to require recounting.[6] Here we need only note that the impact has been dual.

First, the overall level of Jewish identification has receded, because of the interaction of two related factors. On the one hand, the secularizing influence of modern culture has attenuated the scope and intensity of *hizdahut Yehudit* ; on the other, this ideological erosion has coincided with sociopolitical changes which, for the first time in centuries, have made integration into the broader Gentile world a very live and increasingly attractive option. During the last decade, the erosion of Jewish identification has been reflected in an alarming increase in intermarriage. But this is simply the logical culmination of a process that has dulled both the Jew's sense of his own uniqueness and the Gentile's reluctance to forge bonds with him.

Second, the impact of the Emancipation and the *Haskalah* has resulted in greater emphasis upon national, as opposed to religious, modes of identification. This was not true of the early champions of Jewish *Aufklärung*; Mendelssohn and his ideological progeny could have thought of nothing worse. However, nineteenth- and early twentieth-century Jewish society, especially in Eastern Europe, increasingly regarded language, culture, and political aspiration as the focus of both the substance and the mode of Jewish identification. This shift, too, has helped make intermarriage more acceptable and feasible. If religious, especially traditional, thought spoke of Jewish uniqueness and reciprocal covenantal commitment, secular nationalistic ideology could only tell the Jew that he belonged to one nation *inter alia*. Small wonder that so many have found ethnicity no obstacle to intermarriage.

THE ZIONIST IMPACT

The emphasis upon nationality has found its most prominent expression in Zionism; and this brings us to more specifically contemporary aspects of *hizdahut Yehudit*. The two major events that have stamped Jewish life in this generation – the Holocaust and the rise of the State of Israel – have molded patterns of Jewish identification. While the impact of the former has been more traumatic, the impact of the latter has certainly been broader. The existence of the state affects Jewish identification both within and without Israel. At one level, it has restored identities, such as citizenship and soldiering, that had dropped out of Jewish history for two millennia. Concurrently, the resumption of political life has sharpened the need for renewed definition of the relation between the material and spiritual elements of Judaism. At another level, Israel has become the focus of Diaspora Jewry's commitment to Jewish history. It has restored pride and generated anxiety. It has helped Jews relate to the past and reach for the future. For many, it has become the primary medium through which they can identify as Jews.

In practical terms, the sense of identification aroused by the state has found its primary outlet in a remarkable display of philanthropy. But the ethnic consciousness generated by the disproportionate prominence of the state on the international scene is reflected in other ways too. The increased use of Hebrew names in the West, almost unheard of in the thirties, is one manifestation. The quasi-messianic hopes entertained by segments of Russian Jewry are another – if at quite a different level.

Nevertheless, the impact of the state should not be exaggerated. For one thing, with regard to most Jews, it has generated more empathy than self-definition, although, in practice, the two are related. Charity, as either *caritas* or philanthropy, is less demanding, above all less committing, than self-definition. It allows for a wide latitude of multiple loyalties. Second, in terms of Jewish identification, Zionism, along with the rise of the State of Israel, has had negative, as well as positive, results. It has enhanced the affinity of those who might otherwise have become wholly estranged; but by making possible and even encouraging the substitution of national for religious categories, it has diluted the content of Jewish identification for others.

On the collective plane, it has done even more. The gospel of "normal" national existence, that age-old dream which Ezekiel confronted – "We will be as the nations, as the families of the countries" (20:32) – often called, in effect, for collective assimilation, and Jewish identification was accordingly impaired. As it happened, the pressure of history has outrun ideology, and the Yishuv has had to rediscover the reality of Jewish loneliness and even uniqueness. Nevertheless, the danger of assimilation *en bloc* remains very real.

The rise of the state has affected Jewish identification in yet another way. The very normalization of social and cultural life has emasculated the identifying force of certain elements. Language, for instance, once figured prominently as an aspect of *hizdahut*. It need not today. Can a Tel Aviv student appreciate the value of Hebrew in tsarist Odessa? As visions have faded into the light of common day, and as they have often been less consciously sought, their symbolic potency has been reduced.

THE HOLOCAUST EXPERIENCE

The second major experience, the Holocaust, has affected the Jewish identification of those within and without its range. Although the sensibilities of the former have been dulled by time, the searing effect of the torment has molded their Jewish identity and subsequent identification. For some, driven both to defy seemingly elemental forces and to ally themselves with "the powers above," the agony sharpened and deepened *hizdahut Yehudit.* Many either rebelled or were left listless. In some degree, however, virtually all wrestled – none remaining unaffected.

For others, fortunate enough to have been spared the horrors of the Holocaust, the impact upon Jewish identification has been qualitatively weaker; but in their case, too, conflicting results have been produced. Some, overcome by skepticism and despair, have become totally disaffected. Many have reacted by identifying more fully. For those whose response to the Holocaust is peripheral, the change has been limited, frequently confined to sympathy with suffering confreres but largely devoid of keener self-definition. But Jews who are more deeply involved intellectually and emotionally have responded in terms of the latter as well. The very scope of the destruction has stiffened resolve to persist and strengthened Jewish consciousness. Resolve has, in turn, produced a measure of activism. Theoretically, it is formulated in Emil Fackenheim's "614th commandment": not to give Hitler another victory. Practically, it is reflected in expressions ranging from the Jewish Defense League's "Never Again" to aspects of Israeli foreign policy. It has, above all, brought home the need to assert Jewish existence more visibly and forcefully. In the wake of the Holocaust, many have found J.L. Gordon's counsel, "Be a man when you go out and a Jew in your home," totally unacceptable. The victory over Hitler and those whose silence abetted him requires that one not only be Jewish but overtly Jewish.

The acceptance of this lesson, learned with such frightful pain, is the legacy of the Holocaust. It may well have been reinforced by the development of the State of Israel. For the individual, a low Jewish profile may be feasible and, from a practical standpoint, often advisable. For a state, especially one with such a sensitive relation both to the international community and to Diaspora Jewry, such a stance hardly seems possible. To the extent that it draws sustenance from Jews in whom it strengthens Jewish identification, the state must recognize and, overtly or indirectly, declare its Jewishness; and to the extent that its political claims are rooted in Jewish history and Jewish destiny, it is driven to identify with them actively. In this sense, the specifically contemporary aspects of Jewish existence coalesce with the constant elements within it in the persistent quest for new and yet very old patterns of *hizdahut Yehudit.*

Notes

1. Bavli, Ta'anit 11a; translation in *Treatise Ta'anit of the Babylonian Talmud*, ed. Henry Malter, Jr. (Philadelphia, 1928), pp. 74–75.
2. Bavli, Shevuot 39a.
3. Bavli, Sanhedrin 44a. I have treated some of the halakhic ramifications of this question in "Brother Daniel and the Jewish Fraternity," *Judaism* 12 (1963): 260–280, included in the present volume; see third section; pp. 57–83.
4. This point – the balance between spiritual affinity and physical kinship (in the broadest sense of the term) – is bound up with one's perception and definition of Jewish identity and obviously requires fuller elaboration. Here I confine myself to rejecting the total domination of pure ideology.
5. Maimonides, Mishneh Torah, Hilkhot Avodat Kokhavim 11:1; translation in *A Maimonides Reader*, ed. Isadore Twersky (New York, 1973), pp. 74–75.
6. With respect to large segments of Sephardic Jewry, the transition from quasi-medieval to modern culture has coincided with more strictly contemporary developments.

Chapter 10

Jewish Values in a World of Change:
The Role of Jewish Communal Service

A definition of the role of Jewish communal service vis-à-vis Jewish values in a world of change should presumably best begin with the presentation and analysis of the values in question. To adopt that course, however, is to confront, at the outset, one of the prime difficulties besetting the modern Jewish community: the lack of consensus concerning the nature and substance of contemporary Jewish existence. With respect to many readers, such a presentation would run the risk of arousing opposition before its message has even been integrated. There are Jews whose hackles are raised by the mere mention of an avowedly halakhic position. Nevertheless, I opt for an ideological opening, and this, not only in submission to the dictates of logic and methodology (not to mention simple honesty), but out of a deep-rooted conviction, admittedly part of the traditional credo, that whatever its short-term divisive impact, for which there is abundant historical and contemporary evidence, Torah ultimately constitutes a genuinely unifying element in Jewish life; perhaps, in the final analysis, the only unifying element. So I trust that even readers who cannot subscribe to its total *Weltanschauung* will bear with me until the conclusion of this essay, and hopefully discover that it can nevertheless provoke thought and perhaps even provide a measure of direction.

Reprinted from *Journal of Jewish Communal Service* 61 (Fall 1984).

Jewish values exist on two levels. In one sense, Judaism demands the perfection of universal values, moral and religious. In another, it posits new categories, broaching novel and largely particularistic demands. Sinai constitutes both the culmination of an antecedent historical process and a wholly fresh departure. On the one hand, the Rambam concludes a sketch of the gradual proliferation of *mizvot* with the phrase, "until Moshe Rabbenu came and Torah was completed through him,"[1] clearly suggesting that Torah built upon existing historical, and presumably axiological, foundations. On the other, the rabbis describe the Sinaitic entry into the Covenant as an act of conversion,[2] and therefore to be perceived in light of the halakhic dictum that "a proselyte who converts is regarded as a newborn child."[3] Practically speaking, Halakhah is equally normative whether defined as the optimal means of attaining general human goals or as a way of realizing specifically Jewish ones. Philosophically, however, the difference between the two perspectives – and, consequently, the dialectical relation between them – is quite significant.

The universal values themselves break down into two categories, the moral and the religious. Bestriding both is the primal concept of *zelem E-lohim*, "the human face divine" (in Milton's phrase) – faith in the dignity and sanctity of man in both moral and metaphysical terms; and, concomitantly, in the worth and meaning of life. This faith finds normative expression in God's mandate to Adam, who is put "into the Garden of Eden to develop it and to keep it,"[4] i.e., Adam is charged with enhancing and preserving the world he inhabits. This dual call to creative endeavor and sociohistorical responsibility translates, practically, into a clear work ethic; and work, in one form or another, is a cardinal Jewish value.

Judaism proper, however, begins not with Adam but with Avraham; and his universal message is clearly and prophetically defined by Isaiah:

> Hearken to Me, ye that follow after righteousness.
> Ye that seek the Lord;
> Look unto the rock whence you were hewn,
> and the hole of the pit whence ye were digged.
> Look unto Abraham your father,
> And unto Sarah that bore you.[5]

The "passion for righteousness" (as Arnold aptly conceived "Hebraism") and the passion for God; social justice – comprehending not only legal deserts but the outreach of Avraham's hallmark, *hesed*,[6] to the needy and the underprivileged – and radical monotheism; that is the patriarchal legacy to mankind, to be ideally implemented through a Torah existence.

Our particularism, too, springs from Avraham. He was, after all, a convert, and, following his conversion, began to build a people.[7] It was only at Sinai, however, that we attained mature national fruition; and it was there that two new related elements, henceforth cardinal Jewish values, entered the picture. The first was Torah, the content of revelation proper, whose study and perpetuation then became a central Jewish concern. The second was Israel, a covenantal community forged by axiological commitment no less than by historical destiny; and its preservation, too, assumed primary significance.

With Sinai, the panoply of cardinal Jewish values was largely completed, although the entry into Eretz Israel – conceived as the focus of divine immanence, as the matrix of national existence, as the locus of historical and eschatological fulfillment, and as a unique social and, perhaps, even metaphysical entity – subsequently obtruded an additional element, partly instrumental and partly intrinsic. Henceforth, the Jewish world, personal or collective, would rest upon fairly constant foundations: the sanctity of man and the sanctification of life; responsibility to preserve and enhance the human environment; the religious quest for God and the moral quest for a just and compassionate society; commitment to the study and observance of Torah and to the physical and spiritual sustenance of the community of Israel as both a covenantal and a national entity.

But if the basic values have, within the central tradition, remained relatively constant, their implementation and, at times, their interpretation have not. Modes, emphases, priorities, all have been subject to the ebb and flow of historical currents. Even within a seemingly rigorous halakhic regimen, there is far more flexibility than meets the eye, especially that of an outsider.[8] With respect to some of the most critical decisions in a person's life, the choice of a mate or a career, for instance, there are no definitive halakhic norms. Or again, while certain familial obligations are clearly and rigorously mandated, the structure and character of domestic relations remain largely a matter of personal choice. Nothing dictates whether a father be a Prussian *paterfamilias* or a chummy mentor. Likewise on the communal plane. In one context, education may stress the communication of knowledge; in another, the inculcation of commitment. Physical survival takes priority in one generation, spiritual growth in the next. Each hour has its own call, and the vicissitudes of history require flexibility with respect to both strategy and tactics.

The proper perception of change is thus essential to the intelligent direction of private conduct or public policy. It is important, however, that the nature and scope of change be properly evaluated, and the tendency to exaggerate needs to be resisted. Any traditionally oriented worldview is inclined, almost by definition, to the classical position that human nature and human society fundamentally remain, in Hooker's celebrated phrase, "general and universal," and Judaism is no exception. It recognizes the significance of change, yet holds that change is generally overshadowed by constancy; and it insists that we must discriminate between profound and meaningful change and merely superficial difference.[9]

Nevertheless, with respect to our own times, the feeling that we are being swept along by currents of genuine and accelerated change persists. It is probably difficult for us, as contemporaries, to assess this feeling. In part, this is no doubt part of our nineteenth-century legacy of historical consciousness; and, to some extent, it is true that even denizens of what retrospectively appear to have been eminently stable periods often saw their work as marked by transition, if not disintegration. Allowance for these factors having been made, however, the perception of exponential change persists; and I, for one, am inclined to accept it.

The patterns of change are multifaceted and of varying scope and duration. On one level, we are still being buffeted by the cultural forces that have gradually secularized much of the West over the last three centuries. In the Jewish community, these have increasingly led to weakened commitment, as many of its scions – first in Europe, but, more recently, among Oriental Jewry – have run the gamut from secularization, though assimilation, and to the point of intermarriage. On a second level, we are still under the impact of specific twentieth-century developments, primarily the Holocaust and the gestation of a renascent Jewish state. On yet a third level, we are confronted by possibly still inchoate trends affecting the contemporary scene. These are both external and internal. Among the former, the most signfificant, at least in North America, is the dimunition of Jewish political and possibly economic power.

In relative terms, the Jewish community is now less influential than it was a decade or two ago, and the opportunities open to its members are more limited. The potentially omnious ramifications are obvious. Among them, one might cite the ferment concerning the status of women, the declining birth rates, the growing incidence of divorce, the proliferation of "blended" and "reconstituted" families, and the gradual aging of the population – all general phenomena but with particular implications for the Jewish world. Of more singularly Jewish developments, perhaps the most significant is increased polarization, the result of both the constriction of the overall base through attrition and assimilation, and of the contraction of horizons in many quarters. All this, of course, quite apart from more general socioeconomic and cultural factors, such as the ongoing technological revolution and the possibly radical changes in the mode of communication. In sum, the feeling that ours is indeed a world of relatively rapid and substantive change is soundly based.

Given this context, how might we best conceive the role of contemporary Jewish communal service, and what direction can one offer it constituents? I am inclined to open with an admittedly conservative counsel: Don't lose your heads. Given the pervasive sense of rapid change, it is all too easy to lose one's balance and bearings, to be overwhelmed by the razzle-dazzle of social gimmickry and the welter of pseudo-scientific jargon. But precisely because of the scope of current change, the last thing the Jewish world needs is the substitution' of glitter for substance or the pursuit of novelty at the expense of basic values. These remain pretty much what they have always been, historically; and, for our purposes, they can be succinctly distilled into the twin aims of serving God and servicing Jews. That is, of course, a religious formulation, and the first component is barely palatable to the consistent secularist. But for him too, Jewishness,

however he defines it, is presumably not just a sociological but an ideological category – indeed, the historical and philosophic source of many
of his most cherished humanistic values; and he, too, is confronted by the
dual challenge of integrating and inculcating the axiological complex and
of helping his brethren.

Moreover, both purposes are, to an extent, related, inasmuch as aid
to a fellow-Jew is geared not only to sustaining him as an individual but
to enhancing the viability of the Jewish community as a whole; and, as
many have reluctantly come to realize, Jewish communal survival, even
in purely sociological terms, is directly linked to spiritual commitment. In
pursuit of these goals, the ability to adapt, resourcefully and imaginatively,
to change is crucial; but on the condition that in the process, we do not
erode our feeling for the values themselves. And we should once again
beware of luxuriating in an exaggerated sense of the presumed uniqueness
of our own situation, over and above the singularity of every historical
era. We ought, rather, to bear in mind that it is precisely the combination
of resourcefulness and commitment which has stood Jewry in such good
stead throughout the ages.

Thus, our two primary aims, the social and the ideological, are intimately and reciprocally linked. We help preserve our people by enriching
its spiritual fiber; and part of that fiber is the emphatic readiness to help.
Today as ever, therefore, the first priority of Jewish communal service
should be to enhance both the sense of community, as opposed to individualism, and the sense of universalism. This entails, initially, a return
to primal values: work and responsibility. These, conceived not only as
instruments of self-realization but also as avenues to helping others, are
grounded in the altruistic impulse and serve to reinforce it. As such, they
stand opposed to the pleasure principle which in recent decades has so
pervaded Western culture and, through it, Jewish society.

The work ethic is a bit passé in our changing world, and many Jews
tend to regard it as a Puritan relic. In this respect, however, Puritanism's
self-image as the "new Israel" is right on the mark. Work, not contrasted
with study (which is simply a specific and higher labor)[10] or with enriching leisure (what the Greeks called *schole*), but with pleasure, is, as previ-

ously stated, a cardinal Jewish value and one that we should encourage as a means of deepening the sense of giving and sacrifice. Concomittantly, we should strive, by precept and example, to tone down the pleasrues of opulence. The sybaritic self-indulgence, complete with glatt kosher junkets, that has become a way of life for so many who can afford it, and an aspiration for those who can't, stands radically opposed to Jewish tradition and experience. We should recognize this fact and be ready to act upon it. And we should recognize, too, the profound Jewish truth that ultimately self-fulfillment is largely attained through *hesed* and community. This, as Lionel Trilling aptly noted, is the clearest sense of Hillel's celebrated dictum: "If I am not for myself, who is for me? [But] if I am for myself alone, what am I?"[11]

A second manifestation of altruism is even more personal. In an age in which the very status of the family has become an issue, we should encourage Jews not only to raise families but to raise large ones. Neither personal convenience nor presumed universal interest can provide a rationale for merely maintaining the status quo. Whatever the current global merits of zero population growth, for post-Holocaust Jewry it is an intolerable canon. We cannot eradicate the enormity of Auschwitz, but the least we can do as a nation is to "replace" (how frighteningly inhuman the term but imperative nonetheless) its victims. Whatever the career cost, and however parents divide it, a large family constitutes a desideratum in Jewish life today. And here too, with the means at our disposal, we should promote not only the responsibility of parenthood but its self-fulfilling joys. An early Jewish source amply attests to them amply. In response to the divine promise, "Fear not, Avram, I am thy shield, thy reward shall be exceedingly great," Avram asks poignantly, "O Lord God, what wilt Thou give me, seeing I go childless?"[12]

As was indicated above, the emphasis upon community contrasts not only with individualism but with universalism. Conceptually, this in no way entails the renunciation of *hesed* as a catholic category. Just as the rejection of individualism as an ideology does not negate the value of self-fulfillment but instead presents a different mode of attaining it, so the rejection of universalistic doctrine does not entail apathetic insensitivity to mankind but posits a different way of progressively relating to it. In practice, however, there is no denying the fact that a centripetal thrust tends to minimize, if not deaden, concern for outsiders. As such, it often compromises the ideal of *hesed*.

Nevertheless, given our present situation, I see no alternative to turning inward. The combination of rising assimilation and declining power mandates increased concern for specifically Jewish needs – spiritual, physical, and emotional. Despite the best humanitarian intentions, we cannot escape the pressure of priority. "Many are Thy people's needs, and their wit is limited," intones the *piyyut*, and this aptly describes our current situation. Whether certain communal manifestations of our collective generous impulse were in order a generation ago is perhaps debatable; that most can no longer be afforded is not. At the same time, we should make an educational effort to contain the insidious effects of creeping insularity. The notion, altogether too prevalent in some circles (albeit, perhaps not those likely to read this paper), that the concerns or even the suffeirng of mere goyim are irrelevant to us cannot be countenanced. Avraham Avinu and Moshe Rabbenu, at any rate, thought otherwise.

The question of priorities arises, of course, with respect to purely domestic needs as well. It confronts us in two related areas: the choice of values and the choice of population. Ideally, to be sure, Jewish institutions should foster the whole gamut of cardinal Jewish values, all the more inasmuch as those values constitute an organic whole. Practically, however, some must be preferred over others. In determining precedence, the nature of the setting must obviously be considered. No single institution can address itself equally to all aims, although in defining its own focus it should bear the total context in mind. From an overall perspective, therefore, decisions must be made at two levels. First, to what extent should single-purpose institutions be developed at the expense of multifaceted ones, and which? Second, with respect to the latter – I refer primarily to community centers – what is the overriding aim and what relatively secondary?

I do not propose to offer pat solutions to such questions, but I would very much urge that they be approached, both axiomatically and pragmatically, with a vision that can define general national priorities while allowing for local variables. We can hardly equate Lawrence, New York, with Lawrence, Kansas. Broadly speaking, however, in assessing the role of Jewish communal service today, I would assign top priority to the deepening of Jewish identity and commitment. Would that the situation were otherwise, and that communal entities could provide already deeply committed Jews with necessary services. Unfortunately, however, in most places, for the foreseeable future, that is the ball game. Between helping a Jew cope with his problems or satisfy his desires and keeping him Jewish, there is not much room for choice. This may appear to entail the precedence of collective over personal needs, and to some extent it does. It should be borne in mind, however, that from a traditional perspective, Jewish identity is itself a most precious boon.

This is not to suggest that all Jewish centers should be primarily concerned with overtly inculcating commitment. On the whole, that responsibility is better left to schools and synagogues. However, they should strive to create a climate conducive to commitment, one in which it should clearly be regarded as a desideratum. They should, at the very least, instill a basic sense of belonging. At present, this sense is less easily attained than a generation ago. Mere presence in a Jewish setting no longer suffices; youngsters in particular need to be actively engaged as Jews. Gone are the days when basketball and arts and crafts provided an effective barrier against intermarriage.

Given the ambient freedom adolescents enjoy within the general culture, the danger is so pervasive that only meaningful Jewish experience can contain it. This requires positive content – not necessarily "religious," narrowly speaking, but a clear and conscious call to act and exist as part of the Jewish people, and a feeling of the moral and spiritual challenge of that existence. Here again, the readiness to give should be developed and tapped. Jewish communal service provides for those in need. Upon those presumably not in need, it can bestow a sense of giving and belonging, thus realizing a profound Jewish value and imbuing a feeling of Jewish confraternity.

The need for priorities obtrudes upon the selection of target populations no less than upon the choice of values. To which age group, socio-economic stratum, or spiritual level should Jewish communal service address itself primarily? Presumably, no sector should be wholly ignored, but the emphasis can vary, and here again, numerous variables should be weighed. Nevertheless, some policy guidelines can be suggested, with an eye to both private and public interests. Traditionally, Jewish communal service, at least in North America, has been oriented, like American culture generally, toward the young. In the light of current demographic trends and projections, this orientation is open to serious question. The increase in the proportion of the aged, combined with the fact that their social and economic needs are often greater than their grandchildren's, surely calls for some restructuring.

Nevertheless, we should beware of excesses. In establishing priorities, we need to consider not only the socioeconomic factor as an individual concern, but the Jewish element, regarded as both a personal and a communal need. Service to a senior citizen is mandated by *hesed*, and as such is enormously important; but its impact upon the quality of his Jewish commitment is, on the whole, relatively minimal. With respect to the young, however, insofar as service to them molds their Jewish identity, it assumes an entirely different dimension. Relating to this age group, a community center services not only Reb Israel but *K'lal Yisrael*, and this fact should be assigned significant weight in deciding upon the allocation of energies and resoures.

At the same time, we should take heed lest we lapse into the glorification of youth that is so endemic to much current Western culture but so alien to Judaism. Respect for age is deeply rooted in Jewish tradition, and sensitivity to its character is a moral and religious value to be instilled collectively. We cannot expect every older person to sing, with Browning's Rabbi Ben Ezra, "Grow old along with me! / The best is yet to be." But we can strive to impart a sense of dignity and purpose to life's twilight and to imbue concern and respect for it. In this educational effort, communal institutions that serve both ends of the age spectrum directly and can develop an integrated approach to their needs can play a significant role. Indeed, we should strive to relate to both groups simultaneously through imaginative initiatives that challenge the young to serve the old themselves, thus helping not only to bridge the collective generation gap, but also to provide for those in need and to educate toward a life of *hesed*. Moreover, we could thus deepen the sense of community and enable the youngsters to realize that, for all they may help their seniors, there is so much which they can receive from them.

With respect to age groups, I have suggested that priorities be determined not only on the basis of mundane physical and/or emotional needs but with an eye to personal and public spiritual interests. Similar considerations obtain with respect to choosing between more or less committed target populations. Jewish communal service should be primarily oriented to meeting the greatest spiritual needs, to reaching those on the periphery of our world, whose contacts with Jewish educational or religious institutions are tangential at best – the multitude of marginal Jews for whom a community center may be the last barrier to assimilation. Agencies geared to responding to specific needs – vocational guidance, family counseling, and the like – should be equally oriented and accessible to all; but institutions such as centers that initiate programs and provide facilities with structured communal goals should maximize their efforts where the results are apt to be most critical.

Clearly, much thought needs to be given to the likelihood of success. In some cases, an emphasis upon servicing the marginally committed may be unwarranted, as resources and energies may be wasted upon them and better spent elsewhere, and we also need to beware of spreading ourselves too thin. In principle, however, their needs should take precedence over those of others less in danger and better able to fend for themselves.

Coming from an Orthodox rabbi, this may appear to be strange doctrine. But can we responsibly entertain any other? To be sure, we invest substantially in institutions of higher learning, knowing full well that the resources and energies devoted to their enrichment and embellishment could conceivably save some marginal Jew from spiritual disaster. However, these institutions ensure and enhance our collective existence in a way that community centers cannot. They add a cultural dimension, develop leadership, and posit a standard of excellence. Hence, if we are to sustain the quality of our spiritual life, we cannot neglect them out of purely quantitative considerations. The role of communal service is quite different, however; and in defining the scope of its activity, precedence should indeed be given to Jews who, precisely because they are *not* likely to enhance the quality of our collective spiritual life, can derive maximal benefit from it.

If, in one respect, Jewish communal service focuses upon a particular segment of the community, in another it relates to the Jewish world as a whole. I refer to its role as a unifying force. Broadly based and not necessarily identified with any particular sector, its institutions can mold our sorely fractured society in one of two ways. First, they can meet, albeit separately, the specific needs of various groups, whether by providing genuinely special services, such as classes with a given ideological orientation, or by allocating the use of essentially general facilities, as in the areas of sports or music. This is a rather limited unifying mode, but in our present situation, even the moderate interaction resulting from the common use of a single complex is not to be denigrated.

Beyond this, however, communal institutions can provide a focus and a forum for truly cooperative activity and, at times, perhaps for constructive confrontation as well. In this connection, the relation to Eretz Yisrael – the land, its people, and its state – can play a significant role. Through it, one can transcend parochial concerns and relate, horizontally and vertically, to the Jewish people as a whole. Despite the lamentable decline in Zionist commitment in the last decade, Israel is still the object of a broader consensus than almost any other major concern in Jewish life, and this situation is likely to continue for the foreseeable future. Moreover, the unifying force of a relation to Israel is built around positive consent and is not the result of an emasculating blandness whose "unity," beyond a certain point, is simply not worth the candle.

The relation to *K'lal Yisrael*, as a concept and as a reality, brings us back to the issue of Jewish identity and commitment, and to the role of the community center as an educational force. A center is not, of course, primarily concerned with education in the narrow sense of the term. It should, however, be concerned, first, with what the Greeks called *paid-*

eia – the enhancing of powers, the enrichment of personality, and the orientation to values. Second, it can contribute to learning. The study of Torah has traditionally been a major Jewish value; and even where that, strictly defined, is not feasible, the acquisition and internalization of Jewish knowledge, more broadly conceived, remains significant. A community center can advance Jewish learning in two respects. It can simply offer classes in different areas and for various age groups, with an emphasis on adult education, especially for the many who are beyond the reach of schools or synagogues or have become disaffected with them. In this regard, the growing interest in informal education and the projected increase in leisure time offer an opportunity and a challenge. Beyond this, however, a center should strive to develop an openness to learning, to create a climate within which learning is regarded as a value, and respect and appreciation for it are cultivated.

Finally, in a world of change the role of Jewish communal service includes developing the capacity to deal with change. It can effect this in two ways: by transmitting the knowledge and the skills to cope with specific changes, and by providing a proper perspective upon the phenomenon in general. Current social trends clearly intensify the need for the former. In one area, rapid technological development has greatly exacerbated the problem of vocational obsolesence and raised the possibility of widespread middle-age career shifts. In another, as various factors have converged to intensify stress within the structure of the family, divorce has increasingly been sought as a solution, even in long-term marriages. And of course, in a more positive development, the rising actuarial curve has broadened the need for guidance in dealing with the blessings and traumas of longevity.

With respect to perspective, we are concerned not so much with increasing the numerator as with decreasing the denominator, not so much with teaching people how to climb mountains as with enabling them to see mountains as no more than hills. In this regard, Jewish identity and commitment can be of great significance. Quite apart from the sense of greater security that religious faith and trust instill, the feeling of rootedness inherent in identification with a historical tradition makes the current changes seem less threatening. By placing the ephemeral within the context of the permanent, it provides a firm psychological anchor; and the knowledge of a measure of underlying stability that it conveys confers the inner strength to confront change without being overwhelmed by it. This is doubly true with respect to Jewish history, whose tortuous path attests so eloquently to the ability to withstand the vicissitudes of change.

And therein lies a moral for institutions no less than for individuals. Surely, Jewish communal bodies cannot be obtuse to change. They must sensitize their antennae to perceive and even anticipate it, and they must manifest the wisdom and courage to cope with it, flexibly and imaginatively. At the same time, they must, as I have emphasized, beware of losing their bearings – of being frightened by mutation, of being tempted by faddishness. A committed Jew does not quite proclaim that *plus ça change, plus c'est la même chose.* But he senses that change should be perceived, if not *sub specie aeternitatis,* then at least in the context of a long and trying history. This knowledge gives him the strength to deal with its challenges, confident that, if our vision remains clear and our basic values sound, we shall overcome.

Notes

1. Mishneh Torah, Melakhim 9:1.
2. See Babylonian Talmud, Keritot 9a.
3. Babylonian Talmud, Yevamot 22a.
4. Bereshit 2:15.
5. Yeshayahu 51:1–2.
6. The term *hesed* is not readily translatable. It denotes both excess and lovingkindness, and is generally used to describe empathetic *caritas*, based upon the breaking down, or at least the lowering, of interpersonal barriers, and manifested in benevolent aid, not necessarily financial, to one's fellow, be he sick or poor (per Babylonian Talmud, Sukkah 49b).
7. The sequence of Avraham's circumcision as an act of conversion (signified by the change in his name, reflecting a new identity) just prior to Yizhak's birth, and presumably as a condition of it, is surely no coincidence; see Bereshit Rabbah 46:2.
8. I am not referring to possible changes in the normative substance of Halakhah but to differences resulting from optimal factors and modes of realization.

9. This perception may itself vary. In all likelihood, the sense of change was keener in biblical times than subsequently. Nevertheless, the generalization holds.
10. See Babylonian Talmud, Sanhedrin 99b.
11. Avot 1:14.
12. Bereshit 15:2. The Jewish Publication Society version, following the Vulgate's *ego vadam*, renders, "seeing I go hence." However, I prefer the interpretation of the Ramban, ad locum, that the statement refers to present desiccated loneliness rather than to future barren demise.

Chapter 11

Abortion: A Halakhic Perspective

The problem of abortion raises highly complicated halakhic issues, and several of the ramifications interact with a variety of halakhic areas. Moreover, as a number of fundamental issues are the subject of dispute, it is difficult to speak of a definitive halakhic approach in each area, Nevertheless, it is possible to identify the positions that appear to be most faithful to the basic sources and that have been accepted by the mainstream of major halakhic authorities. The purpose of this discussion, then, is to adumbrate the fundamental problems, to summarize the positions of the decisors, and here and there to express my personal view. This is not the forum for a detailed presentation involving subtle analysis of textual proofs and extensive halakhic give-and-take. My purpose is to convey a picture that is general, necessarily incomplete, yet as clear as possible. One hopes that the need for concision in this outline will enhance discussion of the topic.

Aborting an existing fetus is unequivocally prohibited. A famous mishnah records: "If a woman suffers hard labor in travail, the child [fetus] must be cut up in her womb and brought out piecemeal, for her life takes precedence over his life. If its greater part has already come forth, it must not be touched, for the [claim of one] life cannot supersede

---

This article is a translation of testimony delivered to a Knesset committee investigating the law regarding abortion. The Hebrew version appeared in *Beriut ha-Tzibbur* 17:4. The translation was prepared by Rabbi Nathaniel Helfgot and was published in *Tradition* 25:4 (Summer 1991).

[that of another life]" (Ohalot 7:6). The first case mentioned in the mishnah sanctions killing the fetus only because of the danger posed to the mother's life (implying that in general abortion of the fetus is prohibited). Several questions arise regarding the details of this prohibition, particularly respecting its source and scope, the responses to which carry significant practical implications.

Most basic is the origin and the source of the prohibition. Is it biblical or rabbinic? What is the nature of the stricture, and how should it be categorized? As to the first aspect, there is, indeed, a view according to which the entire prohibition on abortion is only rabbinic. Assuming that we set aside certain general ethical and religious norms, such as "You shall do that which is upright and good" (Devarim 6:18), "You shall be holy" (Vayikra 19:1), and "You shall follow in the ways of God" (Devarim 28:9), there would be, according to this view, no biblical prohibition against killing a fetus. However, in my opinion this view should not be accorded serious weight, not only because it is disturbing from a moral standpoint, but also because it seems to contradict an explicit Halakhah. Sanhedrin 57b cites the view of R. Yishmael that a Noahide who aborts a fetus has the legal status of a murderer. Maimonides (Mishneh Torah, Hilkhot Melakhim 9:4) codifies the law in accordance with the view of R. Yishmael; and, though the Talmud cites a differing view, to the best of my knowledge no decisor disputes Rambam's ruling. If so, it is inconceivable that this action would be permitted to a Jew, given the great halakhic principle which states: "Can there be any act that is permitted to a Jew and at the same time prohibited to a Noahide?" (Hullin 33a). In other words, no action forbidden to a non-Jew, of whom the Torah requires a less exacting moral standard, can be permitted to a Jew. Hence, we must conclude that there are some situations in which abortion is biblically proscribed. This indeed is the conclusion of most decisors. The question then remains: What is the specific prohibition? Several possibilities come immediately to mind.

1. *Homicide.* Although a Jew who kills a fetus is not punished by the judicial system as a murderer, he has nonetheless violated the prohibition against murder. It is like the case of someone who kills a *treifa* (an individual with a fatal wound or defect); he is not liable for capital punishment,

but he has violated the prohibition against muder and is liable for divine retribution.

2. *Ancillary to homicide (senif retzihah)*. Abortion falls into a category similar to improper emission of seed, an act viewed by the Talmud as tantamount to the shedding of blood (Niddah 13a) and about which Maimonides writes, "Not only is it a grave prohibition, but he who acts in this manner should sit in a state of excommunication; of him Scripture says: 'Your hands are full of blood' (Yesheyahu 1:15), and it is as if he had killed a human being" (Hilkhot Issurei Bi'ah 21:8). According to this position, abortion does not constitute homicide *per se*; it is part of a network of strictures revolving around the prohibition of murder but extending beyond it. This would be akin to the concept of *abizrahu* (actions ancillary to a specific sin) which appears in other halakhic contexts. For example, according to a number of Rishonim (medieval halakhic authorities), the requirement of giving up one's life rather than transgress the prohibition on idolatry, illicit sexual relations, or murder applies not only to these acts but to their appurtenances.

3. *Tort (habbalah)*. Even if the fetus is not a human being, whose killing comes under the rubric of homicide, abortion should still be proscribed as a consequence of the fetus's being an organic reality bound up with the person of the mother, a status which therefore prohibits intentional injury to it.

4. *Hatzalah* (the obligation to perserve life and the corollary prohibition of negligence). This concept is derived either from the commandment *Lo ta'amod al dam re'akha* ("You shall not stand idly by while your brother's blood is shed"; Vayikra 19:16) or from the obligation of *hashavat avedah* (return of lost property, which includes restoration of the body) or the concept of *va-hay bahem* ("You shall live by them"; Vayikra 18:5). Even if the prohibition of murder applies solely to persons already born, the positive obligation to preserve life may extend to the fetus because of its potential existence. Where an obligation to promote life exists, its truncation would clearly be forbidden.

As noted, I definitely favor the first possibility, based on the proof-text regarding the Noahide. Indeed, the Mekhilta records the position of Isi ben Akiva that whatever is forbidden a Noahide because of the prohibition of murder is likewise forbidden to the Jew: "Before revelation we were enjoined from shedding blood; after revelation, instead of forbidding such an action, shall we now permit it? Verily, they said, people who commit these acts are exempt from human punishment but are liable for divine retribution" (*Mishpatim*, Masekhet Nezikin 4). Although the punishment of the Jew for certain types of homicide may be lighter, the fact that he has violated the prohibition of homicide does not vary. Therefore, it seems clear that in any case where a Noahide abortionist is liable for murder, a Jew is also considered a murderer.

Here, however, we enter the area of the second fundamental issue: the scope of the prohibition. Does it apply to all fetuses in all situations or only to certain ones? If there are limitations, how are they determined? This question can be raised in relation to all the possible rationales listed above. Clearly they are not mutually exclusive. Some abortions may come under all the categories of prohibition; some may be permitted. To return for a moment to the violation of homicide and the proof from Noahide law, it seems to me that the Noahide is liable in those instances where the fetus has developed to the point of independent viability (outside the uterus) at the time. In such circumstances, a Jew committing an abortion is exempt from capital punishment only because of the child's status as a fetus, i.e., not having left the womb and entered the world; this exemption is not granted to the Noahide. Hence the Jew would violate the prohibition of homicide and be subject to divine punishment. In the early stages of pregnancy, however, the missing element of full human life is not merely that birth has yet to occur, but the absence of full development and the fact that in its current state the fetus is not viable outside the womb. It is logical to assume that such an abortion would not be classified as an act of murder. Murder, it would appear, is defined as the termination of currently existing life, and not the curtailment of potential life. Therefore, it would seem that the prohibition of murder should be limited to the latter part of pregnancy – practically speaking, more or less the last trimester.

The less severe cases listed above require a separate treatment. *Posekim* have suggested a number of possible stages within the period of pregnancy.

Each of these can be analyzed regarding the question of whether all, some, or none of the prohibitions apply. The proposed stages are (1) the initial period, (2) after the forty-day mark, (3) after the first trimester, and (4) after the quickening of fetal movement. Of these intermediate categories, the only one mentioned in the Talmud as a criterion is forty days (three months appears as a measure of recognition of pregnancy, not as a measure of the viability of the fetus). Prior to that stage, the Talmud records, the embryo is viewed as *maya be-alma* ("mere liquid"). For instance, a stillborn child ordinarily precludes the halakhic status of firstborn for the next child. Yet a miscarriage that occurs prior to the fortieth day of gestation is disregarded, and the next male offspring is considered the *peter rehem* (first of the womb) (Bekhorot 47a). As a result, it is proper to give greater weight to the forty-day mark, with implications for the detailed discussion below. If we go on to analyze the latter three prohibitions mentioned above in relation to these stages of pregnancy, the following conclusions may be drawn:

1. *Serah retzihah* (ancillary to homicide). If abortion is literally a case of *hashhatat zera* (destruction of seed), and not merely analogous to that category, the prohibition would come into play from the first moment. If, however, we assume that the specific prohibition on *hashhatat zera* does not apply in this case (e.g., if we adopt the view of Hazon Ish that *hashhatat zera* only applies to the person who ejaculates the semen, perhaps only at the moment of ejaculation), we are dealing with a distinct prohibition which is an appurtenance to murder. Then it would be possible to divide the period of pregnancy halakhically; the most reasonable measure is the forty-day mark.

2. *Habbalah* (the prohibition on injuring or wounding human beings, including oneself). This can be further divided into two possibilities. First, one may not injure the fetus because of its status as a living organism. There is no prohibition of murder because that requires the extinction of a self-sustaining life; but the stricture against intentional wounding might apply even to a human organism sustained by another biological organism. Second, abortion is proscribed because of the physical injury to the mother; the fetus is no less signficant than any other limb of the mother which is not to be dismembered unnecessarily.

According to the first possibility, the most reasonable cut-off mark is again the fortieth day of gestation. Before then, this stricture would certainly not apply, and the later stages are not sufficiently clear-cut to be used as standards. According to the second possibility, the fate of the fetus is subservient to its status as part-and-parcel of the mother; if so, the forty-day mark might become irrelevant. Here too, nonetheless, one may suggest that prior to the forty-day mark, removal of the fetus (categorized as "mere liquid") does not constitute injury to the mother, whereas removal after forty days does. This is because the fetus, having become a significant halakhic entity, renders the abortion a significant injury to the mother. This last point, however, is far from conclusive; there is definitely room to consider later stages as standards. Among these, three months seems to me the most reasonable, as it does appear in Halakhah as the stage of "recognition of the fetus" conferring the status of "pregnant" on the mother (Niddah 8b).

3. *Hatzalah* (the obligation to preserve life). Rishonim debate whether the obligation of *pikkuʾah nefesh* (violating prohibitions of the Torah, including those of Shabbat, to save a life) applies to a fetus: May one, for example, violate the Sabbath to avoid an abortion? Some permit this violation because the fetus has the status of *nefesh* (person), although this status applies to the post-forty-day embryo. Others are more lenient, on the basis of the rationale that "The Torah stated, violate one Shabbat for him in order that he may observe many Shabbatot in the future" (Yoma 85b). This justification for the concept of *pikkuʾah nefesh* applies to the pre-forty-day embryo as well. Others, however, forbid the violation of Shabbat in all cases inasmuch as they do not view the fetus as a *nefesh*.

Following the first view, abortion after the fortieth day would clearly be prohibited. Prior to that point, however, it is still an open question, as the exponents of this view only ruled that saving such a fetus does not justify the abrogation of various prohibitions. However, they did not propose that, where the effort to save life does not collide with Torah prohibitions, there is no obligation to preserve the fetus. According to the second view, it is reasonable that abortion would be prohibited even before the forty-day mark. While the fetus does not yet have the status of *nefesh,* it is difficult to imagine that the Torah would, on the one hand, permit abrogation of Shabbat laws to save such a fetus and, on the other, permit its arbitrary abortion. The third view allows both sides of this issue, even after the forty-day mark, perhaps as far as the last trimester, similarly to the position that would be held by the first view regarding the initial stage.

So far we have examined the scope of the prohibition of abortion in terms of certain stages of pregnancy. We now turn to the circumstances and the reasons for the abortion, and give the possible sanction for it in light of various factors. Here too, the scope of the prohibition or, if you will, the scope of the possible exemptions clearly depends on the sources and origin of the prohibition. Here too, we shall analyze the issue point by point.

1. *Homicide.* This prohibition is waived only in the face of actual threat to life. *Pikku'ah nefesh* is generally defined as real danger of loss of life, even if the chances of harm occurring are slim. There are some *posekim* who included in this category even spiritual danger, such as the threat of apostasy, or psychological danger. However, it must be emphasized that even this position was concerned with actual insanity that could be brought on by having the child, and not simply with a sense of frustration, perplexity, bad nerves, or some neurosis or psychosis. Wherever this prohibition pertains (in my opinion, the last trimester), abortion should therefore be sanctioned only when the life of the mother (or in the unlikely event, someone else's life) is in danger, or, according to some *posekim*, if the sanity of the parents is threatened. Furthermore, it must be noted that the expanded definition of preservation of life that derives from the opinion of these authorities was originally stated regarding the suspension of Shabbat, kashrut, and other similar restrictions where saving an individual threatened with insanity does not come at the cost of another life. In our case, by contrast, the parents' "rescue" comes at the cost of fetal life, and it may very well be that in such circumstances even these authorities would view a lenient course of action with reservations. For this reason such leniency must be employed, if at all, only in extreme circumstances. Similarly, the famous principle that "One does not follow probability in cases of preserving a life" (Yoma 84a), which allows for violation of Halakhah to save lives

even when the threat is statistically small, may not be operative when the prohibition to be set aside is murder. Even in cases of physical danger, the gravity of the situation should be carefully weighed.

2. *Serah retzihah.* Here it is clear that saving a life is not the only sanction for permitting an abortion. This is evident from the talmudic passage that permits a nursing mother to cohabitate using a *mokh* (a barrier of cotton or wool) to prevent pregnancy. Strictly speaking, this amounts to *hotzaat zera le-battalah* (improper emission of seed), yet the Halakhah does not decree that the woman practice abstinence during this period. Since this prohibition is waived to facilitate normal family relations (which is why the emission in this context is not "wasteful"), it would follow that other ethical and humane factors may also be taken into account.[1] It would seem to me that issues like *kevod ha-beriyot* (dignity of persons), *shalom bayit* (domestic peace), and *tza'ar* (pain), which all carry significant halakhic weight in other contexts, should be considered in making these decisions. However, it is difficult to set down clear-cut guidelines in this area, especially if we assume that our case is not an example of destruction of seed proper, but a parallel stricture that serves as a type of middle ground between the prohibitions on destruction of seed and homicide. I cannot now offer evidence or a clear-cut argument that can serve as a solid, compelling basis for defining the factors that militate for leniency in this area.

3. *Habbalah.* Here too various factors may be considered. If the prohibition is against injuring the mother, there would seem to be no restriction where the abortion is performed for her benefit, for that would be like surgery. Hence if the health of the mother requires an abortion even though there is no real danger to life, or if her existence will be devastated by bringing to term a seriously crippled child, then perhaps (though, it seems to me, the justification for leniency here is far weaker) out of concern for social and familial stigma or impediments to the child's halakhic marriageability, there is room for leniency in terms of *habbalah* (and that is the only prohibition we are addressing right now). On the other hand, if the problem is damage and injury caused to the fetus proper, this lenient course of action is dubious.

4. *Hatzalah.* This is possibly the most common justification, because it applies to the entire period of pregnancy and is seemingly independent of specific circumstances. At the same time, the obligation to save life may offer the greatest room for flexibility in certain common cases. To begin with, since it is a positive rather than a negative commandment, it brings into play the important principle in Halakhah according to which positive commands are more easily set aside than negative ones. Second, this obligation involves improving the condition of the fetus rather than a prohibition against harming it. Hence, there are situations where one must carefully examine whether the lot of fetus is indeed being improved. Regarding the first point, it should be noted that the parameters of the "cost" one must incur to help another human being, or even to save him, have yet (to the best of my knowledge) to be fully elaborated from the sources. Therefore, this obligation may not apply if the continued pregnancy will cause the parents profound physical or psychological distress. This is true, however, only if the obligation to preserve life is rooted in the command *ve-hay bahem* ("you shall live by them") or *hashavat avedah* (restoration of property, which includes, *a fortiori,* restoration of life itself); if, however, the basis is *lo ta'amod al dam re'akha* ("do not stand idly by while your brother's blood is shed"), there is no room for these considerations.[2] It is certainly possible that the fetus is excluded from the category of *re'akha* ("your brother"), and thus to be judged only from the perspective of *va-hay bahem.* Nevertheless, it is also quite conceivable that the obligation to preserve life is unlimited, extending to the fetus and thus closing off the possibility of leniency.

As to the welfare of the baby, it may well be that there is no obligation to preserve its life during pregnancy if there is a serious chance (or surely a likelihood) that the child, if born, will be so maimed that its life will be filled with suffering. To be sure, neither homicide nor suicide is permitted to end the life of an individual who is suffering intolerably. Yet, Rema (Yoreh De'ah 339:1) states normatively that one is permitted to abstain from acting to prevent the death of a *goses* (an individual in the throes of death) whose natural death is approaching. Moreover, Rabbenu Nissim, in his commentary to Nedarim (40b), states that one is allowed to pray for the speedy demise of an ailing person who is suffering terribly and awaiting death. Here too, nevertheless, caution should be the rule, as there are many opinions, both stringent and lenient, in the halakhic literature.

So far the discussion has dealt with the various possibilities of biblical prohibitions. According to those who maintain that abortion is only proscribed rabbinically (a position which I regard as untenable regarding the last trimester, though it may be considered for the earlier stages, as noted above), the same possible restrictions may be proposed, albeit on a different plane: homicide on the rabbinic level, the obligation to preserve life on a rabbinic level, and so on. In discussing rabbinic laws, there is some room to expand the range of factors that are likely to tilt the equation toward leniency. We should, for example, include issues like pain or domestic peace that warrant leniency in the realm of rabbinic prohibitions but not, according to most authorities, in the realm of biblical prohibitions. Indeed, certain halakhic decisors have responded with lenient rulings in cases of "great need," presumably because they assumed that the prohibition is here only rabbinic. Several points must be noted, however. First, the lenient position is a minority view, perhaps even an isolated one. Second, the concept of "great need" is so flexible and lacking in clear content that it is difficult to apply practically. Third, the lenient respondents saw themselves as dealing with highly exceptional cases rather than charting out a general policy.

On this basis, it seems to me that at least after the forty-day mark, when the critical determinants in my opinion, namely, *serah retzihah* and *habbalah,* are applicable (either biblically or rabbinically), there is little latitude to permit abortions for psychological-social reasons. I do not posit this, God forbid, out of lack of sensitivity to those suffering in these situations, nor out of indifference to their emotional, economic, and social travails. However, in consideration of the halakhic norms that take an extremely serious view of feticide, it is difficult to justify broad sanction for such abortions. To review these norms:

1. There is a possibility, to say the very least, that we are treading upon biblical commands and prohibitions.

2. Even if the prohibition of abortion or the obligation to save the

fetus is rabbinic, it should not be treated lightly. Considering the fetus: who would dare prophesy that its future life is destined to be detrimental? As to the mother, in the overwhelming majority of cases there is no real danger of insanity or physical deterioration. In the absence of such factors, it is difficult to see on what basis we can justify general leniency.

3. Moreover, it is a major principle of Halakhah that one does not set aside a prohibition that conflicts with a positive obligation where it is possible to fulfill both requirements. In a substantial number of cases, alternative means of dealing with these dilemmas exist, including counseling, monetary assistance, etc. Although in particular instances these means and resources are not always available, a general approach and comprehensive policy should clearly work toward this goal rather than for an expansion of the grounds on which abortions are to countenanced.

Let me conclude this overview with two remarks. First, the reader has surely discerned that in a number of places I have refrained from setting down definitive conclusions, but have been satisfied to indicate general principles, tendencies, and possibilities in the Halakhah. This approach is not the product of modesty or hesitation about resolving debates among halakhic titans. It is rooted in a view of the nature of *pesak* in general and of this topic in particular. The question of abortion involves areas in which the halakhic details are not clearly fleshed out in the Talmud and Rishonim, and in addition the personal circumstances are often complex and perplexing. In such areas there is room and, in my opinion, an obligation for a measure of flexibility. A sensitive *posek* recognizes the gravity of the personal situation and the seriousness of the halakhic factors. In one case, therefore, he may tend to view the points of contention one way, while in a second, which exhibits slightly different details, he may tilt the decision on these points in the other direction. He may reach for a different kind of equilibrium in assessing the views of his predecessors, sometimes allowing far-reaching positions to carry great weight, and other times ignoring them completely. He might stretch the halakhic limits of leniency where serious domestic tragedy looms, or hold firm to the strict interpretation of the law when, as he reads the situation, the pressure for leniency stems from frivolous attitudes and reflects a debased moral compass. This approach is neither cavalier nor discriminatory. The flexibility arises from a recognition that halakhic rulings are not, and should not be, the output of human microcomputers, but of thinking human beings; a recognition that these rulings must be applied to concrete situations with a bold effort to achieve the optimal moral and halakhic balance among the various factors. Thus, it is the case that halakhic rulings have more the character of general directives than of specific decisive rulings – within set limits, of course, and when the *posek* is not absolutely convinced respecting the point at issue. However, as we noted above, this application of *pesak* must be the outcome of serious deliberation, in the broadest sense of the term, by committed and observant men of Torah who are sensitive to the human and halakhic aspects of the case at hand, and possess the stature and ability to confront the halakhic problems.

Despite this emphasis, I imagine that some may view the ideas presented above as, overall, excessively severe and inflexible. Hence my second concluding remark. Judged by the standard prevalent today in most of the world, at least the Western world, the halakhic approach presented here appears rather stringent. This requires no apologies. But it is worth making clear, certainly to those who, in seeking a humane approach, are liable to adopt slavishly an overly liberal attitude in this area, that from the perspective of the fetus and those concerned with its welfare, liberality in this direction comes at the expense of humanity, insofar as the caution of the Halakhah is tied to its intimate concern for the values of lovingkindness and mercy. It is not only the honor of God which obligates us, regardless of the cost, to avoid what is prohibited and to obey the commands of the Holy One, blessed be He, that are expressed in this Halakhah. It is also the honor of man in Halakhah, the humane and ethical element that insists on the preservation of human dignity and concern for human welfare, that rises up in indignation against the torrent of abortions. If the Halakhah's course is sometimes onerous for certain families or for those responsible for them – and this fact should neither be denied nor ignored – let us remember, paraphrasing the famous words of Shakespeare, that Halakhah loved not the parents less, but the child more.

Notes

1. Assuming that the warrant for permitting sexual intercourse is not to facilitate normal family life but rather the commandment of *onah* (meeting the sexual needs of one's wife), this equation is no longer valid. However, it seems to me that the sanction for intercourse in this manner, in our case, does not simply involve the temporary suspension of the prohibition but its being uprooted entirely. This is so because the stricture does not apply to any and all acts of emission of seed *le-battalah*, but only to those that involve destruction of seed, *hashhatah*. For certain purposes, there is in fact no "destruction" at all. If so, the equation is indeed significant.
2. See *Shulhan Arukh*, Orah Hayyim 659, which rules that an individual is not obligated to spend more than a fifth of his possessions to fulfill a commandment. This only applies in relation to positive commands; regarding negative prohibitions, a person should give up all his wealth before violating them.

Chapter 12

A Rabbinic Exchange on Baruch Goldstein's Funeral

To my dear colleague,

Greetings, *ha-shalom veha-berakhah.*

We all recognize the great spirit of sensitivity that characterizes the network of *hesder yeshivot* and our mutual cooperation in safeguarding the absolute independence of each yeshiva in regard to educational policy; and we are all quite committed to the appropriate and established tradition of mutual noninterference in this area.

Nonetheless, in these troubled times I feel compelled to temporarily abandon this tradition, not out of a desire to express my opinion, but simply because it is impossible, from a personal and moral stance, to remain silent.

Therefore, I must vigorously protest against what took place last night before all of Israel and the entire world. A person, whatever his former merits may have been, departed this world while engaged in perpetrating an act of awful and terrible slaughter, *tevah ayom ve-nora,* and thereby, beyond the crime itself, desecrated the name of heaven, trampled upon the honor of the Torah and *mizvot,* soiled and sullied the image of *Knesset Yisrael,* and endangered the future of [Jewish] settlement in Judah, Samaria,

Reprinted from *Tradition* 28:4 (Summer 1994); translated by Rabbi Benjamin Samuels.

and Gaza. This man won praise and honor in the yeshiva of his hometown, Kiryat Arba, and was eulogized *ke-Halakhah,* with full ceremonial honors, by its *Rosh Yeshiva.*

Woe to the ears that hear this! But if it has been decreed that we must hear it, at least there should be a clear protest which expresses not just disassociation, but also disgust and shock. We must make this protest not just to protect our public image, but to preserve our self-image.

May He who, "being merciful, forgives iniquity" (Tehillim 78:38), "remove the shame of His people all over the earth" (Yeshayahu 25:8).

> In fear and trembling,
> For the sake of the honor of
> the Torah and its students,
>
> Aharon Lichtenstein
> *Rosh Yeshiva,* Har Etzion

Dear Rabbi Lichtenstein,

Greetings, *shalom rav.*

Let me note that we are opposed to terrorism of any kind – Arab terrorism against Jews, and Jewish terrorism against Arabs. But the rabbi's protest [in the preceding letter] does not sit well with us, in the spirit of "Take the beam from between your eyes" (Bava Batra 15b).

As is well known, your eminence supports the political process and everything that goes with it, which includes, if only de facto, the legitimization in the eyes of the entire world of the arch-terrorist (may his name be blotted out) who has spilled the blood of Jews and others like water, and the terrorist ideology he represents, thereby causing a terrible and awful desecration of God's name, a *hillul Hashem nora ve-ayom,* and indescribable damage to the Jewish people everywhere.

Therefore, although we understand that your eminence has good intentions for the sake of heaven, your distinguished words in this matter are not to be heard. For when God's name is desecrated, one does not grant due respect to sages.

With blessings,

Avraham Kurzweil
Shmuel Haber
Rashei Yeshiva, Karnei Shomron

Dear Rabbi Aharon Lichtenstein,
Rosh Yeshiva of the Yeshivat Hesder in Alon Shevut,

With greetings, *ha-shalom veha-berakhah ve-kol tov sela*, and appropriate solicitude, *ahar derishat shelomoh ke-ya'ut*.

A fax was received in our yeshiva's office, and although my name did not appear on it, so that it was not explicitly addressed to me, it was very clear who it was meant for; because of *kavod ha-Torah*, I think it proper to respond.

Yes, I did eulogize the late Baruch Goldstein (may Hashem avenge his blood), who was lynched by the non-Jews in the Cave [of Machpelah]. A Jew who is killed because he is a Jew must certainly be called *kadosh*, a holy martyr, just as we refer to the *kedoshei ha-Shoah*, the holy martyrs of the Holocaust, without investigating their previous conduct. How much more so in this case, for we knew him intimately as God-fearing and compassionate, as one who loved humanity and saved lives.

Even if someone were to maintain that his final act was improper, *lo haya ke-shura*, why is he not entitled to a eulogy *ke-Halakhah*? In my eulogy, I intentionally did not mention the deed, but focused on his personality and his achievements, and I did not take a public position on the deed.

The eulogy was given in the assembly hall of the yeshiva, not to show that we identified with the deed, but for other reasons, among them the cold and rain, which did not allow for the event to be held outside in the public square.

I marvel that great Torah sages, lovers of Israel, are so quick to judge an individual without knowing the background and circumstances from which he acted and which compelled him to act. Perhaps this was a situation of "his heart coerced him" (Shevuot 26a), for he was the first to see the spilling of blood in the area; people died before his eyes, and [he] also [heard] the cry "Slaughter the Jews!," "*Atbah al-Yahud!*" on Purim night and saw the disgrace of the Jewish people. All these together, I assume, led him to this extreme deed.

I repeat, my purpose in these remarks is not to formulate a conclusive judgment, but rather to judge favorably, *le-lammed zekhut,* as we are commanded to judge our fellow Jews favorably (Avot 1:6).

I hope that the esteemed rabbi will understand the spirit of my words, which are uttered in pain and distress, and may Hashem bind up His people's wounds (Yeshayahu 30:26).

With blessings,
Dov Leor
Rosh Yeshiva, Yeshivat Nir, Kiryat Arba

Dear *Rashei Yeshiva* of Yeshivat Karnei Shomron,
Rabbis Avraham Kurzweil and Shemuel Haber שליט״א,

Greetings, *ha-shalom veha-berakhah.*

Upon returning from a brief trip outside of Israel, I found your astonishing response to my letter.

1. Reading between the lines, it is evident that you agree that my reaction, in and of itself, was correct – that, at the very least, there was a "sliver" (Bava Batra 15b) that required attention – but feel that I am not the appropriate person to speak to the issue, as I am "publicly known" as a supporter of the process that bestows legitimacy upon terrorist ideology.

Thus, the question begs to be asked: Why were *you* silent? Why was no protest heard from those in our community, *mi-pi anshei shelomeinu,* who champion your political views, against the tribute given in a *hesder* yeshiva to (as Rabbi Leor wrote in his response to me) "the late Baruch Goldstein (may Hashem avenge his blood), who was lynched by the non-Jews in the Cave [of Machpelah]. A Jew who is killed because he is a Jew must certainly be called *kadosh,* a holy martyr, just as we refer to the *kedoshei ha-Shoah,* the holy martyrs of the Holocaust, without investigating their previous conduct"?

Was this the time for enlightened scholars with unblemished foreheads, without slivers and without beams between their eyes, perhaps even foreheads adorned with tefillin, to remain silent?

I admit without embarrassment that, from both a practical and a communal perspective, it would have been better if my reaction had been voiced by *Rashei Yeshiva* who have no trace of the taint that in your opinion clings to me. But to my distress, this did not happen. In any event, I doubt if it would have exempted me from the obligation and the desire to take a stand on this issue.

2. Even as we are astonished by the silence relating to the tribute expressed in tears and eulogy, we must likewise question the inaction in our *yeshivot* in regard to the killing itself. I do not suspect my colleagues, God forbid, of giving a seal of approval to the occurrence, even after the fact. But your reluctance to take a public position, in and of itself, calls for inquiry; it has caused moral and public damage to both our immediate and our broader community.

The Chief Rabbis שליט״א have said their piece; Rabbi Menachem Eliezer Shach and Rabbi Ovadiah Yosef, however belatedly, have issued vigorous statements. In the religious-national camp, however, several of the elder statesmen who customarily take positions and issue protests in regard to much less significant events were struck mute.

This fact has given rise to a variety of questions, and many have reached the sad conclusion that "since the rabbis are silent, presumably they are content" (Gittin 56a). I hope that this conclusion is mistaken, but as to the depth and intensity of the discontent, there is room for soul-searching.

3. As to the supposed beam that disqualifies my protest, I am simply amazed.

This is not the place to discuss the peace process, concerning which I too, to some extent, am hesitant and perturbed, because of security considerations. But clearly, any *ben Torah* who supports it – and is prepared, in this regard, to forcibly swallow his objections to someone who has spilled Jewish blood – is not acting out of esteem, even most grudging, for terrorism, but rather to prevent further bloodshed.

To be sure, in your opinion, this assessment of the situation is mistaken, and the entire process leads to "indescribable damage to the Jewish people" instead of progress. But how can we equate a view sincerely based on the hope of saving tens of thousands of lives with the bestowing of honor, even as a kind of last obsequy, a *hesed shel emet,* on a mass murderer?

If you were convinced that the peace process is indeed necessary from the standpoint of saving the lives of many, *pikuah nefesh de-rabbim,* and that it will indeed yield genuine peace to the House of Israel, would you abstain from embracing it only because of fastidiousness (*nekiyut ha-da'at*)?

With blessings of Torah and *mizvot,*

Aharon Lichtenstein

Chapter 13

The Israeli Chief Rabbinate: A Current Halakhic Perspective

The topic to which I have been asked to address myself is "The value and place of a central rabbinic authority in a modern Jewish state: Is there halakhic significance to a central rabbinic authority in a democratic state?" Whoever formulated this topic manifestly saw the issue of the status of the *rabbanut ha-rashit,* or Chief Rabbinate, as related to its existence within a sovereign modern and democratic context. I readily concede that this factor is, quite conceivably, of genuine importance. However, it can only be considered after one has dealt with the prior question (both logically and historically) of the role of a central rabbinic authority. What, we ask ourselves, is the halakhic significance, if any, of a *rabbanut rashit* in any context?

This issue is itself to be analyzed on two levels: the requisite and the optimal. We must first ask ourselves whether the establishment of a central rabbinic body and subsequent acknowledgment of its authority is normatively mandated. Even if we should determine, however, that it is not, it may still be contended that the existence of such an institution is desirable as an instrument toward the realization of clearly perceived halakhic, and not merely social or even moral, desiderata.

As regards the first level, we must obviously differentiate between

This paper was delivered at the Orthodox Forum 1990, and was published in *Israel as a Religious Reality,* ed. Chaim Waxman (Northvale, NJ: Jason Aronson, 1994).

a possible obligation to found a *rabbanut rashit* in the first place and the duty to abide by its dicta once it has been firmly established, by whatever means and for whatever reasons. The case for the former presumably rests upon the precedent of the Sanhedrin, the instituting of which the Rambam posited as the initial phase of the *mizvah* of setting up a judicial system rather than as its culmination: "How many regular tribunals are to be set up in Israel? How many members is each to comprise? First there is a Supreme Court holding sessions in the sanctuary."[1]

Not surprisingly, Rav Kook implicitly drew upon the comparison. In a brief essay written just prior to the founding convention of the *rabbanut ha-rashit,* he expounded his conception of its prospective role and character; and, citing the verse which the Rambam had adduced as proof that the classical *semikhah* could be reinstated,[2] he issued a clarion call: "The revival of the rabbinate means the return of the glory of the rabbinate. Is this not an echo of the prophetic voice that assured us: 'And I will reinstate your judges as at first and your advisors as in the beginning'?"[3]

From a rigorous halakhic perspective, however, the analogy is just that: a suggestive model which may be regarded as embodying certain elements, and, hence, as positing certain values, but having no direct normative relevance. The Sanhedrin was a formally constituted body that, ideally, provided general spiritual leadership and was invested with wide-ranging legislative and judicial authority with respect both to the Diaspora and to Eretz Yisrael.[4] In the Rambam's succinct formulation:

> The Supreme Court in Jerusalem represents the essence of the Oral Torah. Its members are the pillars of direction; law and order emanate from them to all of Israel. Concerning them, the Torah assures us, as it is written: "You shall act in accordance with the directions they give you" (Shemot 17:11). This is a positive command. Anyone who believes in Moses our teacher, and in his Torah, must relate religious practices to them and lean upon them.[5]

Clearly, no modern counterpart exists, or, under present conditions, can exist. Membership in the Sanhedrin was confined to those who had been ordained as a link in an unbroken chain of *semikhah* going back to Mosheh Rabbenu's investiture of Yehoshua. The Rambam held that the institution could be restored in pre-messianic times, but only under conditions, such as the overwhelming consensus of the foremost *talmidei hakhamim* of Eretz Yisrael, that neither currently obtain nor are anticipated on the horizon.[6] Contemporary halakhic sanction for a national rabbinic authority must be sought, then, without regard to the classical Sanhedrin.

This precedent aside, no solid base for the mandatory establishment of such a body exists. Not only does the Halakhah fail to prescribe such a course at the national level, but, to the best of my knowledge, it does not even require it at the local level. We are very much attuned to the concept of *mara de-atra,* a single rabbinic figure or group endowed by a specific community with spiritual hegemony; and, indeed, this model was prevalent in much of the Diaspora and, historically, served *Knesset Yisrael* well. However, the halakhic status of the *mara de-atra* related to his position subsequent to his having been selected. Nothing required the creation of the post *ab initio.* It is true that the Ramban maintained, in light of the wording of the verse "You shall appoint for yourselves judges and officers, tribe by tribe, in every settlement God has given you" (Devarim 16:18), that each tribe is to appoint its own central *bet din* (court). However, as he clearly indicates, this is, in effect, a miniature Sanhedrin: "Just as the Great Sanhedrin is appointed over all the courts of Israel, so one court is appointed over each tribe"[7] – and, hence, of no direct normative relevance to our discussion. The earlier part of the *pasuk* does, of course, mandate the appointment of a *bet din* in every locale, but it makes no reference to the need for a single overarching communal authority, either existing solely or as the pinnacle of a spiritual or even juridical hierarchy.

On the contrary, from the gemara it would clearly appear that several *batei din* can coexist in the same town. It speaks, for instance, of litigants' rights to choose between "the courthouses of Rav Huna and Rav Hisda," both of these being, as Rashi explains, "in one place."[8] Or again, in delineating the scope of the prohibition of "You shall not gash yourselves" (Devarim 14:1), which, *inter alia,* Hazal interpret to include an injunction against divisiveness, "You shall not make separate groups," Abbaye and Rava treat its parameters with respect to contradictory *pesakim* issued by different local *batei din* – taking it for granted that several may exist in the same community, with none designated supreme.[9] *A fortiori,* then, there need be no single supernal national rabbinic authority. Again, it is entirely conceivable that the decisions of such a body, once chosen, may be normatively binding; but its initial designation is, ordinarily, purely optional.

This by no means suggests, however, that the matter is religiously neutral. No spiritually sensitive person, much less a *ben Torah,* can countenance the proposition that, beyond the mandatory, nothing matters. Surely, a halakhic chasm divides a *devar mizvah* from a *devar ha-reshut;* but the latter, too, can be of considerable spiritual moment. It may be judged more contextually than normatively; but judgment, in the light of halakhic categories, is nonetheless significant. At this level, then, we may weigh the impact of a central rabbinic authority upon halakhic interests – often related to the pragmatic but hardly identical with them – with respect to the various functions of the rabbinate; and this, with an eye to both the constant aspects of the problem and its manifestation in the contemporary Israeli context.

Rabbinic functions are many and can be variously classified. For our purposes, they can best be divided into two broad categories as they relate, respectively, to the communal and personal sectors. The maintenance and supervision of halakhically related services, the development of religious institutions, public instruction in Torah, representation of the religious sector in relation to other sectors, or of the general Jewish community vis-à-vis its Gentile counterpart, concern for the Jewish character of the Jewish street – all these form one cluster of roles. Others clearly address themselves to the individual: participation in rites central to the life-cycle, harnessing him or her to halakhic observance, providing pastoral guidance or support. Still others straddle both realms. *Pesak* may be either public or private, depending upon the substance of the question, the channel of query, and the mode of response. General spiritual influence and inspiration clearly has a dual impact, sensitizing *yahid* and *rabbim* alike. Finally, moral initiative clearly relates to both realms. On one level, the enactment of the prophetic mandate "Execute the judgment of truth and peace in your gates"[10] – understood in both its broad general sense and in Hazal's vein as a specific call for settling litigation via amicable compromise[11] – provides a measure of personal relief even as it concurrently promotes communal harmony. On another, commitment to *hesed,* regarded by Rav Hayyim of Brisk as *the* cardinal rabbinic obligation,[12] both sharpens social conscience and enhances the quality of individual lives.

Surveying this spectrum with reference to our problem, we instinctively sense a functional relationship between the public component and the advisability of centralization. On the whole, the instinct is sound, although not uniformly so; it clearly applies to the supervision of kashrut, for example, more than to instruction in Torah. While for many the issue is debatable even with regard to largely administrative sectors (the equivalent of the familiar arguments for community control as opposed to distant and faceless big government can be readily harnessed), in this area, the case for a central authority, with the scope and weight attendant upon it, is palpably strong – all the more so, as the problems occurring in the modern socioeconomic context transcend narrow geographic bounds and are not readily amenable to local jurisdiction. Admittedly, this does not necessarily militate for regarding centralization as the sole option. A measure of cooperation between rabbis or rabbinic groups or some loose confederation might constitute a viable alternative. Nevertheless, with respect to the public sphere, the merits of centralized authority are manifest.

Ishut provides a clear example. Hazal demanded that "whoever does not know the nature of divorce and marriage should not have any dealings with them,"[13] and set a rather high standard for what constitutes sufficient knowledge. Although this statement of Hazal addressed the individual, obviously there is a public need for safeguards to ensure that those who lack the necessary expertise do not, out of irresponsible indifference or ignorance of their own limitations, involve themselves in this sensitive area. To this end, a central authority can be enormously helpful. Conceivably, safeguards could be provided, as in the medical and legal fields, by voluntary professional organizations; and a community can admittedly sustain itself, as in most of the Diaspora today, in their absence. The potential contribution of a central authority is nonetheless self-evident, not to mention its invaluable assistance in coping with the sheer administrative difficulties, such as the maintenance of adequate and reliable records in an age of great mobility.

Chapter 13

With respect to other sectors, however, the balance of pros and cons shifts perceptibly. It is not for naught that the Torah postulated that judges are to be posted *bi'she'arekha* – in Eretz Yisrael, in virtually every hamlet.[14] Presumably, this insistence was not intended solely to afford easy access to judicial redress. It likewise ensures spiritual leadership that is organically related to its ambient society, aware of its problems, and sensitive to its needs; leadership that can communicate effectively with its constituency in light of direct knowledge of its existential milieu; that can intelligently assign priorities and impose demands while yet aware of limitations; that can serve as a transcending spiritual mentor even as, like the Shunamite woman, "amongst my people I dwell".

Bi'she'arekha relates to both the appointment and the exercise of spiritual leadership. The benefits of rabbinic independence in attaining and maintaining a position are obvious. In many cases, however, a leader who is not responsible to a community is also not responsive to it. At times, of course, a stance of defiance (although not of insouciance) is desirable. Over the long run, however, the patient wisdom needed by a spiritual leader to stimulate the spiritual growth of a community, his ability to speak and its readiness to listen, are enhanced by knowledge that he was its choice, without external pressures and sans remote-control politicization.

This is not to suggest that the selection of a *mara de-atra* can be regarded as a purely sociopolitical matter, wholly independent of definitive standards. According to the prevalent view, the Halakhah classically posited *semikhah,* defined by the Rambam as "the appointment of the elders to judgeship,"[15] as a prerequisite to serving on a *bet din* – to membership, that is, in a body which, in Hazal's time and beyond, constituted the primary seat of local rabbinic authority and the matrix of communal spiritual leadership. That, however, only served to qualify a person to occupy such a post, enabling him to sit on an ad hoc constellation or to be a candidate for a more permanent position which the *semikhah per se* had not conferred upon him. Who then determines which *samukh* assumes a specific position is, to the best of my knowledge, nowhere spelled out in the gemara. But if intuitive judgment and prevalent historical practice are any guide, the community within which he is to serve seems the most likely choice.

Appreciation of the significance of the communal factor in no way obviates the possible role of a central authority in making rabbinic appointments. The process can be both general and local, licensing in accordance with proper objective standards being assigned to one level, and selection to another. Halakhically, to be sure, *semikhah* need not be central at all. Any group of three *semukhim* – on the Rambam's view, even a single *samukh* joined by two non-*semukhim*[16] – can confer the title. Moreover, according to the Rivash,[17] licensing was only necessary with respect to classical *semikhah*. That tradition having been terminated, every qualified and knowledgeable person can now serve as a *moreh horaah*. Nevertheless, a median course of essentially dual appointment *can* be adopted; and, under present circumstances, may be highly warranted. The need for maintaining standards and assuring reasonable qualification in all major respects is palpably greater today than in medieval Spain or in the sixteenth-century setting of the Rema, who cited the Rivash with apparent approval. This function can perhaps best be consigned to a hopefully disinterested central authority. "Shall a priestess not be the equal of a hostess?" The concern for standards so properly endemic to secular professions can hardly be ignored in the Torah world; and to this end, a central body can be most effective.

Given a measure of goodwill and readiness to prefer the general interest – admittedly rare qualities when both ideology and power are at stake – analogous cooperative accommodations should probably be attainable, *mutatis mutandis*, in other areas as well. However, one sector is presumably not so amenable and needs to be singled out for special discussion. On a primary level, Halakhah is avowedly pluralistic. Within certain limits, it not only entertains but encourages diverse views, and the world of halakhic discourse is animated by the sense that "these and these are the words of the Living God" (Eruvin 13b). On a secondary level, however, discourse is to issue in decision, presumably authoritative and definitive; and the diversity that is admired in the bet ha-midrash is the object of aversion in the *bet din*. *Mahloket*, the very stuff of which so much Torah study is made, translates, in the context of *pesak*, into divisive dissent. In its stead, univocal summary decision, optimally typified by the Sanhedrin, is posited as ideal.

The implications for centralization are clear. Technically, this discussion may be deemed irrelevant to our present situation inasmuch as the formal Sanhedrin is long defunct. Nevertheless, the axiological aversion to divisiveness may very well be in order. On one level, we might take note of the status of the *zaken mamre*, of whom the gemara says that even if the Sanhedrin whose decision he countermanded wishes to remit him, it is not authorized to do so, "that contention not increase in Israel."[18] Admittedly, one might contend that, given its existence, defying a central authority is indeed punishable as subversion, but that the existence of competing decisions or even contradictory codices is not deplorable *per se*. However, this contention, probably questionable in any event, is clearly undercut by the gemara's lament over the fact that "When the students of Shammai and Hillel whose studies were not complete became many, dissension multiplied in Israel, causing the Torah to become like two Torahs."[19] Clearly, the concern here is not with *lèse majesté* but with fissures in the halakhic universe.

Pushed to its logical conclusion, this position militates for a single universal rabbinic authority – for the establishment, that is, of a Sanhedrin or its equivalent. Some have indeed regarded this vision, animating the essay previously cited, as Rav Kook's ultimate semi-mystical aspiration upon the founding of the Chief Rabbinate in Jerusalem.[20] Failing that, however, one could still yearn for maximal uniformity within a broad geographic area, at least for adherents of the same ethnic tradition.

Individualists bridle at this prospect. Bristling over possible personal constraint and public atrophy, they regard the concentration of authority as a potential threat, all the more so if they have cause to be circumspect or even suspicious with regard to those in whose hands it might be concentrated. They regard the Sanhedrin as a unique institution, effectively relegated to a remote ideal past or envisioned as part of a utopian future, but of little relevance, even as a model, to the present. Rav Hayyim's refusal, early in this century, to join, and implicitly be subordinated to, a nascent *Mo'ezet Gedolei ha-Torah* is typical. Electricity having then been recently introduced in Brisk, he observed that it presumably represented real progress. Yet, he noted, one could not ignore a disturbing fact. Previously, if a kerosene lamp was extinguished in one location, no one else was adversely affected. Henceforth, however, if a failure were to occur at the power station, the whole of Brisk would be plunged into darkness.

Nevertheless, the merits of uniform *pesak* are varied and weighty; and the recurrent historical attempts to attain it, whether through discourse and decision, or, as in the case of the *Shulhan Arukh,* by dint of personally molded consensus, amply illustrate this. One might particularly press this cause with respect to Eretz Yisrael, and not in the light of Zionist ideology, but for sound halakhic reasons. With reference to *pesak,* the concept of place is assigned considerable weight. Thus, with reference to the *issur* of "Do not cause factionalism," Abbaye holds that it only applies to factionalism in a single town but not to conflicting norms propounded or practiced in different towns.[21] Or again, the gemara states that if a *posek* adheres to a minority view, even if he permits what, according to the prevalent position, is prohibited *mid'oraitha,* his license may be relied upon by members of his community.[22] By extension, the use of the phrase "in his place" notwithstanding, it is entirely conceivable that the relevant concept is as much sociological as geographic. Could not a lone Habad hasid in Melbourne rely upon a lenient decision of the Lubavitcher Rebbe even though he is poles removed from Eastern Parkway?

If this be the case, one may contend that for our purposes, the whole of Eretz Yisrael constitutes a single locale, on the basis of the famous gemara in Horayot which postulates, with reference to defining the community whose collective transgression by a majority of its constituents obligates the offering of "a bull sin-offering for an inadvertent communal sin," that only inhabitants of Eretz Yisrael are included in the category of *kahal* ("congregation"): "R. Assi said: In [the case of an erroneous] ruling [of a court], the majority of the inhabitants of the Land of Israel are to be taken into account.... From this it may be inferred that only these are included in the 'congregation,' but those are not."[23] The formulation is primarily negative and is intended to exclude Diaspora Jewry. However, it also has a positive aspect, expressing the conviction, of both halakhic and philosophic moment, that inhabitants of Eretz Yisrael are uniquely bound by a dimension of community absent elsewhere. Hence, the admonition against *mahloket* and the quest for univocal central authority are doubly meaningful with respect to *eretz ha-kodesh*.[24]

In theory, quite possibly. In fact, however, as we turn to examine the current state of the Chief Rabbinate in Israel, one wonders how much of the foregoing is truly relevant. The contribution of the *rabbanut ha-rashit* to the administration and supervision of areas crucial to halakhic existence is obvious. Equally self-evident, however, is the fact that as a quintessentially *rabbinic* authority, whether as spiritual leadership in the broader sense or with regard to the specific area of *pesak,* it now carries relatively limited weight. Secularists and haredim largely ignore it, while the non-Orthodox actively fight it. Its status in the *dati-le'umi* community is more secure, but even there many offer it little more than honorific lip-service, having recourse to it only at their convenience. Moreover, increasingly regarded as the virtual patrimony of a dominant faction, its base of support has narrowed and the number of those who truly look to it for guidance has dwindled. Even in the world of *yeshivot hesder,* there are not many who, confronted with conflicting *pesakim* of the *rabbanut ha-rashit* and, say, Rav Shlomo Zalman Auerbach, would routinely prefer the former.[25]

Nor, halakhically, is there any reason why they must. In an address delivered before the Mizrachi in the mid-fifties, the Rav vigorously upheld the authority of the Chief Rabbinate, citing several instances to prove that, historically, even when greater *talmidei hakhamim* had resided in his community, a *mara de-atra* had been its final halakhic arbiter. Whatever may have been the case then, it is surely difficult to apply this principle today, for the status of a *rav rashi* as *mara de-atra d'yisrael* is precisely what is in question. Champions of a central rabbinic authority must still wrestle with the crucial question of *mi be-rosh*: who is defined as such, by whom, and how? When there is reasonable consensus about the appointive procedure, the status can be readily conferred and assume halakhic force. In its absence, however, the title rings hollow.

As previously noted, it is entirely possible that even if deciding whether or not to choose a central authority is optional, once a community has decided to create the post, the decisions of its occupant may be binding. This only obtains, however, so long as the institution, and whoever is invested with its power, is truly recognized. Royal authority *de jure* rests on a social base *de facto,* so that the Yerushalmi states that during the six months that David spent in flight in Hebron, he did not enjoy full regal status.[26] One may question the extent, if any, to which the principle would apply to the spiritual hegemony of a properly constituted Sanhedrin. It is reasonable to assume, however, that it does apply to a spiritual mentor who lacks this formal designation, and certainly so if the loss of effective control had preceded his investiture.

There is little doubt that the Chief Rabbinate is not at present the master of what it regards as its own domain. To its proponents, it is a proto-messianic precursor. To many, however, it is either anachronistic or premature. One may celebrate this fact or lament it; but I do not see how it can be questioned.

Ought we, then, to conclude that a moribund *rabbanut rashit* should be dismembered with dispatch? Categorically not. Quite the contrary; if the institution did not exist, it would have to be invented, albeit possibly in a different form. In a complex modern Jewish society and state, the apparatus to administer and supervise the halakhic aspects of the public sector and to license those who operate within it is clearly invaluable; and it must be staffed and headed by competent and committed persons whose authority transcends narrow bounds. Moreover, on certain public issues, the state, qua collective agent, needs recourse to a definitive *posek.* And again, inasmuch as the problems transcend narrow jurisdictional bounds, so must the authority that seeks to cope with them. The princely – some might say, the quasi-papal – aspect is less crucial. It is even arguable that there can be a *rabbanut rashit* without chief rabbis. In this vein, some have suggested that the network of *batei din* as a rabbinical court system should be maintained, but that the central rabbinate, as an overarching spiritual authority, should be dismantled. Nevertheless, this element, too, surely serves constructive purposes, whether by positing a visible human symbol of the state's link to traditional Judaism or, beyond pomp and circumstance, by providing a ready spokesman and forum for it.

What certainly needs to be reduced, however, is politics, bureaucracy, and above all, illusion. These are, of course, by no means peculiar to the

Israeli rabbinic establishment, but they are particularly perturbing when encountered in the Torah world. The political connection is dual. There are internal, at times internecine, struggles between various groups over power and influence, extending to involvement in the appointive processes at the local level. These are generally deplorable but understandable – partly inevitable, and at times genuinely *le-shem shamayim*. In addition, however, there is excessive engagement in the broader political process. To be sure, the current official ban, often ignored in practice, against any dayyan's speaking out on sociopolitical issues, even when these have clear moral import, on the grounds of judicial impartiality, is totally at variance with Jewish tradition and its conception of communal leadership. But when a chief rabbi becomes embroiled in negotiations over the composition of the Mafdal's electoral list, he tarnishes both the party and his post.[27] Can anyone imagine the Archbishop of Canterbury publicly determining who should be the Conservative candidate in Kent?

Moreover, even when matters of clear conscience are at stake, one often wishes for a greater measure of discrimination than sometimes now obtains. Certainly, no one would suggest that the *rabbanut ha-rashit* should wholly avoid controversial positions out of concern for cultivating its self-image as a truly national institution. Yet in the choice of issues to be addressed and emphasized, a modicum of prudence and a sense of priority are surely in order. Whatever one's own views, one can understand and respect the impetus to align the Chief Rabbinate with the radical opposition to territorial compromise. To say the least, advocacy of *af sha'al* engenders a factional image; but all recognize that the issue is major, and confronting it arguably well worth the damage. But the Nakash affair, in which the *rabbanut*, on highly dubious grounds, served as a prime vehicle of opposition to the extradition of the convicted Jewish killer of a French Arab, is quite another matter. I trust that even those who enlisted in the crusade at the time recognize, in retrospect, that the passion for righteousness that impelled it should have been tempered by a greater degree of prudence and sensitivity. In their absence, the *rabbanut*'s stature suffered significantly.

Of bureaucracy, presumably little needs to be said, as it is the Achilles' heel of centralization. It should be noted, however, that in our case two complicating factors exist. First, many who work within the *rabbanut* system lack, by dint of their education, the training and the inclination to promote efficiency. Second, much of the population that perforce encounters the system does not acknowledge its basic tenets, so that the spiritual price collectively paid for its failings is magnified.

As to illusion, I have not the slightest intention of impugning the integrity of those associated with the current Chief Rabbinate. I do not believe that they, or their predecessors, have in any way sought to mislead the public. There is, however, a measure of self-delusion, fed in part by quasi-messianic fervor. The wish being grandfather to the thought, the *rabbanut ha-rashit* revels in seeing itself as that which perhaps ideally it should be, but at present palpably is not, and in the foreseeable future is unlikely to become – a central vehicle for the realization of the prophetic promise: "For Torah issues from Zion, and out of Jerusalem comes the word of God" (Yesheyahu 2:3). Of this, the *rabbanut ha-rashit* is, at most, an earnest; and it is best that this fact be acknowledged. A *rabbanut* with a leaner self-image and less grandiloquent tone would also be healthier.

As this article draws to its conclusion, the reader will have noted that relatively little has been said of a democratic state or even of a modern Jewish state. Not by accident. To my mind, the link between centralization and democracy, while real, is, in our context, limited. On the one hand, the basic issues related to the inherent conceptual tension between a focal center and *bishe'arekha* obtain even in a theocracy. How authority is divided, whether jurisdiction is hierarchical, who makes appointments, which *pesakim* are binding: these and similar questions exist independently of the overall governmental system. Having opted for a given political structure, a religious community may still choose between Presbyterian and Congregationalist models, or something intermediate.

On the other hand, the abolition of the Chief Rabbinate would still leave us faced with problems arising out of the conjuncture of halakhic tradition with a pluralistic society and state. In some way, *gittin* and *gerut* would still have to be afforded or denied recognition, locally if not centrally, albeit perhaps less definitively; and the problem of the non-Orthodox would still be with us. Poor rapport between the rabbinic fraternity and much of the populace would continue to bedevil us, at least for some time. Tensions arising out of the meshing of religion and state would not disappear, nor would coercive legislation be more sympathetically received. If these problems are to be confronted, far more radical measures must be considered, with their concomitant, and possibly exorbitant, costs. The thesis that in a pluralistic society there is a trade-off between power and influence, at least on the spiritual plane, and the concurrent contention that in contemporary Israel too much of the latter is being sacrificed for the former, bears directly upon the established *rabbanut ha-rashit*. But it is advanced by its advocates with regard to the religious community as a whole.

I readily acknowledge that relating the problem of centralization to its specific contemporary context does bear upon its analysis. And the impact cuts both ways. On the one hand, the friction attendant upon contact with what is perceived as the heavy and distant hand of central ecclesiastical authority is exacerbated by a liberal and largely secular context; and the exclusiveness more likely to be accorded a central rabbinate may seem less justifiable in an avowedly pluralistic order. In such a context, the difficulty of building and sustaining a broad base of support for the *rabbanut ha-rashit* is virtually intrinsic, particularly as Israeli society becomes increasingly polarized. Rav Kook's dream related to the specifically *national* aspect of the Chief Rabbinate, the dimension of *mamlakhtiyut* so prized by religious Zionism. This dimension entails, however, a presumed relation to a broad social spectrum and the ability to speak for and to divergent cultural and ideological sectors. In the highly charged atmosphere of Israeli religious life, that ability has proved very elusive, and for obvious reasons. Sociopolitically, very few can remain firmly anchored within the Torah and yeshiva world, to which, to some extent, the *rabbanut* looks for credentials and legitimization, and, at the same time develop genuine rapport with the general secular community. The majestic stature of Rav Kook, combined with his very special background, enabled him to come close, but of his successors, no one else has done so consistently.

On the practical level, the problem is graphically illustrated by the electoral process. The chief rabbis are, in effect, elected by (and must presumably appeal to) an assemblage that includes many who are anxious to see them steer a vigorous course, and others, ranging from *dayyanim* who barely recognize the existence of the state to thoroughgoing secularists, who would be happy to see them neutralized. Currently, moreover, the difficulty is further aggravated by the growing polarization and by the alienation of many younger Israelis who find Torah Judaism simply irrelevant.

From a halakhic perspective, it is arguable that a strong *rabbanut rashit* is needed all the more in a democratic state precisely because of its weight as a countervailing force to help sustain the state's Jewish character. Moreover, in at least one respect, the modern mindset is more attuned to a central halakhic hierarchy than its predecessors. During the gestation of the Chief Rabbinate in Eretz Yisrael, it was the secularists who insisted upon the establishment of an appeals court, an institution some traditionalists regarded as halakhically shaky but which was *de rigueur* to a Western sensibility.

The modern component is surely relevant, then, to a proper consideration of rabbinic centralization, as the ambience of contemporary Israeli society inhibits its development in one respect and yet stimulates it in another. All I am suggesting is that we refrain from exaggerating its significance. If I am thus also correspondingly constricting the significance of this paper, that is a small sacrifice to bring for truth.

Notes

1. Mishneh Torah, Hilkhot Sanhedrin 1:3.
2. *Perush Ha-Mishnayot*, Sanhedrin 1:3.
3. *Hator*, 14 Adar I, 5681, reprinted in *Ha-Rabbanut Ha-Rashit l'Yisrael ba-Avar u-va-Hoveh* (Jerusalem, 1973), p. 7.
4. Generically, the term Sanhedrin includes both the central body of seventy-one and the smaller council/courts of twenty-three. In this essay, it is used only with reference to the former.
5. Mamrim 1:1.
6. *Perush Ha-Mishnayot*, Sanhedrin 1:3; Mishneh Torah, Hilkhot Sanhedrin 4:11.
7. Devarim 16:18.

8. Sanhedrin 23a. I have here assumed the view of Rashi that both *batei din* were in the same town. Tosafot, s.v. *kegon,* held that they were in the same general vicinity but at a distance of at least three *parsaʾot* (approximately seven miles); this was not because Tosafot insisted upon unitary jurisdiction, however, but due to consideration of *kevod ha-rav,* as Rav Huna had been Rav Hisda's rebbe.

9. Yevamot 14a. See also *Siftei Kohen,* Yoreh Deʾah 242, subs. 10 of the concluding summary. The *Arukh Ha-Shulhan,* Yoreh Deʾah 242:57, states that since it is now the universal practice to elect a local rav, others may not engage in *pesak* in his town. But he does not state that such an election is mandatory.

10. Zekharyah 8:9.

11. See Sanhedrin 6b.

12. When his eldest son, Rav Mosheh Soloveitchik, assumed his first post as a rav. Rav Hayyim told him that the primary rabbinic task was *zu tohn hesed.* For all the remark's interest and significance, I trust it is self-evident that it needs to be viewed in context and hardly to be confused with presumably identical positions expressed by contemporary liberal religious thinkers. While the emphasis upon social justice is common, the total perspective is not. Rav Hayyim, of course, took rigorous halakhic commitment, as well as its role as the basis of social ethics, for granted, and certainly had no doubts about the significance of a rabbi's duty to sustain it. His comment was unquestionably impelled by a sense that the increasingly defensive pre-World War I Lithuanian rabbinate had lost its balance in one direction. He would have been no less critical of reverse imbalance.

13. Kiddushin 6a, according to Rashi's interpretation.

14. Mishnah Sanhedrin 1:6 states that a community must have a population of at least 120 in order to qualify for a small Sanhedrin, but does not say that establishing one is mandatory. Moreover, the gemara's explanation for the number (Sanhedrin 17b) seems to suggest that the populace must include almost one hundred who can serve as *dayyanim.* However, the Rambam (Sanhedrin 1:2) states that establishing the court is indeed obligatory and, moreover, omits the explanation (which, in light of the term *ke-neged,* he evidently regarded as symbolic), conveying the impression that any 120 would suffice. In any event, this requirement does not apply to a simple *bet din* of three, which, in Eretz Yisrael, must be set up even in small settlements. In the Diaspora, however, *batei din* need only be established in each province; see Makkot 7a.

15. Sanhedrin 4:3.

16. Ibid. Generally, the performance of functions requiring *semikhah* is limited to a *bet din* comprised wholly of *semukhim.* Evidently, in this case, the function does not require *semukhim,* and the need for even a single samukh derives from the specific content of the act of investiture as the transmission of authority. See *Hiddushei Maran Riz Halevi* ad loc.

17. See *Sheʾelot u-Teshuvot Ha-Rivash,* responsum 271; see also the Rema in Yoreh Deʾah 242:14. The Rivash agrees that some authorization may generally be required, but for incidental reasons – in deference to a master or to confirm that one can express himself clearly.

18. Sanhedrin 88b.

19. Loc. cit., quoted from *Tosefta* Hagigah 2:4 and Sanhedrin 7:1. The question of fundamental attitudes toward diversity and controversy has deeper roots and broader implications than can here be treated adequately.

20. See Menahem Friedmann, *Hevrah ve-Dat* (Jerusalem, 1978), pp. 110–111.

21. See Yevamot 14a.

22. Ibid. Of course, this option only exists so long as the point at issue has not been debated and definitively decided by a vote of the Sanhedrin.

23. Horayot 3a. While the gemara's statement relates to a single halakhah, it obviously has major hashkafic implications and has been applied to other halakhic areas. See, e.g., Rambam, *Perush Ha-Mishnayot*, Bekhorot 4:3, and *Avnei Nezer*, Orah Hayyim 314.

24. The emphasis upon the more thoroughly organic nature of Jewish existence in Eretz Yisrael as a factor to be reflected in the structuring of spiritual life runs as a prevalent strain through Rav Kook's address before the founding convention of the *rabbanut ha-rashit*, a contemporary newspaper account of which (most of it a literal rendering) is reprinted in Aryeh Morgenstern, *Ha-Rabbanut Ha-Rashit l'Eretz Yisrael, Yissudah ve-Irgunah* (Jerusalem, 1973), pp. 179–180.

25. In the religious (*dati*) or traditional (*mesorati*) Sephardic community, the standing of the Chief Rabbinate is relatively higher, but this is largely, I believe, because of a perceived link between the *rabbanut ha-rashit* and the centuries-old office of *rishon le-ziyyon*. This is evidenced by the fact that the overall stature of Rav Ovadiah Yosef, who continues to lay claim to the latter title long after leaving *Heikhal Shelomoh*, is manifestly higher than that of his successor.

   I trust I have not overstated the case. In religious Zionist circles, the *rabbanut ha-rashit* certainly does enjoy a significant measure of prestige, and the *rav rashi* carries a perceptible aura. His appearance at any *dati-le'umi* Torah institution would be regarded as an event by its students and faculty, myself included; and at times, as in the case of a recent symbolic *hakhel* convocation, the Chief Rabbinate has demonstrated a capacity for mobilizing a large public. All this is a far cry, however, from genuine general authority or sustained acknowledged leadership. The point is readily exemplified by the failure to establish either Yom Yerushalayim as a truly national day of rejoicing or the Tenth of Tevet as a memorial day for the Holocaust.

26. Horayot 3:2.

27. Of course, in some parties such matters are routinely determined by *gedolim*. They act, however, as masters of an avowedly partisan bailiwick who have not been formally invested with a presumably national mantle.

Chapter 14

Legitimization of Modernity: Classical and Contemporary

Few elements distinguish the typical modern Orthodox Jew from his haredi counterpart more than their respective instinctive relations to authority. To the haredi, authority, both as abstract concept and as human reality, is a wholly unmixed blessing. On one plane, a *gadol* or a *zaddik*, independently considered, is a veritable pillar of the cosmic order, in a mystical vein, or of his ambient society, in purely rational terms. He enhances and ennobles his world by bringing it into contact with levels of wisdom or saintliness that would otherwise lie beyond its purview. On a second plane, that of the individual's relation to his spiritual mentor, the authority of *gedolim* is not only accepted but relished. They are regarded – indeed, experienced – as fountains of wisdom and towers of strength. Theirs is a dual guidance, illuminating as well as inspiring. Where could one receive better definitive counsel than from those of whom it is written, סוד ה׳ ליראיו ובריתו להודיעם, "The secret of the Lord is with them that revere Him, and His covenant, to make them know it"?[1] And who radiates power and generates uplift more than those of whom Hazal say, גדולים צדיקים יותר ממלאכי השרת, "The supremely righteous are superior to the servant angels"?[2]

Moreover, the exercise and acceptance of authority *per se* is reassuring.

This paper was delivered at the Orthodox Forum 1993 and published in *Engaging Modernity: Rabbinic Leaders and the Challenge of the Twentieth Century,* ed. Moshe Z. Sokol (Northvale, NJ: Jason Aronson, 1997).

Apart from the comforting knowledge that *ex cathedra* pronouncements have provided optimal counsel, there is the gratification of relief from the burden of decision-making. At the very least, the submissive embrace of authority spares the adherent the agony of choosing and induces the sense that, whatever the consequences, he cannot be held liable for what is chosen.

Beyond this, some may luxuriate in the admittedly problematic contemplation of the abrogation of choice as a fulfillment, *mutatis mutandis*, of the mandate, בטל רצונך מפני רצונו, "Set aside your will in deference to His."[3]

The modern Orthodox Jew's relation to authority, by contrast, is far more circumspect, if not ambivalent. He regards authority – again as both concept and reality – with an expectant yet jaundiced eye. On the one hand, he recognizes, as a matter of *a priori* inherent necessity and in light of relevant sources, that authority, and submission to it, is critical. It is essential at all times as both a normative and a psychological need, and, particularly so, for himself. Forasmuch as, in some sense, he regards himself as engaged in new departures, he searches for a firm supporting anchor. Sociologically, if he feels – as many do, at present – under attack by the onslaught of a highly vocal and increasingly successful opposition, the need for an authoritative mainstay becomes all the more pressing.

On the other hand, the typical modern Orthodox Jew bridles at the thought of constricting his autonomy. Lacking a hagiographic orientation, he probably holds even his "own" *gedolim* in less awe than the haredi exudes with respect to his mentors. But even if this were not so, he would still be somewhat reluctant, on personal and philosophic grounds, to seek or even accept their counsel. That reluctance is, after all, part of his modernity. From Descartes on, if not since the Renaissance, the concern with personal judgment – whether in Kantian ethics, libertarian politics, Romantic aesthetics, or existentialist angst – is central to modern culture. Moreover, the modern Orthodox Jew would not regard his reluctance as a failing. He would, in all likelihood, insist upon seeing it as a virtue – the result, not of presumptuous vanity, but of a readiness to confront reality as a responsible spiritual being; and he would speak of striking the proper balance between the avoidance of error and the value of personal engagement.

The dilemma is presumably familiar, particularly in this venue, because some of its central aspects were explored in the Orthodox Forum's earlier volume, *Rabbinic Authority and Personal Autonomy*; and it is clearly relevant to the first question with which I have been confronted: "To what extent, if at all, must a contemporary Orthodox Jew look to modern, as against medieval or rabbinic, authorities to legitimate his response to modernity?" *Prima facie,* this is a strange reading. I presume that the question's substance is not factual but normative. The issue is not whether, out of sheer necessity, due to a dearth of classical material, we are driven to look to current lights, but rather, whether we are obligated to do so, as opposed to indulging ourselves in reliance upon earlier sources. If so, however, the formulation is doubly surprising. First, it runs counter to the grain of the Torah world's thought and practice. From childhood, we are involved with the substantive message of a famous gemara: אם ראשונים בני מלאכים – אנו בני אנשים, ואם ראשונים בני אנשים – אנו כחמורים, "If the first were as angels, we are as humans; and if the first were as humans, we are as asses."[4] Even those who do not regard *yeridat ha-dorot* as an ironclad historical necessity are profoundly habituated to acknowledging the superiority of earlier links in the chain of *mesorah*; if not as regards different levels of the same plateau, then at least between successive planes – Hazal as opposed to Rishonim, the latter vis-à-vis Aharonim. What are we to make, then, of the suggestion of the priority of contemporary authorities implied in our question? Confronted with an irrefutable contradiction between the dicta of the Ramban and the Netziv with regard to a halakhic detail of *milah* or *shehitah,* one would surely opt for the Ramban. Why should any *ben Torah* even imagine, then, that the overarching issue of response to modernity should be approached differently?

Second, one senses that our questioner, presumably modern Orthodox, would prefer to look to earlier authorities but envisions adversaries, evidently haredim, who would foreclose that option. But isn't this a reversal of roles? One would have supposed – with respect, say, to the analogous seventeenth-century confrontation between "ancients" and "moderns" familiar from Swift's *Battle of the Books* – that more conservative traditionalists would espouse classical authority, whereas the more innovative would champion the cause of their contemporaries. And yet, our questioner seems to assume otherwise. Have I misread him, or has he misread the scene?

Neither. The nub of the matter is that when a modern Orthodox Jew speaks of looking to the Rambam as opposed to the Brisker Rav, he is confronting us with an optical illusion. With respect to the former, one exercises judgment; vis-à-vis the latter, he faces it. Rishonim can be readily approached as a resource. Statements that coincide, broadly speaking, with our positions can be cited with comforting reassurance. Those that do not can frequently be explained away by noting distinctions between respective sociocultural situations, so that one may contend that the Rishonim, had they been referring to our experience, would have expressed themselves differently.

Have kollels, of whatever vintage, ceased to flourish because of the Rambam's[5] withering critique of much of their underlying rationale? The Torah world simply contends – to my mind, with trenchant cogency – that both the ideological composition of the Jewish community and the pressures of secular vocations have changed to the point that, even if one acknowledges the Rambam's arguments, which some Rishonim[6] challenged vigorously, the *raison d'être* of institutions which guard the spiritual hearth as well as training future leaders seems virtually self-evident. This by no means implies that Rishonim's hashkafic texts are of little moment as they can be circumvented and, at times, even manipulated. Their writings, at the very least, set a tone, point a direction, create a climate, and, to a great extent, determine the parameters of our discourse. They are, very much, the *einei ha-eidah*, our prime philosophic lights, whose concerted and consensual judgment we generally regard as binding. Nevertheless, at the level of specific guidance, particular statements can be parried so that a modernist may feel that he can confront the classical corpus with relative assurance.

No such leeway exists, however, with regard to recent, particularly contemporary, *gedolim*. They have encountered modern culture, and to the formidable extent that they have rejected it, they have addressed a clear message, direct or indirect, to the current Orthodox world. The pronouncements of Rav Elhanan Wasserman or Rav Baruch Baer Leibowitz leave no room for the luxury of subjective recourse or the niceties of differentiation. Their stern and often foreboding denunciations relate to the twentieth-century scene, and they leave the votaries of modern Orthodoxy only one of two options: either recant or live with the knowledge that the authors of *Birkat Shmuel* or *Kovetz Shiurim, seforim* they may very well use and admire, have, in concert with most of their peers, largely disavowed them. Even on sensitive and important issues, sections of the *Moreh Nevukhim* or the *Derashot Ha-Ran* may be effectively neutralized, in the same manner as Duns Scotus or Aquinas dealt with Aristotelian or Augustinian texts. One cannot finesse Rav Schach, however; one must simply decide whether to stand at his bar.

Those who nevertheless persist are confronted by the obvious question: Quite apart from the difficulty of sustaining the requisite psychological stamina, is their stance halakhically and hashkafically defensible? The very formulation of the question reflects the patent fact that the burden of establishing legitimacy clearly rests upon the modern Orthodox camp. No one poses a comparable challenge to their opponents. Advocates of modernity generally recognize – and, to my mind, unquestionably should recognize – the validity of a haredi orientation as one possible rendering of מה ה' א-להיך שואל מעמך, "What doth the Lord thy God require of thee?" (Devarim 10:12), even as they strenuously reject some of its elements.

As we are all painfully aware, however, the favor is hardly reciprocated – and this situation is unlikely to change significantly in the near future. Hence, the respective relations to authority are thoroughly asymmetrical. Quite apart from varied predispositions to authority figures and the fact that most acknowledged *gedolim* have not espoused modernity, the stakes for the haredi and the modernist are substantively different. To the former, legitimacy is not an issue; to the latter it is *the* issue.

Can the authority of the contemporary *gedolim* be denied, then? Who, if anyone, is authorized to challenge their jurisdiction? With respect to the purely halakhic realm, at least two *loci classici* may be cited to support the contention that it can not, and that one may not reject later authorities by relying upon their predecessors. The first is an operative rule of *pesak*:

Halakhah ke-batra'ei," "The Halakhah is in accordance with (the view of) later (*poskim*)." As the *Shakh* summarizes, this rule of thumb postulates that כל מקום שדברי הראשונים כתובים על ספר והם מפורסמים והפוסקים האחרונים חולקים עליהם הולכים אחר האחרונים, "Wherever the words of the earlier (authorities) are on record and are widely known, and later *poskim* challenge them, we follow the later (authorities)."[7]

On the same plane of authority, preference is to be given to later masters, inasmuch as they have presumably had the opportunity to survey and evaluate the views of their predecessors, to whom later contentions may never have occurred. However, the relevance of this principle to our problem is limited. It need not relate to the contrapuntal opposition of the classical and the contemporary but to successive layers of each. It is as much a reason for preferring a *pesak* of the Rosh or the Ran to that of Rabbenu Tam or the Ri Migash as it is for following the *Mishnah Berurah* instead of the *Magen Avraham*. Indeed, in practice, its exercise is generally confined to lateral controversies on the same plateau, between successive amoraim, Rishonim, and Aharonim.[8] Moreover, it is only one rule among many, subject to conflict with more cardinal principles; and a qualified rule at that, the prevalent reservation being that it only applies when later *poskim* were almost surely exposed to the earlier views. Above all, *Halakhah ke-batra'ei* is preeminently a technical tool in the professional hands of a recognized *posek* who applies it in the process of arriving at a decision. It is no lodestar for orienting spiritual existence, personal or communal.

Much more trenchant is a second source, quoted from the *Tosefta*, with significant additions, by the gemara in Rosh Hashanah:

למה לא נתפרשו שמותם של זקנים הללו – שלא יאמר אדם: פלוני כמשה ואהרן? פלוני כנדב ואביהוא? פלוני כאלדד ומידד? ואומר (שמואל א יב) ויאמר שמואל אל העם ה' אשר עשה את משה ואת אהרן, ואומר (שמואל א יב) וישלח ה' את ירבעל ואת בדן ואת יפתח ואת שמואל... שקל הכתוב שלשה קלי עולם כשלשה חמורי עולם, לומר לך: ירובעל בדורו – כמשה בדורו, בדן בדורו – כאהרן בדורו, יפתח בדורו – כשמואל בדורו. ללמדך שאפילו קל שבקלין ונתמנה פרנס על הצבור – הרי הוא כאביר שבאבירים, ואומר (דברים יז:ט) ובאת אל הכהנים הלוים ואל השפט אשר יהיה בימים ההם. וכי תעלה על דעתך שאדם הולך אצל הדיין שלא היה בימיו? הא אין לך אלא אצל

שופט שבימיו, ואומר (קהלת ז) אל תאמר מה היה שהימים הראשונים היו טובים
מאלה.

Our Rabbis taught: Why were the names of these elders not specified? In
order that one should not say, "This person is like Moshe and Aharon, this
one like Nadav and Avihu, this one like Eldad and Medad?" And it is stated,
"It is the Lord that made Mosheh and Aharon" (1 Shmuel 12:16); and it is stated,
"The Lord sent Yerubaal and Bedan and Yiftah and Shmuel" (1 Shmuel 12:11).
Scripture has balanced three of the world's lightest against three of the world's
weightiest, in order to tell you that Yerubaal in his generation is as Mosheh
in his, Bedan in his generation as Aharon in his, Yiftah in his generation as
Shmuel in his. This is to teach you that even lightest of the light, if he has
been appointed a leader over the community, is as the mightiest of the mighty.
And it is stated, "And thou shalt come unto the priests the Levites, and unto
the judge that shall be in those days" (Devarim 17:9). Can it occur to you that
a person would go to a judge who is not in his day? The intent is that you
should follow your contemporary judge. And it is stated, "Say not thou: How
was it that the former days were better than these?" (Kohelet 7:10).[9]

In this *baraita*, we evidently do encounter a firm mandate for
contemporary authority. Not content with validating modern Yiftahs,
independently considered, it obliges us to defer to them rather than to
classical Shmuels, whenever we find them in conflict. As Tosafot noted:
שהימים הראשונים היו טובים מאלה – ולכך יש לשמוע לראשונים יותר מן האחרונים אל תאמר
כך דאין לך אלא שופט שהיה בימיו " 'That the earlier days were better than the
present, and that therefore earlier rather than later (authorities) should
be heeded' – don't say that, as you have only your contemporary judge."[10]
Whatever the reason – I presume it is because, as previously suggested,
direct immediate authority is qualitatively different from possibly selective
recourse to earlier texts – the message is clear.

Nevertheless, the bearing of this source upon our problem is limited. It explicitly relates to an individual or group that has been formally
appointed to a post and, hence, empowered to speak and act *ex cathedra*; and it focuses upon this aspect directly. The contemporary, be he קל
שבקלים, "the lightweight" to whom we are enjoined to hearken, has been
נתמנה פרנס על הציבור, appointed as communal leader, and it is out of deference to the authority with which he has been officially invested that we

are charged to turn to him. One may extrapolate from the *baraita* to our own situation, but the extension of the principle certainly entails a leap. Essentially, with reference to a context within which no formal investiture exists, the question of who stands in judgment before whom, and with respect to which issues – and it is this, as I have suggested, that lies, in a modified and masked form, at the core of the choice between ancients and moderns – here remains unresolved.

Yet, דברי תורה עניים במקום אחד, ועשירים במקום אחר or "The words of Torah are poor in one place and rich in another"; and the relevant halakhic guidelines are accessible and reasonably straightforward. On questionable matters, the ordinary person, even if he be a learned layman or a middle-echelon rav, must accept the consensual view of current *pesak*. Whether the formal prohibition of *Lo tassur* applies after the dissolution of the *Beit Din Ha-Gadol* is a subject of debate,[11] but the fact that one is ordinarily bound by consensus is not. Deviation from it is, in effect, designated as error, even with reference to contemporaries for whom current wisdom has not yet attained the aura of tradition.[12]

And this is so on two levels. In delineating the parameters of judicial error, the Gemara differentiates between *ta'ut bi-devar mishnah*, "an error with regard to a definitive matter," deriving from ignorance of the material, which is invariably invalidated, and *ta'ut be-shikul ha-da'at*, "an error of judgment," which may at times be sustained, with the erring judge required to compensate the wronged party; and it defines both with reference to the prevailing corpus or practice:

אמר ליה רבינא לרב אשי: אפילו טעה ברבי חייא ורבי אושעיא? – אמר ליה: אין. – אפילו בדרב ושמואל? – אמר ליה: אין. – אפילו בדידי ודידך? – אמר ליה: אטו אנן קטלי קני באגמא אנן? היכי דמי שיקול הדעת? אמר רב פפא: כגון תרי תנאי או תרי אמוראי דפליגי אהדדי, ולא איתמר הלכתא לא כמר ולא כמר, ואיקרי ועבד כחד מינייהו, וסוגיא דשמעתא אזלי כאידך – היינו שיקול הדעת.

Ravina said to Rav Ashi: "Even if he has erred with regard to [dictates of] Rabbi Hiyya and Rabbi Oshaya [would this be regarded as an error *bi-devar mishnah*]?" He responded, "Yes." "Even with regard to [dictates of] Rav and Shmuel?" He responded, "Yes." He said to him, "Even with regard to mine and yours?" He responded, "Are we, then, but as reed-choppers in a brush?" What is [an error] with regard to *shikul ha-da'at*? Rav Papa said: "If two *tannaim* or *amora'im* should disagree, and the halakhah has not been resolved like either, and he [i.e., the judge] has happened to decide like one of them, while the prevalent view inclines to the other, that is [an error of] *shikul ha-da'at*."[13]

Presumably, subsequent ages are comparably bound by their Ravina and Rav Ashi or by the prevailing winds of current *pesak*; and contravention of either is wholly out of court.

Thus, for the ordinary person or even the ordinary *dayyan*. With respect to a master, however, himself in the forefront of halakhic exposition and decision, the situation is entirely different. He, too, is generally bound by that which, by common consent, by whatever recognized standard, and by dint of whichever historical circumstances, has attained the status of acknowledged *devar mishnah*. With respect to *shikkul ha-da'at*, however, he enjoys considerable latitude. He is, after all, the equivalent of any two *tannaim* or two *amoraim* engaged in a particular *mahloket*, and inasmuch as the gemara clearly implies that error can here only be ascribed to others, while the *tanna* or *amora* in question can stand by his position, regardless of the inclinations of *sugya d'alma*, any *gadol*, even if he is not the equal of his adversaries, but so long as he is in their league, can postulate a minority view.

The Rosh is fully explicit on this point. In rejecting the Rabad's position that the writings of the Geonim have attained the status of *devar mishnah*, he contends that this may apply to a *dayyan* who contravenes their rulings out of ignorance, but not to one who challenges them knowingly:

אבל אם לא ישרו בעיניו דבריהם ומביא ראיות לדבריו המוקבלים לאנשי דורו. יפתח בדורו כשמואל בדורו. אין לך אלא שופט אשר יהיה בימים ההם ויכול לסתור דבריהם.

But if he disapproves of what they said, and he cites proofs, acceptable to his contemporaries, for his views, Yiftah in his generation is as Shmuel in his; you have only your contemporary judge, and he can contravene what they said.

Further, he argues that the gemara's statement that rulings of leading amoraim were to be regarded as *devar mishnah* applies only to unwitting error, not to frontal opposition:

והיינו דא"ל רב הונא לרב ששת אפילו בדידך ודידי וא"ל אטו קטלי קני באגמא אנן כלומר אם חדשנו דבר מדעתנו שלא נמצא לא במשנה ולא בגמרא ודיין שלא ידע דברינו ופסק בענין אחר וכששמע הדברים ישרו בעיניו כטועה בדבר משנה הוי וחוזר. אבל הדיין ההוא פשיטא שיש שיש לחלוק על דבריהם.

> And this is the import of what Rav Huna said to Rav Sheshet: "Even with regard to your views or mine?" And he responded: "Are we, then, but as reed-choppers in a brush?" – to wit: "If we innovated something, on our own, which was found in neither the mishnah nor the gemara, and a judge who was unaware of what we had said decided otherwise, and when he subsequently heard what had been said, he approved of it, he is to be regarded as erring with respect to a *devar mishnah*." However, that judge can unquestionably challenge their words.[14]

In extending the right of dissent even to material defined as *devar mishnah*, the Rosh breaks fresh ground. With respect to the realm of *shikkul ha-da'at*, however, the right to postulate a dissenting position is unassailable.

Moreover, adhering to this position is not just a personal prerogative. It extends to members of the *posek*'s community. The Rema is explicit on this point: ואם היה מנהג בעיר להקל, מפני שחכם אחד הורה להם כך, הולכין אחר דעתו. "And if the local custom was to be permissive because a given *hakham* had guided them accordingly, they can follow his view."[15] His source is a *teshuvah* of the Rashba, who, in turn, bases himself upon several gemarot, of which the best-known is cited several times in Shas:

תניא נמי הכי: במקומו של רבי אליעזר היו כורתין עצים, לעשות פחמין לעשות ברזל. במקומו של רבי יוסי הגלילי היו אוכלין בשר עוף בחלב.

> Our Rabbis taught: In the locale of Rabbi Eliezer they would chop down trees in order to have charcoal on the Sabbath for the forging of iron [i.e., for a *brith milah*]. In the locale of Rabbi Yossi the Galilean, they would eat chicken meat with milk.[16]

The import of the *baraita* is both clear and far-reaching. A *posek*'s community may – with respect to *humrot*, one should say, must – accept his decisions, even if they constitute a minority or solitary view, and even if they are permissive with regard to a *d'oraita* issue.

The definition of the relevant community, however, is murky. The gemara speaks of locale, but it seems strange that geography should be the sole determinant. Would an enclave of Judean emigres in Galilee be permitted to eat chicken fried in butter? Would only residents of twelfth-century Egypt be entitled to rely upon the Rambam's minority *kulot*? It seems far more likely that other factors – ethnic identity or, above all, spiritual and ideological fealty – should carry no less weight. I believe this is clearly suggested by the Rashba:

ומן הדרך הזה כל שנהגו לעשות כל מעשיהם על פי אחד מגדולי הפוסקים במקום שנהגו לעשות כל מעשיהם על פי הלכות הרב אלפסי זכרונו לברכה ובמקומות שנהגו לעשות כל מעשיהם על פי חבור הרמב"ם ז"ל והרי עשו אלו הגדולים כרבם.

In this vein, if they have been accustomed to act consistently in accordance with the *Halakhot* of Rav Alfasi ז"ל, or, in places which have been accustomed to act consistently on the basis of the codex of the Rambam ז"ל, they have, in effect, established these *gedolim* as their *rebbe*.[17]

Physical proximity is obviously not intended here. What is envisioned is, evidently, a principled and consistent attachment. Its basis is left open; the places cited could have come to be "accustomed to doing all their actions" in accordance with the dicta of the Rif or the Rambam as a result either of accident or choice. The point is, however, that spiritual commitment rather than geographic contiguity is the determining factor. A Sephardi congregation in Warsaw could still be bound by the rulings of the Rishon le-Zion. Would a Gerer hasid cease to be part of the Beth Israel's community just because he had moved to Paris?

The implications for a contemporary Orthodox Jew's legitimization of his response to modernity are self-evident. Were there no genuine *gadol* who had subscribed to the core halakhic positions of what is roughly denominated as modern Orthodoxy, ordinary rabbis and laymen would be hard-put to cling to them. In the absence of an imprimatur from any *gadol* whatsoever, it would be difficult if not impossible to justify the adoption of norms and values in defiance of a wall-to-wall phalanx of *gedolei Yisrael*. Such action would simply be regarded as error, whether *bi-devar mishnah* or *be-shikkul ha-da'at*. One's contemporary authority no doubt bases himself largely, and perhaps selectively, upon classical predecessors. But the ordinary person must base himself upon a *shofet she-be-yamekha*. Even if we assume that, on the personal level, a moderate *lamdan* may, and perhaps must, act in accordance with his own informed and conscientious reading of the sources – a dubious proposition in its own right – surely no such course could be championed in the public sphere.

Who, however, imagines this to be the case? Only the ignorant and the arrogant. Even if we limit our purview to the confines of our own bailiwick, it is self-evident that the imposing presence of our collective *rav muvhak* is sufficient to refute this perception. No objective observer of the American Torah scene – or of the international scene, for that matter – can fail to acknowledge the Rav's position as one of the *gedolim* of this century, and his advocacy of the critical values of modern Orthodoxy. Even Israelis who do not perceive that his spiritual stature towers majestically over that of their *Rashei Yeshiva*; even Americans who are blind to the fact that he bestrides their current *Mo'ezet Gedolei ha-Torah* like a colossus – *eilu ve-eilu* know that he is of the very first rank, fully entitled to develop independent positions on all matters of *shikkul ha-da'at*. And among these positions are several that are generally taken to be the linchpins of modern Orthodoxy. Surely the Rav can in no way be described as a champion of the movement in all its ramifications. Indeed, he has frequently been among its severest critics, castigating manifestations of utilitarian pragmatism, flaccid emotion, tepid commitment, and ceremonialism tinged with vulgarity. On the central issues, however, he has been steadfast and consistent: on the interrelated questions of general culture, confronting the world, and Religious Zionism. There is no denying the fact that among his peers, the Rav, while not alone with respect to any of these views, is decidedly in the minority with respect to all. But there can also be no question of his right to champion his positions.

That right is relevant not only to the Rav personally but to any declared member of his ideological community. Those who identify with his worldview and halakhic orientation can rightly regard their similar views as legitimized by his authority – with the proviso, of course, that they generally submit to that authority. They need not routinely accept every jot and tittle of his every ruling. While the Rashba spoke of communities "which have been accustomed to act consistently on the basis of the codex of the Rambam ז"ל," it seems unlikely that this left no room for exceptions. He himself goes on to distinguish between the status of an accepted historical *posek* and that of a community's actual rav:

ומיהו אם יש שם אחד חכם וראוי להוראה ורואה ראיה לאסור מה שהם מתירין נוהג בו איסור. שאין אלו כרבם ממש דבמקום רבם אילו יעשו שלא כדבריו יקלו בכבוד רבם במקומו.

> However, if, in that community, there is a *hakham*, qualified to decide, who sees evidence for proscribing that which they permit, he should treat the matter as forbidden, inasmuch as these [i.e., general authorities such as the Rif or the Rambam] are not as their actual *rav*. For in the place of their *rav*, if they should act contrary to his views, they shall be slighting the respect of their *rav*, in his place.[18]

They should, however, meaningfully identify themselves as his followers. As is manifest from the Rashba's *teshuva*, to those who meet this standard, a *gadol*'s authority extends beyond his lifetime. The postmortal Rambam could, through his *Mishneh Torah*, still be decisive after several generations; and the Rav, ז"ל, remains, even in death, a bulwark of his spiritual community. Just how long a protective shadow a *gadol* may cast deserves thought. Presumably, it should be confined to the duration of the continuous existence of the sociohistorical entity to which he had belonged and which had belonged to him. As regards the Rav, ז"ל, in any event, we are not at this juncture at the point of expiration.

We are familiar with an elastic conception of the scope of an ideological community from one of the Rambam's best-known responsa. Avraham Avinu's household, he writes to R. Ovadiah Ger-Zedek, includes

כל מי שיתגייר עד סוף כל הדורות וכל המיחד שמו של הקב"ה כמו שהוא כתוב בתורה תלמידו של אברהם אבינו ע"ה ובני ביתו הם כולם

> Whoever shall convert, until the end of all the generations, and whoever shall declare the singularity of the name of God, as it is written in the Torah, is a student of *Avraham Avinu*, and they are all as members of his household.[19]

In our context, the parameters would obviously be much narrower, but the basic concept of an ideological community is analogous. And of course the Rema omitted any reference to overall commitment, speaking instead of specific rulings by a current *hakham* (ואם היה מנהג בעיר להקל, מפני שחכם אחד הורה להם כך, הולכין אחר דעתו. "If the custom in the city was to be lenient because a scholar had directed them in that fashion…") without stipulating that he was the *mora de-athra*. If the omission is intentional, his view is far-reaching. As to the basic concept of a *gadol*'s ideological community and its relevance to the current scene, however, there can be little question.

The point can be illustrated by an apt anecdote. When a group of leading *rashei yeshiva* met to consider promulgating an *issur* against Orthodox participation in the Synagogue Council of America, Rav Reuven Grozowsky, ז"ל demurred. He explained that inasmuch as the prospective participants were mostly "*talmidim* of Reb Yoshe Baer," it was for him to decide how to guide them, and others ought not to intervene.

In one sense, the position I have outlined exalts authority and inhibits autonomy, inasmuch as it posits sanction by a contemporary *gadol* as a condition for the halakhic legitimacy of a movement. And yet in another sense, it ultimately leaves the decision in the hands of the individual, as it is for him to choose in which camp to pitch his tent. The more modernist among us will probably be somewhat uncomfortable with the first proposition. But anyone who has discussed these issues with serious young *benei Torah* knows that they are more perturbed by the second. They are often doubly perplexed. First, they may be fazed, practically or conceptually, by the difficulty of making a choice. How does one know to whom to attach oneself? Second, they may be troubled, ideologically, by what is at once the prerogative and the burden. They recognize that in selecting a mentor to whom one will admittedly be bound, one is exercising an autonomous choice that will largely determine one's future agenda and priorities, so that a measure of personal freedom is definitive, after all. Some are exhilarated, but others are taken aback, if not frightened.

In response, I find myself telling them, in essence, that the second question answers the first. Obviously, one does not choose among *gedolim* by gauging respective degrees of *lomdut* or saintliness. One seeks a leader who speaks to one's own inner sanctum, as a convert to *hasidut* would seek a *rebbe*. The quest for a mentor is integrally and dialectically related to self-definition, a process to which conscience and sensibility are indeed crucial. Hence, as to the second question, it has no answer and needs no answer. Indeed, up to a certain point and beyond another point, one is charged with charting one's own course. But should this frighten or alarm? And what is the alternative? The fact that some are, in fact, alarmed is a reflection of the flight from spiritual responsibility endemic in certain circles. From a genuine Torah perspective it can only be deemed regrettable.

Personal judgment may be relevant with respect to an additional factor. The Rav once quoted his father, Rav Moshe ל״ז, to the effect that the nature of *pesak* was drastically changed when formal classical *semikhah* was terminated. Originally, a *samukh* – at least on the Rambam's view that *semikhah* applies to *hora'at issur ve-heter* as well as to *din*[20] – would pronounce a decision that was binding by dint of his authoritative fiat. Now, however, the *posek*'s personal status has been vitiated, and with it, the standing of his decisions. Now, he essentially serves as a reference guide, providing reliable information about what the tradition and its sources, properly understood and interpreted, state; but it is they, rather than he, that bind authoritatively.

This is a radical thesis, both conceptually and practically, with potentially momentous implications for the implementation of Halakhah. Legal decisions obviously entail two components: elucidation of the code or the rule and assessment of the particular situation to which it is to be applied. Juridic authority is ordinarily empowered to deal with both components; and the obligation to submit to its dicta encompasses both. One violates the injunction, לא תסור מן הדבר אשר יגידו לך ימין ושמאל, "Thou shalt not deviate from the sentence which they shall declare unto thee, to the right or to the left," by challenging the Sanhedrin's factual determination no less than by rejecting its theoretical conclusion. Yet if one accepts Rav Moshe's contention, this ought not to be the case with respect to late periods. If a *posek* is only an interpretive reference guide to halakhic sources, one might accept his rendering of the content of the halakhic corpus, but rely upon one's own judgment in evaluating the facts.

The application of this dichotomy to the contemporary scene would neutralize much of the critique of modern Orthodoxy. But it would also neutralize much else, and I think that one should be reluctant to ground legitimization upon so radical a thesis. On the other hand, it certainly ought not to be dismissed entirely, and it can be borne in mind as an auxiliary factor, a concept that can be appreciated by anyone familiar with the byways of *pesak*. Concurrently, in a far more modest vein, one could harness the element of factual evaluative capacity to our previous discussion concerning the selection of a polestar. The Rosh explains that the choice of a *posek* may be determined, understandably, by his area of specialization:

וכן דעתי נוטה דמאיזה טעם עשו חכמי הגמרא כלל זה לפסוק הלכה כשמואל בדיני וכרב באיסורי בכל מקום. לפי שידעו ששמואל היה רגיל תמיד לפסוק דינין ולכך היה מדקדק בהן ויורד לעומקן ומשכיל על כל דבר אמת. וכן רב היה רגיל לדקדק בהוראת איסור והיתר לכך סמכו על הוראותיו לעניני איסור והיתר.

And this is my inclination, that why did the sages of the gemara establish a principle to accept, consistently, the views of Shmuel with respect to civil questions and those of Rav with respect to ritual questions? Because they knew that Shmuel judged civil issues regularly and therefore would study them carefully and analyze them in depth. Rav, likewise, focused upon ritual decision regularly; hence, his judgments were relied upon with regard to the ritual area.[21]

Analogously, in seeking Torah guidance with respect to modern culture, one would presumably prefer *gedolim* who know it intimately and intensively to those whose understanding of it is both narrow and cursory. The implication for deciding before whose bar to sit for judgment is self-evident.

The whole of the foregoing discussion refers even to purely halakhic issues, allowing for the assumption that questions concerning the legitimacy of modern Orthodoxy are indeed of that order. However, there are many apologists who contend that the primary issues are matters of *hashkafah*, to which authority *per se* is far less relevant, and with respect to which classical sources are arguably self-sufficient. This brings us to the

familiar shibboleth of *daat Torah*. This concept is generally in disrepute
among votaries of modern Orthodoxy, who have sought to challenge
both its historical progeny and its philosophic validity. I must confess
that I find myself, in principle, more favorably disposed to the idea. I readily concede that the concept, in its more overarching permutations, is of
relatively recent vintage; and I base this assumption, apart from Professor
Kaplan's stimulating and wide-ranging essay,[22] on the statement of no less
an authority than the Ba'al Ha-Tanya. Responding, in *Iggeret Ha-Kodesh*,
to a query, evidently about some mundane matter, posed to him by followers, he writes:

אהוביי אחיי ורעיי מאהבה מסותרת תוכחת מגולה לכו נא ונוכחה זכרו ימות עולם בינו
שנות דור ודור הייתה כזאת מימות עולם ואיה איפוא מצאתם מנהג זה באחד מכל ספרי
חכמי ישראל הראשונים והאחרונים להיות מנהג ותיקון לשאול בעצה גשמיות כדת מה
לעשות בעניני העולם הגשמי אף לגדולי חכמי ישראל הראשונים כתנאים ואמוראים
אשר כל רז לא אנס להו ונהירין להון שבילין דרקיע כ"א לנביאים ממש אשר היו לפנים
בישראל כשמואל הרואה אשר הלך אליו שאול לדרוש ה' על דבר האתונות שנאבדו
לאביו כי באמת כל עניני אדם לבד מדברי תורה וי"ש אינם מושגים רק בנבואה ולא
לחכמים לחם כמארז"ל הכל בידי שמים חוץ מיראת שמים

Come now, and let us reason together, remember the days of old, consider the
years of many generations. Was there ever anything like this, and where, then
did you find such a custom in any of the books of any of the sages of Israel,
either Rishonim or Aharonim, that there should be a praiseworthy custom
to ask for worldly counsel, as to what to do with respect to secular matters,
of even the greatest sages of Israel of old, such as *tannaim* or *amora'im*, to
whom no secret was foreign and to whom even the byways of Heaven were
familiar; with the sole exception of the actual prophets. For in truth, all
human matters, except for those of Torah and *yir'at shamayim*, are grasped
by prophecy alone, and bread is not to the wise, as Hazal said: "Everything
is in the hands of Heaven except for the fear of Heaven."[23]

To be sure, the term *yir'at shamayim*, may be broadly interpreted. Nevertheless, the passage is telling.

Moreover, I freely acknowledge that one's faith in the concept is
periodically put to a severe test. As but one instance, the doyen of current
rashei yeshiva, R. Schach, proves the value of Torah as the self-sufficient

repository of all knowledge by asking, rhetorically: "Whence did Hazal know that the earth was forty-two times larger than the moon, and that the sun was approximately one-hundred-and-seventy times larger than the earth (as explained in the Rambam, *Hilkhot Yesodei Hatorah* 3:8), if not from the power of the Torah?"[24] In raising this question, he is wholly oblivious not only of the rudiments of astronomy but also of the fact that the selfsame Rambam explicitly states, with respect to these very issues, that they are beyond the pale of Hazal's authority:

> Do not ask of me to show that everything they have said concerning astronomical matters conforms to the way things really are. For at that time mathematics were imperfect. They did not speak about this as transmitters of dicta of the prophets, but rather because in those times they were men of knowledge in these fields or because they had heard these dicta from the men of knowledge who lived in those times.[25]

To my mind, the strain is palpable.

Nevertheless, I find the alternative view, that *gedolei Torah* are professional experts whose authority and wisdom can ordinarily be regarded as confined to the area of their technical proficiency, simply inconceivable. Our abiding historical faith in the efficacy of Torah as a pervasive, ennobling, informing, and enriching force dictates adoption of the concept of *da'at Torah* in some form or measure. Still, contrary to the historical course of the idea, I find it less applicable today than heretofore. At a time when many *gedolim* do not spring organically from the dominant Jewish community to whose apex they rise, and instead distance themselves from it; and when the ability to understand and communicate in a shared cultural or even verbal language is, by design, limited, the capacity of even a *gadol* to intuit the sociohistorical dynamics of his ambient setting is almost inevitably affected. And while the quasi-mystical element of סוד ה׳ ליראיו ובריתו להודיעם always remains applicable, that, too, presumably is not wholly independent of circumstances.

These considerations bear directly upon our concerns. The limitations cited are of little relevance to the ability to deal with purely internal matters arising in the context of the traditional Jewish community. Hence, to the extent that one subscribes to the concept of *da'at Torah*, at least on the advisory, if not the normative, plane, and bearing in mind the fundamental distinction between *devar mizvah* and *devar ha-reshut,* one may regard it as currently in full force with regard to this sphere. However, the central issues concerning modern Orthodoxy and its legitimacy characteristically focus upon its relation to the outer world; and it is precisely at this juncture that the counsel of those least familiar with that world becomes less reliable. Hence, to the extent – admittedly, in dispute – to which the issues related to the legitimacy of modern Orthodoxy relate to *hashkafah* rather than Halakhah, and insofar as – again, admittedly only up to a point – the debate hinges upon judgment and implementation rather than upon axiological principles, the need for a contemporary legitimizing bulwark is mitigated significantly.

And yet, at bottom, I believe that it still exists, for both intrinsic and ancillary reasons. For one thing, some of the most controversial issues – *Torah u-madda* is a prime example – have clear halakhic import. Second, significant philosophic cruxes are matters of perennial debate, only partially bound to a reading of the modern map. Attitudes to *yishuvo shel olam* or the nature and scope of the Issakhar-Zevulun relationship awaited formulation in the time of the Rishonim no less than in our own.

These considerations aside, however, even if it were wholly licit to sever all links with contemporary *gedolim,* so as to rely instead upon selective, even if avowedly submissive, recourse to earlier authorities, such a course would be grossly mistaken; and this from both a personal and a communal standpoint. The statement attributed to Rav Israel Salanter that both mitnagdim and hasidim are in error, the former in thinking that they can do without a rebbe, and the latter in imagining that they have found one, is apt in this conviction – at least with respect to the former. A person, and not only the ordinary layman, needs a *gavra rabba,* to serve in part as a role-model if possible, and in part as a realization of what Whitehead called "the vision of greatness"; to lift one's sights and aspirations – extending the bounds of what he strives to achieve, and suffusing him with appreciation and admiration for what he senses he cannot achieve; to guide, on the one hand, and inhibit, on the other. This is not a matter of popular hagiolatry or Carlylean hero-worship. It is a spiritual necessity, all the more so within our tradition, for which an *adam gadol* is the embodiment of the *mesorah*, and of *Torah she-b'al-peh*. Rava's statement, כמה טפשאי שאר אינשי דקיימי מקמי ספר תורה ולא קיימי מקמי גברא רבה, "How foolish are ordinary people, who rise in honor of a *sefer Torah* but do not rise in honor of a great person,"[26] makes the point succinctly. Of course, we are all awed and inspired by past masters, too; but the element of contemporaneity, that of והיו עיניך רואות את מוריך, "But thine eyes shall see thy teachers," adds a dimension no one should readily abandon.

The communal factor is no less significant. Were modern Orthodoxy to divorce itself wholly from modern Torah authorities, the effect would be both desiccating and devastating. The movement would lose not only the vivifying power of the *gedolim* but the vibrancy of the Torah world within which they live and function. That world – if you will, haredi society in general – is open to criticism in many respects. But there is no doubting its vitality and its commitment; and from these, modern Orthodoxy has much to learn and draw. The present situation, marked by bifurcation, mistrust, and tension between the two communities, is deplorable enough, and is detrimental to both; after all, the haredim, for their part, have much to learn and draw from their modernist peers. But the chasm created by conscious retreat from recognition of any current authority would exacerbate matters greatly. Some may feel that they have little choice, that the alternative is the loss of spiritual identity. I do not agree; but let awareness of the magnitude of the prospective price provide a powerful stimulus for the development of indigenous Torah authority.

II

The need for modern authority appears to be presupposed in the second question with which I have been confronted: "To what extent, if at all, is it legitimate to base a cohesive modern Orthodox worldview upon selection of elements from the thought of various authorities, e.g., Rabbi D.Z. Hoffmann on academic scholarship, Rav Hirsch on humanism and Rav Kook on Zionism?" Implicit in this formulation is the assumption that modern sanction is vital, the only question being whether it can be attained eclectically. The components cited are philosophic, but in presenting a response, I would like to deal with the question, first, in the light of halakhic analogues; and then proceed to treat the hashkafic issue independently.

Were the question raised with respect to Halakhah, I would regard the projected eclecticism as doubly problematic. There is, first, the need to cope with apparent textual support for the demand for consistent adherence to one's acknowledged *posek*. In popular parlance, the *locus classicus* for this demand is the mishnah's twice-repeated prescription, *Asei lekha rav* – "Establish a *rav* for yourself."[27] The common association notwithstanding, this is, in truth, a rather dubious source. Unquestionably, some classical *mefarshim* have indeed interpreted the *mishnayot* in this vein. Thus, Rabbenu David Ha-Naggid, the Rambam's grandson, writes:

> And inasmuch as in their time students of Hillel and of Shammai flourished and controversy between scholars became rife, therefore, Rabban Gamaliel ordered and said: "Designate for yourself a *rav*, to study Torah from either the school of Shammai or that of Hillel, and don't remain in doubt but rely upon the view of the school of Hillel or of that of Shammai."[28]

Rabbi Yosef ben Shoshan, a fourteenth-century Spanish commentator, is even more explicit:

> The intent is that an individual should select for himself a specific scholar whom he should ask and who will direct him as to what he should do, so that he can rely upon him and not be halting between two opinions, doing on occasion like this one and on occasion like that one, as that would cause him to act in accordance with his own inclination, to the point that he will issue license to himself and turn hither and thither, inasmuch as he has not committed himself to the directives of a specific scholar.[29]

Nevertheless, the bearing of the statement upon our discussion is limited. For one thing alternative interpretations of the mishnah abound. Some explained it as urging the layman to seek expert guidance instead of relying upon his uninformed judgment, rather that instructing him in the quest for that guidance.[30] Others, by contrast, saw it as addressing a prospective *posek*, exhorting him – in case of uncertainty, obviously, but even when he senses that he can decide judiciously, on his own – to consult colleagues or masters before deciding definitively.[31] Still others held, in light of the elaboration in Avot de-Rabbi Nathan (8:2), that the *rav* in question was not a *posek* at all but a *rebbe*, from whom one seeks Torah knowledge rather than *ex cathedra* decision. To be sure, some contended that this was only true of the first mishnah, within which the call is twinned with a parallel charge, "And acquire for yourself a friend," but not of the second, within which it is conjoined with the directive, "And avoid uncertainty."[32] However, the Mahzor Vitri and the Ravan, *inter alia,* described the *mishnayot* as identical, both dealing with *talmud Torah.*[33]

Second, even some who did interpret the mishnah as referring to the area of *pesak* may very well have regarded its exhortation as advisory counsel rather than normative demand. Thus, the Rambam, taking note of the conjunction, in the second mishnah, with "and avoid uncertainty," writes: "That which is ordained here, that one should establish a *rav* for himself, does not refer to learning but to decision. That import is: Establish a person as a *rav* for yourself, so that you can rely upon him with respect to the licit and the forbidden, and thus relieve yourself of uncertainty."[34] Of course, if it is Hazal's, even spiritual advice carries great weight.[35] Nevertheless, as opposed to binding norms, it can be more flexibly considered, with reference to sundry contextual factors, and in the light of possibly conflicting values.

Third, even the latter mishnah appears to encourage the designation of a personal guide, with whom one is presumably in direct contact, rather than, as in the context of our discussion, the adoption of a single intellectual authority, from whom one may be remote in time and place. This selection of a spiritual father is highly significant, in its own right – existentially, it is often of greater moment than the choice of a definitive *posek.* It is, however, on a different continuum than deciding between conflicting schools of *pesak*, and it needs to be approached independently.

Finally, looking beyond immediate commentary, there is scant evidence that this mishnah has served as the normative base for consistent adherence to a designated *posek*. It does not appear as such in any major codex, and a search of major collections of *teshuvot*, from Rishonim down to the present, reveals that the phrase is cited in a bare handful, and without normative thrust. Of far greater import is a directive of the *Tosefta*:

לעולם הלכה כדברי בית הילל, והרוצה להחמיר על עצמו לנהוג כחומרי בית שמאי וכחומרי בית הילל על זה נאמר: הכסיל בחושך הולך. התופס קולי בית שמאי וקולי בית הילל רשע; אלא או כדברי בית שמאי כקוליהון וכחומריהון או כדברי בית הלל כקוליהון וכחומריהון:

The halakhah is always in accordance with the views of the school of Hillel. If a person wishes to impose rigor upon himself, to conduct himself in accordance with the stringencies of the schools of both Shammai and of Hillel, of him it is written, "But the fool walketh in darkness." If one adopts the leniencies of the schools of both Shammai and Hillel, he is wicked. Rather, if like the school of Shammai, then in accordance with both their leniencies and their stringencies; if like the school of Hillel, then in accordance with both their leniencies and their stringencies.[36]

The gemara generalizes the precept:

כל היכא דמשכחת תרי תנאי ותרי אמוראי דפליגי אהדדי כעין מחלוקת בית שמאי ובית הלל – לא ליעבד כי קוליה דמר וכי קוליה דמר, ולא כחומריה דמר וכי חומריה דמר. אלא: או כי קוליה דמר וכחומריה עביד, או כקוליה דמר וכחומריה עביד.

Wherever one encounters two *tannaim* or two *amora'im* who disagree with each other, as did the schools of Shammai and Hillel [i.e., with respect to a wide range of issues], he should not adopt the leniencies of both or the stringencies of both, but, rather, the leniency and stringency of the one or of the other.[37]

The door to eclectic *pesak* would here seem to be effectively barred. However, the directive is possibly open to two major qualifications.

First, with reference to the folly of collecting *humrot,* the gemara later stipulates that it only applies to mutually contradictory *pesakim.* Conceivably, a similar limitation might be posited with respect to the evil of collecting *kulot.*

Second, weight should perhaps be assigned to the motivational factor. If a person qualified to make such judgments[38] finds himself inclined to agree with the Rambam on one issue and with the Rabad on another, he may very well be authorized to pursue his inclinations. The proscription applies to those who have adopted multiple *kulot* purely out of a desire for comfort. It is not the adoption of lenient rulings *per se* but the persistent quest for sloth and slough that is reprehensible.

The second problematic aspect, still with reference to the halakhic realm, brings us back to our prior discussion. It will be recalled that the sanction to subscribe to a minority view derives from reliance upon an authority to whom one is, in some meaningful way, attached, to the point of being part of his societal or ideological community. What kind of adherence is there, however, if one only accepts convenient *pesakim* and deserts his authority when one discerns choicer pickings elsewhere? Hence, to presumed votaries of dissenting orientations, eclecticism poses a special difficulty. It not only invites criticism of their conduct in particular areas but may undermine the fundamental legitimacy of their overarching position.

Transposing these criteria to the axiological sphere, I believe that, while they do not translate into directives, they can serve as guidelines. To start with the second criterion, it is clearly applicable to *mahshavah* no less than to Halakhah. A person who subscribed to Rav Kook's Zionist ideology but preferred the Satmar Rav's view of secular Jews would be as hard put to rely upon his *hetter* on *shemittah* as one who rejected his *pesakim* regarding *ribbit* or the status of *agunot*.

However, at least one major qualification can be suggested. I do not believe that, in order to be regarded as a disciple, one must derive his comprehensive philosophic sustenance from a single authority. Certainly, one can draw wisdom and inspiration from varied sources and blend them within his own spiritual orbit. The crucial question is where one's presumed master stands with respect to what one has imbibed elsewhere. If he is sympathetic or oblivious, if he relates to the area in question with detached geniality or consigns it to benign neglect, surely one may and possibly should turn to others who have studied the matter in depth and feel passionately about it. However, if the positions sought elsewhere are vigorously opposed by one's mentor – especially if they are challenged on ideological grounds as possibly illicit – adherence to them severely strains supposed affinity and the right to capitalize upon it.

Could a votary of astrology readily claim reliance upon the Rambam with respect to allegorical hermeneutics? Obviously, on certain issues, much may depend on the master's response to dissent, even with regard to positions he espouses strongly. No relation to the Rav would have been strained over territorial compromise. Historicistic psychologization of Halakhah would have been another story, however.

The first criterion, the motivational factor, is equally applicable. Whatever one may think of the wisdom of collecting masters – with respect to *talmud Torah,* Hazal saw both pros and cons[39] – the legitimacy of this course appears to me beyond reproach. The impetus is crucial, however. How can we fault a person who composes a mosaic out of elements drawn from varied sources, each of which has been culled because of its resonance with his or her profoundest Jewish instincts? If, on the other hand, one has selected elements because they are the hashkafic equivalent of *kulot,* state-of-the-art philosophically correct, and culturally convenient, the eclectic quest is thoroughly reproachable.

This brings us to our independent philosophic consideration. Quite clearly, we must evaluate not only the subjective motive impelling our modernist seeker but the substantive nature of his materials. In this respect, I must confess that I was slightly taken aback by the conjunction of the three names cited in the question. I suppose part of the surprise was due to their quite different stature in the Torah world. Rav Shlomo Zalman Auerbach once vetoed the addition of a famous *rosh yeshiva* to a board he headed because he had heard that the latter habitually referred to Rav Kook simply as "Kook"; and it was not until the information was vigorously denied that he relented. One cannot imagine him acting similarly with R. Samson Raphael Hirsch, who is routinely cited, even by many *benei Torah,* as "Hirsch"; and not only because one came from his Jerusalem orbit, the other from remote Frankfurt.

The primary cause of my surprise, however, is my perception of the ideological components listed. If we examine them with reference to the quintessential *masorah,* we attain, I believe, distinctly different results. One can view nineteenth-century European nationalism as an appropriate matrix for Rav Kook's thought, and there is no dearth of analogues to Hegel, Bergson, and others in his writings. Moreover, we may cavil at the antinomian elements and the measure of imbalance between classical values in his work. But at no point can there be any question about the radical Jewish authenticity of the traditional wellsprings for his Zionism – much less, of his accommodation and concession to the spirit of the times. Further, his Zionist conviction is in no sense a sociocultural addendum to his fundamental Judaism. His view of *Knesset Yisrael*, Eretz Yisrael, and their relation is the epicenter of his being and credo. It does not stand in relation to his general *Weltanschauung* but constitutes its very essence.

I seriously doubt that comparable statements could be made about R. Samson Raphael Hirsch's humanism. Without in any way maligning him, it must be candidly stated that in much of his work it is precisely the sense of accommodation and concession – at times, even of apologetics – that is persistent, if not pervasive. The humanism is genuine and genuinely Jewish; and yet at many points, the sense that we are dealing with an element that has been engrafted is inescapable. Hence, as with the Rambam's Aristotelianism, the question of the relation of the Western humanistic adjunct to the indigenous tradition inevitably arises. I presume – again, as with the Rambam – that in part we are not dealing with a graft at all but with an interpretation of the tradition; if you will, with a prism through which its thrust and content are perceived. Surely, R. Samson Raphael Hirsch did not regard the degree of universalism which he espoused as an addendum. He undoubtedly saw it as of the woof and warp of *Yahadut,* as the optimal response to an inherent question. Nevertheless, the sense of increment is, I suggest, often inescapable.

Much the same can probably be said of R. David Zevi Hoffmann's relation to academic scholarship. His embrace of much of its approach and many of its findings was genuine – perhaps even enthusiastic; and I am perfectly willing to presume that he regarded its exercise as a means of arriving at a richer and more precise understanding of the tradition and its texts. Yet surely he recognized that much of the material and the methodology was imported. Here, too, we should distinguish between scholarship as implement and as increment; but, in a badly mixed metaphor, it may well be that the prism itself is, in part, engrafted. In any event, if the prospective impact of the deletion of a given element be a litmus test for its significance and authenticity, the result of a comparison can be instructive. Would R. Hoffmann have viewed *Judentum* sans *Wissenschaft* as Rav Kook would have regarded *Yahadut* without *Ziyonut*? It may be contended that the comparison only attests to the elements' respective degrees of centrality, not their rootedness. I am inclined to believe that it reflects both.

It is entirely possible that I am wrong about all three thinkers. I possess expertise with respect to none, and my remarks are broadly impressionistic. For our purposes, however, it is the principle that is important; and it can be formulated clearly. Ideological eclecticism *per se* is thoroughly legitimate. There is no *a priori* reason to object to the selective gathering, properly motivated, of hashkafic components from various Torah thinkers and to the attempt to fuse these into a coherent worldview. However, an important qualifying distinction should be borne in mind. If the elements gathered are thoroughly grounded in indigenous tradition – of which, in effect, they severally constitute a rendering – the quest can be pursued without reservation. If, however, they are accretions appended to the tradition, let the selector beware.

Let me emphasize that I do not advance this distinction out of rejection of accretions *per se*. The caveat relates to the eclectic aspect. It is perfectly legitimate for individuals profoundly committed to Torah to employ categories from their ambient intellectual culture in dealing with major religious issues and to integrate aspects of that culture into their thought and experience, so long as they always bear in mind that these elements have originated outside their Torah ambit. If I may interject a personal note, I have devoted time and effort to the study of literature, and I share, in some measure, the faith of classical humanism, from Plato to Arnold, that literary culture can enhance and ennoble spiritual being. Nevertheless, I am fully cognizant of the fact that this interest and that faith are not included in the patrimony of the *Shakh* and the *Peri Hadash*. Not everyone has opted for addenda, but there is ample precedent to assure the legitimacy of the practice.

Collected appendages are something else. The concern they raise is dual. First, if, with respect to the same sphere, they are piled vertically, we encounter the phenomenon of "the cake of custom," familiar from late-Victorian social theory – the cumulative impact of a series of incremental changes, each of which is limited in scope but the sum of which places a considerable distance between the initial and final termini of the process. Second, if the changes relate, horizontally, to various spheres, we are still confronted by the question of the respective proportions of the core and the appendages. The issue is not only quantitative but qualitative. Context, as Whitehead emphasized, often determines substance. The identical modern component assumes very different meaning when transposed from the world of a profoundly traditional thinker, for whom it may be singular, to that of a reforming modernist. When Buber ripped hasidic tales out of context, they were metamorphosed. Above all, if one is to engage in philosophic eclecticism, one must be animated by a unifying and synergizing Torah commitment, through which organic integration into a meaningful world-order can take place. It cannot be recommended if the result is potpourri and flux – even less so if it is conducted in a spirit that builds a *Weltanschauung* out of secular materials and regards normative Halakhah as a complex of obstacles to be circumvented. If context and proportion are disregarded, we may find ourselves grappling with the conundrum posed by Roman legists: If I construct a wooden ship, and then proceed to replace its planks one at a time, at what point does it lose its initial identity?

I realize that I have proffered little in the way of precise counsel. In approaching, say, two major Sephardi figures, Rav Eliyahu Ben-Amozeg and Rav Uzziel, the prospective builder of a coherent world-order out of disparate elements will have to judge for himself how to relate to their writings, respectively, on universalism and on social justice. But did my questioner really expect to receive a formula in response to the query of "To what extent, if at all...?" I trust, however, that I have indicated a direction, and I hope that it provides food for thought.

Notes

1. Tehillim 25:14. The Jewish Publication Society version renders סוד as "counsel" and יראיו as "those that fear Him."
2. Sanhedrin 93a. The passage is of interest with regard to the controversy between the Rambam and the *mekubbalim* as to whether the human or the angelic state is superior.
3. Avot 2:2.
4. Shabbat 112b. For a discussion of the concept of *yeridat ha-dorot* and its ramifications, see Rabbi Dr. Norman Lamm, *Torah U-madda* (Northvale, NJ, 1990), pp. 86–103.
5. See, particularly, *Perush Ha-Mishnayot*, Avot 4:5, and MT, Hilkhot Talmud Torah 3:10.
6. See, e.g., the wide-ranging rejoinder of the Tashbez in *Sefer Ha-Tashbez*, 1:1421-47.
7. Appendix, *Kitzur Be-hanhagat Hora'at Issur Ve-heter*. *Yoreh Deah* 242:8. The view that the rule extends to post-Hazal *poskim* was espoused by the Maharik, *She'elot U-teshuvot*, 84, but challenged by R. Mosheh Al Askar in his *She'elot U-teshuvot*, 54.
8. See sk, *Hoshen Mishpat* 25:21.
9. Rosh Hashanah 25a–b, cited from *Tosefta*, Rosh Hashanah 1:18. With variations, the substance of the passage is quoted in several contexts. See *Tosefta Ki-feshutah*, p. 1035.
10. Ibid., s.v. *sheha-yamim*.
11. See *Sefer Ha-Hinukh*, 595–6, *Minhat Hinukh*, 595:3, and the sources cited in the opening note to 595 in the Makhon Yerushalayim edition.
12. See S.K., *Pilpul Be-hanhagat Hora'at Issur Ve-heter*, appended to *Yoreh De'ah*, 242.
13. Sanhedrin 33a.
14. *Pesakim*, Sanhedrin 4:6.
15. *Hoshen Mishpat* 25:2.
16. Hullin 116a, and analogue. For the Rashba, see his *She'elot u-Teshuvot*, 1:253.
17. Ibid.
18. Ibid.
19. *Teshuvot Ha-Rambam*, ed. J. Blau, p. 549.
20. See Hilkhot Sanhedrin 4:8.
21. *Pesakim*, Bava Kamma 4:4.
22. See Lawrence Kaplan, "Daas Torah: A Modern Conception of Rabbinic Authority," in *Rabbinic Authority and Personal Autonomy*, ed. Moshe Z. Sokol (Northvale, NJ, 1992), pp. 1–60.
23. *Likutei Amarim im Iggeret Ha-Teshuvah Ve-Iggeret Ha-Kodesh* (Brooklyn, 1956), p. 267.
24. Rav E.M. Schach, quoted in *Toda'ah* 48:2 (Nissan 5752).
25. *Guide of the Perplexed*, trans. S. Pines, III:14; p. 459. The question raised by the passage is self-evident; but the Rambam's position, in any event, is clear.
26. Makkot 22b.
27. Avot 1:6, 1:16.
28. *Midrash David* 1:16.
29. *Perushei Rabbeinu Yosef ben Shoshan al Massekhet Avot* 1:16.

30. See, for example, on 1:16, the commentaries of Rabbeinu Yosef Hayim, in *Mili De-Avot*, and Rabbeinu Yizhak b. Shlomo MiToledo.

31. See, for example, on 1:16, *Yalkut Me-am Loez* and Rabbeinu Yonah.

32. See, for example, Meiri and Rabbenu Bahyye.

33. See both, on 1:6 and 1:16.

34. *Perush Ha-mishnayot* ad loc.

35. This point, of course, needs to be considered within the context of the broader issue of the qualitative range, from pragmatic advice to the normative command, of the content of *Massekhet Avot*. The question is important, but beyond the scope of this article.

36. *Tosefta* Sukkah 2:4 and Eduyyot 2:3.

37. Eruvin 7a.

38. How such a person should be defined is, obviously, of great practical significance, but I have found no clear rishonic guidelines. The Meiri (*Bet Ha-Behirah*, Eruvin 7a) states with respect to any *mahlokot* that have not been decided, יש בחירה ביד התלמיד לפי שקול דעתו לפסוק כאחד מהם באחת ובשני לו באחרת "The choice is in the hands of the student to decide like one opinion in one case and like the second opinion in another case, according to *shikul da'ato*." He does not explain what is meant by a *talmid*. The Rosh (*Pesakim*, Sanhedrin 4:6) appears to set a higher standard: והיכא שנחלקו שני גדולים בפסק הלכה לא יאמר הדיין אפסוק כמי שארצה ואם עשה כן זהו דין שקר. אלא אם חכם גדול הוא גמיר וסביר ויודע להכריע כדברי האחד בראיות ברורות ונכוחות הרשות בידו. "In a situation where two *gedolim* are in dispute, the judge should not say, 'I will decide according to the one I like,' and if he does so, this is a false judgment. Rather, if the judge is a great scholar who is knowledgeable and knows how to decide matters of law with clear-cut textual proofs, he is entitled to do so." Obviously, however, this formulation, too, cannot be applied with precision.

39. See Avodah Zarah 19a and Abot de-Rabbi Nathan 8:2.

Chapter 15

The Future of Centrist Orthodoxy

The topic to which I have been asked to address myself this evening, "The Future of Centrist Orthodoxy," is, to many, a nontopic. What future? they retort; and, armed with sheafs of statistics, projections, and extrapolations, our interlocutors may postulate, with varying degrees of tremor, glee, or professional indifference, that this particular strain of sectarian Judaism will barely survive the present generation. I know full well that many of my confreres who subscribe to the centrist credo and pursue its lifestyle share this gloomy forecast. Retrospectively, regarding the changes that have largely transmuted the Orthodox scene over the last several decades, and translating these, perhaps exponentially, into prospective anticipation, they look to the morrow with dire foreboding. Surveying, all around them, children, their own or their peers', who have shifted right or left, and observing the force of renascent *harediyut*, which has so dramatically altered the balance of power in the religious community in Israel as well as in the Diaspora, many centrists are gripped by a sense of being steamrollered by an inexorable juggernaut.

I understand these sentiments perfectly; and I freely confess, moreover, that on occasion I am not wholly immune to them. Nevertheless, I

This paper is a fusion of an address on "The Strengths and Weaknesses of Modern Orthodoxy," delivered before the bienniel convention of the Union of Orthodox Congregations of America in 1990, and of an address delivered at Queens College in 1991. It also contains new material added in 2003.

submit at the outset that my own fundamental perspective is quite different. First, on the factual level, the centrist situation, as viewed from my
own perhaps excessively insular vantage point, is not quite so bleak. I am
cognizant of sociological and ideological trends, and I follow the Israeli
election returns; and yet, what I sense is hardly unadulterated gloom and
doom. "Do you know," an alarmed Israeli associate asked me last year,
"what percentage of foreign yeshiva students attend black-hat and Zionist *yeshivot*, respectively?" I admitted to my ignorance, but ventured the
assumption that the majority – he subsequently quoted a figure of over
80 percent – attended the former. But, I continued, why the panic? Are
the *batei midrash* of Mir or Brisk thriving at "our" expense? Granted that
the relative position of Zionist Orthodoxy has been seriously eroded, with
a concomitant loss of power and influence; but in absolute terms, has
the community's Torah quotient increased or diminished since I moved
to Israel twenty years ago? As I sit in Yeshivat Har Etzion, the answer is
self-evident. But ours is not an isolated phenomenon. What was the total
enrollment of *hesder yeshivot* then and now? Or, to take the most prominent of non-*hesder* institutions, can anyone compare the current stature of
Yeshivat Merkaz Harav with its relative obscurity in the fifties? Much the
same could be said with respect to secondary education, and even more
pointedly of women's Torah education, which, starting almost from scratch,
has shown such marked progress during the last several decades. Moreover,
a similar picture, *mutatis mutandis*, could be painted with respect to much
of the Diaspora. Far from being consigned to becoming juggernaut fodder,
then, the centrist Torah community is vigorous and growing.

There is, further, a second reason for regarding this evening's topic as
both genuine and serious. To what extent, we must ask ourselves, ought we
to be cowed by futurist projections? Even if one regards such prognoses
as reliable, there is a point beyond which men and women of conviction
simply refuse to let scientific astrologers dictate thought and practice; a
point at which one affirms anew his commitment to the biblical commandment, תמים תהיה עם ה' א-להיך, "You shall be wholehearted with your God"
(Devarim 18:13), which the Ramban interpreted as demanding submissive
fealty to the *Ribbono shel Olam* and trust in Him, to the neglect of the

prognostications of soothsayers, even if they are assumed to have objective validity.[1] Genuine faith, Emil Fackenheim once suggested, consists of the capacity to hold firm even if one is the last believer on earth – or, we might add, as in the case of him who was first commanded, התהלך לפני והיה תמים, "Walk before Me and be wholehearted" (Bereishit 17:1), if one is the first. Intelligent planning cannot obtain wholly oblivious to facts and their extrapolation; but neither can it be reduced to that. He who is excessively intimidated by the projected future forfeits the present – and also, in consequence, the capacity to shape that morrow.

Commitment to principle would need to be commended even if the soothsaying were reliable. But what, in fact, is the track record? Have we, entering upon the *fin de siècle,* forgotten the sardonic humor of the fifties – that in America the optimists were studying Russian, and the pessimists, Chinese? Requiems for centrism are now being composed by those – perhaps not the identical individuals but surely of the same disciplines – who a generation ago were thoroughly convinced they were seeing the last of the haredim. How many of the scholars currently involved in the fundamentalism project of the American Academy of Arts and Sciences imagined, two decades ago, that as of this date, the phenomenon would be around for them to analyze? Did not the conventional wisdom which today often trumpets forecasts of the demise of centrist Orthodoxy once confidently anticipate the passing of all Orthodoxy? I have always been impressed by the skeptical wisdom of Christopher Dawson, who in the mid-thirties asked rhetorically who had anticipated, fifteen years earlier, the collapse of parliamentary democracy in Central Europe. So, while conceding that the obituaries for centrism may yet turn out to be accurate – there are, after all, Tocquevilles in this world too – I shall treat my assigned topic in earnest.

In doing so, I shall proceed, in part, descriptively, seeking to fasten upon the major strengths and weaknesses of centrist – or, if you prefer, modern – Orthodoxy. Primarily, however – given my training, inclinations, and presumed mandate – I shall approach the subject prescriptively, explaining how I understand the phenomenon and its significance, and setting forth how I believe the contours of its future should be limned.

If asked to define centrism, I would distinguish between three senses of the term. The first, largely relative, concerns a specific sociohistorical context. In our case, it corresponds roughly to a given median attitude towards modernity qua both lifestyle and *Weltanschauung*; to a qualified acceptance of certain views – regarding the nature and destiny of man, his relation to God and his place in history, the desired range and mix of human experience, the source and scope of spiritual authority – that happen to be characteristic of the modern world. In this sense, a centrist is one who subscribes to an intermediate position on these issues, being perched, sociologically, between champions of more radical positions on either side.

In this context, the centrist element is largely an accident of culture – not an asseveration of the value of the center *per se* but an assertion of positions that currently happen to lie between renunciation and affirmation of much of what modernity is commonly understood to be. As such, it is also suspect. Does one champion a complex of views regarding basic and ultimate matters – history, nature, the relation of the temporal and the eternal, of secularity and the sacred, even of God and man – because he has probed the issues in depth and these views constitute his innermost convictions? Or does one accept them because they provide a convenient equilibrium between rigorous insular faith and multifaceted culture, enabling him to enjoy the psychological security of remaining firmly anchored in tradition, while yet basking in the social, intellectual, and, yes, economic ambience of his contemporary milieu?

In a second sense, by contrast, centrism is indeed conceived as an intrinsic virtue. Quite apart from the substantive content of a particular trait or position, the very fact that it, and its adherents, are ensconced between two extremes, as measured by some absolute scale, is deemed of merit. The middle in question may have a sociological correlative – say, welfare-state capitalism between thoroughgoing socialism and laissez-faire capitalism in the political arena, or Anglicanism between Catholicism and Calvinism in the religious. But the main point is that it is moderation *per se*, as a *via media* between alternative theoretical constructs, that is sought.

As such, the middle is not primarily sociological, but psychological, moral, and, hence, axiological. In this connection, it is of course the

Rambam – and, in general thought, Aristotle as an antecedent – who comes to mind immediately. First, in *Shemonah Perakim* – the brief philosophical and psychological treatise with which he prefaced his commentary to *Avot* – and, subsequently, in Mishneh Torah, the Rambam explicates the virtues of centrism:

> הדרך הישרה היא מדה בינונית שבכל דעה ודעה מכל הדעות שיש לו לאדם והיא הדעה שהיא רחוקה משתי הקצוות ריחוק שוה ואינה קרובה לא לזו ולא לזו לפיכך צוו חכמים הראשונים שיהא אדם שם דעותיו תמיד ומשער אותם ומכוין אותם בדרך האמצעית כדי שיהא שלם בגופו.

> The right way is the mean in each group of dispositions common to humanity; namely, that disposition which is equally distant from the two extremes in its class, not being nearer to the one than to the other. Hence, our ancient sages exhorted us that a person should always evaluate his dispositions and so adjust them that they shall be at the mean between the extremes, and this will secure his physical health.[2]

Whether the Rambam regarded this quality as absolutely and universally optimal is uncertain. In *Hilkhot De'ot*, he postulates, for the saintly, a higher ideal which entails some deviation from the center, presumably in the direction of an ultimate moral desideratum – ומי שהוא מדקדק על עצמו ביותר ויתרחק מדעה בינונית מעט לצד זה או לצד נקרא חסיד... וזהו לפנים משורת הדין – (א:ה) "Whoever is particularly scrupulous and deviates somewhat from the exact mean in disposition, in one direction or another, is called a *hasid* ... This is supererogation"[3] – whereas, in *Shemonah Perakim*,[4] such deviation is prescribed, in quasi-medical terms, as an instrumental and temporary technique for achieving optimal median virtue. In Mishneh Torah, however, the tilt is confined to narrow parameters, so that the fundamental centrist conception remains; and, in any event, as a general norm, the conclusion is unequivocal:

> ולפי שהשמות האלו נקרא בהן היוצר והם הדרך הבינונית שאנו חייבין ללכת בה נקראת דרך זו דרך ה'... וההולך בדרך זו מביא טובה וברכה לעצמו שנאמר למען הביא ה' על אברהם את אשר דבר עליו (א:ז).

> And as the Creator is called by these attributes, which constitute the middle path in which we are to walk, this path is called the

Way of God ... whoever walks in this way secures for himself happiness and blessing, as it says (Bereishit 18:9), "In order that the Lord might bring upon Abraham that which He spoke concerning him" (De'ot 1:7).

To some, the citation of the *pasuk* as a proof-text may appear circular. But the Rambam's view, at least, is clear.

Finally, we may speak of a center in a third sense – not as a linear median between extremes but as the heart of a circle; as the pivotal hub around which being is structured, activity generated, and movement flows. Centrism in this sense is a spiritual ideology or communal base which relates to the mainstream of human existence rather than to its periphery, and which stresses interaction and integration rather than polarization and bifurcation. It bears both a centripetal and a centrifugal aspect. In terms of James's famous dichotomy, it tends to be world-accepting, but insists upon asserting the hegemony of the spiritual over the world at its core, and not just marginally.

In seeking to assess the current perception of centrist Orthodoxy, and in striving, correspondingly, to chart a course for its future, I think it can be safely stated that the dominant sense and concern at present is the first – that of being a median and possibly mediating movement between "rightists" and "leftists"; and I believe it can be asserted with equal surety that this emphasis should be reversed. The emphasis should be placed, on the one hand, upon the relation of the spiritual to what is ordinarily perceived as the highway of human life, the *derekh eretz* that Rabbenu Tam – speaking, of course, practically rather than axiologically – defined as its *ikkar*;[5] and, on the other, upon the role of Torah, narrowly defined, as central but not exclusive to a value system.

Focus upon the relative aspect of centrism leads to undesirable ancillary results; and, in addition, diverts attention from grappling with issues related to absolute elements of its substantive content. By representing centrism, in effect, as more of a sociological than an ideological phenomenon, one blurs both the image and the reality of the centrist credo. This, in turn, serves almost by definition to undercut self-esteem, inculcating, if only subliminally, the sense that true *lomdut* and *yir'at shamayim* are to be found further to the right, and genuine cultural sweep only on the left, with centrism merely a pale Janus-like shadow of both. Focus upon content, defining centrism in its own terms as a worldview, would drive home the point that it is an alternative rather than a compromise. This would serve the interests of the quest for religious truth and provide a much-needed boon to self-confidence. That confidence – not overweening arrogance and not diffident complacency; without pretensions of exclusiveness, but with a clear sense of intrinsic worth – can only result from greater preoccupation with inherent substantive content. As an approach, the *via media* will never attain full approbation. There will always be critics who, with respect to belief, will paraphrase Newman's comment that there is no real alternative between Catholicism and atheism, with Anglicanism only serving as a halfway house on the right and liberalism as a halfway house on the left. And with respect to vision and experience, others will rail that centrism is too restrained and rational – in Nietzsche's terms, excessively Apollonian. What the centrist community can attain, however, is the elucidation of its own convictions and the recovery of a sense of its own worth.

The optimal centrist course requires, however, far more than a shift of psychological or even ideological focus. The key is implementation – dedicated and creative realization of centrist values. Above all, what is needed is a *heshbon ha-nefesh*: a process of self-examination that should recognize, and hence develop, strengths, but that should also acknowledge, and hence issue an initiative to surmount, weaknesses. Some of the weaknesses are blatant and acute; and it is they, rather than pressure from competing extremes, that constitute centrism's true major concern.

To begin, on a positive note, with the strength, it inheres primarily, I believe, in scope – a scope which, hopefully, also entails a dimension of depth. The range is multifaceted, and is manifested in at least six distinct, albeit somewhat interrelated, areas.

First, centrism is committed, ideologically and practically, to coping with the whole of life, rather than just with its spiritual epicenter. It contends that advancing, individually and collectively, *yishuvo shel olam*, as a realization of divine will as defined, prophetically, – לא תהו בראה לשבת יצרה "He did not create it to be a waste; He formed it to be inhabited"[6] – is, properly perceived and directed, an aspect of spiritual existence. It acknowledges, of course, the validity of the ideal envisioned by the Rambam in the concluding lines of Mishneh Torah – the eschatological aspiration that, ultimately, all secular pressures having been suspended, mankind will be, universally and exclusively, animated by the quest for the knowledge of God:

> ובאותו הזמן לא יהיה שם לא רעב ולא מלחמה ולא קנאה ותחרות שהטובה תהיה
> מושפעת הרבה וכל המעדנים מצויים כעפר ולא יהיה עסק כל העולם אלא לדעת את
> ה' בלבד.

> In that era there will be neither famine nor war, neither jealousy nor strife. Blessings will be abundant, comforts within the reach of all. The one preoccupation of the whole world will be to know the Lord.[7]

However, it contends that so long as that millennial situation does not exist – delicacies palpably not being as common as dust, and the universal harmony only a fanciful dream – the primeval mandate of *l'avdah u'l'shamrah*, empowering and charging man with the responsibility and the authority to preserve and develop the world, obtains. Under present circumstances, we cannot be content with ministering to purely "religious" needs, but must see the social, economic, political, and even military spheres as falling within the purview of Torah existence. Hence, we take our current cue from a more variegated charge formulated by the Rambam elsewhere: שאין ראוי לאדם שיעסוק כל ימיו אלא בדברי חכמה וביישובו של עולם "For it is not worthy for a person to occupy himself all his days other than in matters of wisdom and in the settling of the world."[8] While this world is indeed, in one sense, a mere antechamber to the palace of eternity, we, having been implanted within it and entrusted with its care, need to strike a balance between treating it as a *bet Elokim,* to be tended as the locus of epiphanous immanent *Shekhinah*, and as a *sha'ar ha-shamayim,* an access gateway for transient souls en route to their celestial abode.

On the collective plane, this scope has social and historical import. Concurrently, it also has a personal dimension. It strives to relate to the full range of the human spirit and its existential concerns. It seeks to see *avodat Hashem* as a complex within which emotional maturity, aesthetic sensibility, and human sensitivity find their place alongside central, specifically religious, components, such as commitment to *talmud Torah,* as elements within a broad spiritual existence. In a more mundane context, it emphasizes economic self-sufficiency, which, beyond its pragmatic significance, bears a spiritual aspect, enhancing the sense of dignity so much in keeping with centrism's humanistic inclinations. Minimally, although certainly not as a cap, it strives to assure the mindset that Arnold ascribed to Sophocles,

> ... whose even-balanc'd soul,
> From first youth tested up to extreme old age,
> Business could not make dull, nor Passion wild;
> Who saw life steadily, and saw it whole.[9]

Second, centrists, almost by definition, are attuned to a broader cultural range than their haredi counterparts. They draw upon a broader range of disciplines, and they seek knowledge from beyond our own insular pale.

They take seriously the observation of the *midrash,* אם יאמר לך אדם יש חכמה בגוים תאמין "If a person shall say to you that there is wisdom among the nations, believe him,"[10] and they translate its implications into practice. Optimally, the result may be not only wider horizons but deeper insights – and this, as regards the road to wisdom and not merely the information highway.

Closely related is a third element: the broader human range. On one level, this entails a universal component. Modern though they be, centrists are descendants of Avraham Avinu, who, as *av hamon goyim,* felt a universal responsibility to inculcate faith and *hesed* amongst his Gentile peers. They are heirs to Mosheh Rabbenu who, when he saw some Midianite girls being assaulted by a gang of youths, did not avert his gaze from an incident involving a bunch of *shekazim* and *shikses,* but rallied to their defense. Given our priorities, we cannot ordinarily emulate their acts, but we can at least share their sensibility. On a second level, centrists, again almost by definition, are animated by a sense of kinship with *K'lal Yisrael* as a whole, feeling a responsibility and an existential bond even toward those segments of the community that, lamentably, do not share much of traditional faith and values.

Fourth, in a totally different vein, human range is reflected, internally and domestically, as well as personally, with respect to the status of women. Relative to earlier periods, and in comparison with their haredi peers, centrist women currently enjoy a greater measure of influence and self-determination. Advocates portray this development as laudable progress within the context of indigenous Jewish tradition; critics regard it as assimilatory capitulation to the culture of sociologically correct feminism. Both may be partially correct, but, in any case, the bare facts are reasonably clear. Without getting involved in the welter of controversy surrounding various highly profiled hot-button issues, it can be fairly stated that the centrist climate is, ideologically and pragmatically, more conducive to the furtherance of women's ambitions – some, admittedly, not shared by many haredi women – than heretofore. This is manifest, in part, in the public realm, in which women are now more actively and vigorously engaged, and in which their specific concerns figure prominently in the forum of discourse and agenda. In part, it is evident with respect to the domestic sphere. While, from any traditional Jewish standpoint, marriage and family, as opposed to purely egocentric self-fulfillment, are central values, there remains much Halakhic and hashkafic flexibility as regards the nature and character of the home. The degree of equipoise, the division of labor, authority, and responsibility, the extent of the respective balances between career and family – all, without abandoning the general concept of role-differentiation, are open to interpersonal resolution; and – the core issue often being the quality of respect rather than the scope of authority – the imprint of centrist values is likely to be felt with regard to all. Even more significantly, the expectations attendant upon the marital relationship itself may vary, with centrist couples often striving to maximize (and, hence, the increased danger of disappointment) the sense and the reality of existential partnership.

Apart from the public and the interactive, there is a third, purely personal, dimension; and it is perhaps most visibly reflected, albeit in relation to a limited sector, with reference to serious Torah study. From a religious perspective, concern with stature is not confined to issues of empowerment or entitlement. Its focus is the enhancement of spiritual personality; and, in this respect, the common element of *zelem E-lokim* serves as both a leveling and a bonding factor. Realization of spiritual potential can, of course, assume many forms, and, within our world, has not been gender-neutral. Surely, however, in a tradition which has, persistently, placed so high a premium upon study, significant engagement in quality *talmud Torah* should – at the very least, for the desirous and able – serve as a portal of access to the Ribbono Shel Olam, for women as well as for men. The purgative and deterrent force which Hazal ascribed to Torah as countervailing passional sinfulness – בראתי יצר הרע בראתי לו תורה תבלין, "I created the evil impulse, and I created its antidote, the Torah" (Kiddushin 30b) – presumably affects both. Comparably, the Sifre (Vaethanan, 33) states that one mode of fulfilling the all-embracing normative ideal of love of God consists of learning His word:

"והיו הדברים האלה אשר אנכי מצוך היום על לבבך" – למה נאמר? לפי שהוא אומר "ואהבת את ה' א־לקיך בכל לבבך" איני יודע באיזה צד אוהבים את הקב"ה, ת"ל "והיו הדברים האלה אשר אנכי מצוך היום על לבבך" – [תן] הדברים האלה על לבבך, שמתוך כך אתה מכיר את הקב"ה ומדבק בדרכיו.

"These words, which I command you this day, shall be upon your heart" (Devarim 6:6) – why is this stated? Since he says, "You shall love the Lord your God with all your heart" (ibid. 6:5), I [am confronted by the question that I] do not know how one is to love the Holy One, blessed be He. Therefore, the [next] verse teaches, "These words, which I command you this day, shall be upon your heart" – place these words upon your heart, for, through this, you come to know the Holy One, blessed be He, and to cling to His ways.

That assertion, too, is presumably unrestricted. Surely, then, women's pursuit of *ahavat Hashem* through serious *talmud Torah* is more than laudable; and a community which has fostered its advance can take just pride in the accomplishment.

That advance has, of course, not been confined to centrism. Much water has flowed under the general Jewish bridge since the Hafetz Hayyim threw his support beyond the then incipient and semi-radical Beis Yaakov movement. Nevertheless, to the extent that the cutting edge – particularly the study of primary texts, including *gemara* – has been more manifestly encouraged within the centrist community, this development, and the more general position of women which, in some measure, it both reflects and enables, is rightly perceived, for better or for worse, as one of its hallmarks.

Positive ramifications have been dual. At the purely personal plane, increased exposure to Torah has not only advanced knowledge but has, concomitantly, generally stimulated growth in religious sophistication and meticulous Halakhic observance. To be sure, many – including some within centrist or *dati-leumi* circles – have expressed reservations about the spread of women's learning. Quite apart from possible Halakhic objections, they contend that benefits cited have been attained at the expense of innocence; that advance in insight and information have been accompanied by the attrition of the naive piety historically ascribed to our largely unschooled great-grandmothers. This may be, to a degree, correct, but barely relevant. The naivete of women exposed to the modern world has unquestionably been sapped – as has that of men; but, overwhelmingly, not because of learning but in spite of it. For all but a most limited circle of centrist women, *tzenna u-r'enna* yiddishkeit – even if it were to be idealized as the optimal and ultimate religious telos – is not a live option. Dare any one suggest, then, that it is better supplanted by vacuous leisure than by serious study?

The primary value of women's Torah study inheres, then, in the potential stimulus to *avodat Hashem*, and its advocacy is to be construed as aimed neither to parry the thrust of feminist pressure nor to ward off insidious secularism, but as grounded in its intrinsic contribution to personal growth. There are, however, derivative social implications as well, themselves dual. When imbued with a genuine Torah *hashkafah* – and this is the crucial sine qua non – better educated and, hopefully, more deeply committed, women, will expand their constructive contribution to public life, enabling the community to mobilize a fuller range of human resources to cope with its challenges. Concurrently, a *bat Torah* should be better qualified and motivated to function, spiritually, in her traditional roles of wife and mother within a Torah-centered home.

Fifth, with respect to the particular area of *talmud Torah* in general, centrist or modern Orthodoxy perceives it as sweeping a wider arc than the traditional fare of most haredi *yeshivot*. While the overwhelming emphasis upon *devar Hashem zo halakhah* remains, and while *Torah she-b'al-peh* – the linchpin, as Hazal tell us, of the covenant between *Knesset Yisrael* and the *Ribbono shel Olam*[11] – is the primary focus, *yeshivot* with a modern bent have sought to extend the narrow bounds of the recent Eastern European Torah world and to return to the more variegated tradition of the Rishonim – particularly, of *hakhmei Sefarad* – who included the study of Tanakh, *parshanut*, and *mahshavah* as integral elements of a total Torah education.

Finally, the centrist community generally has a far sharper sense of history than ordinarily obtains in the haredi world. On one plane, this is relevant to a proper understanding of the past, particularly insofar as the recognition of difference or development is concerned, with an aim to striking a balance between permanence and flux, *yemot olam* and *shenot dor ve-dor*. It is even more critical, however, with respect to the present and the future. And this, in two senses. First, as the example of Religious Zionism amply illustrates, the centrist community – roughly speaking, (although there are significant differences), the sociological and ideological analogue of the *dati-le'umi* sector in Israel – is informed by a sharper sense of historico-national goals. As compared with the haredi world, it assigns a higher priority to these goals and is imbued with a keener conviction of the ability of human effort to help attain them. Second, broader historical awareness provides a base for more intelligent and effective action, enabling a clearer definition of what F.H. Bradley called "my station and its duties,"[12] and a flexible response grounded in an awareness of the specific character of the contemporary challenge.

Ideally, scope also confers a measure of depth. True range is not merely a potpourri of concerns and commitments. It is grounded upon integration, understood as both comprehensiveness and harmony. As such, it confers, objectively, a greater degree of organic unity upon communal and personal existence, and provides, subjectively, a clearer and profounder perspective upon the interrelated totality of existence and upon the substance and significance of its components. The mosaic *ketonet passim* symbolizes richness of texture and depth of color no less than mere variety.

So much for centrist Orthodoxy's strengths. What of its weaknesses? These, I suggest, can be broken down into two primary categories: those that are the possibly inevitable obverse of its strengths, and those that are unadulterated weaknesses, manifestations or results of lassitude, indifference, or incompetence. Range and scope have much to recommend them, and in many respects, the precept and practice of Hazal to mandate them. But they do ordinarily command a price. Obviously, a community or an institution that harps incessantly upon a single theme should inculcate greater adherence to it than one that advances several simultaneously. The monochromatic pursuit of Torah, narrowly defined, will presumably result in greater expertise than a more diverse approach; and an ideology committed to the proposition that nothing but *talmud Torah* is of intellectual worth should instill a more passionate commitment than one which contends that, for a *ben Torah*, learning may be central but need not be exclusive.

Those who nevertheless opt for a *ketonet passim* do so out of the conviction, consonant with Hazal's statement that כל העוסק בתורה בלבד דומה כמי שאין לו א-לוה "Whoever engages in Torah only, is as one who has no God,"[13] that Torah and its study must, ideally, exist within the context of the totality of *avodat Hashem* and human life. But they recognize that they pay a price for their *Torat hesed*, even if they deem it worthwhile.

Likewise with respect to the dominant tone of centrism's perspective upon life. Its overarching comprehensive balance may be majestic, noble, but is unlikely to be fiery. Its pervasive sense of "the depth, and not the tumult, of the soul"[14] – how Jewish and even halakhic Wordsworth's formulation sounds! – may well exact a toll in the passionate quotient of religious experience. This inherent defect is frequently compounded by insufficient awareness of the price and by failure to assess or monitor its dimensions. Unfortunately, the modern Orthodox establishment, captivated by its own moral and educational rhetoric, is often remiss in failing to scrutinize the possible spiritual fallout of its positions. There are, after all, situations in which, regardless of ideology, one must simply conclude that the game is not worth the candle and prefer narrowness.

The failure to monitor the inevitable fallout is serious. Far more grievous, however, is the existence of a weakness that logically does not inhere in the centrist outlook, and sociologically need not flow from it. What in the quest for scope mandates, for example, that children in a *mamlakhti-dati* school in Jerusalem should go home at noon, while their peers in a *heder* learn till evening? What degree of historical sensitivity dictates that a haredi of high school age make do with three weeks' summer vacation, while his modern counterpart has well over two months? Does a universalist concern require that youngsters – and hence most adults as well – know a good deal about the Rolling Stones but nothing of the *Avnei Nezer*? That they be familiar with batting averages but unable to identify Reb Menahem Zembe?

The sad answer is self-evident. Not just the exigencies of budgeting energies, resources, or time, not the balancing of needs and the assignment of priorities, but sheer shallowness or callousness with respect to yiddishkeit is responsible for such aberrations. These are the weaknesses that truly hurt, both because they are so avoidable and because of the mindset they presumably reflect. Juggling priorities and balancing opportunities, determining orders of importance among values, deciding what to emphasize or what to defer: this is all part of the inevitable complexity of spiritual existence, personal or collective. Neglect of spiritual values or a casual approach to their pursuit is not. Resolving the question of how halakhic living should be structured and what its possible models are is a perennial challenge. That Halakhah should be central to a Jew's existence, and not merely a limiting factor defining the parameters of his options, is, however, beyond question. This truth, unfortunately, is not always sufficiently appreciated in the centrist community; and this failing lies at the heart of some deplorable weaknesses.

Let me focus upon three. A recent impressionistic study of haredi society in Israel opens with a graphically descriptive account of the community's intensity.[15] Haredi intensity, at times visceral and even physical to the point of violence, often has frightful consequences. But in many respects it has a positive aspect that is sorely missing, by and large, in the centrist world. The lack of intensity – in some measure, admittedly, the obverse of centrism's virtues but often far exceeding those bounds – is perceptible in at least two critical areas. Much of the modern Orthodox world lacks, first, intellectual intensity – by which I mean, specifically, that it is marked by constriction and mediocrity with respect to *talmud Torah*. Its primary and secondary school systems produce many wonderful individuals and committed observant Jews; but it is a sad fact that their median Torah knowledge is quite limited. The problem concerns both skills, particularly textual, and scope, although the latter is especially severe. In an age of relatively easy access through reference works, encyclopedias, and CD-ROMs, this is less critical than previously. But the shortfall is still acute – and it has the · additional effect of stifling ambition. It is difficult to thirst with aspiration to master Shas if one has barely learned one hundred blatt by the time he graduates from high school. And this, I repeat, is not purely the result of competition between gemara and chemistry. It springs also from either pampered indolence or diversion to a host of interests and avocations that contribute nothing to intellectual growth of any kind. In this setting, the Rambam frequently does not so much compete with Michelangelo as with Michael Jordan, or even, lamentably, Michael Jackson. Small wonder that he often loses. Clearly, there is need to exert an effort to ensure that the ambition to become a *talmid hakham* becomes a primary aspect of youthful dreams, and that provision be made for their optimal realization.

The deficiency is, at times, encountered even where, theoretically, least expected – with respect to women's commitment to *talmud Torah*. It is not unusual to find young haredi women who would, at best, have great difficulty in mastering a primary text of *midrash* or *parshanut* – let alone, *mishnah* or *gemara* – but who give of themselves, unstintingly, in order to enable their husbands or their sons to develop into serious *talmidei hakhamim*. It is, alas, also not unusual, to find their centrist peers – more knowledgeable, both generally and Jewishly – unwilling to make similar sacrifices, and less passionately committed to ensconcing Torah study to a position of centrality in their homes. This is, again, not to advocate a return to the bliss of ignorance. As previously noted, for the centrist community, this is neither a serious nor a desirable option. What is needed, critically, is a more powerful impulse, personal and communal, to structure a more intensive Torah universe.

Analogously, the centrist world further lacks emotional, and especially religious, intensity. Whether this be the result of excessive rationalism or of religious lassitude, many centrist *batei knesset* lack the palpitating angst and radiant fervor that should characterize *avodat Hashem* at its best.

One *pasuk* exhorts עבדו את ה' בשמחה "Serve the Lord with joy;" another, עבדו את ה' ביראה "Serve the Lord with fear;" and concludes, conjoining, וגילו ברעדה "and rejoice with trembling"[16] – and yet, in so many synagogues, the gamut runs from the drab to the tepid to the rigid. I was once told of a North American rabbi who occupied a prominent modern Orthodox pulpit but was ideologically far more attuned to Conservatism. Upon being asked why he didn't cross over, he responded, "Because they don't cry at Ne'ilah." His reply was well taken; and yet a nagging question persists. In many of "our" congregations, in which, at dusk, all intone, יהי רצון מלפניך שומע קול בכיות שתשים דמעותינו בנאדך להיות "May it be Your will, O Hearer of the sound of weeping, that You store our tears in your flask" – how large a flask would the tears fill?

Would that the reason were Wordsworthian engrossment in "thoughts that do often lie too deep for tears."[17] More likely, it can be set down, lamentably, to passionless blandness. Habad folklore recounts that the Ba'al Ha-Tanya, as a young man, was on his way to Vilna, with the aim of learning under the Gaon. En route, he encountered an elderly Jew – later reputed to have been Eliyahu Hanavi – who asked him where he was headed; and, upon being told, responded: לערנען קענסט דו עטוואס, דאוונען קענסט דו גארנישט; גיי בעסער צום מגיד אין מעזעריטש ("You can learn somewhat, but don't know how to daven at all. Go, rather, to the *maggid* at Mezeritch"). How aptly this applies to many a centrist Jew! But where is the maggid to provide guidance and inspiration? It is perhaps all part of a more general modern malady. One recalls Arnold's lament over "the wintry clime" and "this iron time," and Eliot's view of a whimpering culture. But whatever the cause, the problem is both urgent and serious.

A second, related weakness is best described as the prosaic character of much of the centrist world. And this, too, in two respects. There is, first, as previously suggested, a lack of the soaring passion characteristic of one strain of poetry. But there is also a prosaic quality with respect to the other end of the literary or emotional spectrum, which is more closely identified with "dry" intellectual poetry. "I always think," wrote T.E. Hulme,

> that the fundamental process at the back of all the arts might be presented by the following metaphor. You know what I call architect's curves – flat pieces of wood with all different kinds of curvature. By a suitable selection from these you can draw approximately any curve you like. The artist I take to be the man who simply can't bear the idea of that "approximately." He will get the exact curve of what he sees whether it be an object or an idea in the mind.[18]

This quest for precision, "the avoidance of conventional language in order to get the exact curve of the thing" (p. 572), is impelled, first and foremost, by an inner sense of the importance of the enterprise – "But it is the zest with which you look at the thing which decides you to make the effort" (p. 571) – and secondarily, by the ability to translate perception into language; and it has, for our purpose, its analogue in halakhic observance. Here, too, zestless commitment can be content with approximation. Standards may be middling and their implementation shoddy, so long as "more or less," one is leading a halakhic life. The *zehirut* and *zerizut*, as postulated in the spiritual ladder of Rabbi Phinehas ben Yair, and elucidated by the *Mesillat Yesharim*, are frequently regarded as beyond the ken of the ordinary Jew. As a result, the typical centrist is at times bereft of the passion of *hasidut* and of the compensatory halakhic precision of mitnaggedut. I am not intimating that every *humra* is desirable. Many, by dint of their substance and motivation, are not. What I am advocating is the maintenance of a high level of rigorous halakhic observance.

A third problem is that of leadership, specifically of Torah leadership. To some extent, albeit in different form, the issue confronts the entire American Jewish community today, but I confine my present remarks to its centrist component. This sector has long been remiss in failing to mobilize the requisite material and human resources to cultivate first-rank *talmidei hakhamim*; and to the extent that its ranks have been blessed with them, it generally has not appreciated them sufficiently, often consulting them at its own convenience. This is blatantly so in the political context in Israel, but I believe that the Diaspora scene is not markedly different.

The deplorable result is threefold. First, with respect to many issues of spiritual, albeit not necessarily halakhic, import, the community is bereft of some insightful guidance. Second, the critical sense of historical continuity, of which *gedolei Yisrael* as *hakhmei ha-mesorah* are an integral part, is partially jaded. Third, what Whitehead called "the vision of greatness," so essential an educational tool, particularly in a world to which both inspiration and authority are central, is undermined. In this area, recent decades have seen considerable progress; and yet much remains to be done. The issue is not one of establishing an overarching *moʾezet gedolei Torah,* a matter to be considered on its own merits. It is rather a question of assuring the role of Torah leadership as an informing presence at the head and heart of the centrist community.

In making these remarks, I have not sought to challenge the viability or legitimacy of a centrist orientation. Were I addressing a haredi audience, I could expatiate on *its* shortcomings; and many are quite serious. Or rather, putting the matter positively, I am fully appreciative of the worth of both modes of *avodat Hashem,* as well as of the potential – alas, insufficiently exploited – for their mutual fructification. What I am seeking is to stress the need for introspective commitment and committed introspection; the need for centrist Orthodoxy to probe the measure of its fidelity to its own avowed ideals.

As the litmus test of that fidelity, a single text may suffice. In the popular mind, the marks of centrism are college education, Yom Ha-Atzmaʾut, or, on a more superficial plane, the color of one's hat or yarmulke. As symbols, these are obviously not without substantive significance, but the essence inheres in the interpretation and implementation of the counsel – possibly, a cross of the normative and the hortatory – of the mishnah in Avot: וכל מעשיך יהיו לשם שמים "And all your actions shall be for the sake of Heaven."[19] In one sense, this may be taken as defining the scope and substance of human activity, i.e., that one's actions should be such as palpably, demonstrably, and directly are "religious" and clearly identifiable, in halakhic terminology, as a *devar mizvah*. This is the sense often favored by many in the haredi camp. Centrists, however, are inclined to prefer an alternative interpretation – that whatever one does, even if it is an optional and legitimately sanctioned *devar ha-reshut*, be oriented to the *Ribbono shel Olam* as an aspect of a comprehensive and integrated life committed to *avodat Hashem*. The orientation may revolve around the motivation or the *telos* of action; but in either case, this construction is clearly distinguishable from the narrower. It is this which the Rambam, in particular, emphasized, with almost radical force and sweep,[20] and its spirit is reflected in parallel texts: רוחץ אדם פניו ידיו ורגליו בכל יום בשביל קונו שנאמר כל פעל ה' למענהו "One washes his face, hands, and feet daily for the sake of his Creator, as it says, 'All that God has created is for His sake'";[21] or, startlingly: דרש בר קפרא איזוהי פרשה קטנה שכל גופי תורה תלויין בה בכל דרכיך דעהו והוא יישר אורחותיך אמר רבא אפילו לדבר עבירה "Bar Kappara expounded: What is a short passage upon which all the bodies of the Law depend? 'In all your ways know Him, and He will make your paths straight.' Rava said: Even in a matter of sin."[22]

From my perspective, one can accept the validity and viability of either construction. What is critical, however, is that the adherent of either feel bound by fealty to his own worldview and committed to its implementation. This is often the Achilles' heel of centrism; and it is this issue which holds the key to a reasoned response to the question posed at the outset: Does centrist Orthodoxy have a future? The answer has been classically formulated: מעשיך יקרבוך ומעשיך ירחקוך "Your actions will bring you near and your actions distance you." The critical problem for modern Orthodoxy is not theoretical but practical. Its hashkafic basis is sound, its resources reliable, and its precedents evident. Its destiny will be determined, however, not so much by a set of principles as by the measure of fidelity to those principles – by the scope and intensity of the commitment to their realization. The cardinal and immanent problem of the centrist Jew inheres in the fact that he often derives legitimizing sustenance from the affirmation that even a *devar ha-reshut* may be sanctified *le-shem shamayim*; and yet – whether because of religious superficiality or because, as Wordsworth lamented, "The world is too much with us, late and soon"[23] – he fails to invest his actions with this character. His besetting sin is not so much in his being rebellious as in being obtuse or oblivious. At some level, there often obtains a degree of distracted *hessah ha-da'at* – the frightful sense of Laplace's reply when asked why he had omitted any mention of God from his *Mécanique Céleste*: "Je n'ai pas besoin de cette hypothèse." That is to say, one manages without Him.

This is the ultimate challenge to centrist Orthodoxy; and how it is met, personally and collectively, holds the key to its future. In this regard, spiritual leadership can, one hopes, do much. But the final answer lies with you, my narrower and broader audience. If Torah and Halakhah become marginal to centrism, it shall be marginal to Jewish life. If they become focal, it can enjoy a long and vibrant future.

Notes

1. See his comment to Devarim 18:13, and his addendum at the end of the section on *mizvot aseh* in the Rambam's *Sefer Ha-Mizvot*, no. 8.
2. Hilkhot De'ot 1:4. The question of the relation between the Rambam's formulation and Aristotle's Nicomachean Ethics has been much discussed, but it lies beyond my scope here.
3. Hilkhot De'ot 1:5.
4. See chap. 4. The contrast is significant for an understanding of the concept of *lifnim mishurat ha-din*.
5. The controversy between Rabbenu Tam and Rabbenu Elhanan as to whether Torah or *derekh eretz* is *ikkar* is cited, with minor variations, in *Tosafot Yeshanim*, Yoma 85b, s.v. *teshuvah*; *Haggahot Maimuniyot*, Talmud Torah 3:2; and *Tosafot Rabbenu Yehudah he-Hasid, Berakhah Meshuleshet*, Berakhot 35b, s.v. *v'assafta*.
6. Yeshayahu 45:18. While presented in the *pasuk* as a definition of primordial purpose, the formulation also assumes normative halakhic force; see Gittin 41b.
7. Hilkhot Melakhim 12:5. The universal element, beyond the specific *mizvah* of *talmud Torah*, is noteworthy.
8. Hilkhot Gezelah ve-Avedah 6:11.
9. Arnold, "To a Friend."
10. Eikha Rabbati 2:17.
11. See Gittin 60b.
12. See his *Ethical Studies* (New York: Library of Liberal Arts, 1951), pp. 98–147.
13. Avodah Zarah 17b.

14. *Laodamia*, 1, 75. The following line, "A fervent, not ungovernable, love," if applied to love of God, raises interesting questions.

15. See Amnon Levy, *Ha-Haredim* (Jerusalem, 1989), chap. 1.

16. Tehillim 100:2 and 2:13, respectively.

17. *Intimations of Immortality*, l. 10.

18. Hulme, "Romanticism and Classicism," in *Speculations: Essays on Humanism and the Philosophy of Art* (London, 1924); reprinted in *Criticism: The Major Texts*, ed. W.J. Bate (New York, 1952), p. 570.

19. Avot 2:12. The range of interpretation of this mishnah, as reflected in the *perushim*, is worthy of further study.

20. See Hilkhot Deʿot 3:2–3 and *Shemoneh Perakim*, chap. 5.

21. Shabbat 50b.

22. Berakhot 63a. Rava's comment, cited by the Rambam in *Shemonah Perakim* but omitted in the Mishneh Torah, has apparently antinomian overtones that obviously raise certain problematic issues. However, some texts then continue, היינו דאמרי אינשי גנבא אפום מחתרתא רחמנא קרי (עיין "דקדוקי סופרים" על אתר וכתבי רבנו בחיי (ירושלים, תש"ל), עמ' עד. This casts Rava's comment as more descriptive than normative. On the other hand, Rashi, s.v. *daʾe'hu*, does regard it as a directive, but evidently confines it to situations such as that of *Eliyahu be-har ha-karmel*, for which license is cited elsewhere, albeit perhaps only with respect to a navi; see Yevamot 90b.

23. The opening line of a sonnet. As noted by C.S. Lewis in the chapter devoted to the term in his *Studies in Words*, "world" has had a multiple and complex history; and, depending on its sense, the lament may vary widely.

Chapter 16a

The State of Orthodoxy

THE QUESTIONS

1. Do you believe that recent developments warrant the triumphalism exhibited by important segments of Orthodoxy which predict the total disappearance of non-Orthodox movements?
2. What do you regard as the basic challenges facing the Orthodox movement?
3. Are there common elements shared by the diverse groups comprising Orthodoxy or is Orthodoxy merely a coalition of separate movements held together only by common opposition to non-Orthodox groups?
4. How do you view the resurgence of right-wing Orthodoxy? Does it portend the eclipse of modern Orthodoxy?
5. Do you regard modern Orthodoxy as a philosophy of compromise or as an authentic version of Judaism?
6. How do you view the current *teshuvah* movement?
7. How should Orthodoxy respond to the State of Israel?
8. What have been Orthodoxy's greatest achievements and greatest features on the American scene?

As an expatriate who enjoys direct contact with Orthodoxy in America only in the course of brief annual visits, I respond to *Tradition*'s invitation with a

Reprinted from *Tradition* 20:1 (Spring 1982).

measure of diffidence. If proverbial wisdom can be twisted, I approach the questions it has posed endowed, I hope, with a transient's perspicuity; and yet I feel sadly bereft of the sense of immediacy so essential for measuring a pulse or perceiving nuances. Nevertheless, as the questions are by and large general – and since, moreover, most are, *mutatis mutandis,* no less relevant to the Israeli than to the American scene – I trust the response will be to the point.

Any assessment of the current state of American Orthodoxy must relate to two distinct issues: (1) its position vis-à-vis schismatic movements, and (2) the degree of success or failure in coping with challenges which confront American Jewry as a whole. With respect to the former, it is clear that over the past two decades the relative strength of Orthodoxy has been considerably enhanced. This change is due, in part, to the decline of Conservative and Reform Judaism, many of whose traditional constituents have either become totally disaffected or have moved in the direction of consistent halakhic living. In large measure, however, it stems from the resurgence of Orthodoxy itself. Much to the dismay and disbelief of our adversaries (and, quite candidly, weren't there some premonitions among our adherents as well?), it turned out that the projections of our anticipated demise were not only premature but quite simply erroneous. Revitalization has been perhaps most clearly manifested in the growth of advanced (and often protracted) Torah study; and the development of this area probably constitutes our greatest single recent achievement. How many truly believed, 20 years ago, that the yeshiva proper would today be the heart of Yeshiva University, its bet midrash filled to capacity, evening after evening? I wonder if even Rav Aharon Kotler זצ״ל, visionary as he was, thought that close to a thousand *benei Torah* would now be learning in Lakewood.

Moreover, the growth has not been confined to major centers; *yeshivot* have sprung up in what were once regarded as spiritual steppes; nor has it been purely quantitative. The quality of Torah learning has been enhanced, as regards both depth and scope, and commitment to it, rooted in a sense of its transcendence and unfazed by the imperious pressure of an engulfing secular culture, has been sharpened.

The enrichment of Torah study has of course been accompanied by an ideological and sociological shift to the right; and this, in turn, has led some in the modern Orthodox camp (I very much dislike this stereotyping nomenclature, but in a brief essay it is almost indispensable) both to doubt their own credentials as the bearers of an authentic Torah position and to fear that the intensification of commitment must *ipso facto* generate forces which may sweep them aside. The doubt is sheer nonsense. If by modern Orthodoxy one means the attempt to relate the truth of Torah to the social and intellectual milieu of a more general culture; if it entails realizing Torah values within the context of an integrated life, seen steadily and seen whole, it needs no apology. One may accept it or reject it, but can anyone cavalierly dismiss the tradition of Rav Saadya Gaon and the Rambam as pallid compromise?

As to the fear, it is certainly not without foundation. It should be emphasized, however, that the decline of modern Orthodoxy is by no means an inevitable result of the growth of the right-wing Torah world; and that, despite some unquestioned and unjustified belligerence from certain quarters, if modern Orthodoxy is eclipsed, the primary reason will not be the resurgence of the right but the fragility of the complex and tenuous balance it offers and, alas, some of its own shortcomings. For too long, while it was clearly the main show, modern Orthodoxy was apologetic toward the left and condescending to the right. Often more concerned with image than with substance, it evaded some of the challenges posed by its position and frittered away opportunities offered by it; and some of its spokesmen confused making the *Times* with the *summum bonum*. None of this is inevitable, however; and there is no reason why a chastised and therefore chastened modern component, itself rooted in intensive commitment to Torah and drawing sustenance from it, cannot flourish within the overall context of revitalized Orthodoxy. Although persistent internecine struggles have somewhat obscured the fact, that which unites the diverse factions of Orthodoxy is far more basic and far more comprehensive than that which divides them; and if only we all develop greater sensitivity, tolerance, and empathy, we should be able to attain a mutually fructifying relationship within our common halakhic community.

The improvement in the relative position of Orthodoxy – largely based, in turn, upon its absolute resurgence – is both impressive and, to us, gratifying. With respect to our second topic, however – Orthodoxy's success in meeting the challenges confronting collective American Jewry – the picture is far less sanguine. Even as the hard core of Orthodoxy has strengthened and deepened its commitment, the community as a whole has become polarized, with most of it increasingly apathetic if not alienated with respect to its Judaism. During the past 20 years, assimilation has become ever more insidious, intermarriage rampant, Jewish identity eroded, and disaffection with *any* religious affiliation widespread; and upon all this Orthodoxy has had almost no significant impact. Consequently, I, for one, fail to understand the smug satisfaction which envelops some of my colleagues. With intermarriage running close to 50 percent, when studies indicate that over three-fourths of our brethren do not enter *any* house of worship on *any* day of the year, while the fabric of the Jewish family is impaired (just think of the purely halakhic problems this raises, not to mention the broader implications), can anyone rest content because several thousand *benei Torah* (whose importance I do not, of course, minimize in the slightest) are now more committed? We are justifiably gratified by the growing number of *baalei teshuvah*. Yet, even as we recall Hazal's emphasis upon the significance of every individual as a whole world, can we forget that these represent a minuscule part of their alienated peers?

Nor do I share the glee some feel over the prospective demise of the competition. Surely, we have many sharp differences with the Conservative and Reform movements, and these should not be sloughed over or blurred. However, we also share many values with them – and this, too, should not be obscured. Their disappearance might strengthen us in some respects but would unquestionably weaken us in others. And of course, if we transcend our own interests and think of the people currently served by these movements – many of them, both presently and potentially, well beyond our reach or ken – how would they, or *K'lal Yisrael* as a whole, be affected by such a change? Can anyone responsibly state that it is better for a marginal Jew in Dallas or in Dubuque to lose his religious identity altogether rather than drive to his temple?

Our collective difficulties are, under present circumstances, perhaps largely unavoidable. The deck is simply stacked. However, I am afraid that Orthodoxy's failure to cope with them has been exacerbated by some of our own failings. These are primarily two. The first – to some extent, I am afraid, the obverse of intensified commitment – is a certain narrowness which has gripped much of the Orthodox world. At its worst, this has bred a measure of arrogance and intolerance, and has even shockingly led to corruption derived from the sense that one is above mere civil law or civil behavior. Even where these are absent, however – and I fervently trust such instances are not widespread – narrowness manifests itself in cultural insularity and limited horizons; in pettiness and smugness; above all, in misplaced priorities and skewed perspectives. This last is reflected in the prevalent attitude toward the State of Israel, which is generally regarded favorably but not recognized as a momentous historical development. It is also evidenced, however, with respect to the American scene. On one of my visits I recall being almost overwhelmed by the impression that the major challenges confronting American Orthodoxy were neither demographic nor ideological, not how to deepen Jewish identity and weld the community, and not how to come to grips boldly with the social and intellectual impact of secular culture. These were, rather, determining the status of metropolitan *erubin* and finding the right tuna fish. I do not, of course, minimize in the slightest the need for dealing with the minutiae of Halakhah very seriously and responsibly. But this must be done, as *gedolei Yisrael* always insisted, with sensitivity, with perspective, with sweep. And of these we currently have too little.

The second failing – not unrelated to the first, concerns the quality of leadership. American Orthodoxy has produced some fine *talmidei hakhamim,* many capable and conscientious rabbis, and a group of thoughtful and articulate intellectuals; and, under the circumstances, this achievement has been remarkable. Nevertheless, the fact remains that it has produced almost no indigenous *gedolim,* neither in the narrower sphere of Halakhah nor in the broad realm of public leadership, and no first-rank creative thinkers or artists. Their absence, at a plane beyond competence and commitment, is sorely felt; and it is partly responsible for the myopia which often besets us.

In closing, let me stress that in making certain criticisms I have not sought to minimize the accomplishments of American Orthodoxy. These have been, under circumstances which rendered sheer survival a major achievement, very substantial. However, I feel we would do best to leave the kudos to others and to focus more on what yet remains to be done. Looking before and after, we should regard our recent resurgence as providing both the opportunity and the responsibility to proceed "Tomorrow to fresh woods and pastures new."

Chapter 16b

The Condition of Jewish Belief

THE QUESTIONS

1. In what sense to you believe the Torah to be divine revelation? Are all 613 commandments equally binding on the believing Jew? If not, how is he to decide which to observe? What status would you accord to ritual commandments lacking in ethical or doctrinal content (i.e., the prohibition against clothing made of linen and wool)?

2. In what sense do you believe that the Jews are the chosen people of God? How do you answer the charge that this doctrine is the model from which various theories of national and racial superiority have been derived?

3. Is Judaism the one true religion, or is it one of several true religions? Does Judaism still have something distinctive – as it once had monotheism – to contribute to the world? In the ethical sphere, the sphere of *ben adam le-chavero,* what distinguishes the believing Jew from the believing Christian, Moslem, or Buddhist – or, for that matter, from the unbelieving Jew and the secular humanist?

4. Does Judaism as a religion entail any particular political viewpoint? Can a man be a good Jew and yet, say, support racial segregation? Can a man be a good Jew and be Communist? A Fascist?

5. Does the so-called "God is dead" question which has been agitating

From *The Condition of Jewish Belief: A Symposium Compiled by the Editors of "Commentary" Magazine* (New York: Macmillan, 1966), pp. 132–39.

Christian theologians have any relevance to Judaism? What aspects of modern thought do you think pose the most serious challenge to Jewish belief?

(1) The Torah, both the written text and the oral law, constitutes divine revelation in three distinct senses. It was revealed *by* God, it reveals something *about* Him, and it reveals Him. First, the Torah comprises a specific narrative or normative *datum,* an objective "given" invested with definite form and content, which was addressed by God to Israel as a whole or to its leader and representative, Moses. This datum consists of two elements:

(a) The *revelatum,* to use the Thomistic term, whose truths inherently lie beyond the range of human reason and which therefore had to be revealed if they were to be known at all; and

(b) the *revelabile,* whose truths – be they historical facts or the norms of morality or natural religion – could have been discovered by man in any event, and whose transcendental status therefore derives from the relatively extrinsic fact of their having been divinely expressed. The present character of both as revelation, however, is crucial. After the fact, both constitute God's living message to Israel.

Secondly, the Torah reveals something about God, and this in two ways: it presents direct statements about divine attributes: and, inasmuch as it is not merely a document delivered (*salve reverentia*) by God but composed by Him, it constitutes in its normative essence an expression of His will. As such, it affords us an indirect insight into what is otherwise wholly inscrutable. He who is hidden in His numinous "otherness" – *E-l mistater be-shafrir hevyon, ha-sekhel ha-ne'elam mi-kol ra'ayon* – or transcendent in His luminous majesty – (Milton's "Dark with excessive bright thy skirts appear") – has chosen, *mutatis mutandis,* to condense His infinite will in the very act of its expression. Finite man is thus enabled, though ever so haltingly, to grasp it somewhat. Hence, as the *Tanya* emphasized, the tremendous importance of the study of Torah for traditional Judaism. It is the one means of embracing and absorbing, as it were, God's presence as manifested through His revealed will. It becomes, therefore, not only an intellectual exercise but a religious experience.

But the revealed character of Torah does not exhaust itself in propositions imparted by God or concerning Him. It is realized, thirdly, as a revelation of the divine presence proper. Revelation is not only an objective *datum* or the process of its transmission, important as these may be. It is the occasion, exalting and humbling both, for a dialectal encounter with the living God. Revelation is not only a fixed text but, in relation to man, an electrifying I-and-Thou experience. Moreover, this experience is not confined to the initial moment of divine giving and human taking of a specific message. It is repeated recurrently through genuine response to God's message which ushers us into His presence. The rapture and the awe, the joy and the tremor of Sinai were not of a moment. They are of all time, engaging the Jew who truly opens himself to the divine message and God's call. "Every day let them [the words of the Torah] be in your eyes as if newly given." The experience of revelation is repeated through response, be it study or action, to its content, and conversely, the awareness of its content is sharpened through an intensive sense of its experience.

To the committed Jew, this experience, at Sinai or at present, is not simply a momentarily rapturous encounter. It is enthralling in *both* senses of the word. It imposes binding obligations. The Torah, although it includes sizable narrative segments, is, in its quintessence, normative. Indeed, the rabbis felt constrained to explain why it had not begun with the first command addressed to Israel (Exod 12) rather than with the story of creation. At its core, the Torah is a body of law, Halakhah, its heart and soul. To respond to the Torah, at whatever level, is not just to undergo mystical or even prophetic trauma, but to heed a command. Or rather, to heed God as the giver of commands. To the pure ethicist, obligation may perhaps be rooted in an autonomous moral law. Religiously speaking, one is bound by the person-to-person encounter. Not just the law but the King, not only the *mizvah* but the *metzavveh*. "Why [in reciting the Shema] does the portion of Shema precede that of *Ve-hayah im shamoʿa*? In order that he [who recites] should first accept the rule of the Kingdom of Heaven and then the rule of *mizvot*." This is the crux of the precedence in Exodus 24:7, of *naʿaseh*, "we shall do," to *ve-nishma*, "we shall hear," which the Rabbis saw as being so basic to Israel's acceptance of the Torah.

From this perspective, it is obvious that all 613 commandments are equally binding. Not that they are all of equal importance. Some outweigh others, and in cases of conflict, the Halakhah provides criteria between them. All are similarly obligatory, however, for it is their source rather than their content which binds – and for Him they share in common. Whether a particular commandment has "ethical or doctrinal content" is not the heart of the matter. The crucial point is that it *is* a commandment, that it elicits a response to the divine call. To put it more sharply, there always is ethical or doctrinal content. In the age-old controversy – dating from Plato's *Euthyphro* – as to whether things please God because they are good or they are good because they please Him, traditional Judaism has certainly held with Socrates that the divine will is not arbitrary but rational. As regards commandments, however, even if we ignore the intrinsic content, perhaps hidden from us, of a specific *mizvah,* its merely being such has moral and religious import. It widens the scope of religious awareness. It inculcates the habit of acting in response to the divine will in all areas of endeavor. It develops a sense of the divine presence. It integrates all of human life into a normative and purposive existence. It enables the Jew to attain not only dignity but sanctity.

(2) This normative existence is the key to Israel's election as God's chosen people. Generally speaking, our election may be viewed as the result of the interaction of divine grace and human merit, of supernal love and yearning aspiration. Specifically, however, the vehicle through which this election has come into being has always been the covenant. And a covenant – be it with the patriarchs, in Egypt, at Sinai, upon entering the promised land, or, in a slightly different sense, with every individual Jew throughout the generations – has invariably entailed a key element: the acceptance of divine norms. Not Luther's feminine waiting for the seed of grace but active submission to a divinely ordered discipline – that has been the core of the process. Moreover, the normative element is not only the genetic historical source of our election. It defines, in large measure, the heart of the concept proper. In what does our chosenness consist? It consists in being singled out as a unique instrument for the fulfillment

of God's purpose in history. This, in turn, entails commitment to unique responsibilities and special obligations – a "Jewish man's burden," if you will. It involves a closer relation to God; responding more fully and more frequently to divine command. There is, to be sure, an obverse – the dispensation of special grace and the bestowal of particular favor. Furthermore, our covenantal relation being dynamic rather than static, it has led us to develop through the years a distinctive national character. The essence of our election, however, remains our unique commitment and its attendant responsibilities: these may, no doubt, produce special consequences. For better: "Rabbi Chananya son of Akashya used to say, the Holy One, blessed be He, wished to render Israel more worthy. Therefore, he provided them with much Torah and commandments." Or for worse: "You only have I known of all the families of the earth; therefore I shall visit upon you all your iniquities." These are ancillary, however; the basic ground of our election is normative existence and obligation.

The concept of Israel's chosen status is therefore substantively different from the theories of racial and national superiority formulated by Gobineau, Treitschke, and their confreres. Chosenness, as we understand it, resides in our covenantal relation with God rather than in any inherent superiority. It is, of course, quite conceivable that the doctrine of Israel's national election has indeed served as the model for these theories. I am not historian enough to judge. It should be clear, however, that there is no real analogy. We do not boast of our prowess. We lay no claim to aboriginal merit. Rather, we humbly thank God for assigning us a unique destiny, and we strive to fulfill the responsibilities of the covenant which he proffered and we accepted. To the relativist, this will no doubt still sound naive. But the believing Jew can assume no less.

(3) This concept of normative existence, of a life governed by divinely ordained law and organized as an all-embracing religious discipline, constitutes Judaism's most distinctive contemporary hallmark. Halakhah is its *principium individuationis*. The ideal of personal dedication to God's purposes in the broadest sense is by no means uniquely Jewish. However, our means of attaining it – and therefore the specific content of the ideal

proper – clearly is. Life dominated in every area and for every individual by constant reference and response to divine commandments is qualitatively different from an existence generally committed to religious goals. The Jew's whole life is permeated by an awareness of his relation to God. In every sphere of endeavor – be it social or economic, physical or intellectual – conscious choice and religious response are operative. The Halakhah, through its numerous laws concerning various areas, directs the Jew in the sanctification of himself and his environment. It suffuses his life with spiritual significance, and integrates his activity into a divinely ordered whole. It gives the Jew a sense of purpose.

While the halakhic ideal of normative existence represents the distinctive hallmark of Judaism, it has both particularistic and universal implications. In its specific form, the Torah's total discipline was addressed to the Jew and to the Jew alone. It constitutes the crux of our covenant with God and we neither expect nor encourage the world as a whole to adopt it. Within a purely monotheistic framework, we regard the Gentile world as fully entitled, indeed mandated, to develop its own true and valid religious approaches – to institute modes of worship, to formulate religious philosophies, to seek out, and, if it so wishes, to invest with a public character vehicles of bringing man closer to God. Hence, our view of the relation between the Jewish and the Gentile worlds with respect to the overall Torah discipline differs radically from that which obtains with respect to monotheism. Monotheism is an idea which we may have developed but which is nonetheless universally binding. It was not only something which the world could observe *in* us but which we insisted it should learn *from* us. The halakhic discipline, on the other hand, is specifically Jewish and bears no normative relation to the Gentile. And yet it too has universal implications. While the details of halakhic living and its formal regimen do not relate to the non-Jew, the ideals and values embedded within the Halakhah addressed themselves to mankind as a whole. The degree and the obligatory means of attaining these ideals, as well as the normative and covenantal framework within which they exist, are Israel's and Israel's alone. However, the central underlying purposes – of integrating the secular and the holy, of suffusing all human activity with a pervasive sense of religious meaning and direction – these belong to everyone and to no one. Imprinting them upon the universal consciousness of all men would constitute Judaism's greatest contribution to the modern world.

The pervasive character of Torah discipline permeates the ethical sphere as well as the "religious." Indeed, the inner logic of the halakhic ideal clearly dictates that social and personal ethics (the ethical includes much more than interpersonal *ben adam le-chavero*) are an integral aspect of religion proper. The impact of this ideal upon ethical thought and behavior is, in part, simply the general impact of religion upon morality. It provides a conception of the nature of man as a moral agent; it posits an absolute rationale for moral action; and it defines a set of desiderata toward which such action ought to be directed. It thus transmutes morality from a drifting pursuit of relative goods – in the naturalistic universe of the secularist, even were an autonomous morality conceivable, it would have no absolute goals to seek – into a dedicated quest for the intrinsic Good. The ethical thrust of Halakhah goes beyond this, however. It extends to positing specific ideals and designating modes and standards of their fulfillment. While genuine morality can never be legislated in detail – virtue, justice, or wisdom ultimately depend upon inner commitment – the Torah's guidelines, besides setting a minimum standard, provide a direction for, and add a religious dimension to, moral action.

Hence, the Torah ethic – together with numerous other factors, of course – distinguishes the committed Jew from both a secular humanist on the one hand and a Christian or Moslem on the other. He differs from the one with respect to the elemental questions of the nature and destiny of man. And while he would essentially agree with the other as regards the basically religious character of human existence, he would challenge him with respect to specific goals. Nor are these minor questions of technical implementation. Our opposition to the dualism pervading much of Christian thought is hardly a petty trifle.

(4) As with the ethical sphere, so with the political. Judaism could hardly countenance political systems or philosophies which regard man as nothing but *homo economicus*; which deny the essential worth of the individual;

which renounce the concept of distributive justice; which arbitrarily discriminate against one group in favor of another; or which disregard the concept of collective responsibility for the welfare of each and every person. In this sense, Judaism definitely entails a particular political viewpoint. A spiritual conception of man and society and dedication to a just social order are a *sine qua non* of any political outlook which a Jew could legitimately adopt. As to the optimum means of attaining these goals, however, Judaism – despite the fact that the Halakhah does provide specific direction on certain points – could allow for considerable latitude. Indeed, it is the acolyte of a political ideology who finds himself with little practical leeway; his specifically political "system" often binds him with dogmatic pronouncements of a party line geared to this very area. The religious devotee, whose ideology is essentially spiritual rather than political, may have far greater pragmatic latitude. Never, of course, an unlimited spectrum; but still a fairly wide range.

(5) Such, in summary substance, is the bedrock upon which the Torah *Weltanschauung*, as both belief and experience, rests, It is a position which has always been under attack – in modern times, more so than previously. What aspects of contemporary thought challenge it most severely? There are, unfortunately, numerous candidates for this dubious distinction, but a few may be singled out for special mention. They – I refer to intellectual rather than social pressures – fall roughly into two classes: those which undermine religion generally and those which challenge Judaism – and to an extent, all revealed religion – specifically. Foremost among the first are: materialism, Marxist or other; pseudoscientism, especially as manifested in the social sciences; deterministic psychology, especially behaviorism; and, in the sphere of both ethics and religion, utilitarianism. Within the second group, the major challenge is presented by liberalism (I use the term in Cardinal Newman's sense, i.e., rampant intellectualist individualism) and, though to a lesser degree than at the turn of the century, biblical criticism. Probably the greatest over-all challenge is posed, however, by two elements which straddle both categories: positivism, legal or otherwise;

and historicism, not so much because of its critique of specific traditions as because of the relativism which almost inexorably attends it.

Not to be included in this list, however, is the so-called death-of-God issue currently being bandied about in Christian circles. To the extent that this notion is more than so much doublethink and disguised atheism, it constitutes a reaction against sentimental anthropomorphism – the "Grandfather in Heaven," to use C.S. Lewis's phrase, of popular liberal theology. Despite its appeals to realism and morality, however, it represents a reaction which has gone haywire. Essentially, its advocates hold a transitional position. It is only a matter of time before they fragment into two groups – secular moralists, and devotees of what will turn out to be a conception of God after all, if a somewhat unconventional one. I do not quite see how one can hold this position seriously and remain a believing Christian, but that no believing Jew could hold it is beyond question. And not only because Jewish dogma contravenes it. It is not just that the believing Jew *may* not hold it. He *cannot*. "The lion hath roared, who will not fear? The Lord God hath spoken, who can but prophesy?" (Amos 3:8). To the Jew who is called upon to respond to Him constantly, can God be anything but a living presence?

Chapter 16c

Directions for American Orthodoxy

QUESTIONS

1. Considering the ease with which a Jew can relate to the outside culture, how can we help him/her maintain a proper between the general culture and the Jewish community in all its facets? What are the responsibilities of the contemporary and future Jew to the general culture with respect towards *tikkun ha-olam*?

2. Notwithstanding the strength and growth of Orthodoxy, are we satisfied that there exists a spiritual depth which makes us feel confident in the future of American Orthodoxy? Are the centripetal forces pulling towards the religious core a match for the centrifugal forces pulling away from the center? Can we create the works of *musar and mahshavah* [Jewish thought] that speak to our own generation? And more importantly, what can we do to help develop the living role models which can inspire us to aspire to higher *madregot* [levels] in our personal *Yiddishkeit*?

3. The feminist issue is perhaps the most explosive issue facing Orthodoxy. How can we preserve the special quality of the traditional Jewish woman in the face of the incessant demands of the American feminist agenda? How can we distinguish between legitimate requests for improvement and change from those which are echoes of the surrounding society?

This article first appeared in the Fall 1998 issue of *Jewish Action,* the magazine of the Orthodox Union.

Do you believe the feminist issue will estrange feminists and their supporters from the rest of Orthodoxy? One well-known feminist has recently forsaken Orthodoxy over feminist issues. Do you believe we need to fear further defections? What can be done to heal the developing breach between the opposing factions?

4. What do you think will be the effect of the information and communications explosion on Orthodoxy? How can we best utilize the new opportunities afforded by the new technology for education, outreach, communal interaction, etc.?

5. Our generation has seen the passing of numerous Torah giants from our midst. How can we encourage the development of knowledgeable, inspiring, and forceful leaders?

6. What can be done to improve the relations between the different groups within Orthodoxy? Are we in danger of greater polarization or can we look forward to greater unity?

7. Do you foresee the greater yearning for *Yiddishkeit* as a spur to non-Orthodox Jewry becoming more traditional and closer to authentic Judaism? How can we help them draw closer? Do you think the rapid increase in the rate of intermarriage and the disastrous impact of "patrilineal descent" have made it too late to effect a turnaround?

8. What do you see as the major role of the Orthodox Union in the next century? What are some of the areas which will require greater attention? Would it be of value to convene a gathering of some of our best minds to engage in interactive brain storming in order to anticipate the crucial challenges of the future and articulate imaginative plans? Should they prepare a blue print for the future?

9. What do you see as the future relationship between American Israeli Orthodoxy? Can American Orthodox Jews help heal the religious-secular Israeli rift?

10. How can we express our opposition to blatant violations of Halakhah without creating confrontations which frequently have disastrous counterproductive consequences?

11. How can we educate our children to be more sensitive to *hillul ha-Shem*

and the extreme gravity of that sin? Are we placing sufficient emphasis on the merit of honesty in the education of our children?

12. How serious is the problem of defections from Orthodoxy? What are the chief causes of this little-discussed phenomenon and what should be done to remedy it?

Confronted by the phalanx of questions included in this symposium, I find myself responding instinctively with two reservations. The first is the obvious rejoinder that such a range can hardly receive adequate treatment in the space allotted to each participant. The second, in a more personal vein, is recoil from futuristic projections, in general, and from the implication (here, admittedly quite muted) that they should intimidate us into falling in step with the presumed inevitable. On second thought, however, I note, with respect to the first point, that the editors have mercifully only asked for answers to one or more questions; and, as to the second, I shall take the liberty of assuming that, in accordance with my vocation and predilection both, I have the license to seek to prescribe rather than to predict.

While the issues raised cut a broad swath, as might have been anticipated, *a priori*, with respect to the examination of any religious community, they may be condensed into two primary categories: areas which, substantively, relate to the internal structure, character, and direction of American Orthodoxy itself, and those which concern its interaction with other segments of society, Jewish or general. This, in turn, invites two further, and somewhat related, questions: (1) Upon which area ought we focus, collectively? (2) How, and to what extent, do these areas intersect, and how does one inform the other and impinge upon it?

Given my spiritual perspective, on the one hand, and my reading of the contemporary scene, on the other, I have little doubt but that American Orthodoxy – especially, albeit not exclusively, its more modern wing – should best concentrate upon molding and holding its own character and constituency. And this, across a broad spectrum, and with respect to a range of issues. Thus, at one pole, the problem of defections – whether out of philosophic skepticism, egocentric libertinism, or societal disaffection –

certainly needs to be acknowledged and addressed. Assuredly, the figures are nowhere nearly as calamitous as those of pre-World War II Europe, but they are nevertheless quite worrisome. Moreover, the current initial base is considerably smaller and the defections often graver. At stake, in some cases, is not just the move from the *heder* to the Bund, but the rejection of Jewish identity to the point that *"Bashem bagadu ki vanim zarim yaladu"* ["They betrayed God for they gave birth to alien children," Hoshea 5:7] and, at that level of apostasy, even isolated instances should concern us.

At the other extreme, the quest for vigorous and sensitive spiritual leadership should retain high priority. The current dearth of first-rank *gedolim* is generally acknowledged and bemoaned. One can think of no indigenous American *gadol* certain to be remembered with wistful awe a century hence; of no current *hibbur* [work] assured of a place in a standard bet midrash library in the next generation; of no giant majestically bestriding the contemporary scene and securely moving American Orthodoxy into the future. On that plane, however, I am not certain that much can be said or done. The social and/or educational infrastructure out of which emerged the Hazon Ish, Rav Shlomo Zalman Auerbach, or Rav Yosef Ber Soloveitchik, זצ״ל, is, at least for the foreseeable future, probably beyond replication. Yet, much can and should be done to stimulate Torah leadership at a secondary plane. The key is obviously educational – identifying and inspiring talent, channeling energies and resources, promoting institutions and providing opportunity. Above all, ours is the task of infusing and idealizing the blend of piety, knowledge, imagination, sensitivity, and commitment so critical for the persona of a *talmid hakham* who can also serve as a mentor and a leader; and we are challenged to strive for a proper balance, in his development and personality, between insular concentration and relatedness to his ambient society. Over the past generation, much has been done in this direction – far more than even optimists had previously envisioned. Yet, in the perennial quest for replenishing leadership, much lost ground remains to be recovered.

In the interim, American Orthodoxy as a whole – each "camp" with its own specific problems and priorities – needs to strengthen and deepen its moral and religious base. The form and direction to be taken may very well vary. Some, for instance, ought to be encouraged to intensify passion, others to inhibit it. Two general comments may be in order, however. First, one cannot escape the impression that American Orthodoxy is now excessively politicized, its attention often riveted upon power and confrontation, be it *le-shem Shamayim*, and hence somewhat diverted from matters of the spirit. Secondly, this community has become increasingly engrossed with what is done – and, from a halakhic perspective, this is of course crucial – to the neglect of how or why it is, or should be, done; and this imbalance requires redress. Hopefully, as Orthodoxy becomes more confidently secure, the urge to concentrate upon defining externals, so characteristic of an embattled community whose very survival is under siege, may diminish, and more spiritual energy can be directed to modality and motivation. As *le-ovdo* (service to God) becomes a more prevalent reality, we should be able to focus more upon what, in the wake of the Ramban, the best of *Mitnagdut* and *Hasidut* both, has been regarded as the epitome of halakhic living – *be-khol levavkhem* (with all your heart).

This spiritual emphasis must obviously include a powerful moral component. Woe unto us if dishonesty of *anshei shelomenu* (our own people) be regarded primarily as a potential catalyst of *hillul ha-Shem*. It is, of course, that, but much more. Chicanery is a tragedy of spiritual rot which has, at times, infested and infected some individuals and institutions in our community, and has thus traduced if not travestied the commitment for whose sake corners were ostensibly cut; and this should be painfully acknowledged.

Greater unity, likewise, should be defined as a spiritual desideratum. From a certain point of view, this is a preeminently political issue, as it obviously impacts upon the relation of Orthodoxy to other groups. While this aspect cannot be denied – clearly, a community consumed by internecine strife is less poised to defend its turf and promote its agenda than a united front – the quest for greater harmony is fundamentally spiritual, and its absence exacts a moral and religious toll from all our "wings." Quite apart from the positive search for *ahavat* – and *ahavat Yisrael* as a *mizvah* and a value, and quite apart from the simply human worth of empathetic comity, there is so much to be gained, objectively, from reaching out instead of lashing out. Mutual fructification can expand horizons and sharpen insights, induce sensitivity and deepen commitment. Expressed negatively, the prevalence of either *mahloket* (conflict) or mutual benign neglect poses the threat that sectarian factionalism – and concomitant recrimination and condescension – may set the shrill tone for our communal climate. In that case, all sectors of the Torah world would be adversely affected – and this, I repeat, not just politically or economically, but spiritually.

Of course, we all have – and should have – our Rubicons; and I am no exception. But how often and where we draw the line in the sand; with what degree of verve we enter the lists; what are our priorities and emphases, and do we at least have the urge to walk the extra mile – these questions can affect our personal and communal stance significantly. As to projection concerning the prospect for greater polarization or unity, on the whole – I hope this is not just a wish as father to the thought – I am sanguine. I believe that reciprocal denigration has peaked and that the sense of a chasm between mainstream elements in respective factions is receding, so that a greater sense of a continuous spectrum is emerging; and that while we may see greater disaffection and splintering at the fringes, the overall climate will be less militant and more congenial. Responsibility and self-interest both, properly conceived, dictate that we strive, collectively, to restrain confrontation and triumphalism, while developing initiatives which, within difference, will encourage not only cooperation but genuine community.

Inner spiritual growth, through more intensive, rigorous, and passionate engagement with Torah, *mizvot,* and the *Ribbono shel Olam,* is the *unum necessarium per se,* at both the personal and the communal plane. It is also the key to fruitful interaction with general culture and possible contribution toward *tikkun ha-olam.* That culture is, in one respect, the object of prospective *tikkun,* moral and religious. In another, it may be, defined by Arnold as "the best that has been thought and said in the world," an agent of *tikkun.* As such, it serves the Jew dually. It can enhance his or her own spiritual growth; and it can stimulate and enable him or her, in the spirit of *le-ovdah u-leshamrah,* to sustain and develop the world around them, either through material *yishuvo shel olam* (societal stability), what Bacon denominated, "enlarging the bounds of human empire," or by humanizing its values and mores.

This concern with *tikkun olam* is itself an element of spiritual growth, inasmuch as it is grounded in the transcendence of egocentrism. Nevertheless, two caveats should be noted. First, at the level of implementation, personal or communal, it needs to be weighed against other priorities. We cannot do everything concurrently, and, even as we internalize concern about the broader world, our primary responsibility, for the foreseeable future, is certainly to our own. Secondly, the ability to imbibe from general culture and to impact upon it, while maintaining proper Torah values and perspective is, again, very much a function of one's own spiritual state. Hence, in surveying the current scene, I find need for considerable improvement. Much of the Haredi community cares little, apart from considerations of *parnasah* (livelihood), about *yishuvo shel olam*, not quite regarding the world, in Augustine's terms, as *massa perditionis*, but not overly concerned about its destiny, either; and it has almost no inclination for understanding or appreciating its *hokhmah*. Many modernists or centrists, on the other hand, do not manifest the religious resolve needed to produce individuals with the scope and intensity which are the hallmark of *bnei Torah* – individuals for whom *devar Hashem* is not simply a set of directives defining the parameters of existence but a consuming passion at its center.

If time and space permitted, much more could be said about the issues discussed or others omitted. Given the constraints, however, I shall rather content myself with a single concluding observation. The symposium suggests that the future of American Orthodoxy can be viewed with "triumph and trepidation." As we look ahead, these twin senses, properly conceived and realized, are certainly in order. Looking before and after, we have considerable cause for both gratification and concern. Yet, if our resolve as Orthodox Jews is to be meaningful, we must also be informed and animated by much else. Between celebration and anxiety lie responsibility, determination, commitment, and, above all, faith. The conclusion of the gemara in Makkot 24a is equally apt for the individual and for the community: *ba Habakkuk vehe'emidan al ahat, she-ne'emar ve-tzaddik be-emunato yihyeh,* "Habakkuk came and grounded them (i.e., Torah and *mizvot*) upon one, as it is stated, 'And the *tzaddik* shall live by his faith.'"

Chapter 16d

The State of *K'lal Yisrael*

QUESTIONS

1. What do you see as our generation's greatest acheivement?
2. What do you see as the most significant issues/problems facing *K'lal Yisrael* today?
3. What suggestions would you propose for their solution or amelioration?
4. What should be he approach to improving the current polarization between religious and irreligious Jews and between different groups of Jews?

A symposium which opens by asking participants to identify "our generation's greatest achievement" was, presumably, planned by an optimist; and I'm afraid that, within its context, the designation of "survival and continuity" as a response must seem disappointingly pessimistic. Yet, what else can one say? In 1942, or in 1945 for that matter, did anyone envision any more pressing need? Continuity should never be taken lightly and, in the latter half of the twentieth century, surely cannot be taken for granted. Ours is an epoch, in which, *mutatis mutandis,* one may say of *K'lal Yisrael* what Hazal said with respect to the *Ribbono shel Olam:* His awesomeness is manifested, even as His domain is ravaged and His people subjugated,

This article first appeared in *Jewish Action* 46:4 (1986).

by the very fact that His people are able to survive, solitarily, amongst the nations of the world (Yoma 69b).

Not, of course, mere passive survival; ours is an age in which diastolic and systolic alternations are frequently compressed into a single movement. Laboring under the pressures of the time, we consolidate by creating and, albeit to a lesser extent, create by consolidating. Yet, our primary thrust has been advisedly conservative. We have been impelled to fulfill the *mizvah* of *peru u-revu,* literally and figuratively. But it has largely confronted us in its second manifestation, as mandated to Noah rather than Adam. Building a pristine world-order would be both invigorating and ennobling. For our generation, its background the macabre ruins of European Jewish channels, the first priority and the primary achievement has been the restoration and sustenance of decimated Jewry. Even should ten generations lapse before an Avraham reappears, we shall have been those who rekindled the Torah and passed it along.

Survival and continuity – of which or of whom? At one level, of *K'lal Yisrael* itself. The ravages of migration and assimilation notwithstanding, Jewry of several continents has sustained itself as a vibrant community, whatever the mode of identity. At a second level, of the State of Israel. Its gestation and birth are to the credit of the previous generation, but its maintenance in our own, as a remarkable instance of the interaction of ferment and consolidation, is a remarkable achievement in its own right. In its thirty-ninth year, we regard the state pretty much as a given, and hope its neighbors will do likewise. But we ought not forget just how tenuous its existence has been.

At a third level, of the Torah world. Limited in scope but qualitatively central, that world has enjoyed a truly remarkable renaissance. Despite the currently popular idealization of pre-1939 Eastern Europe as a spiritual bastion, the fact remains that there, as elsewhere, within both the Ashkenazic and Sephardic world, in Eretz Yisrael as well as in the Diaspora, the status of *talmud Torah* was seriously and continuously eroded. Among adherents and opponents alike, the prevalent perception – obviously, not always verbalized or admitted – was that the yeshivas had little future, other than as a fossil on the periphery of modern society; and the war, of course, exacerbated this feeling. The contrast with the present is self evident. Much current Torah production is admittedly Alexandrian in nature – collation, summary compilation, monographic codification. But that is precisely the point: survival and continuity.

Merubim tzarkhai amekha – the array of problems confronting *K'lal Yisrael* today is formidable, *veda'atam ketzarah* – and the wisdom needed to cope with them is in relatively short supply. As regards the former, the external threat of anti-Semitism is, of course, perennial, but despite recent worrisome tendencies, Russian Jewry possibly excepted, it is not presently primary (the threat to the State of Israel posed by its Arab adversaries belongs in a different category). Our major, current problems are internal. First and foremost, there is the frightful decline in sheer numbers, of simple *yiddishkeit.* "Not with a bang, but with a whimper." Vigorous ideological opposition is now, except in some circles in Eretz Yisrael, relatively muted. However, an amalgam of ignorance and indifference has produced a severe spiritual crisis, of almost unprecedented scope and intensity. Widespread radical *am ha'artzut* would have been bad enough, *per se*, but in the modern context it has gone hand in hand with loss of faith. The resultant abondonment of religious values and observance has issued, at the juncture of the internal and external, in rampant assimilation and intermarriage. These have led to well publicized jeremiads about the impending *fin du peuple juif.* These projections, written with sociological expertise but with jaded faith, reflect genuine alarm; but they do not faze *ma'aminim bnei ma'aminim.* (One also wonders when futurists, given their anemic composite batting average, will practice humility in earnest.) Even a surviving people is concerned about its sons and daughters. The current disaffection of most is our greatest single problem. Mass Jewish education is in shambles; and unless we recognize the depth and scope of the crisis and mobilize in response to it, it is likely to remain as such for the foreseeable future.

Our spiritual conflagration is aggravated by the paucity of resources needed to fight it. Funding is a familiar issue but here I refer primarily to our overriding need: human resources. At one level, we are sorely in need of qualified communal and educational personnel. At another, we are confronted by a crisis of leadership. Within the Torah world and without, in Israel as well as in the Diaspora, we lack first-rank individuals in whom knowledge and charisma, sweep and vision, perspicacity and sensitivity, fuse to mold an authentic and authoritative leader. There are, for instance, many eminent *talmidei hakhamim,* even some *gedolim,* in Eretz Yisrael today; but, as a leader, is there anyone who invites comparison with the Hazon Ish?

The problem of leadership is exacerbated by the sharpened divisiveness that, like a festering sore, has infected our body politic. Polarization makes it difficult to hear even figures of stature across ideological chasms. Divisiveness is, however, primarily a central problem in its own right. It has weakened *K'lal Yisrael* morally and materially. It has encouraged pettiness and aggressiveness, and it has diverted energies from creative growth to internecine strife. Disunity and distrust sap our collective strength, and let us bear in mind that we are paying a spiritual price as well. Self-righteousness often obstructs true righteousness.

This catalogue consists of familiar and largely general problems, but conclude it with a more specific issue – *yohsin*. Historically, the question of personal halakhic status, particularly with respect to marriage, has been a major public concern in some periods, while confined to isolated instances in others. Our generation has been, in this regard, an age of sad transition. Sexual libertarianism, rising divorce rates, dubious conversions, and deviant definitions – all have combined to foster an exponential growth in the number of beclouded Jews. Their plight portends a dangerous national cleavage, on the one hand, and posits possible personal tragedy, on the other. Yet, despite its potentially alarming proportions, the problem has been treated by many with a complacent equanimity that is frightening in itself.

The problems are more easily formulated than their solutions. Nevertheless, some general directions and tentative suggestions may be delineated. With respect to our most critical problem, the construction of Jewish commitment, no pat solutions can be offered, especially since many of the relevant factors are mostly, if not entirely, beyond our control. However, one element is clearly and urgently needed: the examination and recommendation of priorities, and this at the highest level. We are what we are, and simply don't have enough fingers to dam all the dikes. However, given a clearer sense of strategy and purpose, we can surely reduce duplication and waste, and by raising certain questions, we can strive to utilize our resources most effectively. Should, for instance, the effort currently being expended to maintain standards of *kashruth* superior to those of the *Shulkhan Arukh* be better diverted to education? How many of the average *talmidim* filling our *kollelim* could serve *K'lal Yisrael* better through outreach? Does our educational structure strike the optimal present balance between quantity and quality? In an age in which, as Rav Michel Feinstein recently lamented, more than half of *K'lal Yisrael* does not even know *Shema Yisrael,* are we sufficiently assessing the importance of minimal mass commitment as opposed to the need for maintaining a small intensive core? Are we doing enough to communicate a sense of the initial urgency of the problem? In the process of determining priorities, these questions, and many more, need to be asked – radically, honestly, and, if need be, painfully. Perhaps, in the end, the answers will change little; but at last, then we will know that we are acting based on conscious choice rather than from haphazardness, inertia, or possibly even a measure of self-interest.

Reappraisal would presumably ameliorate the dearth of human resources – first, by attracting to the field of Jewish communal service (broadly defined, to include education) qualified people who are now deterred by poor salaries and low status; second, by directing individuals to areas in which their contribution can be maximal. It would not, in and of itself, produce leaders, of whom it may largely be said that *nascitur non fit* – he is born rather than made. Here, too, the impact of reassigned priorities could be significant. During the past generation, some segments of the Orthodox world have almost totally neglected significant investment in providing opportunity for leaders to develop; others have recognized – in a sense, even exaggerated – this need but have largely produced scions capable of shepherding their own flock, to a point, but quite incapable of addressing themselves to most of contemporary *K'lal Yisrael,* whose social dynamic and inner spiritual reality they do not truly understand.

Some progress has been made of late in this direction, and we must beware of losing heart should the early crops be disappointing. Given collective will and recognition of the importance of the issue, a better spiritual and material climate for growth can be provided, and in time, there shall be a harvest.

With respect to reducing polarization, I am convinced that the best approach does not call for minimizing difference but rather for maximizing community. Basic ideological differences do exist, and to dismiss or blur them is both irresponsible and anti-halakhic. Orthodoxy cannot accord secularists or dissenters the *hekhsher* they so insistently demand. We can, however, place greater emphasis upon the factors which, without denying difference, transcend it; upon confraternity, upon historical and existential ties, upon essential components of a shared moral and spiritual vision, upon elements of both a common fate and a common destiny. We should not only concede but assert that, whatever their deviations, other camps include people genuinely in search of the *Ribbono shel Olam*; that secular Jewry, too, harbors moral idealism and a commitment to *K'lal Yisrael*, and that while we reject leveling compromises, we strive for understanding and respect. This will no doubt seem excessively liberal to some and terribly patronizing to others; but such responses should hardly faze us.

With respect to *yohsin*, finally, we need to act out of a sense of both the importance and the urgency of the problem. There is a real danger that by the time the seriousness of the issue sufficiently penetrates the Torah world to the point that it may entertain solutions we would ordinarily shun, the magnitude of the problem will, in the interim, have grown to such an extent that even those palliative solutions will then only dent it. Possible approaches – all partial, none palatable – should be considered now. Conditional *kiddushin*, problematic though they be, should be reexamined – in the light of present pressures, as regards both *mamzerut* and *agunot*. With respect to *geyrut*, we ought at least probe the option of a *modus operandi* whereby we might recognize conversions that would be effected under the aegis of others, but which, in practice, would be administered according to *halakhic* guidelines and meet prevalent Orthodox standards. Such a proposal touches the raw nerve of legitimization, an issue towards which we are probably sensitive. However, in an age in which the "tears of the oppressed" are potentially so common and abuses so widespread, it, at least, bears exploration.

This brief discourse has broken very little fresh ground, nor was novelty its intention. If, however, it will help focus thought and stimulate discussion, it shall more than have served its purpose.

Chapter 16e

The Source of Faith Is Faith Itself

"Who prop, thou ask'st, in these bad days, my mind?" Thus opened Matthew Arnold an early sonnet, *To a Friend*. I believe that, unlike the Rambam, I do not generally experience the days as bad; and I am quite certain that if I did, Arnold's choices – Homer, Epictetus and Sophocles – would not provide the requisite solace. But as to the formulation of the question: In my case, at least, the critical factor is indeed "who" rather than "what."

Without question, during my formative years and, to a lesser extent, beyond, the source and bulwark of my commitment was not so much a cluster of abstract factors or arguments as key persons. This may make my response less valuable for readers who have no access to my sources of strength and inspiration. Moreover, such a response raises obvious questions about determinism and inequity which, in a different context, would need to be addressed philosophically. But any other response would be not only partial but false.

I refer, of course, to those who, in the words of the Mishnah, put me on the path to temporal and eternal life: my parents, ז״ל, who were also my primary (in several senses of the term) teachers, and my *rebbeim*, of whom three – Rav Hutner זצ״ל, the Rav זצ״ל, and Rav Ahron Soloveichik זצ״ל – stand out far above the rest. At home, I received trust and strength, imbibed (although did not always implement in youth) a

---

Published in *Jewish Action* 53:1 (Fall 1992); reprinted in *The Jewish Action Reader* (NY: Orthodox Union, 1996).

work ethic, and initially breathed an atmosphere within which a balance between criticism and rootedness was consistently maintained. Both of my parents, each in his own way, habitually raised serious questions about the religious world or about various textual or philosophic aspects of Torah – but always radiated a sense of profoundly engaged commitment.

The impact of my *rebbeim* was obviously varied. That of the first two is presumably self-evident. They – the Rav, as *rabbi muvhak,* in particular – both limned the contours of my religious and intellectual universe and filled it with content. In addition, they communicated a powerful sense of relation to the past, immediate and distant, of *k'illu kiblah mehar Sinai,* of being and becoming a link in the unbroken chain of the *mesorah.* Perhaps more needs to be said, however, about my relation to Reb Ahron. From him too, I learned much, but above all, he served as a role model. The *Rosh Yeshiva* (as his *talmidim* invariably called Rav Hutner), *gavra d'mistafina minei* par excellence, simply overwhelmed. The Rav overawed. I could entertain no rational illusions about attaining their status or stature. But Reb Ahron, while an inspiring vision, yet somehow seemed within reach, and truly presented a model. It wasn't so much what he said or did. I was simply enthralled by what he was – a remarkable fusion of mastery and simplicity, of vigor and humility and, above all, a pillar of radical integrity. To an extent probably far beyond what he knew or could even have imagined, he was to me, for many years, a polestar. Upon attaining fuller maturity, I came to realize that the notion that I could attain his level was pretentiously vainglorious. But his hold upon me, and the ambition and commitment it generated, have not waned to this day.

What I received from all my mentors, at home or in *yeshivot,* was the key to confronting life, particularly modern life, in all its complexity: the recognition that it was not so necessary to have all the answers as to learn to live with the questions. Regardless of what issues – moral, theological, textual or historical – vexed me, I was confident that they had been raised by masters far sharper and wiser than myself; and if they had remained impregnably steadfast in their commitment, so should and could I. I intuited that, his categorical formulations and imperial certitude notwithstanding, Rav Hutner had surely confronted whatever questions occurred to me.

Later, I felt virtually certain the Rav had, so that the depth and intensity of their *avodat Hashem* was doubly reassuring.

Newman has emphasized the difference between difficulty and doubt, noting that of all his beliefs, the existence of God was the most fraught with philosophical questions, and yet none was borne in his mind and heart with greater certitude. This is the crucial distinction between judging faith and its tenets as an outsider or probing its contents while firmly ensconced within. The bulwark of my mentors' support assured that my own situation would be the latter; and the motto I inscribed I my college notebook was David's plea: *Tuv taʿam ve-daʿat lamdeni ki be-mizvotekha heʾemanti* (Tehillim 119:65). Answers, I of course continued – and continue – to seek, and have found many. But commitment has not been conditioned upon them. I have never been attracted to fideism and I regard Tertullian's *credo quia absurdum est* as alien to the spirit of Judaism. Clearly, however, faith cannot be contingent upon having all the answers. Its essence is implied in Rav Yohanan's rejoinder to a student who had initially ridiculed a palpably implausible statement but who then recanted upon finding empirical support for it: "Neʾer-do-well, had you not seen, you would not have believed. You ridicule the words of the wise" (Bava Batra 75a).

The source of my support was not confined to my immediate *rebbeim*. At one point, during my late teens, I was troubled by certain ethical questions concerning Amalek, *ir ha-nidahat*, etc. I then recalled having recently read that Rav Chaim Brisker would awaken nightly to see if someone hadn't placed a foundling at his doorstep. I knew that I slept quite soundly, and I concluded that if such a paragon of *hesed* coped with these *halakhot*, evidently the source of my anxiety did not lie in my greater sensitivity but in my weaker faith. And I set myself to enhancing it.

That faith has been persistently reinforced by Jewish history. And this, in two respects. First, I have envisioned Providence as revealed and refracted through the uniqueness of Jewish history, in the spirit of the response Hazal ascribe to *Anshei Knesset Ha-gedolah*: "These are His awesome effects, for were it not for awe of God, how could one nation survive among the nations?" (Yoma 69b). Of course, I realized that, from a purely logical standpoint, one could rejoin with an analogue to Newman's statement that he saw design in nature because he believed in God, not vice versa. But given the substratum of faith, our singular history had provided much reinforcement.

Secondly, Jewish history has served as a corpus with which – to some extent, even through which – to identify, and on which behalf to continue. That sense has received added impetus through the Holocaust. Some may regard this as paradoxical; but it is thoroughly genuine – and from my perspective, not paradoxical at all. The theological philosophic difficulties posed by this frightful *hester panim* are self-evident. They are, however, so insoluble and intractable that a person of faith is led to look beyond their sheer magnitude to evoke and formulate a practical response. For me, that has meant a redoubled commitment – a sense of mission to take the flickering torch from my predecessors and move with it toward our common goals.

The greatest source of faith, however, has been the *Ribbono shel Olam* Himself.

At the level of rational demonstration, this is, of course, patently circular. I hold no brief for Anselm's ontological proof, and I recognized the theoretical possibility of self-delusion long before I had ever heard of Feuerbach. Existentially, however, nothing has been more authentic than the encounter with *Avinu Malkeinu,* the source and ground of all being. Nothing more sustaining, nothing more strengthening, nothing vivifying.

The encounter, of course, has been varied. In part, it has been channeled – primarily through *talmud Torah* (this is no doubt an aspect of *maor she-bah,* "the light within it," of which Hazal spoke), but also through *tefillah* and the performance of *mizvot*; or, if you will, by the halakhic regimen in its totality. In part, it has been random – moments of illumination while getting on a crowded bus or watching children play in a park at twilight. Obviously, it has also been greatly varied in intensity. In its totality, however, whatever the form and content, it has been the ultimate basis of spiritual life.

This will obviously provide little guidance for those to whom attaining encounter is precisely the problem. To those "struggling to develop faith," one can, however, proffer first the reassuring assertion of the religious significance of the quest *per se*, as, in the footsteps of *Avraham Avinu,* they have already become *mevakshei Hashem*; second, the prospective hope of successful resolution, as "The Lord is good unto them that yearn for Him, to the soul that seeketh Him" (Eikhah 3:25); and third, the counsel to focus persistently, in terms of Coleridge's familiar distinction, upon faith rather than belief, upon experiential trust, dependence and submission more than upon catechetical dogmatics. Intellectual assent is normative and essential; but, at the personal level, it is generally not the key. In the final analysis, the primary human source of faith is faith itself.

Sources of Essays in

Leaves of Faith, vol. 1:
The World of Jewish Learning

Chapter 1, "Why Learn Gemara?" is published here for the first time.

Chapter 2, "The Conceptual Approach to Torah Learning," was delivered at the Orthodox Forum 1999.

Chapter 3, "Torat Hesed and Torat Emet," was presented at the Bernard Revel Graduate School, Yeshiva University, in 1984.

Chapter 4, "A Consideration of Synthesis from a Torah Point of View," appeared in *Gesher* 1 (1963).

Chapter 5, "The End of Learning," was a Torah U-Madda lecture at Yeshiva University in 1986.

Chapter 6, "Get You Wise Men," was an address to Yeshiva University Rabbinic Alumni in 1966.

Chapter 7, "The Ideology of Hesder," appeared in *Tradition* 19:3 (Fall 1981).

Chapter 8, "The Human and Social Factor in Halakhah," was delivered at the Orthodox Forum 1998, and appeared in *Tradition* 36:1 (2002).

Chapter 9, "The Rav at Jubilee," was presented at a conference of the Union of Orthodox Jewish Congregations in 1992 and appeared in *Tradition* 30:4 (Summer 1996).

Chapter 10, "The Rav ל″צז in Retrospect," appeared in Hebrew in *Mesorah* 9 (Adar 5754; Feb. 1994).

Chapter 11, "A Portrait of Rav Shlomo Zalman Auerbach ל″צז," appeared in *Jewish Action* 56:1 (Fall 1995).

The index of volume 1 was prepared by Samuel P. Groner.

General Index

A

Abbaye, 35

Abortion, 241–253

  concern for human dignity, 252

  different stages in pregnancy, 245–250

  flexibility afforded for individual cases, 250–252

  nature of the prohibition, 242–244

  prohibition to Noahide, 242, 244

  scope of possible exemptions, 247–251

  scope of the prohibition, 244–247

  source of prohibition, 242, 250

Abraham, 66, 72, 73, 76, 86, 192, 197, 226–227, 231, 232, 238n7, 317, 356, 367

Acton, John, 73

Adam, 226

Aeschylus, 117

Ahavat Hashem (Love of God), 121–124, 127–129, 319

  relationship to disdain for the world, 127–128

  six characteristics, 123

  through women's Talmud Torah, 319

Akiva, Rabbi, 121–122, 132

  Aleinu, 70, 86

Amalek, 365

Anselm of Canterbury, 366

Anthropomorphism

  conflicting perspectives of Hazal and Rambam, 140–141

  perspective of Knesset Yisrael, 141–143

Apostate

  see Meshumad

Aristotle, 21, 43, 313

Arnold, Matthew, 148, 227, 305, 317, 325, 352, 363

Asceticism, 128

Ashrei, 147

Aquinas, Thomas, 283

Auerbach, Rav Shlomo Zalman, 270, 303, 350

Augustine, 283, 353

Averah lishmah (idealistic transgression), 38, 54n25

Avnei Nezer, 323

B

Bacon, Sir Francis, 9, 353

Baer, Yitzhak 34

Bahya, Rabbenu, 35, 121,128

Source Index

Index prepared by Doron Friedlander and Myles Brody

B. *Other*